› Becoming an
ARCHITECT

Other Titles in the Series

THIRD EDITION

❯ Becoming an
ARCHITECT

A Guide to Careers in Design

Lee W. Waldrep, Ph.D.

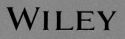

Cover Design: C. Wallace

Front cover image: Quadracci Pavilion, Milwaukee Art Museum courtesy of Lee W. Waldrep, Ph.D.

Back cover images (clockwise from top left): Jay Pritzker Pavilion courtesy of Lee W. Waldrep, Ph.D.; Illustration courtesy of Ashley Wood Clark; The Miller House © Susan Hanes; Smithsonian Donald W. Reynolds Center for American Art and Portraiture courtesy of Bryan Becker

Inside back flap image courtesy of John Myefski, Myefski Architects, Inc.

This book is printed on acid-free paper. ∞

Published by John Wiley & Sons, Inc., Hoboken, New Jersey

Published simultaneously in Canada

For general information about our other products and services, please contact our Customer Care Department within the United States at (800) 762-2974, outside the United States at (317) 572-3993 or fax (317) 572-4002.

Wiley publishes in a variety of print and electronic formats and by print-on-demand. Some material included with standard print versions of this book may not be included in e-books or in print-on-demand. If this book refers to media such as a CD or DVD that is not included in the version you purchased, you may download this material at http://booksupport.wiley.com. For more information about Wiley products, visit www.wiley.com.

Library of Congress Cataloging-in-Publication Data:

Waldrep, Lee W.
  Becoming an architect : a guide to careers in design / Lee W. Waldrep, Ph.D. -- Third edition.
      pages cm
  Includes bibliographical references and index.
  ISBN 978-1-118-61213-2 (pbk.), ISBN 978-1-118-85719-9 (ebk.); ISBN 978-1-118-85738-0 (ebk.)
  1. Architecture--Vocational guidance. I. Title.
  NA1995.W35 2014
  720.23--dc23
                                                              2013042097

Printed in the United States of America

10 9 8 7 6 5 4 3 2 1

To Cassidy, Karli, Anslie,
and my loving wife, Sherry

To close friends
Doug Garofalo, FAIA (1958–2011)
Barbara Laurie, AIA, NOMA (1961–2013)

CONTENTS

FOREWORD

"Education is not the filling of a pail, but the lighting of a fire."

WILLIAM BUTLER YEATS

THE SECOND MOST IMPORTANT WORD in the third edition of *Becoming an Architect* ("architect" is obviously the first) is "becoming." Why focus on process rather than the object or goal? Because to strive to be an architect is always a matter of moving forward and beyond, a matter, in short, of *becoming*. It has to be. Ever since the first human beings climbed down from trees and stepped out of the shadow of caves to build structures of thatch, wood, clay, and stone, the art and science of architecture have evolved in response to technology, cultural imperatives, and climate change. Whatever design and construction skills we brought with us in our journey had to be modified and adapted to the new realities of available materials, site, and weather. This growing body of knowledge then had to be transferred from one generation to the next to keep from literally reinventing the wheel every time we set tool to stone and wood or hand to clay.

The fact that the art and science of architecture is constantly in a state of becoming, of pushing outward at the edges of the known, is the unmistakable handprint of a great irony or paradox: What at first glance seems to be the most static of the arts, upon closer inspection and affection reveals itself as constantly shape-shifting. It becomes, if you will, the most personal, revealing, and lasting signature of the unique values of a culture. In fact, to paraphrase Churchill, architecture shapes cultures and entire civilizations, whether it be the Great Wall of China, the pyramids, or Europe's great cathedrals.

Yet we are not simply passengers headed for new ports. We ourselves are in a state of becoming as our awareness of how little we know drives our thirst to explore and create new knowledge and new ways of applying our maturing skills. This capacity for growth is bestowed on every artist. Consider the early compositions of a Beethoven or the art of Goya or the work of Louis Kahn; compare this to their later or final work. Something profound happens in their "becoming." Often it is the honing down, the grasp for greater simplicity as vision is refined. The body grows older, but the soul grows lighter; insight becomes more profound. More is accomplished by a few well-wrought lines than protracted arm wrestling with the muse.

Although architecture is a collaborative art (which, thank goodness, is its glory), the endlessly unwinding path to "becoming" can be lonely: It's long past midnight, the screen in front of us is blank, and the client (not to mention our partners) expect a presentation later in the day. Times like these—all too frequent—reveal one of the great strengths of this book, one that's not nearly commented on enough. Within the covers of *Becoming an Architect,* author Lee W. Waldrep has convened some of the most interesting and eloquent voices in our profession. They respond to the questions you would ask if you could beam them down to your living room, studio, or on a long hike through the woods. You may not agree with everything you read. But let it rest a few months, then go back. After all, you will be in a different place.

When I look back through the rear view mirror of my own career, I am not the architect I was when I was fresh out of architecture school. Whether better or worse, I leave to the judgment of others. But wherever I am going, I know other architects have been there before me. What has varied is the speed of change and the many surprises in its wake—not all of which are welcomed. What hasn't changed is the support, guidance, and, yes, necessary reality checks offered by fellow architects who are on a similar journey of becoming. Men and women who, like me, will be grateful for the companionship of the valuable resource that is *Becoming an Architect*.

HELENE COMBS DREILING, FAIA
2014 President of The American Institute of Architects
Executive Director, Virginia Center for Architecture

PREFACE

IN SECOND GRADE, my career ambition was to become a clown. Only later did I desire to become an architect. One of my older brothers first pursued architecture in college (he later switched to music). A ninth-grade drafting class was my first formal introduction to what I thought was the profession. At the same time, I had the opportunity to meet with an architect in my hometown. In high school, I interned in an architect's office, drafting and making models. All of these experiences helped me decide to pursue architecture in college.

After six years of college, two architecture degrees from Michigan and Arizona State University, a year as national vice president of the American Institute of Architecture Students (AIAS), and three months working in a firm, I decided architecture was not a good fit. However, from my experiences in architecture, I discovered that I wanted to help others in their pursuit of becoming an architect. Thus, the idea for this book has been over 30 years in development.

Becoming an Architect: A Guide to Careers in Design, 3rd edition, will help you navigate the process of becoming an architect. Its purpose is to provide you with an outline of the process: (1) a National Architectural Accrediting Board (NAAB) accredited professional degree in architecture, (2) the experience or internship component (IDP), and (3) the Architect Registration Exam (ARE). Further, it will help you launch your professional career in architecture.

Chapter 1, "The Definition of an Architect," introduces the basic duties and tasks of an architect. After reading this chapter, you will be better able to decide if you are suited to become an architect. The chapter outlines the basic skills, characteristics, attitudes, motivations, and aptitudes of architects. Finally, it provides a profile of the architecture profession.

Chapter 2, "The Education of an Architect," outlines the education to becoming an architect. It emphasizes that the education of an architect is lifelong and does not end with the receipt of a formal degree. The first of the chapter's three parts focuses on preparation—the courses and activities you can pursue to prepare for an architectural education. The second part provides insight into selecting an architecture program. It delineates the three paths to graduation with a professional degree program. Further, it outlines the attributes—individual, institution, and academic unit—to consider when selecting a program. The third part of the chapter describes the typical architecture curriculum.

As training is a required element of becoming an architect, Chapter 3, "The Experience of an Architect," concentrates on gaining experience both while in school and upon graduation. First, it discusses strategies to gain experience while in school through part-time, summer, or cooperative education opportunities; afterward, the chapter outlines gaining experience as an emerging professional. An additional portion uses the acronym A.R.C.H.I.T.E.C.T. in support of the search for positions that provide useful experience. The chapter also provides a basic overview of the Intern Development Program (IDP), a required program in almost all 50 states for documenting your experiences under the supervision of a licensed architect. Further, the chapter introduces the requirements and process of the ARE.

Chapter 4, "The Careers of an Architect," outlines the career designing process (assessing, exploring, decision making, and planning) and the career paths available to graduates of an architectural education—both those within architectural practice and outside and beyond architecture.

Finally, the Chapter 5, "The Future of the Architecture Profession," provides insight into the future of the profession of architecture. Terms associated with the future of the profession are outlined and, along with those focused on throughout the book, answer the question, "What do you see as the future for the architecture profession?"

Career profiles of architecture students, emerging professionals, educators, and practitioners appear throughout the book and are a wonderful resource for personal stories. Some profiles highlight the traditional path of an architect within a private architecture firm, while others describe related settings in which an architect might work—corporations, government agencies, and education and research. A series of pointed questions related to the profession and the responses of those individuals profiled are also distributed throughout.

The first of three appendixes lists resources for further information. Note especially the first five associations listed: the American Institute of Architects (AIA), American Institute of Architecture Students (AIAS), Association of Collegiate Schools of Architecture (ACSA), NAAB, and National Council of Architectural Registration Boards (NCARB). Also included are career-related associations and other useful resources, including websites, and recommended reading.

The second appendix lists institutions offering NAAB/Canadian Architectural Certification Board (CACB-CCCA) accredited programs in the United States and Canada. The third appendix lists those students, interns, and professionals profiled in the book.

As you will soon discover, becoming an architect is a satisfying and worthwhile endeavor. Enjoy the process of becoming and being an architect, as it will provide a long and meaningful career path.

LEE W. WALDREP, Ph.D.
May 2014

ACKNOWLEDGMENTS

WHEN I COMPLETED my doctoral dissertation, I stated that authoring it was the closest I would ever come to designing architecture. This statement remains true, but in terms of work, authoring this book far exceeds writing my dissertation. I still may never design a residence or a skyscraper, but I hope this book helps future architects design their careers.

First, I wish to extend my love and appreciation to my parents, *Carl E.* and *Marsha L. Waldrep,* who will never see the results of my labor but were certainly an inspiration to me. Although they both passed while I was a child, they continue to live within me to this day.

Next, and just as important, I would like to acknowledge the support of my family—my wife, *Sherry,* and my triplet daughters, *Cassidy, Karli,* and *Anslie.* Without their willingness to let me escape from family obligations, I would not have completed this project. Now that the book is complete, I am ready to swim in the new pool.

I also wish to express my appreciation to the many students, emerging professionals, educators, and architects profiled throughout this book, many of whom I have known throughout my career (see Appendix C). Without exception, all were more than willing participants to this project and are as much the authors of this book as I am.

Thanks are also extended to *Brian P. Kelly,* AIA, director of the architecture program and associate professor in the School of Architecture, Planning, and Preservation at the University of Maryland; *Michelle A. Rinehart,* EdD, assistant dean for academic affairs and outreach in the College of Architecture at Georgia Institute of Technology and *David Zach,* futurist for all sharing their insights. Additional thanks are extended to *Andrea Rutledge,* executive director of NAAB, my colleague and friend.

Special kudos to the following individuals: *Jenny Castronuovo,* who more than assisted me with the collection of images for the first edition of the book; *Margaret DeLeeuw, Shawna Grant, Allison Wilson, Robyn Payne,* and *Deana Moore,* who provided insight as the manuscript was being written; and *Michal Seltzer,* for mocking up a cover design for daily inspiration. Also, I wish to express my appreciation to *Dr. Kathryn H. Anthony,* a special friend who knows all too well the challenges of authoring a book. My appreciation is also extended to *Grace H. Kim, AIA,* a friend who first recommended to John Wiley & Sons that I would be a good author for this project. She was also instrumental in providing images.

I wish to express my appreciation to *Kathryn Bourgoine,* my editor, and *Nancy Cintron,* senior production editor, both at Wiley, for guiding me throughout the process.

Finally, I wish to thank all the architecture students and colleagues within the architecture discipline with whom I have interacted with over my 20-plus-year career; you have been the reason I so much enjoy my work.

1 The Definition of an Architect

He looked at the granite. To be cut, he thought, and made into walls. He looked at a tree. To be split and made into rafters. He looked at a streak of rust on the stone and thought of iron ore under the ground to be melted and to emerge as girders against the sky. These rocks, he thought, are here for me; waiting for the drill, the dynamite and my voice; waiting to be split, ripped, pounded, reborn, waiting for the shape my hands will give to them.

AYN RAND, *The Fountainhead*[1]

AFTER READING THE PRECEDING TEXT from *The Fountainhead* by Ayn Rand, what are your thoughts and feelings? Can you relate to the main character, Howard Roark, in this passage? Are you overcome with the possibilities of creating with the materials around you?

Do you want to be an architect? Do you wish to study architecture? If your answer is "Yes" to any of these questions, this book is for you.

What is the definition of an architect? T*he American Heritage Dictionary of the English Language*[2] defines *architect* as:

1. One who designs and supervises the construction of buildings or other structures. *är-ki-tekt,* n. [MF architecte, fr. L architectus, fr. Gk architekton master builder, fr. Archi- + tekton builder]

Of course, this definition simply scratches the surface. Becoming and being an architect are much more.

◀ Newseum, Washington, DC. Architect: Polshek Partnership Architects LLP.
PHOTOGRAPHER: LEE W. WALDREP, Ph.D.

1

What Do Architects Do?

People need places in which to live, work, play, learn, worship, meet, govern, shop, eat—private and public spaces, indoors and out; rooms, buildings, and complexes; neighborhoods and towns; suburbs and cities. Architects, professionals trained in the art and science of building design and licensed to protect public health, safety, and welfare, transform these needs into concepts and then develop the concepts into building images that can be constructed by others.

In designing buildings, architects communicate with and assist those who have needs—clients, users, and the public as a whole—and those who will make the spaces that satisfy those needs—builders and contractors, plumbers and painters, carpenters, and air conditioning mechanics.

Whether the project is a room or a city, a new building or the renovation of an old one, architects provide the professional services—ideas and insights, design and technical knowledge, drawings and specifications, administration, coordination, and informed decision making—whereby an extraordinary range of functional, aesthetic, technological, economic, human, environmental, and safety factors are melded into a coherent and appropriate solution to the problems at hand.

This is what architects are, conceivers of buildings. What they do is to design, that is, supply concrete images for a new structure so that it can be put up. The primary task of the architect, then as now, is to communicate what proposed buildings should be and look like.... The architect's role is that of mediator between the client or patron, that is, the person who decides to build, and the work force with its overseers, which we might collectively refer to as the builder.

SPIRO KOSTOF[3]

Parthenon, Athens, Greece. PHOTOGRAPHER: R. LINDLEY VANN.

Design Process

But how does an architect truly design? It begins with a client with the need for a building, a project. To design and build this project, an architect follows the architectural design process. This process begins with the schematic design phase, with the architect first gaining an understanding of the scope of the project to be built from the client. With the program determined, the architect develops preliminary concepts and ideas for the project and presents these to the client for approval or revision. In addition, the architect researches zoning or other restrictions. Next is the design development phase.

In design development, the initial concepts and ideas are further refined. The architect begins to determine the building materials of the project as well as detailing the mechanical, electrical, plumbing, and structural aspects of the project. The architect will formally present the project, at this stage of development, to the client for approval. Next is the construction document phase.

During the construction document phase, the architect produces detailed drawings and specifications of the project to be used for construction. These construction documents include all pertinent information necessary for construction. Once completed, the construction documents (CDs) are provided to potential contractors for bidding. Next is the bid or negotiation phase.

In preparation for actual construction, the architect prepares the bid documents. The bid documents include a number of documents for potential contractors to use in preparing a bid (cost estimate) to construct the project. Once bids are received from contractors, the architect will assist the client in evaluating and selecting the winning proposal. In the end, a contract is awarded to the selected bidder, which allows construction to begin. Next is the construction phase.

During construction, the architect's responsibilities will vary depending on the agreement with the client, but most commonly the architect will assist the contractor to construct the project as specified in the construction documents. As questions or issues arise on the construction site, the architect is there to address them. Depending on the issue, the architect may be required to issue additional drawings.

Thus, an architect must be equipped with a number of talents and skills to take a project from its initial idea to final construction. In the profession, architectural firms consisting of teams of architects, related professionals, and consultants undertake almost all projects, although there may be some smaller projects, usually residential, that a sole architect might lead.

Why Architecture?

Why do you desire to become an architect? Have you been building with Legos since you were a child? Did a counselor or teacher suggest architecture to you because of a strong interest and skills in mathematics and art? Or are there other reasons? Aspiring architects cite a love of drawing, creating, and designing; a desire to make a difference in the community; an aptitude for mathematics and science; or a connection to a family member in the profession. Whatever your reason, are you suited to become an architect?

Is Architecture for You?

How do you know if the pursuit of architecture is right for you? Those within the profession suggest that if you are creative or artistic and good in mathematics and science, you may have what it takes to be a successful architect. However, Dana Cuff, author of *Architecture: The Story of Practice,* suggests it takes more:

There are two qualities that neither employers nor educators can instill and without which, it is assumed, one cannot become a "good" architect: dedication and talent.

DANA CUFF[4]

Because of the breadth of skills and talents necessary to be an architect, you may be able to find your niche within the profession regardless. It takes three attributes to be a successful architecture student—intelligence, creativity, and dedication—and you need any two of the three. Also, your education will develop your knowledge base and design talents.

Unfortunately, there is no magic test to determine if becoming an architect is for you. Perhaps the most effective way to determine whether you should consider becoming an architect is to experience the profession firsthand. Ask lots of questions and recognize that many related career fields might also be appropriate for you.

For the architect must, on the one hand, be a person who is fascinated by how things work and how he can make them work, not in the sense of inventing or repairing machinery, but rather in the organization of time–space elements to produce the desired results; on the other hand, he must have an above average feeling for aesthetics and quite some ability at drawing, painting, and the visual arts in general.

EUGENE RASKIN[5]

What Is Architecture?

❭ The creation of space.
John W. Myefski, AIA, Principal, Myefski Architects, Inc.

❭ Architecture is the design and manipulation of the built environment to create a sense of place. It is a confluence of science and art that addresses programmatic and aesthetic requirements within the constraints of budget, schedule, life safety, and social responsibility.
Robert D. Roubik, AIA, LEED AP, Project Architect, Antunovich Associates Architects and Planners

❭ Architecture exists in the harmony between sophisticated form, fulfilling a purpose and the tactile nuances of joining materials together.
Rosannah B. Sandoval, AIA, Designer II, Perkins + Will

❭ Architects take big ideas and turn them into reality. Architects build cities, buildings, parks, communities—physical and virtual. They are visionary and incredibly practical at the same time.
Leigh Stringer, LEED AP, Senior Vice-President, HOK

What Is Architecture? (Continued)

❯ Architecture is the perfect combination of creativity and practicality. It is the opportunity to create an experience for the user through the design of spaces. It is the careful art of designing a space that is functional, enjoyable, and practical.

Elsa Reifsteck, BS Architectural Studies Graduate, University of Illinois at Urbana-Champaign

❯ Architecture is the art and science of planning and designing structures and environments to house the activities of humans.

H. Alan Brangman, AIA, Vice President of Facilities, Real Estate Auxiliary Services, University of Delaware

❯ Architecture is the art of designing buildings and spaces within a given set of parameters that include the programmatic needs of the project, the client's budget, building code regulations, and the inherent properties of the materials being used. Great architecture finds the best solution to a design problem by using both creativity and practicality. Part sculpture, part environmental psychology, part construction technology, architecture is the combination of many separate forces into a harmonic whole.

Carolyn G. Jones, AIA, LEED AP, Principal, Mulvanny G2

❯ The development of architecture is as much a design process as it is a simulation of inhabitable space(s) and building vocabularies. I will go as far to say that architecture is not architecture unless it was developed by means of an analytical process.

Thomas Fowler IV, AIA, NCARB, DPACSA Professor and Director, Community Interdisciplinary Design Studio (CIDS), California Polytechnic State University—San Luis Obispo

❯ Architecture is the built environments that shape the daily lives of people.

Grace H. Kim, AIA, Principal, Schemata Workshop, Inc.

❯ Practical and artistic development of our environment. Winston Churchill once said, to paraphrase, what we build in stone we remember, so

at some level architecture is about the creation of the making of memories and developing a sense of place.

Mary Katherine Lanzillotta, FAIA, Partner, Hartman-Cox Architects

❯ Architecture is the design of the built environment through the programming of needs, three-dimensional design, and the application of appropriate building technologies.

Eric Taylor, Associate, AIA, Photographer, Taylor Design & Photography, Inc.

❯ Architecture is the synthesis of art and science utilized to develop a solution to a challenge in the built environment.

Beth Kalin, Job Captain, Gensler

❯ Spaces that give shape to our lives.

Murrye Bernard, Associate AIA, LEED AP, Managing Editor, Contract Magazine

❯ Architecture is about light, shadow, texture, rhythm, form, and function. To me, architecture is the practice of creating and affecting the built environment. The practice of architecture is to understand the problem and finding a solution that is aligned with the vision for the project.

Sean M. Stadler, AIA, LEED AP, Design Principal, WDG Architecture, PLLC

❯ As the Greek origin of the word defines it, architecture is both art and science. It is the practice of bringing these two objectives together in a manner of achieving "form, function, and design."

Kathy Denise Dixon, AIA, NOMA, Principal, K. Dixon Architecture, PLLC; Associate Professor, University of the District of Columbia.

❯ In its simplest terms, architecture is the design of the built environment—spaces where we live, work, worship, gather, vacation, or simply occupy.

Jessica L. Leonard, Associate AIA, LEED AP BD+C, Associate, Ayers Saint Gross Architects and Planners

Walt Disney Concert Hall, Los Angeles, California. Architect: Frank Gehry. PHOTOGRAPHER: TINA REAMES.

❯ To me, architecture is anything that can be designed—a chair, an app, a light fixture, a website, a logo, a film, a building, or a city.

William J. Carpenter, Ph.D., FAIA, Professor, Southern Polytechnic State University; President, Lightroom

❯ Architecture is the stage we live on. It enables activities to take place and shapes how those activities happen. It can link us to nature and reveal relationships we might not have noticed. Architecture is most unsuccessful when it is primarily designed to protect us from the elements and most successful when it improves our quality of life.

Allison Wilson, Intern Architect, Ayers, Saint Gross

❯ Architecture is not limited to buildings, interiors, or covered spaces; it is a designed response to a programmatic necessity where one either does not exist, or where one exists yet lacks integrity.

Tanya Ally, Architectural Staff, Bonstra | Haresign Architects

❯ Architecture is the design of buildings and spaces. The experiences that are created by a design can have more of an impact than the program within the building or space.

Nicole Gangidino, B.Arch. Candidate, New York Institute of Technology

❯ Architecture is the physical and spiritual transformation of chaos into order, darkness into light, and space into place.

Nathan Kipnis, AIA, Principal, Nathan Kipnis Architects, Inc.

Interior, Johnson Wax Building, Racine, Wisconsin. Architect: Frank Lloyd Wright. PHOTOGRAPHER: R. LINDLEY VANN.

What Is Architecture? (Continued)

❯ The way the built environment is designed to interact with people in their daily lives.

Megan S. Chusid, AIA, Manager of Facilities and Office Services, Solomon R. Guggenheim Museum and Foundation

❯ Architecture is the creation of buildings using a synthesis of art and science to better human existence. Buildings are designed to support the activities within them while evoking a sense of beauty and belonging.

Jordan Buckner, M.Arch./MBA Graduate, University of Illinois at Urbana-Champaign

❯ Architecture is the collaboration of art, design, and technology in buildings and the urban land-scape that is simultaneously enjoyed and criticized by the people it serves.

Kevin Sneed, AIA, IIDA, NOMA, LEED AP BD+C, Partner/ Senior Director of Architecture, OTJ Architects, LLC

❯ Architecture is about shelter; crafting the places in which people live, work, and play—the art and science of designing and constructing buildings. All humans really need to survive is food and shelter. Architecture is a basic pillar of human existence.

Amanda Harrell-Seyburn, Associate AIA, Instructor, School of Planning, Design and Construction, Michigan State University

❯ Architecture is the creation and communication of ideas. It is the creative and technical process for the design, management, and construction of the built environment. It represents a collaboration and coordination with a broad range of experts to get a building built.

Robert D. Fox, AIA, IIDA, Principal, FOX Architects

❭ Architecture is the study of inhabitable space, the relationships between human interaction and thoughtful design. Architecture can be created anywhere with anything, with any materials, on any terrain, in any climate as long as long the design is intentional and inhabitable.

Anna A. Kissell, M.Arch. Candidate, Boston Architectural College, Associate Manager Environmental Design, Reebok International Inc.

❭ Architecture is the creation of the environments in which we live, work, learn, and recreate. It is more than just constructing a building or designing a beautiful piece of sculpture—it is about understanding the wants and needs of the users, and creating an environment that exceeds their expectations. Architecture has the power to determine how we live and the responsibility to move our society forward.

Cody Bornsheuer, Associate AIA, LEED AP BD+C, Architectural Designer, Dewberry Architects, Inc.

❭ Architecture is the intersection of vision and creation in the built environment. However, I do not necessarily feel that architecture is limited to describing buildings alone, nor *architect* a term used to only describe one who designs "buildings."

Ashley W. Clark, Associate AIA, LEED AP, SMPS, Marketing Manager, LandDesign

❭ In the late nineteenth century and early twentieth century, one might have heard architecture described as the "mother of the arts," but today that sort of categorization sounds a bit limiting and perhaps somewhat elitist. Architecture is located at the intersection between the fine arts, applied sciences, technologies and engineering, and the social sciences.

Architecture involves the design of the physical environment at all scales from that of household objects and furnishings to entire portions of cities and landscapes, and everything in between! Consequently, it is both a discipline and a profession that actively works between bodies of knowledge to analyze problems and synthesize useful and meaningful solutions to the problems of the built environment.

Brian Kelly, AIA, Associate Professor and Director, Architecture Program, University of Maryland

❭ Architecture is everywhere and everything. Frank Lloyd Wright said it best, "I know that architecture is life; or at least it is life itself taking form and therefore it is the truest record of life as it was lived in the world yesterday, as it is lived today, or ever will be lived. Architecture is that great living creative spirit that, from generation to generation, from age to age, proceeds, persists, creates, according to the nature of man, and his circumstances as they change. That is really architecture.

Amanda Strawitch, Level 1 Architect, Design Collective

❭ Architecture is the process and products that we wrap our lives around.

Katherine Darnstadt, AIA LEED AP BD+C, Founder and Principal Architect, Latent Design

❭ Architecture is the art, science, business, and collaboration of people to make (great) buildings. Architecture is the thoughtful shaping of our environment for desirable inhabitation.

Joseph Mayo, Intern Architect, Mahlum

❭ Architecture is the physical manifestation of art, science, economy, craftsmanship, and sociology, masterfully blended to meet human needs for shelter and comfort.

Kimberly Dowdell, Project Manager/Director of Marketing, Levien & Company

What Is Architecture? (Continued)

❭ Architecture is the built environment that impacts the human experience. Architecture influences the way people interpret and use space, therefore shapes society and its efforts.

Danielle Mitchell, B.Arch. Candidate, Pennsylvania State University

❭ Architecture is the shaping of environments, real or imagined, that affect the way people think, feel, act, or respond to their surroundings. In this context, architecture can be both a noun and a verb; in other words, it can be the painting itself, or the act of painting.

Architecture appeals to the senses. It can comfort us or intimidate us. It can make us feel welcome and home, or alone and cold. Architecture can be as much about the intended desires of the designer's imagination or the unintended consequences delivered when architecture is not considered more fully in its proper context. Real or imagined, the environment we live, work, and play in is directly influenced by the architecture that surrounds us. In essence, architecture is humanity.

Shannon Kraus, FAIA, MBA, Principal and Senior Vice President, HKS Architects

❭ Architecture can be most broadly described as something that is consciously designed. Some interpret this to be a concern about aesthetics, but I would argue it has nothing to do with that. It is about engaging the world with insightful and reflective intention, ranging from the analytical and experiential to the political or social. While architecture is most often associated with the built environment, it may also be identified in anything that is thoughtfully organized, including institutions, education, and even writing.

Karen Cordes Spence, Ph.D., AIA, LEED AP, Associate Professor, Drury University

❭ Spaces where "dwelling" can occur; dwelling meaning *existing both physically and metaphysically in time and space.*

Sarah Stein, Architectural Designer, Lee Scolnick Architects & Design Partnership

❭ Architecture is a framework for civilization, a stage for life. It is the network of places and spaces we use to gather, celebrate, achieve, ponder, and reflect. Yet today, "architecture" is a field of increasingly blurred borders. As urbanized areas across the globe expand at unprecedented speed and scale, the discipline of architecture is continuously challenged to address the complexity and interconnection of the world's cities, including their impact on public health and the broader natural environment. Delivering a relevant twenty-first-century vision of the built environment requires an increasingly multidisciplinary and cross-cultural approach to design thinking.

Andrew Caruso, AIA, LEED AP BD+C, CDT, Head of Intern Development and Academic Outreach, Gensler

❭ To me, architecture is like a puzzle. It contains components that you, as the designer, are tasked with putting together into a cohesive form. But unlike the conventional puzzle, you not only have to put the pieces together, you also have to create them.

Makenzie Leukart, M.Arch. Candidate, Columbia University

❭ From my perspective, the process of creating architecture is puzzle solving on a majestic scale. This translates into the critical thinking and problem-solving aspects of the profession that architecture programs are so good at teaching and that our clients rely on us for as we help them accomplish their goals.

The architecture project/puzzle contains an infinite number of variables. Some are static; some are dynamic. The attributes of some are known and

Stonehenge, England. PHOTOGRAPHER: KARL DU PUY.

universally understood; for others, the attributes are unique to the person investigating them or experiencing them. The puzzle is constantly evolving, and no one has control over it! Most interesting of all, the result of the architecture project/puzzle is never complete, and no one ever sees it the same as someone else or even experiences it themselves in the same way.

Kathryn T. Prigmore, FAIA, Senior Project Manager, HDR Architecture, Inc.

❯ Architecture is a physical form of art that transforms our communities and has the ability to generate a sense of emotional pride. Architecture defines elements as small as neighborhoods to elements as large as cities, states, and regions. The recognition of specific countries and regions can

be acknowledged by the remarkable architecture it possesses.

Jennifer Taylor, Vice President, American Institute of Architecture Students

❯ Architecture is everything. It is where we all eat, sleep, and live. It is how we interact with our environment and how that environment interacts with the rest of the world. Architecture is not defined by buildings but by the space within them and the space that surrounds them. The art of architecture is about using physical materials to define the space that we cannot see. It is about taking everything in, analyzing relationships, not just in the physical context. Architecture is the world.

Elizabeth Weintraub, B.Arch. Candidate, New York Institute of Technology

Past Is Prologue

MARY KATHERINE LANZILLOTTA, FAIA

Partner, Hartman-Cox Architects

Washington, DC

Why and how did you become an architect?

〉 Having an idea develop into drawings and then a building where one lives or works is thrilling. My parents added onto our home and then built a new home when I was a child. The reality of this experience and living through the construction was very exciting. I knew by the time I was a teenager I wanted to find some way to be involved in the building process.

Why and how did you decide on which school to attend for your architecture degree? What degree(s) do you possess?

〉 As I was trying to decide whether to pursue engineering or architecture, the University of Virginia (UVA) offered a summer program for high school students on the "grounds" in Charlottesville. My parents agreed to let me attend the program to determine if architecture was a good fit for me. As part of the program, I attended morning lectures on history, visited job sites, and then had a "studio" program in the afternoon. The experience was very positive, and I knew I wanted to pursue the bachelor of science in architecture at UVA.

After four years and a dozen or so architectural history courses at UVA, I knew I wanted to be more involved with the preserving the built environment. For graduate school, I applied only to programs that offered a combination of architecture and preservation; I completed a master of

Lincoln Gallery, Smithsonian Donald W. Reynolds Center for American Art and Portraiture. Smithsonian Institution, Washington, DC. Architect: Hartman-Cox Architects.
PHOTOGRAPHER: BRYAN BECKER.

architecture at the University of Pennsylvania and a Certificate in Historic Preservation.

What has been your greatest challenge as an architect?

〉 Reminding myself to stay focused on the big picture and not to get bogged down in the details. To do this often requires me to step back and think creatively about how to solve the challenge in a different way.

As a partner at Hartman-Cox Architects, what are your primary responsibilities and duties?

❭ One primary responsibility is to pursue, secure, and execute good work. As one who is interested in preservation, I tend to look for more work in this same area but am also open to exploring new opportunities. My other duties are "as assigned," as we do not have rigidly set roles but look to see what is needed and where.

A handful of Hartman-Cox Architects projects relate to historic preservation, adaptive reuse, and rehabilitation. How and why are these issues important to architecture?

❭ Most of the Hartman-Cox projects relate to providing a continuity of the sense of place. This can be achieved by preserving existing buildings, adding onto existing buildings in a sensitive and appropriate manner, or by building a new building that respects its neighbors and reinterprets the sense of place. Our firm believes in building timeless buildings of their place. The continuity of history is important culturally as there are specific reasons why particular materials are used in some locations and not in others and, in the process, they leave us with a lesson about the use of local materials and technology.

Smithsonian Donald W. Reynolds Center for American Art and Portraiture. Smithsonian Institution, Washington, DC. Architect: Hartman-Cox Architects. PHOTOGRAPHER: BRYAN BECKER.

Luce Foundation Center for American Art. Smithsonian Donald W. Reynolds Center for American Art and Portraiture. Smithsonian Institution, Washington, DC. Architect: Hartman-Cox Architects. PHOTOGRAPHER: BRYAN BECKER.

In the case of the Old Patent Office building, now the Smithsonian Donald W. Reynolds Center for American Art and Portraiture, we can see the evolution of much of the nineteenth-century technology and architectural history from the restraint and classicism of Robert Mills with the solid masonry vaults to the exuberance and mannerism of Adolph Cluss as seen in the Luce Foundation Center. Buildings also share the cultural memories of place from the soldier's carving his initials in the shutter of a window to the inaugural ball of President Lincoln.

Buildings also embody an enormous amount of energy, and to reuse or renovate buildings appropriately to keep them in use is a responsible approach.

In 1958, the General Services Administration considered tearing down the Old Patent Office Building that occupies two city blocks and turning the site into a parking lot. The amount of wasted materials would have been vast, and the history would have been lost.

What is the most/least satisfying part of your career as an architect?

❯ The most satisfying experiences are watching people in the buildings and seeing how they are enjoying the building and seeing if they are experiencing it in the manner we expected. Of course, when you find the public is not as pleased with some aspect, these are the most instructive moments. All architects should visit their own buildings to see what works and what does not so they can improve upon their experience.

Can you provide details on Architecture in the Schools and why it is important for you to serve the profession in this way?

❯ A program of the Washington Architectural Foundation, Architecture in the Schools (AIS) teams volunteer architects with pre-K to 12th-grade classroom teachers to use architecture and design concepts to reinforce learning standards across the curriculum. Established in 1992, the Architecture in the Schools program originated in the District of Columbia and expanded to the greater Washington metropolitan area in 2002.

Students in the program (1) learn problem-solving techniques, (2) explore different ways to express their ideas, (3) examine their environment through the classroom projects they design, (4) apply abstract concepts to real-life scenarios, (5) develop a cross-curricular understanding of subject matter, and (6) cultivate civic awareness of how the children can influence their environment.

Since its inception over 400 schools and over 10,000 students have participated in the program. The Architecture in the Schools program has expanded to include professional development programs for teachers to learn more about how to integrate design and architecture into their curriculums and a series of architectural walking tours for children in Washington, DC, neighborhoods. With the opening of the District Architecture Center in 2011, we began to offer monthly Saturday programs for K–12 students who are interested in architecture. The programs have ranged from the basics of site design, drawing, and model building to set design and green roof tours. All of these programs allow students to explore the architecture and the built environment.

The experience of opening the eyes of children to the world around them and having them think critically about choices in their neighborhoods has had a profound impact on me. The opportunity to share my understanding of design and architecture with these students has forced me to learn to speak about architecture in a readily understandable way. The students' questions helped me to think critically about how to present ideas in a new approachable manner. Further, these students will grow up and become homeowners or members of a citizen's advisory committee. When this next generation has to think critically about a design issue that may impact or influence their communities, I hope they will have some frame of reference on which to base their decisions.

Who or what experience(s) has been a major influence on your career?

❯ Without setting out to do so, I have found myself gravitating toward projects that have an educational theme. The preservation projects are educational in what and how the buildings are preserved and the missions of the organizations themselves, whether it is preserving the Lincoln or Jefferson Memorials or ren-

Load Testing Columns, Oyster Elementary School Third Grade, Washington, DC. Washington Architectural Foundation, Architecture in the Schools. COURTESY OF THE WASHINGTON ARCHITECTURAL FOUNDATION.

ovating the UNC Morehead Planetarium Building. The Architecture in the Schools program is more directly educational, but the program attempts to encourage children to look at their world and think critically about it while they are still open-minded.

A major influence on my career has been my current partners, Lee Becker and Graham Davidson, and emeritus partners, George Hartman and Warren J. Cox, and all of the members of the Hartman-Cox team over the years.

My parents encouraged me to explore architecture both as a young child by building and, then, as a student when I wanted to pursue architecture as a

career. My parents also were role models for getting involved in and giving back to the community through their own service.

In addition, another influence is the hundreds of Architecture in the Schools volunteers who have given so freely of their time to share their knowledge of architecture and the built environment with the schoolchildren in DC and the metropolitan area to bring AIS program to life in the schools.

Rolaine Copeland, Hon. AIA, was the Architecture in Education program director at the Foundation for Architecture in Philadelphia who encouraged me to start the Architecture in the Schools program in DC.

Daring to Lead

SHANNON KRAUS, FAIA, ACHA, MBA

Principal and Senior Vice-President

HKS Architects

Washington, DC

Why and how did you become an architect?

❯ I became an architect simply because it was a lifelong goal. A life's goal achieved. A passion delivered. It was something I set my mind on from the time I was in fourth grade when the only class I had true interest in was art; my mother had the vision to open my mind to architecture as an occupation that would fit my interests.

It was through art and imagination that I could express myself. I did this through the pictures I would draw, the models I would build, and the

forts I would enlist the neighborhood kids to help construct. From there, becoming an architect simply felt right.

However, in the end I did become an architect to make a difference. While I pursued architecture because that is where I could express myself, I have found that what I enjoy most about this amazing profession is having the ability to work with diverse groups of people to solve complex problems so that others can fulfill their dreams—thus really making a difference by turning vision to reality.

From my first day on campus at Southern Illinois University (SIU) to gaining registration as an architect in the state of Texas, my journey took approximately 12 years—four years of undergraduate work, one year as American Institute of Architecture Students (AIAS) vice president, three

Ahuja Medical Center, Beachwood, Ohio. Architects: HKS Architects. PHOTOGRAPHER: HKS.

years in graduate school for the master of business administration (MBA) and master of architecture, and four years of internship at RTKL finished concurrently with the ARE spread over 18 months.

Why and how did you decide on which school to attend for your architecture degree? What degree(s) do you possess?

❯ Coming out of McArthur High School in the central Illinois town of Decatur, with the ambition to pursue architecture, I found myself at a small but terrific undergraduate program at Southern Illinois University at Carbondale. How I ended up there was primarily the result of not enough information and economics. They had a four-year architecture program, and it was less expensive than most any other school in the area. What I did not know was that the reason it was less expensive was that their

architecture program was not accredited. In the end, this turned to be a blessing—SIU was one of the best, if not luckiest, decisions I made.

Through SIU I learned the art of architecture. I learned to think, draw, paint, sketch, and resolve complex variables into rational solutions. While not known for design, the school was heavily based in the fundamentals, including learning how buildings go together—more so than most schools cover. My education at SIU provided me with the best foundation for becoming an architect I could have asked for.

For graduate school I ultimately chose the University of Illinois at Urbana-Champaign. Having just completed my term as national vice president of the American Institute of Architecture Students, a full-time job in DC following my

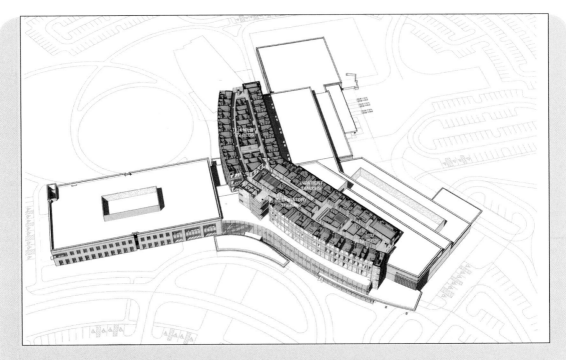

Ahuja Medical Center, Beachwood, Ohio. Architects: HKS Architects. PHOTOGRAPHER: SHANNON KRAUS, FAIA, MBA.

undergraduate studies, I came to realize that the single biggest gap in the amazingly rich and diverse education that architecture provides was business. As such, I chose to apply to universities where I could also attend business school—a decision that ultimately led to my acceptance into the school of architecture and the school of business at the University of Illinois, where I graduated summa cum laude with a master in business administration, and a master in architecture. Where the MBA equipped me to think more holistically about business and refined my communications skills, the M.Arch. filled in the remaining gaps with a curriculum more focused on design and design theory.

Reflecting back on how I chose the schools I did, I do believe that the profession does not have an adequate guidance system for assisting students interested in architecture. I say this because in many ways the school you choose will ultimately go a long way toward determining the type of professional you become.

What has been your greatest challenge as an architect?

❯ My view on this has evolved. Early in my career it was definitely Hadassah Medical Center in Jerusalem, Israel, due to the inherent social, political, and physical challenges of the location. However, now it would have to be managing an office and region of our global practice. Architecture school doesn't quite prepare you for office management and all that goes with it: mentoring, performance reviews, project staffing, recruiting, strategic marketing, and business planning. In many ways it is like being the general manager of a professional sports team where you look for new talent, look to mentor and coach your existing talent in order to position them to succeed and outperform your competitors. The biggest challenge, what keeps me awake at night, is making sure I am doing all I can not only to provide great project opportunities for my staff, but to bring enough project opportunities to keep everyone productive and employed—while doing so by shaping a studio culture within which any individual can thrive and is inspired to be entrepreneurial and innovative. Before my concerns centered around what I could do to improve a project, now my responsibility is to approximately 75 direct reports and their families.

Why did you pursue two graduate degrees— master of architecture and master of business administration—during your graduate studies?

❭ I believe in the notion that an architect is a generalist. The architectural education is extremely com-

prehensive and provides the foundation suitable for many careers; however, business seemed to be the one missing ingredient.

After serving as AIAS national vice president, I quickly came to realize that architecture is a business and that there was much more to learn—so I decided to go back to school and round out my education by earning an MBA in addition to the master of architecture. After speaking with others, I also knew that if I were to ever pursue the MBA, the time to do it was then—as there were no guarantees that such an opportunity would be available later in life.

Ultimately, I felt the MBA would help me simply by providing additional tools for me to draw upon. However, in addition to the business skills, the MBA had many other benefits that I did not anticipate. The program I went through proved valuable

John Dempsey Hospital Addition, Hartford, Connecticut. Architect: HKS Architects.

in helping me to hone my communication skills, problem-solving ability, and leadership skills. In many ways, the business degree was not as much about accounting or finance as it was about maximizing resources and leadership.

As one of the youngest vice presidents in the history of the AIA, what would you say was your most significant achievement?

❭ During my tenure as AIA vice president, I had the fortune of being involved in several meaningful things that I feel truly help the profession. One of the most significant was working with my fellow executive committee members to help the AIA craft and adopt a policy supporting the 2030 Challenge. Other milestones include the development of a national ARE scholarship, as well as the creation of a National Research fund for evidence-based design. My goal as vice president was simply to have made a difference—to have a positive impact on the

evolution of the institute, no matter how small. In doing this, it is now my hope that others who are as passionate about the profession as I am will be similarly encouraged to get engaged and get involved.

As a relatively young architect in a large firm, what are your primary responsibilities and duties?

❭ Currently I am the managing director of a 35-person office and am the regional director for our mid-Atlantic and East Coast region that encompasses around 75 staff. My responsibilities include not only developing our healthcare practice by bringing in new work and working with clients to deliver those projects, but it also now includes managing the office culture, empowering young staff to take on leadership roles, hiring and performance reviews, and mentoring. I took on this role after serving as director of design for about five years in two different offices. That role would include serving as the senior design lead on multiple projects, cultivating new work,

Shore Health Medical Center, Easton, Maryland. Architect: HKS, Inc. PHOTOGRAPHER: HKS.

working with clients to deliver on their expectations, and working with the team to adequately staff projects, develop talent, and nurture new leaders.

Some of my recent projects include Shore Health Medical Center, University of Connecticut John Dempsey Tower, Ahuja Medical Center in Cleveland, Ohio, and Flower Mound Hospital in Flower Mound, Texas. In all of these projects, regardless of my role, my goal is to understand the clients' needs, listen to their dreams, and work with them to identify innovative design solutions that they can implement on time and on budget.

What is the most satisfying part of your career as an architect?

❯ Without a doubt the most satisfying part of my career has been helping others succeed. Knowing you helped recruit someone into the practice, helped influence their career, empowered them, and then witness them begin to take off on their own successful career is quite invigorating. This really is more than mentoring; it is for me the essence of leadership. Mentoring programs come and go, but empowering others to succeed and investing in their development is to me the responsibility of every firm and should happen regardless of any formal mentoring. Second to this is seeing projects you pour your heart and soul into get built. When you are pursuing something you love and look forward to, there is not a greater feeling in the world than to see not only your vision realized but that of your team and client.

What is the most important quality or skill of a healthcare designer?

❯ Patience, communication, and knowledge are the most important skill sets of a designer in healthcare, or any area for that matter. As a programmer and designer in healthcare, we work directly with clients, physicians, nurses, equipment specialists, contractors, builders, project managers, and business leaders. In each case, the architect must be knowledgeable enough of the subject matter being programmed to effectively communicate in the language of the particular user being met with. Most issues and challenges are the result of poor communication, so having the patience to work through misconceptions and differences of opinions is key to resolving issues as you develop a program or a project design solution. The knowledge of healthcare facilities comes through trial and error and is learned more on the job than in school. You have to be "heads-up" in the office, seek out every opportunity to participate in a meeting or go on a tour.

Who has been a major influence on your career?

❯ There have been many great influences on my career, but none greater than my parents and my wife. While I have benefited from many great mentors, and try to learn from all of those around me, it is my parents who helped shape me into the man I am today, teaching me to believe that I could do anything I put my mind to. And it is my wife who helps keep me focused, motivated, and on track with an even-keeled perspective that brings with it humility and grace. Without a doubt I am blessed to have them as positive influences in my life and I know that I would not be where I am today if not for them.

What has been your most rewarding endeavor as a professional?

❯ Having a hand in the creation of the HKS Design Fellowship is so far my most rewarding endeavor as a professional. In 2006, motivated by a desire to empower architects in the community while also linking young architects with political leaders to solve community challenges all at the same time, I initiated the first HKS design fellowship. The program, run and led by emerging architects, features a social or community problem that would benefit from a three-day design charrette intervention. The results then are offered to local leaders and related community organizations at no cost to them.

The program has expanded opportunities for the firm's young professionals by giving them direct client experience and speaking opportunities. It also works well with civic leaders to show how good design can be used to solve challenges and shape communities. For the first two years, HKS focused on projects in Dallas. Since then, the program has expanded to be offered each year in DC, Detroit, Dallas, and Atlanta, and now includes students partnering with interns in charrette teams from over 20 architecture schools.

Second Modernism

WILLIAM J. CARPENTER, Ph.D., FAIA, LEED AP

Professor

School of Architecture and Construction Management

Southern Polytechnic State University

Marietta, Georgia

President, Lightroom (www.lightroom.tv)

Decatur, Georgia

Why and how did you become an architect?

❯ I grew up in Mattituck, New York. I became an architect because of my sixth-grade teacher, Robert Fisher. I was his first student to go to architecture school, and I could not have done it without him. He invented classes for me, such as eco-tecture, that emphasized sustainable design before it was in vogue. He collected donations from many of the businesses in our town to create a scholarship for me that he gave me at high school graduation. This summer I went to visit him and he had all of the drawings and books I had sent him displayed in his library. I would not have known what architecture was without him.

I was able then to apprentice for two great architects: first, Norman Jaffe, FAIA, in New York, and then Samuel Mockbee, FAIA, in Mississippi. Mockbee later received the America Institute of Architects (AIA) Gold Medal.

Why and how did you decide on which schools to attend for your architecture degree? What degree(s) do you possess?

❯ Bachelor of architecture, master of architecture, and Ph.D. in architecture. I went to Mississippi State for my undergraduate studies because I asked Richard Meier at a career day what school he would attend and he said he had just returned from there and something interesting was happening there. At 17, I packed my bags and arrived from New York. He was so right—I was able to study with Robert Ford, Christopher Risher, and Merrill Elam.

I chose Virginia Tech for graduate studies because of its emphasis on urbanism and tectonics. No school in the world offers a better balance of these pedagogical intents—of course, I am an alumnus. Jaan Holt and Gregory Hunt were amazing professors and left an indelible imprint on me.

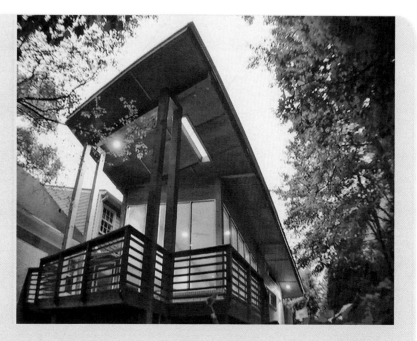

The Breen Residence, Atlanta, Georgia. Architect: William J. Carpenter, FAIA, Ph.D. PHOTOGRAPHER: KEVIN BYRD.

For my doctorate I wanted to go to England. I was able to study with Professor Thomas Muir before he retired. I studied at the University of Central England at Birmingham Polytechnic, which is one of the oldest programs in the United Kingdom. Muir, Alan Green, and Denys Hinton gave me an appreciation for Europe, how to live and where to find the best pubs. I have never met anyone with a deeper commitment to architectural education and learning.

What has been your greatest challenge as an architect?

❯ The greatest challenge I have is balancing my time. I have two wonderful daughters and desire to be an integral part of their lives. I have amazing students to teach, and I work for great clients on architectural commissions. The biggest challenge is getting it all done well. One of the ways I keep it all together is to keep a journal/sketchbook, in which I try to keep new ideas or work on existing ideas at many different scales.

How does your work as a faculty member inform your architectural practice and vice versa?

❯ My students constantly inspire me and help me see things in new ways. I invite them to my studio to see new projects. I try to be involved in their lives during and after school. They are why I teach; I also try to involve students in actual projects such as our community outreach in Reynoldstown (in downtown Atlanta).

What are your primary responsibilities and duties as an architect and a faculty member?

❯ I am president of Lightroom, an architecture and new media firm in Decatur, Georgia. In the past few years we have won awards in a number of different disciplines, including being on the team who won the international 48-hour film festival, being on the team that had a short film accepted to Cannes, and two major awards of excellence from the AIA and from *Print* magazine. I do not think awards define you, but I appreciate that they are from very diverse organizations, all for excellent design.

►Lightroom Studios, Decatur, Georgia. Architect: William J. Carpenter, FAIA, Ph.D. PHOTOGRAPHER: LIGHTROOM.

▼Lightcatcher, Decatur, Georgia. Architect: William J. Carpenter, FAIA, Ph.D. PHOTOGRAPHER: LIGHTROOM.

I teach in the thesis studio, which is very enjoyable. I like teaching at the fifth-year level. I also teach a theory class on modern architecture and design. My duties as a professor are also centered on connecting academic with the profession. To accomplish this, I serve on the National AIA board of directors as a regional director.

You authored the book Modern Sustainable Residential Design: A Guide for Design Professionals *(Wiley, 2009). What is sustainable design and why is it important for design professionals?*

❯ Sustainable architecture is designing efficient buildings that can produce their own energy and allow for the least damage to the earth possible—such as using recycled buildings or materials. It is important for design professionals because economy (part of the Vitruvian triad) is an essential element of great design.

About two years ago the editor of *Dwell* magazine contacted me to write their first book. I have always been impressed with how they humanized modernism with pictures of people and looking comfortable in their homes. Sustainability is often seen as a fad amongst architects and the public. I believe it is an integral part of architecture and the best modern buildings I know—such as the Second Jacobs house by Frank Lloyd Wright and

his Rosenbaum House—are great examples of sustainable modern buildings. I am concerned today about sustainable buildings that look modern-"ish" and not "modernist." This is the difference between style and commitment and authenticity. In the future I believe that sustainable architecture will produce power for us— whether it is a house or an entire city. An important sustainable principle that students need to remember is that the adaptive reuse of buildings can be one of the most sensitive moves an architect can make.

Enhancing Your Business through Design

ROBERT D. FOX, AIA, IIDA, LEED AP

Principal, FOX Architects

McLean, Virginia/Washington, DC

Why and how did you become an architect?

❯ My father was an architect, and I grew up in the offices of Louis Kahn and Romaldo Giurgola when I was a kid. It was during this time that I fell in love with architecture because I could appreciate the tangible nature of design.

Why and how did you decide on attending Temple University for your architecture degree? What degree(s) do you possess?

❯ I have a bachelor of architecture from Temple University. My father taught there so it made the decision easier.

What has been your greatest challenge as an architect?

❯ Design is an incredibly impactful profession. We are all able to create buildings and spaces that are beautiful and functional, but it's our clients that challenge us to go beyond that. Our clients want their offices to be performance tools. It is our job as commercial design specialists to look beyond the pragmatic to create places that enhance the daily lives of our clients.

Earlier in your career, you specialized in corporate interiors. How does interior architecture differ from architecture?

❯ Interior architecture is more intimate than architecture. People spend a majority of their day in the office so it needs to be comfortable and functional. In designing an interior, I work closely with our clients so I get to learn more about them and under-

440 First St., N.W.
Washington, DC.
Architect: FOX Architects.

stand their specific needs, and I get to see the impact of our design on their employee morale and productivity. Today, my firm specializes in both architecture and interiors. This integrated approach allows us to take an "inside-out, outside-in" approach to design.

As a principal of a firm, what are your primary responsibilities and duties?

❯ My duties as a principal include all the aspects of business management: financials, marketing, human resources, legal, insurance, real estate, information technology (IT), software, and contracts, and so on.

More important, I enable design. My primary responsibility is to create a highly specialized team of experts. Starting with our leadership, our firm is composed of subject matter experts who make us an asset on any project.

Beyond that, I am responsible for listening first to our design team and my partners and then developing and communicating the direction of the firm in a clear and concise manner. I strive to find the strengths in others and enable them to perform at very high levels and to continually offer my experience and expertise.

FOX Architects specializes in architecture, interior design, graphic design, multimedia design, and signage. How do these different design disciplines interact within your work?

❯ The reason that FOX has a multidisciplinary design practice is to expand and engage the dialogue of our work. We cannot achieve breakthrough ideas if we do not have a holistic approach to all aspects of design. Different perspectives enable us to stay fresh and develop innovative ideas in an industry that is constantly evolving.

What is the most/least satisfying part of your career as an architect?

❯ The most satisfying part is seeing our clients "get it." The moment they realize their business potential—that is really exciting. I also enjoy learning about other businesses and seeing different business models.

We carry quite a bit of financial liability in what we do; few design professionals really understand the risks that they take on—they just want to design. While design is fun, you cannot grow or evolve unless you are making a decent profit.

Who or what experience has been a major influence on your career?

❯ First, my father was a big influence. Second, I am constantly influenced by a number of the developers with whom we work and seeing how they conceive, construct, and operate a building, from debt and financing, to management, maintenance, sales, and leasing.

▲ American Society for Microbiology, Washington, DC. Architect: FOX Architects. PHOTOGRAPHER: JOHN COLE, JOHN COLE PHOTOGRAPHY.

▶ FOX Offices— Virginia Office, McLean, Virginia. Architect: FOX Architects. PHOTOGRAPHER: RON BLUNT, RON BLUNT PHOTOGRAPHY.

A Gentle Woman's Profession

KATHY DENISE DIXON, AIA, NOMA

Principal

K. Dixon Architecture, PLLC

Upper Marlboro, Maryland

Associate Professor

University of the District of Columbia

Washington, DC

Why and how did you become an architect?

❯ My becoming an architect is the result of several influences during my childhood, not the least of which is the fact that my father was an architect for the Army Corps of Engineers. In a sense, I think I inherited the desire to be an architect. But, moreover, the fact that I had a creative nature, drawing ability, and good math skills also led me to pursue architecture.

▲ Potomac Consolidated TRACON, Federal Aviation Administration, Warrenton, Virginia. Architect: Jacobs Engineering. PHOTOGRAPHERS: KATHY DENISE DIXON/YUYAN ZHOU.

◄Assembly for Worship Church, Brandywine, Maryland. Architect: K. Dixon Architecture, PLLC / Millennium Design Architects.

Why and how did you decide on which school to attend for your architecture degree? What degree(s) do you possess?

❭ It was a fairly easy choice to decide to pursue architecture at Howard University due to the fact that they were the only institution that offered me a five-year scholarship. After my bachelor of architecture, I also pursued a master of arts in urban planning at the University of California at Los Angeles (UCLA) with a focus was housing and community development.

Why did you pursue the additional degree—master of arts in urban planning—from UCLA?

❭ I felt that pursuing a degree in planning would enhance my perspective as an architect. Even the best architecture has to respond to context. On a broader scale, understanding context, community, environment, and our society is essential for a well-rounded architect. I believe all architects should learn more about urban planning, planning policy, and urban design so we are not designing in a vacuum.

How and why did you decide to start your own firm, K. Dixon Architecture, PLLC in 2010?

❭ I decided to start working for myself in 2010 to fulfill a lifelong desire to have my own architecture firm and steer my own destiny. I had actually created the business entity, K. Dixon Architecture, PLLC, in 2003, knowing that one day I would be ready to work for myself, but I had no timeline for when that might occur. In 2010 several factors came together that allowed me to make the transition. One of those factors was the opportunity to teach at the university level in the Department of Urban Architecture and Community Planning at University of the District of Columbia. Teaching evenings at UDC enabled me to work for myself during the day.

How does teaching differ from practicing architecture?

❭ Teaching differs from practicing architecture in that there are no client deadlines. However, I believe it is very similar to practice due to the need to always be prepared for presentation (lecturing), always keeping up to date on current events and trends (continuing education), and always synthesizing large amounts of information (design process) into a format that can be easily understood by others.

What has been your greatest challenge as an architect?

❭ Personally, my greatest challenge has been gathering up the personal confidence to do well in the profession. I was licensed at 29 years of age and had two professional degrees, plus I had obtained additional certifications. However, with all the education and achievements, I was not confident that I could make the decisions and lead the design process and team on my own. I remember having a talk about the lack of confidence with a colleague who had recently started his own consulting business. He told me that I just had to believe in myself and be confident that I can make the decisions and do what is required. He suggested that everyone has this challenge and he had to deal with the same issues in starting his business. It still took more years of experience before I felt I could lead a design team, but I have overcome that personal and internal self-challenge.

What is the most/least satisfying part of your career as an architect?

❭ Seeing the finished product of your labor is probably the most satisfying of any career one can choose. To visit, experience, and reflect over the completed structure and the decisions that went into its creation is a satisfaction that few others will experience.

Probably one of the least satisfying aspects of being an architect is the length of time it takes to see your work come to fruition. Other careers generally have immediate results. However, the length of time to design and construct a building can be 18 months or longer. It is challenging, especially as a young architect, to have to wait so long to see the realization of what you have been working on.

In 2013–2014, you served as the president of the National Organization of Minority Architects (NOMA). What is NOMA, and how has serving in leadership positions within NOMA benefited your professional career?

❯ Founded in 1971, NOMA is a professional networking organization founded to assist minority architects in their career development. Although the number of minority architects is increasing, there are currently only approximately 300 licensed African American women architects in the country. This presents challenges for individuals pursuing the field of architecture and requires a great deal of mentoring. Prior to deciding to pursue a career in architecture, I did not know a single African American woman architect. I only met a couple during my college studies. Although I became licensed on my own, it would have been very beneficial for me to have known and potentially been mentored by a woman architect. As a result, I am involved with the NOMA and have a particular interest in mentoring young African American women in the field of architecture.

Serving in NOMA has been beneficial for my professional development due to the wonderful network of individuals in the organization that I can turn to if I need assistance making decisions about my own career or my practice. It is great to have the NOMA Network as a resource as my firm grows. I also benefit from being the leader of the organization as a result of increased visibility and networking. Given my leadership role, I recently

Galina Perova Fine Art Gallery, National Harbor, Maryland. Architect: K. Dixon Architecture, PLLC.

participated in a White House workshop on STEM (science, technology, engineering, and mathematics) minority inclusion—an opportunity I may not have otherwise ever experienced.

Who or what experience has been a major influence on your career?

❯ Of course, my father was a major influence in my decision to become an architect. I am very much like my father in character and interests.

I was also fortunate to have Barry Washington, an interior designer, serve as a role model early on in my career. On my first job working as a computer-aided design and drafting (CADD) operator for the U.S. Department of Justice, I worked with Mr. Washington on various facility management projects. Barry required a high level of professionalism and quality of work during my three-year internship. His expectation for design excellence has remained with me throughout my career.

The Architecture of Leadership

CAROLYN G. JONES, AIA, LEED AP

Principal

MulvannyG2

Bellevue, Washington

Why and how did you become an architect?

❯ After taking an Introduction to Architecture class at a summer camp program in junior high, architectural design became one of my favorite hobbies. I would spend summers at my drafting table designing floor plans and building foam core models of houses. Despite my interest in architecture, I never thought of it as my career; I started college as an international studies major. During the second semester of my freshman year, I decided to try Introduction to Architecture. Three weeks later, I switched majors. I was instantly captivated by the buildings we were studying and could not imagine anything more rewarding than creating the built environment for a living.

Why and how did you decide on which school to attend for your architecture degree? What degree(s) do you possess?

❯ I received a five-year bachelor of architecture from the University of Notre Dame. Since I did not go to college planning to study architecture, it was pure luck that I even ended up at a school with an architecture program. I chose Notre Dame for its well-rounded liberal arts undergraduate program, its size, the campus atmosphere, and the student life it provided. It was more important to me to be at a school that felt like a great fit for me overall, with the strength of the specific program I was interested in being a secondary consideration.

As it turned out, the program there did provide a very strong background and foundation for the study and practice of architecture. However, I believe that the most important part of my education, which has helped make me the architect and person that I am today, was based more my *entire* Notre Dame experience and not the specifics of the architecture program.

Anthropologie—Urban Outfitters, Vancouver, British Columbia. Architect: MulvannyG2 Architecture. PHOTOGRAPHER: RAEF GROHNE.

What is retail design, and how might it be different from architecture design?

❭ What makes retail design unique is the focus beyond just the traditional shell building to the interior architectural design as well as the visual merchandising. The design of the entire environment, from the building itself to the smallest detail of a merchandise fixture, is part of what creates retail architecture.

I have never felt that interiors and architecture are two separate, distinct fields, and in retail design, the two are inseparable. From the architectural standpoint, retail design needs to be a seamless connection between interior and exterior spaces, forms and functions.

The key is that in retail, the architecture serves as a backdrop for the merchandise. You have to understand how product is displayed, how it best sells, how the customer interacts with or "shops" the space, the impact of lighting, and the importance of setting a certain atmosphere through a combination of built environment, furniture, fixtures, and finishes.

As a principal, what are your primary responsibilities and duties?

❭ As a principal of a very large firm, my responsibilities are much broader than working on individual projects. At one point I managed a large client account and team of over 50 people, which was similar to running a small office. My duties included being the primary contact for the client to coordinate and manage workflow, project quality, schedules, and budgets. Internally, I worked with staffing to keep the project teams balanced with the right individuals, and also monitored the execution of the projects as well as being responsible for the financial performance of the team.

Now, working in a broader capacity, I work with leadership throughout the firm on setting strategy around our retail practice, developing business plans, developing business with new clients, and participating in and leading initiatives, task forces, and other broader business and operations functions of how the office runs. I also have a number of client accounts that I personally manage as principal in charge. Additionally, a key responsibility as a principal is spending an extensive amount of time on personnel issues, helping others set and work toward their goals, dealing with problem situations, helping to maintain morale of the staff, and so on. As principal overseeing projects across the country,

I am also responsible for signing drawings and thus maintaining licenses in most states.

What has been your greatest challenge as an architect?

❯ My greatest challenge as an architect has been learning the necessary skills for my position that were not taught in school, mainly teamwork, management, financial, and leadership. School focused heavily on the achievement of the individual, but in the working world, success relies on working with others. It took me quite a few years to realize that my hard work or talent meant very little, and I would not be successful, if I did not cooperate with and respect the input and contributions of others.

I am probably less confident now than I was when I was first starting out in architecture. The longer you practice, the more you know, but you also become increasingly more aware of what you do not know. Sometimes that can be very overwhelming, but in the end you have to remember that you have an amazing support system in the resources and colleagues around you. Those people become part of your personal and professional "team" who can help you achieve more than you ever could on your own.

What is leadership in the context of architecture? Why is it important, and how does one develop it?

❯ Leadership in the context of architecture can mean many things, especially within the setting of various types of firms where different leaders may be in charge of account leadership, practice or operations leadership, and design leadership. In a broader sense, I think leadership involves having a passion for the craft of architecture, both the design and the construction. It means being a champion for good design and having respect for the other consultants and disciplines that contribute to successful projects, as well as for those in the construc-

tion trades that know their craft and execute the buildings. Leadership is being involved with your community, not just with industry-related groups, but other causes you care about, including supporting sustainability. It includes supporting the profession as a whole, but also being involved with your client's industry or business as well.

Globally, leadership is important to make our communities and world a better place through the built environment. It supports the profession of architecture in the eyes of the public and our clients. Within firms, leadership is important to ensure success of the business, especially during challenging economic times, and it is vital to support, mentor, and grow the next generation of architects.

Honestly, not everyone is cut out for or interested in leadership at a certain level—especially because taking on more leadership in a business often means doing less of the actual "architecture" that we love. But even those who are not interested in a future role as a CEO have other ways to be leaders. Within a firm you can get involved with certain initiatives or activities from coordinating an office volunteer effort to supporting a quality assurance task force. Outside of work, volunteering with other groups you are interested in provides many leadership opportunities. For those who do want higher leadership positions in the firm, be proactive in asking for challenging assignments and projects. Volunteer, as mentioned earlier, for a range of activities inside and outside the office. Find opportunities to learn more about the business and operations of a firm—even if you are in a design role. Support and mentor others, remember that the success of those around you is the only way a leader can be successful. And get licensed; doing so shows that you respect your profession enough to make the effort.

What challenges do you find in being both an architect and a mother?

❯ I am sure that I face the same challenges as a working parent in almost any profession. Balancing work and family is never easy, and with architecture there is, of course, the occasional added pressure to work extra hours or late nights on project deadlines. Learning to work more efficiently in the time you have is critical and often feels counterintuitive to what we have learned since the studio model in school. I think most working parents would agree that it is frustrating to feel like you are never really able to give 100 percent either at work or at home. After becoming a parent, it can be difficult to realign expectations of yourself and your career.

What I do find very challenging in architecture is the lack of role models of other working moms at the leadership level. Perhaps this is not unique to our profession, but it has been difficult to find many women in more advanced roles that also face the challenges of parenting young children and I have found myself to be an exception in this regard. What I have come to realize is that I need to embrace the fact that I actually *am* that role model. It is an honor to be an example for others as a firm leader and mom, learning the ropes of balancing a career and a family every day. I hope, by being a role model in this regard, I can help encourage the next generation of young architects, men and women, to find their own work/life/family balance. As a bigger vision, I also hope to help find a way to keep more talented women architects in the profession in the long run by encouraging them to find creative solutions to integrating their own families and careers.

H&M, Auburn, Washington. Architect: MulvannyG2 Architecture. PHOTOGRAPHER: JUAN HERNANDEZ.

Nordstrom–City Creek,
Salt Lake City, Utah.
Architect: Callison.
PHOTOGRAPHER: CHRIS
EDEN.

What is the most/least satisfying part of your job?

❯ What we often refer as "people issues" are both the most and least satisfying parts of my job. On the least satisfying side is dealing with office politics, staffing problems, or personnel issues. This might include how I get along with and fit in with other leaders in the company whom I do not always agree with or who have different agendas, as well as helping staff who do not get along with each other learn to cooperate and communicate. More challenges include delivering tough messages to staff that are having serious performance issues and, in the worst case, having to lay off or even fire coworkers. Many days, the architecture challenges we face on projects seem quite manageable compared to keeping so many talented and unique individuals working together in a positive, constructive way.

On the flip side, people issues are also the most rewarding part of my job. I truly enjoy working with staff to help them create and work toward their professional goals. Whether through our performance review process or more informal day-to-day coaching and mentoring, it is very rewarding to help facilitate the growth and learning of those around me. Although seeing a building you worked on get completed is a peak experience as an architect, it is just as satisfying to see people around me grow and succeed

in their careers. It can often be challenging to find the time to spend with others in this development capacity, especially when you have so many pressing needs on your own projects, but the time spent connecting one-on-one with those you work with has intangible rewards. It is an honor to be in a leadership position where I can work with young architects in this capacity.

Who or what experience has been a major influence on your career?

❯ By far the greatest influences on my career have been the mentors I have had. Three individuals in particular, two managers and one client, were extremely supportive of my career growth and were champions for me at a young age. As a result, I have enjoyed rapid growth in my career and a chance to expand my skill set and knowledge base very quickly. These opportunities have helped fuel my success within my firm as well opened up opportunities for me to learn new skills on various project types.

Although finding a mentor is not always easy, there are things a young architect can do to help facilitate finding one. The more interest, initiative, drive, and enthusiasm you show in your career, the more likely you are to attract the attention of a mentor who can support you along the way. Look for others that you respect or have an interest in, and do not be afraid to reach out to them to input and advice.

Profile of the Profession

According to the Bureau of Labor Statistics, U.S. Department of Labor,[6] 113,700 architects were practicing in the United States in 2010, the last year for which statistics are available. Employment projections for architect are expected to grow by 27,900 (24 percent) between 2010–2020, faster than average for all occupations.

Much of this growth is dictated by current demographic trends. As the population continues to live longer and Baby Boomers retire, there will be a need for more healthcare facilities, nursing homes, and retirement communities.

There will be a demand for architects with knowledge of green design; rising energy costs and increased concern about the environment have led to many new buildings being built green.[6]

With this projected growth of the profession, should you consider architecture? Before you answer, consider the following. According to the National Architectural Accrediting Board (NAAB), 25,958 students were studying architecture in professional degree programs in the United States during the 2012–2013 academic year, a slight decrease from the previous year. Newly matriculated students enrolled in NAAB-accredited degree programs equaled 7,169.[7]

Further, 6,347 students graduated with the NAAB-accredited degree. If you assume that the number of graduates with the accredited degree remains the same for 2010–2020, the projected time frame, 63,400 graduates with a NAAB-accredited degree may be competing for the projected 27,900 openings. Clearly, based on employment projections, the competition for architectural positions will be keen over the next decade. Take solace, though, because graduates with an architectural education may enter many career fields; see Chapter 4, "The Careers of an Architect."

In its 2013 survey of registered architects, the National Council of Architectural Registration Boards[8] (NCARB) reports 105,847 registered architects living in the 55 reporting jurisdictions, including all 50 states, the District of Columbia, Guam, the Northern Mariana Islands, Puerto Rico, and the Virgin Islands. This total represents a negligible increase from the previous year's survey.

While the AIA[9] does not represent the entire profession, its membership does constitute a majority. Therefore, it is worth reporting its facts and figures. The AIA reports a membership of 81,000 members of the AIA. Of the full AIA architect members, 74 percent practice in architecture firms, 2 percent practice in the corporate sector, and 2 percent practice in government and 1 percent in construction, while the remaining practice at design firms, universities/colleges/associations, contractors' or builder firms, and engineering firms.

SALARY

According to the Bureau of Labor Statistics, U.S. Department of Labor,[10] the 2012 median annual earnings of wage and salary architects were $73,090. The lowest 10 percent earned less than $44,600, and the highest 10 percent earned more than $118,230. Salaries fluctuate, depending on the region of the country, the amount of experience an individual has, and even the type of employer.

Finally, data from the 2013 AIA Compensation Survey[11] report the average compensation for an architect is $76,700, a slight increase from the 2011 survey. The following salaries are almost identical to the previous survey in 2011: managing principal, $133,000; senior project designer, $91,100; architect, $72,500; and interns, $45,400. Of course, these salaries were also collected during the latter part of the economic downturn in the latter part of 2012 and early 2013.

At all experience levels, large architecture firms offer higher compensation than smaller firms. In addition, most firms offer a salary premium to staff with a master of architecture and those that have completed the Architect Registration Exam (ARE) and become licensed, and a full third of firms offer higher salaries for staff that have sufficient experience in building information modeling (BIM).

DIVERSITY

What is diversity, and why is it important? The following answer is from *Designing for Diversity,* by Kathryn H. Anthony, Ph.D:

> Diversity is a set of human traits that have an impact on individuals' values, opportunities, and perceptions of self and others at work. At minimum, it includes six core dimensions: age, ethnicity, gender, mental or physical abilities, race, and sexual orientation.[12]

In the context of the architectural profession, diversity is extremely important because, for many years, the profession has been known as a white man's profession. This label may no longer be quite appropriate, as the profession is beginning to make strides, but consider the representation of women and individuals of color. Again, the AIA is the most reliable source for estimates.

According to the AIA, about 13,500 (16 percent) are women, and 8,000 (10 percent) are ethnic minorities.[13] The National Organization of Minority Architects states that fewer than 2 percent (~2,100) of the 105,000 architects are African American. Within the schools, the numbers are dramatically better. According to the NAAB, the number of female students pursuing architecture in accredited professional degree programs is 11,456 (42.6 percent). The number of students of color is 8,765 (32.6 percent).

As of September 2013, the Directory of African American Architects lists currently 1,896 licensed African American architects (301 female and 1,595 male).[14] Sponsored by the Center for the Study of Practice at the University of Cincinnati, the directory is maintained as a public service to promote an awareness of African American architects and where they are located.

What Are the Most Important Skills an Architect Needs to Be Successful?

❭ The most important skill is listening. I find that too many architects do not listen well; it takes practice.

William J. Carpenter, Ph.D., FAIA, Associate Professor, Southern Polytechnic State University; President, Lightroom

❭ Leadership is the most important skill an architect can possess. As the client's advocate and the head of the consultant team, the architect must maintain an overview of the project and provide consistent guidance to ensure its success as well as the long-lasting relationships developed during its course. A great leader is skilled at listening empathetically, creating a vision, and enabling others to act.

Grace H. Kim, AIA, Principal, Schemata Workshop, Inc.

❭ Creativity, design, technical skills, management, communication, and excellent leadership skills are required. It requires a very high level of maturity.

Robert D. Fox, AIA, IIDA, Principal, FOX Architects

❭ Communication skills. Though architects are often regarded as lone wolves, the reality is that completing a project takes teamwork. You must practice clearly articulating yourself through email, over the phone, and in person.

Murrye Bernard, Associate AIA, LEED AP, Managing Editor, Contract Magazine

❭ The most important skills are *communication*, imagination, *communication*, problem solving, and *communication*. Architects must have the imagination to dream up the vision of clients, the communication skills to articulate that vision so the client can understand it, and the ability to resolve complex variables in order to make that vision a reality. The fundamentals of math, science, and art are rel-

evant, but they are tools that support imagination, communication, and problem solving.

Shannon Kraus, FAIA, MBA, Principal and Senior Vice President, HKS

❭ An architect is the person that dwells at the confluence of the left and right brain. They are able to translate the creative impulse and technical realities into the physical world. A successful architect is able to balance those abilities with the needs of the individual and society.

Amanda Harrell-Seyburn, Associate AIA, Instructor, School of Planning, Design and Construction, Michigan State University

❭ To be successful, you must be able to adapt to your surroundings. You must be a good communicator and, more important, a good listener. You must be open to taking risks and looking at things in a different way.

H. Alan Brangman, AIA, Vice President of Facilities, Real Estate Auxiliary Services, University of Delaware

❭ Creative, analytic, and communication skills. An architect needs to be able to conceive, draw, build, and effectively communicate their ideas as well as find solutions to design obstacles or limitations.

Anna A. Kissell, M.Arch. Candidate, Boston Architectural College, Associate Manager Environmental Design, Reebok International Inc.

❭ Patience for process and appreciation for design is a telescopic continuum in which you cannot skillfully address any point of the scale without being mindful of the others.

Rosannah B. Sandoval, AIA, Designer II, Perkins + Will

❭ Patience, willingness to listen, good personal skills in dealing with clients, and last but not least, ability to design.

John W. Myefski, AIA, Principal, Myefski Architects, Inc.

Cosmonaut Museum, Moscow, Russia. PHOTOGRAPHER: TED SHELTON, AIA.

❯ To achieve *good* design, an architect needs to be sensitive to many things; observing, listening, reacting, inventing, creating, activating. For an architect to design a solution, he/she must first understand and analyze the problem. Without this, architecture lacks an overarching concept— a critical part of a functional, iconic, successful design.

Tanya Ally, Architectural Staff, Bonstra | Haresign Architects

❯ Architects must have the following skills (the order depends on the individual): (a) excellent com-munication skills (e.g., writing, speaking, and tra-ditional and digital drawing ability); (b) tolerance for ambiguity; (c) agility; (d) an analytical mind; (e) attention to both the macro and the micro; (f) humility; and (g) graphical diagramming.

Thomas Fowler IV, AIA, NCARB, DPACSA Professor and Director, Community Interdisciplinary Design Studio (CIDS), California Polytechnic State University—San Luis Obispo

❯ Observation; graphic and verbal communication skills; tenacity, perseverance, and fortitude.

Mary Kay Lanzillotta, FAIA, Partner, Hartman-Cox Architects

❯ Verbal, written, and graphic communication skills are the most important needed to be a suc-cessful architect. Since there are many players in-volved in a building being designed and built, clear communication is imperative to convey your ideas to others.

Robert D. Roubik, AIA, LEED AP, Project Architect, Antunovich Associates Architects and Planners

❯ Drive to get through the rigorous education and training is paramount. After the initial education of an architect, the development of strategic thinking, strategic planning, and efficient thinking continu-ally need to be fine-tuned.

Megan S. Chusid, AIA, Manager of Facilities and Office Services, Solomon R. Guggenheim Museum and Foundation

❯ All architects must be able to communicate well in a variety of media. Other important skills include speaking, writing, critical thinking, and problem solving. Also, an understanding of busi-ness finance is important, as the measure of a successful project is more than aesthetics and func-tion. My personal goal on every project is to learn such that it will enable me to increase my creativity or productivity.

Kathryn T. Prigmore, FAIA, Project Manager, HDR Architecture

What Are the Most Important Skills an Architect Needs to Be Successful? (Continued)

❯ An architect is an artist, who needs to be a master of input and output. An architect needs to be a leader and know how to manage time effectively. Most important, an architect needs to be able to understand and analyze information, as well as be able to interpret it and communicate information effectively. An architect needs to be able to work with different media to create the desired outcome.

Elizabeth Weintraub, B.Arch. Candidate, New York Institute of Technology

❯ Architects also need to be good communicators, and in this case that means they need to be able to skillfully craft the written word, they need to be able to speak in public clearly and persuasively, and they need to be able to effectively utilize visual media to communicate their intentions. Architects need to understand the wide range of technical, social, formal, and ethical dimensions in which they design.

Architects are like orchestra conductors in that they don't need to be able to play every instrument; rather, they need to know what every instrument can do and be able to successfully coordinate their activities.

Architects need to be good collaborators. The age of the sole genius architect is over, that is if indeed the myth was ever a reality. Architecture is the product of collaboration within design teams, with consultants, clients, regulatory bodies, and more. The architect who is unable to collaborate is likely to be an unemployed architect.

Brian Kelly, AIA, Associate Professor and Director, Architecture Program, University of Maryland

❯ Collaboration, teamwork, and people skills are probably the most important and most undervalued skills an architect needs in today's professional practice. But perhaps most important,

McCormick Tribune Campus Center, Chicago, Illinois. Architect: Rem Koolhaas. PHOTOGRAPHER: LEE W. WALDREP, Ph.D.

the ability to work collaboratively with clients, to lead them through the project process, can make the difference between a good project and a great one.

Carolyn G. Jones, AIA, Principal, Mulvanny G2

❯ Being an architect involves solving problems, overcoming challenges, and making all the parts and people involved work in just the right way. It is not human nature for this to be an easy task, and it takes much patience in order to do so.

Ashley W. Clark, Associate AIA, LEED AP, SMPS, Marketing Manager, LandDesign

❯ Passion, patience, and communication skills. Our work is most fun when we are fully committed to it and when we are excited about it. As design and construction are not straightforward processes, it helps to be patient with the team of professionals involved in a project, as many issues will be revisited repeatedly. Great ideas never become reality if no one else can understand and build them, so verbal, graphic, and oral communication skills are a must.

Allison Wilson, Intern Architect, Ayers, Saint Gross

❯ An architect must combine creativity and ingenuity. One must have a passion for understanding people and designing environments for them.

Jordan Buckner, M.Arch./MBA Graduate, University of Illinois at Urbana-Champaign

❯ Architects have to be able to see the larger issues at hand in any situation—they need to understand possibilities beyond the basic requirements, addressing everything from community, education, health, and social conditions to sustainability and technology. They also need the ability to see a way to address these challenges and take on this work. This is why architects have always been associated with critical changes throughout history—their abilities to both identify the difficult topics and envision potential ways to attend to them directly engages world problems and begins to develop solutions.

Karen Cordes Spence, Ph.D., AIA, LEED AP, Associate Professor, Drury University

Vision. Creativity. Passion. Persistence. Resilience. Listening. Communication.

Kimberly Dowdell, Project Manager/Director of Marketing, Levien & Company

❯ The most important skill is communication. You can be a fantastic designer and have a great project, but that is useless if you cannot communicate your ideas to the client. That being said, the ability to draw is also extremely important. Communication, especially in architecture, does not have to be entirely through words. It is helpful to be able to quickly sketch your ideas on the spot for a client or professor.

Elsa Reifsteck, BS Architectural Studies Graduate, University of Illinois at Urbana-Champaign

❯ Architects must exhibit social and cultural awareness as it relates to specific projects at hand. This may include being aware of the project's history and the people it will serve and effect. Not only must architects design and relate to the building, they must also have a sense of business and the legal responsibilities that come with the profession.

Jennifer Taylor, Vice President, American Institute of Architecture Students

❯ An architect must be resourceful. The myriad of regulations, building codes, materials, products, and rules of thumb are impossible to commit to memory. An architect must know where to go to find answers to best solve the design problem. Moreover, because the architect is responsible for coordinating an entire team of professionals, he/she must have very good organization skills and people skills. Finally, the ability to imagine objects in three dimensions is paramount.

Kathy Denise Dixon, AIA, NOMA, Principal, K. Dixon Architecture, PLLC; Associate Professor, University of the District of Columbia

What Are the Most Important Skills an Architect Needs to Be Successful? (Continued)

❯ Because architecture exists at the intersection of numerous disciplines, those who practice it require a wide range of knowledge and skills. Consequently, the best architects today are the products of sound liberal education, not simply professional education.

Courage and insatiable curiosity. The world's best architects are not just problem solvers, they're problem seekers. They look to design solutions that address some of the most challenging aspects of the environments in which we live. Architects have the capacity to integrate multiple perspectives—to see the connections between the arts, science, technology, engineering, and culture—into informed solutions that provide value to communities.

Andrew Caruso, AIA, LEED AP BD+C, CDT, Head of Intern Development and Academic Outreach, Gensler

❯ An architect needs to be an integrative thinker who can pull the assets of a place into a design trajectory that shapes the project and tell the story of space.

Katherine Darnstadt, AIA LEED AP BD+C, Founder and Principal Architect, Latent Design

❯ An architect must love the environment, both built and natural. As a professor of mine once said: the love of architecture comes first. Without love first and foremost, the challenges and complexities of architecture can be mentally exhausting.

Joseph Mayo, Intern Architect, Mahlum

❯ The ability to process and convey information from a multitude of [mental] perspectives; more specifically, this would include drawing

Rotunda, University of Virginia, Charlottesville, Virginia. Architect: Thomas Jeffereson. PHOTOGRAPHER: R. LINDLEY VANN.

skills, the kind that allow one to convey an idea through an image; and traveling, which exposes the senses and psyche to more and varied information than can be received from a textbook.

Sarah Stein, Architectural Designer, Lee Scolnick Architects & Design Partnership

❯ The most important skill is the ability to communicate. One needs to be able to communicate the ideas they have to someone who may not completely understand. If you are unable to communicate, your idea will not progress.

Nicole Gangidino, B.Arch. Candidate, New York Institute of Technology

❯ Creativity, *true* creativity: A creative mind will be able to analyze this unique set of problems and discover the best solution, ensuring the best product for our clients.

Teamwork: Architects must work collaboratively with a diverse set of stakeholders to achieve the best result for the collective. In many cases, different stakeholders will have conflicting definitions of what the "best result" is for the project, and they will all look to the architect for leadership.

Empathy: Architects must possess the ability to listen to and understand the needs of our clients to ensure we are making the right decisions.

Cody Bornsheuer, Associate AIA, LEED AP BD+C, Architectural Designer, Dewberry Architects, Inc.

❯ Adaptability. We must infuse in our contributions to the built environment adaptive traits. That is, we too often think of our buildings as locked in a moment in time serving one function. They must do that and do it well to be useful in their time, but to be useful to our society, the buildings must be willing to adapt to changes we cannot even pretend to predict.

Adaptability also serves us well professionally. The world is full of change, and we must evolve with it and adapt. For some, this means changing how they approach projects, communication, or even design philosophy. For others, it means pursuing creatively other interests and passions.

Joseph Nickol, AICP, LEED AP BD+C, Urbanist, Urban Design Associates

❯ Communication and problem-solving skills are the most important. An architect needs to be able to communicate their idea and vision to coworkers, clients, and consultants, whether through drawings, diagrams, or words. Problem-solving skills are also very important in architecture, interior design, and planning; you need to be able to analyze a problem critically and create a safe, accessible, and beautiful solution.

Amanda Strawitch, Level 1 Architect, Design Collective

❯ A talent—one that is often lacking in our profession—is an in-depth understanding of the business side of architecture. Possessing the relevant knowledge of and skill in finance, negotiation, and strategic planning are critical keys to a successful practice.

And the aptitude to successfully both offer and accept criticism is an oft-overlooked skill, in architecture as in so many other fields. When offering criticism, take care to frame your thoughts in a way that will be respectful of, and constructive to, your colleague. In taking criticism, listen carefully to any concerns, and do not take them as a personal attack. Criticism may not be comfortable, but it is necessary in our profession at every level.

Kevin Sneed, AIA, IIDA, NOMA, LEED AP BD+C, Partner/ Senior Director of Architecture, OTJ Architects, LLC

What Are the Most Important Skills an Architect Needs to Be Successful? (Continued)

❯ Communication, dedication, and perseverance.

Sean M. Stadler, AIA, LEED AP, Design Principal, WDG Architecture, PLLC

❯ To be a great communicator, to be able to influence others, and to think like a designer. Design thinking, unlike traditional models for developing new ideas, involves abductive reasoning—imagining an end state and then building a plan on how to get there. It also really helps to be well versed in more than one discipline. Great thinking and ideas come from having multiple perspectives. Some of the greatest "architects" of our day have backgrounds in physics, environmental science, biology, psychology, engineering, computer science, or industrial design.

Leigh Stringer, LEED AP, Senior Vice-President, HOK

❯ Patience. Patience is key in almost every aspect of the design process. Patience to let your idea run its full course. Patience to continue with your concept despite roadblocks that might pop up along the way. Patience when deadlines loom and the natural urge is to panic and possibly compromise.

Another skill would be balance. Learning to balance the demands of architecture and studio with the rest of your interests is challenging. Having a narrow focus based solely upon architecture limits your abilities as a designer. Your experiences outside of architecture will help define yourself. Do not be afraid to leave the studio and go do something entirely unrelated to the project at hand!

Makenzie Leukart, M.Arch. Candidate, Columbia University

❯ An architect needs to constantly question—question existing situations, find the problems, and discover the best solution. This is the definition of the architectural design process.

Danielle Mitchell, B.Arch. Candidate, Pennsylvania State University

Creator of Space

JOHN W. MYEFSKI, AIA

Principal

Myefski Architects, Inc.

Evanston, Illinios

Why and how did you become an architect?

❯ I wanted to shape the future built environment. I feel that architects have such a profound impact on the way we live that I thought it would be great to create. I also had the chance to work for an architect as a high school senior. This experience really set the stage for my future.

Why and how did you decide on the University of Michigan to attend for your architecture degree? What degree(s) do you possess?

❯ I grew up in the upper peninsula of Michigan, and the idea of going to a school that was in the Midwest was important because of cost; cost was a strong consideration when selecting the University of Michigan. I was fortunate to have one of the best public schools in my state. I attended the pre-architecture program at Northern Michigan University for my first two years. All of my credits transferred to the University of Michigan. This saved me money and allowed me

Private Residence, 317 Adams, Glencoe, Illinois. Architect: John W. Myefski, AIA, Myefski Cook Architects, Inc. PHOTOGRAPHER: TONY SOLURI PHOTOGRAPHY.

1220 J St., San Diego, California. Architect: John W. Myefski, AIA, Myefski Architects.

to flourish in a small university before graduating from Michigan with my bachelor of science. Because I really enjoyed the architecture program, I stayed to graduate with my master of architecture two years later.

After receiving your master of architecture, you had the opportunity to study abroad in Denmark as the recipient of a Fulbright fellowship. Please describe this experience and how it shaped your career as an architect.

❯ Because I received both my degrees from the same school, I felt that my education needed a boost or outside shock to complete my studies as a well-rounded student. My solution was to attend a program in Europe; the Fulbright provided me that opportunity in Copenhagen, Denmark. The Royal Danish Academy was a great chance to study abroad and spend the time traveling throughout Europe. I cannot tell you how this changed my life as an architect and person. The exposure to living in Denmark and what I saw enriched my soul and improved my work. Travel is the most important part of your education!

Private Residence. 1319 Lincoln, Evanston, Illinois. Architect: John W. Myefski, Myefski Architects. PHOTOGRAPHER: TONY SOLURI PHOTOGRAPHY.

What has been your greatest challenge as an architect?

> Waiting to peak! Now that I have turned 50, architecture is just beginning to be fun again. With an encouraging amount of activity in the profession, it is clear the recession is behind us. The Great Recession was clearly a step backwards for anyone interested and working in architecture, but for those who prevailed through the troubling times, the future is bright. The demand for architectural services has been growing and we are seeing an abundance of clients requesting new work. Architecture students graduating within the next five years will become an integral part in this increased demand for work.

It takes time to build a practice and even more dedication if you want your work to be substantial, and not a momentary flash in a magazine. Starting your practice is similar to constructing a home from the ground up. At this point, I feel I have laid a solid foundation and have reached the second floor … I cannot wait to get to the roof! I think most architects hit their stride at age 55 to 60, so I have plenty of time to improve.

What are your primary responsibilities and duties as the principal of your own firm?

> Everything! In a practice of 15 architects with two principals, you really do everything. That is the best part. I find the work, do the design, oversee the building of the project, maintain contact with the client, fix just about any problem that exists, and run the day-to-day of a business. Most people do not understand that it is the architect's job to solve problems. Life is a series of logjams, and I am constantly trying to keep the water flowing.

Why did you decide to open your own firm?

> I had been working for Helmut Jahn and loved my job but needed to look to the future and develop my own work. I started the firm because I found a historic home that I was saving by literally moving it to a new site; it went so well that the owners of the home asked me to take over the new home they wanted. This was my first job, and saving the home made me a hero in my small community—the rest is history.

When designing a project, how do you begin? What is your inspiration?

> I pull the pen out and sketch on whatever I can find. The ideas are created from inside but they are influenced by the program, client, site, locale, history, and so on. I love to feel and experience the site and its surrounding context. Buildings do sometimes have a metaphor, but mainly it comes from someplace within. I think if you could discover the exact point, you would unlock the future.

Who or what experience has been a major influence on your career?

> My childhood was key, and that is because I spent much of it traveling. The exposure opened my eyes, and I have a hard time closing them to this day. My education was a strong second, and that is because I had great professors and a wonderful facility to explore at the University of Michigan. It is simple; you need pen and paper; the rest comes from your exposure and professors. My first position at Murphy/Jahn was the best and gave me the chance to work on wonderful projects.

Making a Positive Impact

KATHRYN T. PRIGMORE, FAIA

Vice President, NCARB, NOMA, CDT, LEED AP BD+C

HDR Architecture, Inc.

Alexandria, Virginia

Why and how did you become an architect?

❯ Architecture allows me to make a living doing everything I like and everything I am good at. These are not necessarily the same thing!

My interest in architecture began when I was in middle school. The City of Alexandria Public Library had an extensive collection of architecture books and journals. After I had read all of them, I ventured out to the Fairfax County library and the library at the AIA headquarters. Living in the Washington, DC, area is such a great thing!

Architecture is a dynamic discipline. Throughout my career as a practitioner, an educator, and a regulator, my education in architecture has allowed me to utilize multiple abilities and skills to expand my knowledge base or to pique my interest in other ways. Architecture provides flexibility. As a result, I have always been able to find satisfying career paths in the profession as I have matured or as life situations created challenges and opportunities—often unexpected.

Why and how did you decide on which school to attend for your architecture degree? What degree(s) do you possess?

❯ My high school physics teacher suggested I apply to Rensselaer Polytechnic Institute (RPI), partly because at least a dozen of my classmates were applying to my first-choice school and he knew the pro-

New Federal Building, Washington, DC. Architect: HDR Architecture, Inc. PHOTOGRAPHER: HDR ARCHITECTURE, INC.

gram was just as good, although not as well known. I visited RPI and immediately became intrigued with studying architecture there. The university was smaller than most of the other programs I had applied to, and it was in the heart of a small, very "walkable" city. I also liked the fact that the school of architecture was relatively self-contained and that the entire faculty had active professional practices. Although located within a technical university, the creative aspects of architecture were infused into the pedagogical approach.

Another reason I decided to attend RPI was that I would be able to obtain two degrees within five years—a bachelor of science in building science and the accredited bachelor of architecture. After I began to take courses, I found out that it was very easy to receive minors and that my advisor did not prevent me from taking overloads as long as I did well in my courses. I also took courses during the summer at various universities in Washington, DC. I ended up graduating four-and-a-half years after I matriculated with both degrees, with a minor in architectural history and one in anthropology/sociology, and with a few extra credits related to the history of technology during the Industrial Revolution.

This background was invaluable. During the early part of my career, the technical aspects of my education prepared me to take the lead on aspects of architectural projects my peers had little interest in and no foundation to perform. Later in my career, my social science background has provided tools and insight that have been invaluable as a manager and studio head.

What has been your greatest challenge as an architect?

❯ I am sure there have been lost opportunities because I am both African American and female, but the most blatant discrimination I have faced seems to be because I look 10 to 20 years younger (on a good day) than I am. Invariably, when I show up for an interview or to a first job meeting, it is clear that the participants do not believe that a person my age could have my credentials.

What are your primary responsibilities and duties as an architect?

❯ In recent years, my focus has evolved from leading a wide range of project types that are outside of the firm's regular portfolio to being an expert in the management and design of facilities that support high-profile critical missions. Many of these projects have been for the federal government and include the Pentagon and the DHS Headquarters

2001 M St., Washington, DC. Architect: Segreti Tepper Architects, PC. PHOTOGRAPHER: KATHRYN PRIGMORE, FAIA.

consolidation currently under way. These are multifaceted projects for which effective client management and team development strategies are important to the success of the project. A lot of time is spent doing proposal development and contract management, which some may not consider architecture, but if we didn't do them, we would not have projects to work on!

Challenges of working for clients include managing client expectations relative to available technology and available budget; creating and documenting a process that could be easily followed as the composition of the teams constantly evolve; and maintaining the morale of the design team, which often work for months under a relentless schedule.

A colleague and I lead a studio of about 20 architecture and interior design staff within an office of about 140 staff. (HDR Architecture, Inc. has about 1,700 employees; the company as a whole has about 8,000 employees.) The studio system is relatively new to our organization. Over the past months we have been trying different ways to create an identity for the studio and develop it while supporting the individual goals of our colleagues. Managing and developing studio resources (staff) presents a set of challenges much like those I would encounter if I had my own firm. The financial accountability aspects of studio management are not much different from managing projects, but work-life balance and similar considerations are just as important to maintaining a healthy, productive work environment.

What is the least/most satisfying part of your position?

❯ The most satisfying aspect of architecture is the ability to make a positive impact on others through my work. On a daily basis, it is building teams or helping a designer and an engineer resolve a problem. In the long term, it is seeing the glow on a client's face as they enter a completed building for the first time or having a former student tell you they just got licensed.

I sometimes feel internal conflicts because I like what I do so much that I often work too many hours. This is sometimes to the detriment of maintaining good relationships with my family and with others outside of the workplace.

Previously, you taught at Howard University; why did you choose to teach?

❯ I spent 13 years at Howard University teaching and nurturing the students. During about half of these years, I also served as associate dean. Teaching has been my most rewarding undertaking, with the exception of being a parent. To teach, you have to learn, especially when you teach technology-based topics as I did.

The ideal career situation for me would be to teach and practice. I started and finished my teaching career doing both, and I plan to return to doing both at some point in the future. In the interim, I have found opportunities at the firms I have worked with to satisfy some of the yearnings that draw me to teaching. I currently lead a professional development group that encourages staff to pursue licensure and the various certifications that have become critical to the success of our practice.

The reward of teaching, however, surpasses everything else I have done as an architect. There are no words to adequately express the satisfaction I feel for the gift of being able to inspire others to learn.

What was your role in serving on the board for Architects, Professional Engineers, Land Surveyors, and Certified Interior Designers and Landscape Architects (APELSCIDLA) in the state of Virginia? What does a state board do?

❯ State board members are responsible for upholding the laws and regulations related to the practice of architecture. This includes approving candidates for examination and acceptance of individuals for licensure. The board also hears and decides disciplinary cases brought against individuals and entities with professional credentials. During my tenure on the board, we reviewed and updated the regulations and assessed the need for continuing education.

Through my appointment to the APELSCIDLA board, I was able to serve on many NCARB committees. I was a writer and grader for the Architect Registration Exam (ARE) and chaired the Committee on Examination—the committee that is responsible for development of the ARE. I have also served on the Broadly Experienced Architects (BEA) Committee that reviews the qualifications of individuals without a professional degree to determine if they are eligible for an NCARB certificate. After completing a number of years of service to the NCARB, I was appointed to, and eventually chaired, the AIA National Ethics Council. All of these service activities support my commitment to improving the profession and to opening up opportunities for younger architects in leadership roles.

1001 Pennsylvania Ave., N.W., Washington, DC. Architect: Segreti Tepper Architects, PC–Architect of Record; Hartman Cox–Design Architect. PHOTOGRAPHER: KATHRYN T. PRIGMORE, FAIA.

I found an article that talked about your mentoring students—do you still mentor students? Why do you feel mentoring is important?

❯ I have been mentoring students who have been interested in architecture since I was in college. A few years ago, I found out that a young lady I started mentoring when she was in eighth grade eventually did graduate from architecture school. I continue to mentor students, former students, and others.

Mentoring is important because it makes a better world for all of us. I also know that mentoring can change people's lives. I have two primary mentors, one for over 20 years and the other for almost 30 years, who have helped me plan my destiny. They have supported my decisions along the way whether they would have chosen the same path or not. Therein lies their legacy to me. Mentors do not dictate; they do not impose their will on their protégées. They listen, offer options and support, and open doors when they can. Like your parents, mentors are there no matter what.

About five years ago, three other African American women (Barbara G. Laurie, Kathy Dixon, and Katherine Williams) and I presented *Vortex: African American Women Architects in Professional Practice* at the AIA National Convention. Since then, it has been presented across the country as part of a dozen AIA programs or National Organization of Minority Architects (NOMA) programs. Vortex has evolved and taken firm roots as a mentoring and leadership development vehicle. Its success seems to come from its flexible format, its dedication to giving a voice to the unknown at every presentation, and for the way it encourages audience participation in honest dialogue about the challenges African American women and others face within our profession.

You were one of the first African American women licensed to practice architecture—why do you think that was the case?

❯ When I became licensed in 1981 there were fewer than 20 African American women licensed to practice architecture in the United States. As of today, there are approximately 300 African American women out of about 1,876 African American architects. There are approximately 280 women architects. I was the fifth African American women elevated to fellowship in 2003.

As the legend goes, the practice of architecture is a rich, white, male profession. Even as opportunities opened up, we were often relegated to the back rooms of offices. This practice persisted blatantly well into the 1970s in many firms for both women and minorities. Rather than face discrimination, many opened their own firms, some married partners who were the "face" of the office, but unfortunately many were driven away. Today, the hearts of many are in the right place, and we are taking our places in the front offices of many firms. For some firms, however, the risk of diversifying their senior leadership is still perceived as too great.

Environmental Design Excellence

NATHAN KIPNIS, AIA, LEED BD+C

Principal

Kipnis Architecture + Planning, Inc.

Evanston, Illinois

Why and how did you become an architect?

❯ Near where I grew up, along the North Shore of Chicago, there are amazing homes designed by everyone from David Adler to Frank Lloyd Wright. The residences in the area were built starting in the late 1800s, with construction peaking between 1910 and the late 1920s. Many of the homes located right along the lake on Sheridan Road are textbook examples of great European homes mixed in with the very first Prairie homes designed by Wright. In addition, there are also various contemporary designs, though not as numerous.

My parents would drive into Chicago, and we would occasionally travel along Sheridan Road to get there. I would be glued to the window watching these great homes.

Later, the 1973 Arab-Israeli war and ensuing Middle East oil embargo opened my eyes about America's dependence on foreign oil. I felt that designing energy-efficient buildings would help decrease our reliance on that volatile energy source.

Why and how did you decide on which school to attend for your architecture degree? What degree(s) do you possess?

❯ I applied to several schools but chose the University of Colorado. I wanted to attend a school that offered an architecture program but also

was not a very large university. The University of Colorado had a pre-architecture program and was not an overly large school.

At the time, I misunderstood the implications of a pre-architecture program, which means that the degree I would receive, a bachelor of environmental design, was not a professional degree and would require that I obtain a master of architecture to complete my studies. (My well-meaning career counselor in high school assured me that this was the same as either a bachelor of architecture or a bachelor of arts in architectural studies.)

I also chose Colorado because of its highly renowned solar architecture program. Located in Boulder, the university was a natural center of interest in solar design. The climate and location are nearly perfect for studying solar design, being up at 5,000 feet above sea level and having more than 300 sunny days a year. Boulder is known for its liberal thinking, which went along with alternative energy research.

For my graduate studies, I researched more on where to attend. Arizona State University (ASU) in Tempe, Arizona, was recognized internationally for its solar and energy-conscious architectural design. Along with the University of California at Berkeley and Massachusetts Institute of Technology, I felt that ASU was one of the best schools for this field of study in the country. I was provided a partial scholarship, which made the decision very simple. I enrolled at ASU and graduated in the master of architecture program with an emphasis in energy-conscious design.

Mid-Century Modern Addition, Glencoe, Illinois. Architect: Kipnis Architecture + Planning. PHOTOGRAPHER: WAYNE CABLE PHOTOGRAPHY, http://selfmadephoto.com.

What has been your greatest challenge as an architect/principal?

❯ Originally, my greatest challenge was convincing clients to let me push the envelope with what I want to do with "green" design. I would try to nudge them into going to a higher level. With the recent explosion of interest in green design, I now actually have the opposite problem. I have people coming to me with so many green ideas for their projects that I have to spend time prioritizing their goals and selecting the ones that are most appropriate for the project location and budget.

Another major challenge is to be constantly bringing in high-quality projects in a timely manner. I have been very fortunate to have had a nearly constant increased demand for our services, while rarely running slow periods or periods of too much work. I have also been able to obtain commissions that allow me to do quality design that generates positive publicity, which in turn provides me with the ability to bring in work of that caliber or higher. This is the kind of cycle that feeds upon itself in a positive manner.

What are your primary responsibilities and duties as an architect?

❯ My specific responsibilities are threefold. The client comes first and foremost. It is very important that I carefully listen to their requests and make sure we achieve them, even reading "between the lines." I let them know that is it is their project, but my name is also associated with it. As a result, there are certain design and technical standards that I want to make sure are achieved.

The next responsibility revolves around my office. I have to make sure we are properly compensated for the work we do, make sure the contracts are correctly set up, and be smart about how we market ourselves. Marketing is an ongoing commitment that requires constant attention to make sure we have new ongoing media material "in the pipeline."

And, finally, I have significant responsibilities to the people in the office. They must feel that they are part of the team and that their input is important to me. I have them attend various "green" seminars or events to further their education. I also try to get them to sample a very wide range of experiences in the office, from computer-aided design (CAD) work, client meetings, and field administration to public presentations. It is mutually beneficial.

◀ Sturgeon Bay Green Vacation Home, Sturgeon Bay, Wisconsin. Kipnis Architecture + Planning. PHOTOGRAPHER: WAYNE CABLE PHOTOGRAPHY, http://selfmadephoto.com.

▼ LEED Platinum North Shore Home, Glencoe, Illinois. Architect: Kipnis Architecture + Planning. COMPUTER RENDING: KIPNIS ARCHITECTURE + PLANNING.

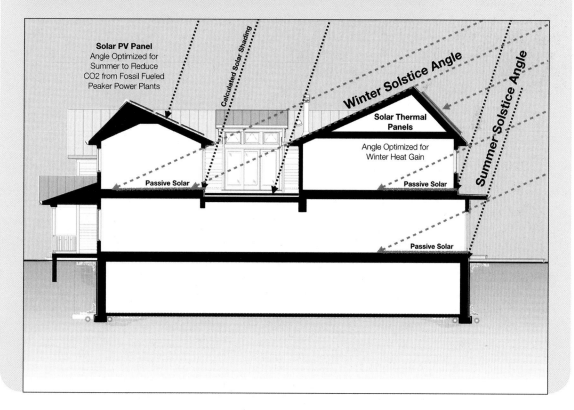

Your firm is strongly committed to integrating excellence in design with environmental awareness. Can you provide more detail to this statement and describe how it is accomplished?

❯ What my firm attempts to do with as many projects as possible is to incorporate "green" principles at as many stages as possible. We try to do this in an integrated way, as opposed to "tacking on" green technologies and materials and as early as possible.

At the beginning of the project, I try to see what design decisions make the most sense in terms of "green" design and in response to the project's specific goals. If there is a solution that I feel works to satisfy both, I pursue it in detail. There is usually a single overall theme that unifies a design. Finding it is really the challenge. If I can get that one big idea to solve the project's key problem and make it work "green," it usually can be done in an economical way and helps the client support it. To me, designing a green project is an opportunity to make the pure design even better and have more meaning. It should not be a burden to design green.

Where do you see the field of green architecture heading in the future?

❯ I believe that in the short term green design will be integrated into local and national codes on such a level that the term *green design* will disappear and become ubiquitous. Beyond that, however, there will be significant challenges as natural resources become scarce enough that it impacts people's lives on a daily basis. The consequences of the disappearance of cheap oil are becoming more and more evident.

This is not a political problem that can be solved by drilling for more oil to the corners of the earth, but requires a fundamental change in how society

functions. Politics being what they are, this message will no doubt be twisted every which way, but in the end, the path away from a fossil-fuel-dependent society is critical for its very survival. Renewable energy and appropriately designed built environments are the only way to accomplish this. Because existing buildings use so much energy and generate such enormous amounts of CO_2 emissions, architects are in a unique position to lead this change by designing super-efficient homes and communities. The difficult aspect for this is to make people understand that in fact life influenced by cheap and abundant power will need to be scaled back. Hybrid Escalades are not the answer; they are the problem.

How did your education help you prepare for these challenges?

❯ By their very training, architects are able to think outside the box and look for solutions where others see only problems. "Celebrate the Problem," we used to call it in school. A specific part of that training is the ability to look back at historical precedents to see how they could inform a current problem. I like to examine how homes functioned before cheap oil and see what can be gleaned from those time-tested designs and integrate them aesthetically into the twenty-first century.

Who or what experience has been a major influence on your career?

❯ As I mentioned, the single biggest influence in my career was the 1973 oil embargo and how I thought I could contribute to a solution to it. This event is what started my career in energy efficiency, which has grown into "green" design in all of its forms.

Steiner Electric Headquarters, Elk Grove Village, Illinois. Architect: Kipnis Architecture + Planning. COMPUTER RENDERING: KIPNIS ARCHITECTURE + PLANNING.

Professors Philip Tabb at the University of Colorado, and John Yellot and Jeffery Cook at Arizona State University influenced the way I practice environmental design by showing me the importance of integrating energy efficiency into architectural design and understanding where the historical roots of environmentally sensitive architectural design were derived from. Amory Lovins, who taught a summer school class at Colorado, made a huge impression on me relative to how architecture, energy, and national security can be interrelated.

I was also fortunate to have worked in two very good, though very different, firms. At Porter Pang Deardorff and Weymiller in Mesa, Arizona, the design principal, Marley Porter, had a great outlook on how fun design should be. It was an infectious quality that spread through the office. The other partners were also very generous in sharing their skills. It was a great work environment.

At PHL of Chicago, it was much more production based and very serious. Once you were at the project manager level, you ran a project like it was your own firm. They really taught me how to run an office.

Creating a Framework for Collaboration

GRACE H. KIM, AIA

Principal and Founder

Schemata Workshop, Inc.

Seattle, Washington

Why and how did you become an architect?

❯ My path to architecture was not a deliberate one. As a high school senior, life beyond graduation was far from my mind. I listed three "areas of interest" on my college application, one of which was architecture. My guess is that the admissions officer chose alphabetically and I was assigned to architecture for freshman advising.

From my first day of classes, I really enjoyed the architectural courses and I never looked back. The problem solving and ability to shape the built environment was fascinating and challenging. And the idea of positively impacting the people who would occupy the buildings was a strong motivator.

Why and how did you decide on which school to attend for your architecture degree? What degree(s) do you possess?

❯ I have a bachelor of science in architectural studies and a bachelor of architecture from Washington State University—the only in-state school to which I applied. At the time, I did not know I wanted to study architecture, so it worked out great that I ended up starting in a five-year bachelor of architecture program. The program structure provided the fundamentals to put me on a level playing field with my classmates in terms of skills and knowledge by the end of the first semester.

After over a decade of practice, I decided to return to school to complete a post-professional master of architecture at the University of Washington. I chose this program because I was a working professional, managing a small practice, and needed a program that would be adaptable to my educational goals (research in a specific topic) as well as my work schedule.

Aqua Lair, Seattle, Washington. Architect: Schemata Workshop, Inc. PHOTOGRAPHER: SCHEMATA WORKSHOP, INC.

Cosmetology Institute, Seattle, Washington. Architect: Schemata Workshop, Inc. PHOTOGRAPHER: SCHEMATA WORKSHOP, INC.

What has been your greatest challenge as an architect/principal?

❯ Maintaining balance in life and work. Unfortunately, I am not always successful at this.

Within the studio, it means balancing the time to draw, manage, and obtain new projects. We try to achieve this balance by the flat structure of the office. As the principal, it is not healthy to control everything. Our employees have a lot of autonomy in creating the work, and they are privy to and accountable for the budgets of their projects as well as the office.

In my life, it means balancing work with time for my husband and daughter, friends, and family. All are important, and despite the fact that my husband is my business partner, we try to make a conscious effort not to spend all our time talking about work or the firm. While philanthropy and community service were of high priority a few years ago; nowadays my top priority is exploring the city and seeing the world through the eyes of my five-year-old daughter.

How is being a principal of Schemata Workshop different from being an intern at Skidmore, Owings, and Merrill?

❯ As in intern at Skidmore, Owings, and Merrill (SOM), I felt like a cog in a large machine. I did my job and understood that others were also doing their part to make sure the project was successfully completed, but I never had a sense of the greater picture, not just architecturally but also from a management standpoint.

As a principal of a small firm, I have a comprehensive view of both the business and practice of architecture. I also make sure that everyone else in the studio is aware of this as well. Open communication and a clear understanding of our business objectives ensure that we all satisfy the contractual requirements to our clients while helping the company make a profit, which ultimately translates to bonuses and profit sharing.

The other major difference is in the projects. At a large firm, you don't have the ability to influ-

Roanoke Residence, Seattle, Washington. Architect: Schemata Workshop, Inc. PHOTOGRAPHER: SCHEMATA WORKSHOP, INC.

ence the types of projects to pursue or the clients for whom you work. As a principal of Schemata Workshop, I am able to strategically select clients who share our values of sustainability, community, and livability.

How did you arrive at the name Schemata Workshop and how does that describe the philosophy of your company?

❯ My partner and I did not want the name of our newly incorporated firm to be our last names— meaning we did not want to be the "bosses" with our names on the door. Instead, we wanted to create a collegial studio environment, where everyone felt that they contributing as an integral member of our team.

A *schema* is a framework or outline. It describes the overarching ideals of the studio and our design approach—to focus the creative efforts of the entire design and construction team during the schematic design phase to create a strong conceptual framework that is then carried throughout the detailing

and construction of the project. It is also a psychology term used to describe the way people perceive and organize information—as architects, this is what we do. We paired the plural, schemata, with workshop to signify that it was a hands-on kind of place where serious work got done, but that it wasn't a rigid corporate environment.

We are dedicated to a collaborative design process that provides innovative and client-specific design solutions. Schemata Workshop produces great design work, but as a secondary goal to client satisfaction.

As the first recipient of the Emerging Professionals Mentorship Award and the 2008 Young Architects Award, can you define "mentorship" and describe how an aspiring architect finds a suitable mentor?

❯ Mentoring is more about leadership than it is about satisfying Intern Development Program (IDP) requirements. A good mentor is a role model, giving others the courage and confidence to tackle a situation in a way that is appropriate for the individual.

Mentorship is not about being a seasoned professional imparting sage advice to someone their junior, but in fact, a continuum of learning throughout one's career. At any point, one should be both a mentor as well as the recipient of mentorship.

For this very reason, I started the "Laddership" mentoring program in Seattle. Laddership is a group-mentoring model where a licensed architect facilitates a group of 5–7 emerging professionals with differing levels of experience. As a group, they share their own experiences and insights in order to enable an individual seeking advice to make an informed decision that suits their particular situation.

Mentorship is also a bit like dating. You might be lucky to find a mentor easily and organically, or it may be hit-or-miss with formal mentoring programs. Your needs will evolve over time, so it is important to seek out multiple mentors throughout your career. Remember, mentors don't always have to be older than you.

When seeking a suitable mentor consider someone in your office, such as a supervisor. But be sure to seek out formal mentors outside your firm as well. This will help in the long run as your career develops within the office and the "politics" come into play. It may be difficult for a supervisor to advise you about a job change if they are motivated by keeping you on their team to complete a project.

Following are some avenues for finding a mentor:

- Ask your professors about colleagues or alumni who might be interested.
- Consider asking the principal of that firm with whom you interviewed and had a great conversation, but who had no available position to offer.
- Attend AIA or other professional organization functions and seek out the familiar faces.

- Ask a fellow young architect serving on a committee with you if they could recommend their supervisor or someone else from their firm who might be a good mentor.
- If you work in a large firm, you could possibly consider finding a mentor from another studio within the firm.
- Contact your state IDP coordinator and ask for help in locating a mentor.

What are your primary responsibilities and duties?

❯ *Vision:* Setting direction for the firm and helping the staff see their role in "steering the boat" toward that direction.

Mentorship: Leadership through actions.

Marketing: Strategically pursuing new projects and nurturing relationships with current and potential clients.

Design direction: Working with the project team to establish a strong design concept and provide critiques/reviews as the design progresses.

Technical oversight: Ensuring that codes are adhered to and documents satisfy permit and constructability requirements.

Client management: Guiding the client through decisions and helping them identify opportunities that add value to their project.

What is the most/least satisfying part of your job?

❯ Most satisfying is making a positive impact on people's lives through architecture. Least satisfying: expending countless hours on a Statement of Qualifications and an extensive public interview process only to receive a letter from the owner stating that the project was awarded to another firm but that we were a close second.

McDermott Place Apartments, Seattle, Washington. Architect: Schemata Workshop, Inc. PHOTOGRAPHER: DOUG SCOTT.

Who or what experience has been a major influence on your career?

❯ Donna Palicka, an interior designer at SOM, whom I worked with for eight months on the programming for General Motors Global Headquarters. From her, I learned the importance of building relationships and that, as a woman architect, I could be feminine and still maintain a professional presence.

Mark Simpson, AIA, and Jennie Sue Brown, FAIA, are two principals of Bumgardner, a Seattle architectural firm that has been in business for over 50 years. Both were instrumental in helping me develop the necessary skills that would eventually enable me to start my own architectural practice.

My husband, Mike Mariano, AIA, has played a critical role in my career development—first as a classmate and fellow intern in the profession, and now as a business partner. Mike has supported me through difficult career decisions and has been patient with challenging work schedules.

And a major event that profoundly influenced my career was Masonry Camp, a weeklong design-build program sponsored by the International Masonry Institute. Spending a week with apprentice tradespeople and other young architects, I realized that the adversarial relationship between architect and contractor that is typically seen on jobsites could easily be avoided if all parties had a mutual respect for each other and an open line of communication. While I was accustomed to working collaboratively with engineers and allied disciplines, I adopted a collaborative attitude with contractors as well. This has resulted in great experiences during construction for all parties involved.

Making an Unrelated Degree Count

LYNSEY JANE GEMMELL SORRELL, AIA, LEED AP

Principal

Perimeter Architects

Chicago, Illinois

Why and how did you become an architect?

❯ My undergraduate studies were art history and psychology. My emphasis was architectural history and my exposure to the theory and history of the practice of architecture led me to consider how I could continue my interest in the built environment. I no longer wanted to write about other people's buildings but to be involved in the design of buildings. In addition, I wanted to teach, and with architecture the possibility is open to teach both during and after practice.

Why and how did you decide on which school to attend for your architecture degree? What degree(s) do you possess?

❯ I chose an accredited graduate program at a school with a good, international reputation located in a large metropolitan setting. My undergraduate degree is a master of arts (first class) and my graduate degree is a master of architecture.

After many years in another firm as project architect, you are now a principal in the firm Perimeter Architects. How did this transition occur and was it on your career path?

❯ After 10 years at my first firm, I was in upper middle management and heavily involved in marketing and business development efforts. Many of my day-to-day tasks were rather removed from the practice of architecture. I took a teach-

Lakeview Residence, Chicago, Illinois. Architect: Perimeter Architects. PHOTOGRAPHER: MIKE SCHWARTZ.

ing position at the Illinois Institute of Technology College of Architecture and balanced teaching and practice for a year. This gave me a greater connection to design and refreshed me. With the birth of my first child, I took two-year break from practice and taught undergraduate and graduate design studios. I missed building buildings and "real–world" challenges; I also feel a responsibility to young female architects to ensure that there are enough women mentors and role models working in the field, especially those balancing a young family with work.

I did not want to go back to working in a big firm. I wanted to have greater control over the process and the design outcomes. In a large firm, one becomes pigeonholed or specialized, and I wanted to return to doing everything and being involved in all phases and scales of issue. If I had not taken the teaching position, I am not sure I would have changed the path I was on. I was challenged and had reached a level of success at my previous firm, but I suspect if I had stayed another five years, I would have become dissatisfied. Building your own firm is exciting and nerve–wracking, but I feel that

the past 15 years have been preparation for where I am now in my career.

As a principal, what are your primary responsibilities and duties?

❯ As a principal in a small firm, my responsibilities are finding new work, defining our business model, creating marketing and business development materials, and ensuring that my team have the resources and support they require. We work on design collectively and charrette design solutions as a team. I also coordinate the work of any and all consultants, oversee the technical content of the documents, develop office protocols and standards, safeguard client satisfaction, and maintain project and internal budgets and schedules. I manage our employees and mentor them as they are learning their craft.

What has been your greatest challenge as an architect thus far?

❯ I cannot identify a single greatest challenge, but learning to accomplish as much as possible in the time available without working enormous amounts of overtime is a challenge. I continue to try and

Tasty Trade Office, Chicago, Illinois. Architect: Perimeter Architects. RENDERING: PERIMETER ARCHITECTS.

keep in mind the difference between professional responsibility and the end goal of the task at hand rather than one's ultimate design ambitions.

What are your 5-year and 10-year career goals relative to architecture?

❯ As principals in a new firm, we are focusing on short- and medium-term goals. We have broken the next two years down into quarters and have business development goals for each quarter—external and internal goals. We have defined the sectors we want to pursue and are aggressively pursuing these markets through our network of previous clients. In 5 years we want to have grown from five to about seven people and have two or three big jobs per year to support smaller, more boutique pursuits and to do some competition work.

In 5 to 10 years I would like to go back to teaching, as I have had to suspend teaching at the College of Architecture at IIT in order to focus on building the new firm, and I miss the energy and challenge that teaching provides.

What do you feel when you see a project completed?

❯ No matter your role in a project, the opening of a building that you helped create and hearing that a client is thrilled with their space makes all the hard work and painful experiences of coordinating projects large and small worthwhile.

Who or what experience has been a major influence on your career?

❯ In my undergraduate studies, I had an art history professor, Professor Margaretta Lovell at the

Spec House 1, Chicago, Illinois. Architect: Perimeter Architects. PHOTOGRAPHER: ANA MIYARES.

University of California at Berkeley, who pressed me to talk about what I wanted to do in the future. She encouraged me not to be afraid of the mathematics and physics that I thought would be involved in architecture (this has proved to be correct) and exposed me to the three-year master of architecture program for nonrelevant degree holders.

Leading by Design

SEAN M. STADLER, AIA, LEED AP
Design Principal
WDG Architecture, PLLC
Washington, DC

Why did you become an architect?

❭ It is the only career I ever wanted as far back as I can remember. I think as early as third grade it was decided. The funny thing is that I did not know anyone who was an architect. Legos were definitely where it all started. I would spend every waking hour as a kid either drawing or building Legos, and I think everyone just told me from an early age that, wow, this kid is going to be an architect.

Why did you decide to choose Kent State University? What degree(s) do you possess?

❭ I have a bachelor of science and a bachelor of architecture, a NAAB-accredited professional de-

gree. Unfortunately, I had no help in understanding how to evaluate schools, and I had no money to just pick the best school out there. So, for me, Kent State was affordable, and the little understanding that I had was it had the best program for Ohio schools of architecture.

What are your primary responsibilities and duties as a design principal in your firm? Please describe a typical day.

❭ As one of the three design principals of the firm, I lead the vision/direction of our design efforts for my projects and mentor staff. As the design leadership for the firm, we also work to develop a design process for our projects that is understandable by the staff and our clients. We are responsible to set the clients' expectations of how we deliver a building from a concept to a built project.

Northwest One,
Washington, DC.
Architect: WDG
Architecture, PLLC.
RENDERING: WDG
ARCHITECTURE, PLLC.

National Harbor
(Aloft National
and Fleet Street
Condominiums),
National Harbor,
Maryland. Architect:
WDG Architecture,
PLLC. PHOTOGRAPHER:
© MAX MCKENZIE.

Raising the level of design in the office is not just about the particular project, but it is also about the image of the firm. This requires us to not only design great buildings but also promote the work we do. Photography, design drawings, project narratives, design award submissions, marketing brochures, and our website presence all speak about our design abilities. As design principals, we are responsible to make sure that all of this is consistent and meets the standards we set.

Additional duties include hiring, marketing, and bringing in new business and operational and financial decisions for the business.

I am not sure that any day is typical these days. I come into the office thinking I am going to accomplish one task, and then quickly something comes up that needs immediate attention, and by the time I get to what I had planned to do it is late in the afternoon. Prioritizing what has to get done during a day is the only way I can make sure that everything gets done.

In 2011, you were the recipient of the 2011 AIA Young Architects award; the jury noted "you are a unique individual of outstanding talent and clear commitment." Can you describe the meaning of receiving this award and what does it mean to have outstanding talent?

❯ The meaning of the award is a personal confirmation that my peers recognize the energy and effort I have committed to my practice and the profession. I do not think it is an award that too many people are aware of or take notice of, but for me it was a milestone that I wanted to achieve. I constantly set goals for myself that keep me focused on being a better architect, husband, father, and human being. Setting a goal to be recognized as a Young Architect recipient was one of the goals I had. I valued my predecessors who had been recognized with this award and looked up to them as role models in the profession. They set high standards, and I never felt that I deserved to be in the same list as they were. This kept me focused on how I wanted to make contributions to my projects, my office, and the profession.

Talent is a difficult word to define in the realm of architecture. There are so many ways that an individual can be a leader in the profession. My path has always begun with a commitment to design excellence. Everything that I am involved with I feel has to meet up to a certain standard that I believe is acceptable. Sometimes I am my own worst critic.

During your career, you have been involved with the AIA at its many levels, including the Young Architects Forum (YAF) and Intern/Associates Committee. Why has this involvement been important to you? Is it important for an architect to be a leader?

❭ My involvement in the AIA has been an important part of my professional development, and I immediately got involved with the local chapter during my first year after graduation. It was amazing how many opportunities were available through the organization during the early stages of my career. My involvement provided me an opportunity to speak and work on tasks that interested me or concerned me about the profession. These were things that I would not have done in the office setting.

During those early years of my career, the ARE was just making the transition from the one-week paper exam to the computer-based exam. We were, in fact, the guinea pigs for how the exam is administered today. I believe that my involvement in the AIA helped to make the transition easier and better for interns.

My involvement progressed from putting together social activities to leading committees at the local and national levels of the Institute. It is here in leading that I found the most reward. The skills that I learned by leading committees soon became skills that I could use in the office to lead certain aspects of the practice. As I matured and was more responsible for our projects, the leadership skills

Verdian, Silver Spring, Maryland. Architect: WDG Architecture, PLLC. PHOTOGRAPHER: © MAX McKENZIE.

carried over to interactions with our clients and with the community and agencies.

What has been your greatest challenge as an architect?

❭ I think the challenges change from year to year, but I definitely think that starting a family and raising children with a spouse that is also a professional has been the biggest challenge I have faced. There is a delicate balance between the time and effort I spend with my involvement in the office and the profession versus the time and effort I dedicate to my family. It is difficult not to drop any of the balls that are in the air.

What is the most/least satisfying part of being an architecture student?

❭ The least satisfying part of being an architecture student is that the curriculum is so demanding that architecture students spend too much time with architecture students and not enough time with the rest of the university. I know this is an age-old problem, but there is little time for architecture students to take art classes, business classes, or philosophy classes. These general studies could also help architects in their profession.

Who or what experience has been a major influence on your career?

❭ I had an opportunity to study abroad for a semester in Italy and Switzerland while in school. The en-

tire class did not take advantage of this, but for me it was the first time I was ever out of the country and at that point I had not even traveled very much within the States. The experience was overwhelmingly powerful for me to have a semester to emerge myself in another culture and society. It really opened my eyes to things that I could have never related to growing up in suburban Ohio. It was that experience that really helped me understand what "urban" meant. It also made me realize that I enjoyed urban living and the scale of urban architecture. These realizations are what guided me when pursuing my first jobs out of college and eventually my relocation to Washington. That experience continues to have a strong influence on my interest in the type of work that we pursue.

NOTES

1. Ayn Rand, *The Fountainhead* (New York: Penguin, 1943), 16.
2. *The American Heritage Dictionary of the English Language* (Boston, MA: Houghton Mifflin, 2011).
3. Spiro Kostof, *The Architect: Chapters in the History of the Profession* (New York: Oxford University Press, 1986), v.
4. Dana Cuff, Architecture: *The Story of Practice* (Cambridge, MA: MIT Press, 1991), 153.
5. Eugene Raskin, *Architecture and People* (Englewood Cliffs, NJ: Prentice-Hall, 1974), 101.
6. Bureau of Labor Statistics, U.S. Department of Labor, "Architects," in *Occupational Outlook Handbook, 2012–13 Edition.* Retrieved January 19, 2013, from www.bls.gov/ooh/architecture-and-engineering/architects.htm.
7. *NAAB Report on Accreditation in Architecture Education.* Retrieved February, 12, 2014, from www.naab.org.
8. National Council of Architectural Registration Boards. *2013 Survey of Registered Architects.* Retrieved January 18, 2014, from www.ncarb.org.
9. American Institute of Architects. *The Business of Architecture: The 2012 Survey Report on Firm Characteristics.* (Washington, DC: AIA, 2012), from http://aia.org/practicing/economics/AIAB095791.
10. Bureau of Labor Statistics, U.S. Department of Labor, *Occupational Outlook Handbook, 2012–13 Edition.*
11. American Institute of Architects. *2013 AIA Compensation Survey* (Washington, DC: AIA, 2013).
12. Kathryn Anthony, *Designing for Diversity* (Urbana, IL: University of Illinois Press, 2001), 22.
13. L. Oguntoyinbo, "In Architecture, African-Americans Stuck on Ground Floor in Terms of Numbers." *Diverse Issues in Higher Education.* Retrieved August 18, 2013 from http://diverseeducation.com/article/55050.
14. *The Directory of African American Architects.* Retrieved September 8, 2013, from http://blackarch.uc.edu.

2 The Education of an Architect

The architect should be equipped with knowledge of many branches of study and varied kinds of learning, for it is by his judgment that all work done by the other arts is put to test. This knowledge is the child of practice and theory. Practice is the continuous and regular exercise of employment where manual work is done with any necessary material according to the design of a drawing. Theory, on the other hand, is the ability to demonstrate and explain the productions of dexterity on the principles of proportion.

VITRUVIUS POLLIO, *The Ten Books on Architecture* (ed. Morris Hicky Morgan)

TO BECOME AN ARCHITECT, there are three major steps: education, experience, and exam. The most critical is education. While completing your formal education (obtaining a National Architectural Accrediting Board [NAAB]-accredited degree) may take five to seven years, your actual architectural education will continue throughout your lifetime. This chapter will help you learn how to prepare for an architectural education, discuss the degree paths, outline the selection process, and describe the experience of an architecture student.

Depending on where you are on this path, the process of becoming a licensed architect may take between 9 and 12 years, from entering an architecture program to passing the Architect Registration Examination (ARE). When does this process begin? For many, it starts very early. Some architects say their interest in becoming an architect began in elementary school or even earlier. For others, it was later—after college or later.

◄ Alexandria Central Library, Alexandria, Virginia. Architect: Michael Graves + Associates/PGAL. PHOTOGRAPHER: ERIC TAYLOR, ASSOCIATE AIA. PHOTO © EricTaylorPhoto.com.

How does their desire to become an architect develop? Some say they enjoyed drawing; they enjoyed constructing or building with blocks, Legos, erector sets, and similar toys. In addition, a drafting course in high school may have piqued an interest in architecture. As architecture is both a science and an art, some pursue the discipline from either science or art or both.

What should you do if your desire to become an architect emerges in high school or earlier? From the academic coursework you choose to a part-time position in an architectural firm, you can pursue many activities to further your interest in architecture and begin the process of becoming an architect. If you have completed a degree in another discipline and now wish to become an architect, many of these same activities may also be helpful.

Preparation

ACTIVITIES

Cultural institutions sponsor events or activities to expose the public to the world of architecture. For example, the National Building Museum in Washington, DC, holds a Festival of the Building Arts each fall. During the festival, visitors of all ages can build a brick wall, participate in a nail-driving contest, try stone carving and woodworking, learn the techniques involved in surveying, build a city out of boxes, or create a sculpture out of nuts and bolts. The Frank Lloyd Wright Home and Studio near Chicago offers an opportunity for young teens to serve as tour guides. Contact area museums or other cultural institutions for exhibits, lectures, or classes related to architecture and the built environment.

PROGRAMS

Organizations such as Center for the Understanding of the Built Environment (CUBE), Built Environment Education Program (BEEP), Chicago Architecture Foundation, Learning by Design in Massachusetts, and Architecture in Education host programs for both individuals and teachers who desire to help younger children learn about architecture. In fact, the Association of Architecture Organizations (AAO) is a network of organizations that strive to enhance the public dialogue about architecture and design.

Learning by Design in Massachusetts gives young people the opportunity and the skills they need to communicate their ideas about the built and natural environments, about community, and about themselves. This organization has developed children's design workshops with themes that include designing dream houses, designing the community, neighborhood walking tours, places to learn, history through structures, block play, and block design. The Center for Architecture Foundation (New York) promotes public understanding and appreciation of architecture and design through educational programs for K–12 students and teachers, families, and the general public.

Many of these programs and others are listed in A+DEN—Architecture + Design Education Network (www.adenweb.org), an online resource of programs designed to help students learn about the design process and built environment.

ACADEMIC COURSEWORK

Because becoming an architect requires a college education, your high school academic curriculum should focus on college preparatory courses, including four years of English and mathematics. Pursue as many honors and advanced placement (AP) courses as possible. AP credit may allow you to carry a lighter academic load or pursue additional coursework, such as electives or minors.

While the mathematics requirement may vary among architecture programs, most either require or encourage you to take calculus. You should pursue or take the highest-level math course your high school offers and even consider taking it at an area community college prior to entering college.

Marina City, Chicago, Illinois. Architect: Bertrand Goldberg.
PHOTOGRAPHER: LEE W. WALDREP, Ph.D.

In addition, you should take a course in high school physics instead of biology or chemistry. If you have already completed college, note that many graduate programs require or strongly encourage your taking calculus and physics as prerequisite courses; these typically can be done at area community colleges, but check the requirements of the graduate program. A handful may also require completing a history of architecture course. Again, check with each program regarding its requirements.

Also, take art, drawing, and design classes rather than architectural drafting or computer-aided design (CAD). Your interest in architecture may have surfaced from a drafting course, but art courses will be more helpful in your preparation to become an architect. Art, drawing, and design courses develop visual aptitude and literacy, while expanding your ability to communicate graphically. Take a freehand drawing course or a three-dimensional course such as sculpture or woodworking. In addition, art courses provide you with material for your portfolio, a requirement for many architecture programs; this is absolutely true if you are applying to graduate programs.

St. Peter's Lutheran Church, Columbus, Indiana. Architect: Gunnar Birkerts. PHOTOGRAPHER: LEE W. WALDREP, Ph.D.

Do your best with every academic course you take! While grades are not the only criterion by which college admissions offices judge applications, they certainly are one of the more important ones.

Besides academics, what can you do to begin your preparation for a career in architecture? Consider the following: (1) exploration of the built environment, (2) visits to architecture firms and schools, (3) participating in a summer program sponsored by an architecture program, and (4) participating in an after-school program. All of these provide you a head start on the path to becoming an architect.

EXPLORATION

An important skill to acquire in becoming an architect is the ability to see. By learning to observe buildings, spaces, and their relationships, you become sensitive to issues that concern architects. Explore your surroundings by looking closely at the built environment every day.

What detail can you describe from memory about a building you know well—a school or nearby store, for example? Now, visit the building and note all the details you did not remember or notice before. Draw sketches of the overall building or details.

MARGARET DELEEUW, University of Maryland

Tour and observe your neighborhood or city, and take visual notes about the architecture you encounter. Seek out guided tours of significant buildings in your city, and learn about their architectural features.

Purchase a sketchbook and begin to draw. Sketch from real life to develop your drawing skills and sharpen your awareness of the existing environment. Sketching from life trains you to observe, analyze, and evaluate while recording your surroundings. Do not worry about the quality of the sketches; focus instead on developing your skill of seeing.

> When I was a summer intern, I sat outside and sketched during my lunch break. One day I sketched a landscape, as the office overlooked a waterfall. Another day I drew my shoe or my handbag. Yet another day I found some object in the office to draw, like a lamp. Some days I sketched my hand or my foot. This simple exercise was greatly beneficial, as it taught me that the key to producing an excellent drawing is to train your eyes to see.
>
> MARGARET DELEEUW, University of Maryland

One way to develop your drawing skills is to dedicate a specific amount of time—one or two hours—per day to sketching. Be committed to drawing each day. Practice, practice, and practice!

Begin reading books, magazines, and newspaper articles on architecture and the profession of architecture. Check the Web or your nearby public library for ideas.

VISITS

Tour the design studios of a nearby school of architecture to become acquainted with the experiences of an architecture student. Speak with current architecture students about what they do. If possible, attend a few classes to learn about the courses you may take. As most schools sponsor lectures highlighting architects and their work, consider attending one. Typically, these are free and open to the public.

Visit with a local architect to gain a broader understanding of the nature of an architect's work and the value of the profession. To locate an architect, contact the local chapter of the American Institute of Architects (www.aia.org). Ask your parents, teachers, or friends of your family if they know any practicing architects. Remember, these connections may be valuable when you apply to architecture programs or for possible summer employment opportunities.

Visit construction sites to learn how buildings are constructed. Talk with carpenters, builders, and others in the building industry to learn their perspectives on architecture. In addition, travel throughout your community, throughout your region of the country, or to other countries to experience architecture from various perspectives. As you visit, sketch!

SUMMERS

Many colleges and universities offer summer programs (www.archcareers.org) designed for high school students, college students, or adults who desire to learn about the field of architecture. Lasting from one to several weeks, these programs are an excellent opportunity to determine if architecture is the right career choice. Most include design, drawing, and model-building assignments; field trips to firms or nearby buildings; and other related activities. These can all assist you in determining if architecture is for you. Summer programs are also a good way to learn about the architecture program of a particular institution.

Each summer, the Graduate School of Design at Harvard University offers Career Discovery, a six-week program during which students of all ages are introduced to design through a core program of morning lectures, panel discussions, and field trips. Almost 100 architecture programs nationwide offer such summer programs. Entities such as museums and community park districts may also offer such programs.

The summer before my senior year, I attended two architecture programs: *Discover Architecture* at the University of Illinois and *Experiment in Architecture* at the Illinois Institute of Technology. Both exposed me to what college would be as an architecture student, and the field trips to architecture firms showed me a glimpse of how life would be as an architect. I drew, created, and recreated … just like a real architect. These experiences helped solidify my decision to pursue architecture in college.

Both of these experiences were invaluable in preparing me for college. They helped influence the colleges to which I applied. The final projects I created during these summer programs provide me with materials to incorporate into my portfolio. Bottom line—I highly recommend taking advantage of as many architecture summer programs as you can!

ROBYN PAYNE, University of Illinois at Urbana-Champaign

Alternatively, obtain a summer internship with a construction company or architectural firm; you may be limited in the tasks you do, but the experience will be far more rewarding than a typical summer position. If you are unable to secure a summer internship, find an architect to shadow for a day or a week. Some high schools offer programs designed to connect students with career professionals.

Chicago Harbor Locks, Chicago, Illinois. Architect: AECOM. PHOTOGRAPHER: LEE W. WALDREP, Ph.D.

If such opportunities are not possible, consider volunteering at or providing community service with a design-related organization such as a museum. Depending on your location, volunteer with Habitat for Humanity; always look for opportunities to become involved with the built environment.

AFTER-SCHOOL PROGRAMS

ACE Mentor Program (Architecture, Construction, and Engineering, www.acementor.org) is for high school students interested in learning about career opportunities in architecture, construction, and engineering. It is an after-school program held throughout the school year in which professionals mentor students, who work on a design project and learn about the career fields of architecture, construction, and engineering.

Other after-school programs include the Boy Scouts of America Explorer Post and Odyssey of the Mind. One program, Saturday Sequence, offered by Carnegie Mellon University in partnership with Carnegie Museum of Art, is offered during eight consecutive Saturdays in the fall and winter and includes hands-on projects and three-dimensional representation.

Additionally, there are competitions that you may enter; the Newhouse Program and Architecture Competition, sponsored by the Chicago Architecture Foundation (CAF) and the Chicago Public Schools, offers opportunities year-round for students interested in architecture and design. The CAF also sponsors DiscoverDesign.org, a free 24/7 interactive tool and the DiscoverDesign.org National High School Architecture Competition. Contact various organizations within your community, including local AIA chapters or architectural foundations to determine if they have programs designed to connect you with the built environment.

What Advice Would You Provide to Someone Who Wants to Be an Architect?

❯ Build, build, build at whatever scale you can because it informs how assemblies come together, which will give one a better understanding when designing.

Mary Kay Lanzillotta, FAIA, Partner, Hartman-Cox Architects

❯ Have a passion for observing the environment around you. Learn to translate what you see into lines on paper.

H. Alan Brangman, AIA, Vice-President of Facilities, Real Estate Auxiliary Services, University of Delaware

❯ I would suggest a period of self-reflection. It is a challenging and competitive career that one cannot enter half-heartedly. If the desire and determination are there, then I would encourage the person to pursue it.

Kathy Denise Dixon, AIA, NOMA, Principal, K. Dixon Architecture, PLLC; Associate Professor, University of the District of Columbia.

❯ Do not let them talk you out of it—most importantly, a strong skill set in math does not matter.

John W. Myefski, AIA, Principal, Myefski Architects, Inc.

❯ Do not allow yourself to get discouraged when it gets tough, and you will find that it is the most worthwhile experience. The ability to create something that has never existed before can be intoxicating.

Be ready to defend why you did what you did. Within the designs you create, it will be necessary to be able to articulate the reasoning behind your choices. This can sometimes be the greatest challenge, but it is also the most rewarding.

Makenzie Leukart, MArch Candidate, Columbia University

❯ Pursue art classes before starting architecture. I did not have good guidance early on to what architecture was about or what the different aspects of the practice were. I realized my passion was designing and creating. I am inspired by the artistic and romantic side of the profession.

Sean M. Stadler, AIA, LEED AP, Design Principal, WDG Architecture, PLLC

❯ Choose a path in which you are extremely passionate. The design profession has many facets. Architectural education offers a broad set of skills that can be applied in diverse ways. Find your niche in the design world (which goes beyond just architecture) and stay true to yourself, making your work all the more imaginative. The best artists are agile in the way they work and find inspiration in the overlapping of experiences.

Rosannah B. Sandoval, AIA, Designer II, Perkins + Will

❯ We are a profession of generalists; you have to know a little about a lot of different things. You cannot be egotistical and think you know how to design without the involvement and successful collaboration with a variety of experts. You need to make sure that you ask the right questions. Schools need to be involving more and different disciplines. The traditional way of thinking about design is dead.

Robert D. Fox, AIA, IIDA, Principal, FOX Architects

❯ Talk with as many practicing architects as possible before applying to architecture school. And if you later learn that a traditional path is not for you, then apply those skills you learned in school—perseverance, design thinking, and problem solving—to a related (or not) profession.

Murrye Bernard, Associate AIA, LEED AP, Managing Editor, Contract Magazine

First Christian Church, Columbus, Indiana. Architect: Eliel Saarinen. PHOTOGRAPHER: SUSAN HANES.

❯ Gain experience in an architecture office to gain a better idea of what the profession is really all about. An architectural intern may find that perception and reality are very different in terms of what actually occurs in an architect's office on a daily basis.

Robert D. Roubik, AIA, LEED AP, Project Architect, Antunovich Associates Architects and Planners

❯ Go see buildings and have experiences in them. Understand why you like certain spaces and not others, and ask other people why they like or dislike spaces. Pursue a wide variety of experiences so that when you design a building, you can imagine a variety of situations for which its spaces will be used.

Allison Wilson, Intern Architect, Ayers, Saint Gross

❯ Set your sights high! Go find amazing architects and work with them. Go knock on Alvaro Siza's door or travel to London and work for Zaha Hadid or John Pawson.

William J. Carpenter, Ph.D., FAIA, LEED AP, Professor, Southern Polytechnic State University; President, Lightroom

❯ Do it. Do not be scared. You cannot let the amount of work it requires to hold you back. You need to want to do all of the amounts of work. The more work you produce throughout the semester, the better the outcome. Make sure you travel.

Elizabeth Weintraub, B.Arch. Candidate, New York Institute of Technology

❯ Be passionate! You must feel in your heart that you want architecture to be a part of your life. Learn to be creative and to challenge linear thinking. Expand your world through travel, reading, drawing, conversation, music, and every other way possible. Learn to enjoy and be rewarded by the challenges of discovery and risk.

Clark E. Llewellyn, AIA, Director of Global Track and Professor, University of Hawaii

❯ Shadow an architect before deciding to pursue architecture; several shadowing experiences are ideal. Take all classes available in freehand drawing, painting, photography, sculpture, furniture making, and related arts and crafts. Invest in a sketchbook. Explore a new part of your city or take a trip to a different city. Participate in the summer high school programs offered by many architecture programs.

Beth Kalin, Job Captain, Gensler

❯ Architects come in many forms. Some are public architects working for communities and city governments; others design skyscrapers, schools, hospitals, churches, houses, and everything in between. Reach out to architects and ask questions. Develop a feel for the challenging and rewarding world that lies before you.

What Advice Would You Provide to Someone Who Wants to Be an Architect? (Continued)

As you follow your dreams, reach out to an architect in your community. Even if you do not know one, pick up the phone book and look some up, give them a call, and simply ask to tour the office. Ask lots of questions—what they like and dislike, what school they went to, what type of projects they work on. Stay in touch with them as you go through your education.

Last, be a heads-up professional. While the profession emphasizes mentorship, know that you must be responsible for your own development by being aware of what you are working on and how it fits in with the overall process, and by asking questions. When you seek increased responsibilities in the office and exercise your judgment when needed, you will find your opportunities to grow are limitless.

Shannon Kraus, FAIA, MBA, Principal and Senior Vice-President, HKS Architects

❭ Work hard and be patient—the process of becoming an architect is one of the most rewarding and demanding experiences you will have in your life. Also, do not be afraid to pursue an alternate

Celebration, Celebration, Florida. Architects: Cooper, Robertson with Robert A. M. Stern Architects
PHOTOGRAPHER: GUIDO FRANCESCATO.

career in architecture. Having an architecture degree and being a licensed architect prepares you for a number of related and careers beyond architecture.

Jessica L. Leonard, Associate AIA, LEED AP BD+C, Associate, Ayers Saint Gross Architects and Planners

❭ Discover more about what architects do beyond the naïve things you hear. Take as many drawing, painting, and sculpture courses as you can. Learn software applications that expand your ability to tell a compelling story about what you are trying to do. Even though the ability to write well is not usually emphasized, it, along with the ability to speak well, is of great importance. A clear narrative, whether written or oral, has the most impact.

Thomas Fowler IV, AIA, NCARB, DPACSA Professor and Director, Community Interdisciplinary Design Studio (CIDS), California Polytechnic State University–San Luis Obispo

❭ Take courses in art, math, writing, and science. If one or two of these skills do not come naturally to you, do not let this inhibit you from your dreams. It is true that some are born with it, but do not forget that one gets better at what they do often. Once you learn to draw and how buildings are put

together, you can stand proud of your hard work and dedication and explain to the next generation how it is done.

Jennifer Penner, Master of Architecture Graduate, University of New Mexico, Regional Associate Director, AIA Western Mountain Region

❯ Keep in mind that the architecture profession encompasses many careers and many firms, each with its own distinctions.

Eric Taylor, Associate AIA, Photographer, Taylor Design & Photography, Inc.

❯ If you do not love what you do, it will reflect in your work. When something needs passion and it is not there, it is noticeably deficient.

Tanya Ally, Architectural Staff, Bonstra | Haresign Architects

❯ As the path to becoming an architect is a challenging and rewarding field, you must love what you're doing in order to be successful.

Jordan Buckner, M.Arch./MBA Graduate, University of Illinois at Urbana-Champaign

❯ The architectural education is one of the most versatile foundations you can achieve. It is one that prepares you for interacting with all facets of society. What you learn in school and what you learn with practice is not just about building objects and spaces, but also how they affect everyone in every way. The average person has no concept about how architects shape all the spaces we use every day.

Megan S. Chusid, AIA, Manager of Facilities and Office Services, Solomon R. Guggenheim Museum and Foundation

❯ Gain real-world experience in architecture. School is very important, but it doesn't always reveal what architects really do. Gaining experience will help you get a taste for what it is actually like to be an architect.

Elsa Reifsteck, BS Architectural Studies Graduate, University of Illinois at Urbana-Champaign

❯ Make sure you understand what it really means to be an architect. Do not rely on portrayals of architects in movies or television. You are reading this book, so that is an excellent first step. For most, architecture is more of a calling. It is a very demanding, high-stress occupation that carries with it a larger reputation than paycheck.

I am confident in my decision because of the great amounts of personal satisfaction I get from my work. Also, do not let your skill set give you a false impression. There is a place for anyone in this field, so do not think that because you might not be a great at drawing, or are not so good at math, that this profession is not for you. Let your passion guide you.

Cody Bornsheuer, Associate AIA, LEED AP BD+C, Architectural Designer, Dewberry Architects, Inc.

❯ Take the time during school and your work experiences to understand the disciplines that influence the built environment that will ultimately inform the work that you plan on developing as an architect. Finding a parallel, alternative, and subversive education from general contractors, engineers, mayors, community leaders, and editors will greatly enhance your understanding of the machinations behind a building.

Katherine Darnstadt, AIA LEED AP BD+C, Founder and Principal Architect, Latent Design

❯ Seek out as much information about the profession as you can find. Design education will give you a solid foundation in the skills and abilities you need as a design thinker, but it often omits some of the professional capacities that make or break a career, such as the importance of networking, building relationships, and communicating your brand. Early involvement in professional organizations provides an overview of the issues and trends in the industry and helps you to create an informed point of view on how to construct your career within this context.

Andrew Caruso, AIA, LEED AP BD+C, CDT, Head of Intern Development and Academic Outreach, Gensler

What Advice Would You Provide to Someone Who Wants to Be an Architect? (Continued)

❯ Architecture school is a wonderful and dynamic education, but it gets interesting when you enter the workforce. Not unlike many other professions, what you learn in school and how it is applied in a position are not well aligned, and this lends itself to dissatisfaction. Spending time with architects in their work environment to learn more about what the day-to-day is like would be beneficial to many who are considering becoming one.

Ashley W. Clark, Associate AIA, LEED AP, SMPS, Marketing Manager, LandDesign

❯ If you want to become an architect you have to make sure you really want it! Throughout your education there will be ups and downs and your professors may not agree with you, and no matter how much work you put in, they may still hate it. You have to have to ability to take criticism because not everyone will agree with you. Architecture is a difficult major and time consuming, but do not forget what is most important to you whether it is your family, friends, or whatever. Never lose sight of what matters because if you want it bad enough you will become an architect.

Nicole Gangidino, B.Arch. Candidate, New York Institute of Technology

❯ A solid liberal educational foundation is absolutely essential for all would-be architects. Even if you select a five-year B.Arch. program, make sure you understand how the required general education courses can contribute to your overall education. Do not just select courses because they are easy; rather, you should select courses that challenge your pre-conceptions, building knowledge and skills that are outside a strictly architectural curriculum.

Learn to write and speak effectively. Make sure that you have an opportunity to develop your skills of reasoning and critical thinking. Pay as close attention to history, theory, media, professional practice, and technology courses as you do to design studio. There is nothing worse than a talented designer who fails to develop the array of knowledge and skills needed to successfully implement her or his designs.

Brian Kelly, AIA, Associate Professor and Director, Architecture Program, University of Maryland

❯ Intern, intern, intern. Do whatever it takes to gain a summer position in an architecture firm and discover what professional practice is really like. Find out as much as you can about the profession and the career paths you can pursue, but be open to all sorts of experiences. Stay flexible and open to new challenges. Realize that, even after college, your education in architecture has hardly begun; your career path can be a rewarding adventure.

Carolyn G. Jones, AIA, Principal, Mulvanny G2

❯ Start sketching your observations and ideas whenever you can. I am always sketching, whether it is a 10-second sketch of a building or scene, or a random thought or creative idea. It is a great way to not only document your thought process, but to learn and analyze where an idea came from, what you captured in the sketch or script, and how you can apply that to your future work.

Anna A. Kissell, M.Arch. Candidate, Boston Architectural College, Associate Manager Environmental Design, Reebok International Inc.

❯ Talk to as many architects as you can and ask about not only what is right about the profession, but what makes it challenging. Develop a strong love for buildings and design to stay energized. Learning about the challenges of architecture early will help inform whether it will be the right career choice for you. In addition to asking questions of others, it will also be critical that you ask questions of yourself: why do you want to be an architect? If your "why" is deep and important to both you and society, then architecture could be the right choice. If you are looking for fame, riches, and ample free time, architecture may not be the profession for you.

Joseph Mayo, Intern Architect, Mahlum

❯ Make the most out of the relationships you build with your peers throughout your architectural education. In most cases, it is the students that you will ultimately learn the most from through the collaborative environment in studio. The relationships I have made with my colleagues have proven to be the strongest of bonds and the most influential to my education and career.

Danielle Mitchell, B.Arch. Candidate, Pennsylvania State University

❯ Start as early as possible in your endeavors to become an architect. Whether it is an interest in art,

science, or even a computer drafting class, nurture the skills you have and acquire the ones you do not with as many training opportunities as present themselves to you. Only a lifelong commitment to learning will help in perfecting your craft.

As you discover obstacles, do not let them overwhelm you; instead, find a way to turn them into new strengths.

If not for a few key people whom I see as mentors, I would not have reached my goal to be an architect. Try to have more than one mentor to be part of your support group. Have at least one who is seasoned in the craft, and another who may be just ahead of you and understands the next step in your journey.

Kevin Sneed, AIA, IIDA, NOMA, LEED AP BD+C, Partner/ Senior Director of Architecture, OTJ Architects, LLC

Notre Dame de Paris, Paris, France. PHOTOGRAPHER: R. LINDLEY VANN.

What Advice Would You Provide to Someone Who Wants to Be an Architect? (Continued)

❭ Architecture is a passion-filled profession. Becoming an architect is not just a career decision—it is a lifestyle choice. You rarely leave work "at the office"—architecture becomes the focus of travels and the subject of party conversations. Architecture can be rewarding if you have realistic expectations about what to expect. Truly understand what an architect does, and commit your life to that.

Know why you want to be an architect—to end homelessness, to become rich and famous, to serve others, to become published. This goes back to the passion. Talk to practicing architects to see if the profession can really meet your career objectives.

Grace H. Kim, AIA, Principal, Schemata Workshop, Inc.

❭ It is a profession for which your appreciation will grow, the more you comes to understand. Accept new information and new ideas; do not limit your ability by things you "already know," but seek to understand more about what you "do not already know" … and try not to take things too personally.

Sarah Stein, Architectural Designer, Lee Scolnick Architects & Design Partnership

❭ Have a vision for yourself and how you would like to impact the world. Then take risks. I have been handsomely rewarded for every risk I took in my career and in my personal life.

Leigh Stringer, LEED AP, Senior Vice-President, HOK

❭ Do your research to understand as much about the profession as possible. Speak with architects and architecture students about their experiences and ask questions about everything from salary to benefits, time commitment, challenges and opportunities, the job market, exams, internships and licensure, fees, training, career paths, work/life balance, technology, expectations in practice, etc.

In general, the more informed you are about the profession, the better you will feel about making the decision to enter or not.

Kimberly Dowdell, Project Manager/Director of Marketing, Levien & Company

❭ Apprentice on a job site, learn a trade such as woodworking, masonry, electrician, painter, plumber, roofer, framer, etc. This is a great foundation for any calling. If your curiosity still stirs, pursue architecture.

Start higher education with a focus on the classics, writing, speaking, painting, mathematics, philosophy, and logic. This education will allow you to pursue anything you desire (i.e., adaptable). Finally, should you still want to practice architecture, use this book to chart a course for your career. Currently, a professional degree in architecture (with a basis in urbanism, if possible) is a prerequisite for professional practice.

But make no mistake, there will be days, weeks, or whole years in your early training where you question your trajectory. This is normal. It is not an easy field, nor is it for the faint of heart. Look around you. None of these obstacles, however, should discourage you if this is your calling. And, if it is, know that your passion and creativity will bring an insatiable thirst for making our civilization and our world much better equipped to respond to the challenges and opportunities we face. It can be a most rewarding profession.

Joseph Nickol, AICP, LEED AP BD+C, Urbanist, Urban Design Associates

❭ I recommend that everyone, no matter what his or her aspirations, seek one or more individuals for help with career development. I have had two primary mentors—one for nearly 30 years and one for almost 25 years—and many friends and associates along the way who contributed to my success. I would not have achieved as much as I have without their support. I also developed a 25-year plan early in my career. This, too, has been invaluable.

Kathryn T. Prigmore, FAIA, Senior Project Manager, HDR Architecture, Inc.

Practice the following: observation and communication. Architects who make a difference see the world in a particularly insightful way and are able to clearly define perplexing situations. In addition, good architects are able to communicate ideas well. Anyone who is interested in architecture needs to start to critically observe the world, becoming aware of both the visible and invisible forces at play, and begin to explore communication methods, whether that is drawing, writing, or physical or digital modeling.

Karen Cordes Spence, Ph.D., AIA, LEED AP, Associate Professor, Drury University

❯ Becoming an architect today means having a direct hand in shaping the twenty-first century. Architects are engaging in cutting-edge building science that is reshaping our world to correct the last century's shortsighted construction practices based on cheap energy.

Architecture has become a global practice, and you leave a physical legacy that impacts not only the people where you live for generations but also worldwide as an architect.

Amanda Harrell-Seyburn, Associate AIA, Instructor, School of Planning, Design and Construction, Michigan State University

❯ Architecture is the type of profession for which you must be passionate in order to succeed. You must work hard and be willing to sacrifice plans and weekends to make progress, work through problems, and meet deadlines. Architecture school has demanding projects and many deadlines, finding a job is very competitive, and the hours may be long. On top of all of this, you must be maintain a portfolio, manage your Intern Development Program (IDP) experience, and prepare for the ARE. A passion for architecture makes all of this worth it. I also think that it is really important to go into the profession with knowledge of the licensing process and realistic expectations. Not every job you have will be working on buildings like those you design and study in school or that make it to the covers of magazines.

Amanda Strawitch, Level 1 Architect, Design Collective

❯ As a student, studio experience is far different from professional experience. Continue to learn and gain experience by participating in competitions, design charrettes and shadowing architects in their professional settings. Participating with Habitat for Humanity hands-on projects have been a big help in understanding structures and construction. These activities taught me the most and that I was most appreciative of the internships and learning experiences I was afforded as an undergraduate student.

Starting the Intern Development Program (IDP) at an early stage also has its benefits of jumpstarting students on the way towards licensure. Many of the previously mentioned experiences offer opportunities to earn IDP hours. As a student, seeing these hours accumulate offers a sense of accomplishment at an early stage and pushes students toward the ultimate goal of becoming a licensed individual.

Jennifer Taylor, Vice President, American Institute of Architecture Students

A Teacher's View

THOMAS FOWLER IV, AIA, NCARB, DPACSA

Professor and Director

Community Interdisciplinary Design Studio (CIDS)

College of Architecture and Environmental Design

California Polytechnic State University

San Luis Obispo, California

Lumeire Ghosting Portable Theater Project, CIDS Project at California Polytechnic State University–San Luis Obispo, CA. Faculty: Thomas Fowler, IV, AIA.

Why and how did you become an architect?

❯ My primary motivation for pursuing architecture began with an interest at a very young age and a desire to understand how everything worked by taking things apart and sometimes getting them back together (not always). I did not know of another profession at the time that would give me a global sense of how things worked and how to document discoveries of what I found through drawings and model making. I had very naïve but romantic notions of what architects supposedly did—but this was just the vehicle that propelled me into going to school to learn about more about architecture.

Why and how did you decide on which school to attend for your architecture degree? What degree(s) do you possess?

❯ I possess a bachelor of architecture from New York Institute of Technology/Old Westbury and a master of architecture from Cornell University. My decision for selecting my undergraduate institution was based on what I could afford to pay, the location, and which schools would admit me. Selecting the graduate program was because of an opportunity to work as an administrator and do graduate work at the same time. The reason for pursuing

graduate work was to obtain additional design theory and to explore the possibilities of teaching.

What is the greatest challenge facing the future of the profession?

❯ The greatest challenge is the lack of accessible and visible role models in the profession and in the academic environments for aspiring ethnic minority and women students interested in pursuing this field.

From my own experience, I was fortunate to have a cousin that practiced architecture in New York City who allowed me to work in his office from high school through my undergraduate studies. This was the component of my education that actually kept me in school, since my challenge was to see the relevancy of my schooling to the eventual practice of architecture. For all students, some linkage to role models is helpful when things do get tough to sort out while in school.

From my undergraduate education and beyond, I have always been very fortunate to find role models to keep me on track and to expose me to opportunities that I would not had known about otherwise. I think it is important to have a strong sense of your destination but have some flexibility as to what the path might be to achieve this goal. Ultimately, stay agile in your ability to modify your future goals as they relate to experiences acquired on your path of learning.

How does your work as a faculty member inform your architectural practice and vice versa?

❯ Being constantly surrounded by the same age group of bright minds, always made up of a diverse range of individuals, who are able to generate a collective range of other ways of seeing a problem is a valuable learning experience to the teacher. Teachers learn at an accelerated rate from their students. Students will always challenge the conventions on how things go to together.

As an academic whose practice of architecture is embedded in working with students in the design and construction of a range of full-scaled building mockups, prototypical structures, temporary structures, and a range of community design projects has developed a form of practice that has been helpful in acquiring examples to show students regarding the intimate process of how design and the construction process works at a smaller scale. The academic involved in practice always has a voice in the back of his/her mind asking the question "How can I capture this process in such a way as to explain it to students so they will be able to learn from it?"

What are your primary responsibilities and duties as an architect and as a faculty member?

❯ I think some practitioners want to see faculty as practicing architects first and as academicians sec-

ond—since it seems to be a logical way to ensure that students will be learning the skills that they need to become architects. From my experience, being a practitioner first does not ensure this linkage to practice, but this depends more on what teaching strategies that are developed to provide students with the tools for understanding these connections.

Practitioners need to understand that they play an important role in the education of architects too. There is also talk about needing students to deal with more of a complexity of design issues while in school, but I would argue issues have to be simplified so students can develop ideas beyond the planning stages of a project into constructible architectural vocabularies. Acceptable levels of design development are lacking in many studios since too much time is spent on thinking about the complexities.

Project Iris, Cody Williams, Independent Study Project at California Polytechnic State University-San Luis Obispo, CA. Faculty: Thomas Fowler, IV, AIA.

How does teaching differ from practicing architecture?

❯ What a teacher does is very much a mystery to those who do not teach, which I think is more of a problem for universities to solve regarding how to decode the process for what academics do as opposed to non-academics. I often hear that the role of an architecture professor is to teach students the skills to build buildings. I would argue the role of an architecture professor is far greater than just this. Teaching is more of a modeling of future citizens who will make great contributions to society as upstanding citizens in addition to also having the knowledge to create architecture. Good teaching is where both the student and teacher learn from the interaction. This is why most are attracted to teaching—since this role provides a continuous mechanism to learn.

During your career, you have been a member of more than one of the national boards of the collateral organizations. What has that involvement meant for your career?

❯ It is often the perception that individuals who become involved as volunteers with associations have limited interest in the broader issues that affect the profession (i.e., design, etc.). I actually have the opposite view that active involvement with the collateral organizations has given me a broader view and appreciation for the profession. Navigating association work is the ultimate design problem for consensus building as you move through this kind of bureaucracy. I served as national president of the AIAS (1984–1985), and served as Association of Collegiate Schools of Architecture (ACSA) faculty advisor (2001–2003), served as secretary for the ACSA (2004–2006), and board member for National Architectural Accrediting Board (NAAB) (2006–2008) and sec-

Tobacco Barn Collage, Horry County, South Carolina. Architect: Thomas Fowler, IV, AIA.

retary (2007–2008). Involvement in association work allows you to establish a macro view of the profession through a variety of networks that over time disperse and expand as people move on to different things.

The Adventures of Nicole

NICOLE GANGIDINO

Bachelor of Architecture Candidate

New York Institute of Technology

Old Westbury, New York

Why did you become an architect?

❯ I became an architect because I enjoy creating something from nothing. I want to be able to design spaces for people to experience. Architecture is more than just building buildings; it is about creating spaces for people and their environment.

Why did you decide to choose the school, New York Institute of Technology? What degree(s)/minor do you possess? Why did you choose to study the bachelor of architecture degree?

❯ I chose to attend New York Institute of Technology because they have an accredited five-year bachelor of architecture degree and a four-year interior design degree. I was unsure if I wanted to pursue architecture or interior design and NYIT has both degrees. Both degrees start off with the same fundamental studios and would have given me the option to enter either program without losing a year once my decision was made.

I chose to study the bachelor of architecture because of its benefits. My goal has been to become a licensed architect. The bachelor of architecture allows you being taking your exams immediately after graduation. I am from New Jersey, and attending an accredited program in New York allows me to take my exams in New York. This was important to me when choosing where I wanted to attend.

Prior to your studies at NYIT, you pursued studies in architectural technology at Brookdale Community College. Why did you begin your post-secondary education at a community college, and how was that experience?

❯ I was accepted into NYIT right from high school, but due to financial burdens, I did not want to start at a new school with financial worries. This was the smartest decision I made. The program at NYIT is very intense and requires a minimum of 17 credits a semester. Architecture is a very intense major and requires a lot of work and time.

At Brookdale, I was able to take an AutoCAD course that taught me all the basics that I needed to know. Being able to complete a year at Brookdale allowed me to enter the program with a better knowledge of what architecture is all about. It also allowed me to take fewer credits and focus on the work that I needed to get done.

You served as AIAS treasurer at NYIT? How has this experience been helpful in preparing for your career?

❯ I was an active member for two years before I ran for the executive position of treasurer. As a member, I helped build the school store as well as help recruit and get other members involved.

This was a great way to get involved on campus, and more involved with people in the profession, as well as, students aspiring for a common goal. I was given the opportunity to attend the AIAS Grassroots, Forum, and Quad conferences while on the executive board. This helped me build connections with different professionals in the architecture profession. Being AIAS treasurer not only helped build connections but also allowed me to have a

Palazzo Angelo Massimo Façade. Model by Nicole Gangidino at New York Institute of Technology.

leadership roll. This gave me the opportunity to help run an organization, which will help me run an office or a company.

During your undergraduate studies, you served as an intern at an architectural and structural firm. Please describe this experience and how it has proved valuable to your education.

❯ For my first internship, I served as an intern at a one-architect architecture firm. This was a great experience because I was able to work on all the projects. I was given a taste of multiple different projects. Because the firm had a contract with Burger King, I was given the opportunity to create layouts for many different size Burger Kings. Also, I went on site visits for residential renovations. This firm gave me firsthand experience working in the field.

I also served as an intern in a structural engineering firm during my third year. After taking all of the required structural classes, I was very interested in structure. I was able to work with many differ-

ent structural programs to determine the required strengths of the structural steel going into a building. Working in this firm showed me the technical aspects that go into the construction of a building.

These two different experiences helped me throughout my educational career. Working with structure during the design process allows you to view things in a different way. Being able to have a different perspective on how it can be constructed during the design phases can either help or hurt your design, but is always important to understand.

What has been your greatest challenge as an architecture student?

❯ My greatest challenge as an architecture student was balancing work, classes, and executive board positions. During my educational career, I lived at either resident halls or an apartment. Living away from home was an adjustment that I had to make. This required me to balance my time, which was not always easy. Working is a necessity, but with the large amount of work that is required, it is difficult to do both at times.

What is the most/least satisfying part of being an architecture student?

❯ The least satisfying part of being an architecture student is the professors. The work that has to get done is something most of us enjoy doing, but the attitude of some professors can make or break your entire semester. Your grade depends on what your professor is looking for, but it isn't always easy to know what that may be.

The most satisfying part is finals time when you have a project for which you are so proud. When you are able to really convey your design to a panel of critics and receive positive feedback, you know all the long hours and hard work truly paid off.

◀ Highline Fashion Headquarters. Rendering of Studio Project by Nicole Gangidino at New York Institute of Technology.

▼ Water Works. Drawing of Studio Project by Nicole Gangidino at New York Institute of Technology.

What do you hope to be doing 5 to 10 years after graduation with regard to your career?

❯ In 5 to 10 years I plan to be licensed in the states of New York and New Jersey. Once I am licensed, I would like to go back and get my master of structural engineering. For right now, my main goal is to be licensed and working in an office as an associate architect.

Who or what experience has been a major influence on your career?

❯ My track-and-field coach in high school, Mr. Phil however, was pushing me to take his course, Architectural Technology. He was the one who introduced me to architecture and what it is all about. After taking his class, I knew that I wanted to be in this profession. After I graduated high school, he was still there for me throughout my career and helped guide me where to go next. I had the privilege to go back to my high school to give a presentation to students about furthering their education in architecture. I had brought some of my projects from Architecture Fundamentals I. Being given that opportunity to go to a group of students and explain what architecture is about was an amazing experience.

I also consider myself a self-motivator. I have always had that drive to succeed. I am constantly pushing myself to do better and thinking about how I can get there. Becoming involved with my campus and community has influenced my career. Architecture can be a way to better your community and influence the people around you. That is why I chose to get involved with my campus community, as well as the surrounding area.

Design for People

ANNA ALEXANDRA KISSELL

Master of Architecture Candidate

Boston Architectural College

Associate Manager–Environmental Design

Reebok International Inc.

Boston, Massachusetts

Why did you become an architect?

❯ I became an architect because of my influences: family, friends, and travel experiences, as well as my desire to design for people. I believe architecture can change the way we live.

Why did you decide to choose the University of Maryland and Boston Architectural College? What degree(s) do you possess?
Please describe the transition between the two degrees.

❯ I chose the University of Maryland with its bachelor of science in architecture primarily for its architecture program; the location, campus, athletics, and community were other greatly contributing factors. The architecture program allowed a greater exposure to non-degree courses during the first two years and an aggressive studio approach and focus on degree courses for the last two years.

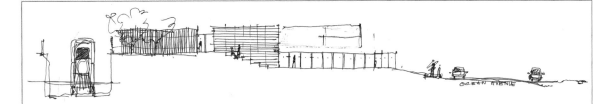

▲ Revere Beach Public Bath House. Studio Project by Anna Kissell, Boston Architectural College.

▶ The Great Wall of China, Zhuanduo Pass, China. PHOTOGRAPHER: ANNA KISSELL.

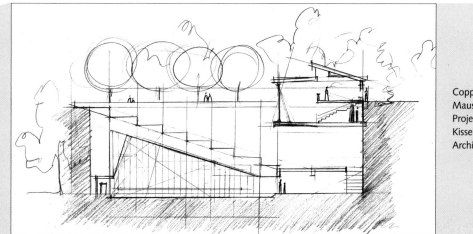

Copps Hill Mausoleum. Studio Project by Anna Kissell, Boston Architectural College.

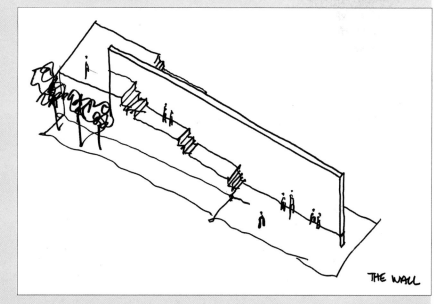

The Wall. Sketch by Anna Kissell, Boston Architectural College.

I chose the Boston Architectural College (BAC) for the flexible structure of the master of architecture and ability to gain professional experience in parallel to my education. The program is designed to fit the schedules of working architectural professionals who would like to continue working full-time yet have the ability to achieve a master of architecture. In the profession today, non-academic experience is an advantage in a competitive field of talent.

I decided to start the master of architecture program part-time at the BAC in the fall after receiving my degree from Maryland because my employer provided educational assistance. Now that I am pursuing my graduate degree, I wish I had taken a longer period of time off between undergraduate and graduate studies. Starting a career in architecture is exciting and tiring at the same time, so it would have been beneficial to focus solely on my career at the beginning, to have more personal time at the end of the day. The path you discover you want to pursue does not necessarily require graduate education or a licensure.

Looking back, it is much harder working full-time and pursuing a degree part-time jointly. I recently took a year off from my graduate studies to focus on my career and personal life, the time off reaffirmed what I wanted to do with my career without forcing a degree.

During your graduate studies, you have had the opportunity to work at Reebok International. Please describe these experiences and explain to what extent they are helpful in your studies.

❭ The integration of academic and professional work is a valuable opportunity I continually experience during my education at BAC and will use beyond my endeavors at graduate school. The integration is applicable semester to semester, whether in design studio, structures, or graduate writing. Drawing and presentation techniques are exchanged and experiences are shared. My professional knowledge enhances my academic work by providing real-world expertise and application of skills not typically built upon in an academic setting, such as time management and concise, effective communication skills; applying an architectural detail, construction technique, or an idea to a professional project we learned in class the past week or bringing my professional knowledge to the classroom to share with fellow classmates and instructors. My academic knowledge breathes life into my professional work.

What are your primary responsibilities and duties with Reebok?

I do the following:

- Schematic design, design development, and implementation of global environmental design projects.
- Provide administrative and on-site project management to global markets to ensure successful execution of global store design.
- Review architectural and MEP (mechanical, electrical, plumbing) drawing sets, construction drawings, and shop drawings in collaboration with architects, engineers, general contractors, and vendors.
- Research new materials, design technologies, and techniques.

What has been your greatest challenge as an architecture student?

❭ Time management has been a great challenge. Managing 40 to 50 hours of professional work, 6 to 9 hours of class time, and 12-plus hours of assignments each week has been the most challenging aspect of the entire academic process. It is a demanding commitment once you are out of undergraduate studies, because you are now dedicating your personal time to pursuing a higher degree. Education is no longer your only focus.

What is the most/least satisfying part of being an architecture student?

❭ The most satisfying part of being an architecture student is the exposure to new colleagues and their ideas, as well as getting to explore your own ideas on practically limitless design projects, and no budget or approvals to go through.

The least satisfying part of being an architecture student is the long nights working on assignments.

During my education, I do not get a lot free time to spend with friends and family, travel, and relax.

What do you hope to be doing 5 to 10 years after graduation with regard to your career?

❯ In 10 or more years after graduation, I hope to have my architectural license. I would love to be focusing on small-scale design, whether residential, retail, or civic architecture. I would like to open a small studio, where I can practice architecture, build things, and paint.

Who or what experience has been a major influence on your career?

❯ Travel, near and far, has been the most influential on my career. I have a yearning for experiencing different cultures, climates, land, food, people, and architecture. Sensory experiences are the most impactful on my designs; they give me multiple ways to approach a design project or problem, while focusing on what part of the design is most important.

Preservation and Architecture

MAKENZIE LEUKART

Master of Architecture Candidate

Columbia Universtiy

New York, New York

Why did you become an architect?

❯ I was led down the path of becoming an architect without even knowing it. The combination of following my engineer grandfather around during the summer and being dragged to early morning art classes taught by my grandmother definitely had a subconscious impact that helped to shape the way I thought about things. I was raised to think things through and make the best decision based on a series of variables. But all the while, I was encouraged to never let those factors get the best of my imagination.

I always enjoyed creating and figuring out how things worked. As my education and experience progressed, the things I made got more sophisticated, and my level of discovery and understanding increased. I discovered that I could turn this joy of creating and solving puzzles into a career, into a passion, into architecture.

The final piece that convinced me to pursue design on the collegiate level was a class I took in high school. My high school offered an architecture design course in which students were tasked with creating a residential house and building a quarter-inch scale realistic model. We entered our designs into a statewide competition in which certificates of recognition and scholarships were given out. I placed second in the state two years in a row; this accomplishment provided me the confidence to believe that this was something I was good at and something worth pursuing.

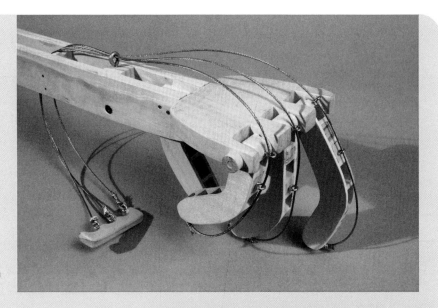

Arm Extension. Project by Makenzie Leukart at Hobart and William Smith Colleges.

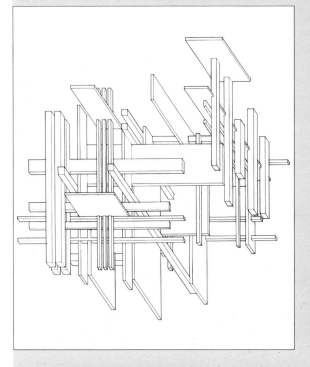

Studio Model. Axonometric Drawing by Makenzie Leukart at Hobart and William Smith Colleges.

Why did you decide to choose the schools Hobart and William Smith Colleges and Columbia University? What degree(s)/minor do you possess?

❯ When starting the process to look at colleges, I focused my search on the more traditional five-year institution offering the bachelor of architecture. I had no idea I would end up in a place like Hobart and William Smith Colleges (HWS). I discovered HWS through a series of acquaintances and references, and while I did not know much about the school, I figured I might as well apply. When I stepped foot on campus for the first time at the accepted student orientation, I fell in love with it.

I fell in love with the campus set on Seneca Lake and the large green spaces dotted with old brick buildings. It was exactly what I had imagined as the quintessential college campus. The architecture department and all the design studios were located in a Victorian mansion that sat away from main campus. It was an amazing space to discover, create, and cultivate my imagination. My professors were amazing and encouraged me and gave me opportunities I did not know I wanted. They pushed me to take a leadership role as a sophomore in the student architecture society. This helped me develop who I was as a person, as a student, as a leader, as a colleague, and more. I graduated from HWS with confidence and with a bachelor's degree with majors in architecture and environmental studies and a minor in art history.

When choosing Columbia, I had a similar feeling to how I selected HWS. I knew at the beginning of the application process that I wanted to earn a dual degree and stay on the East Coast. It was important to be close to family, and there were only so many institutions that offered that possibility. I realized that the one constant was always Columbia. It was my dream school located in the city I really wanted to live in. Columbia just fit the mold of my ideal graduate institution. I again experienced that feeling of knowing this is where I needed to be the instant I stepped foot on campus. I knew that I would do whatever I had to do to make it a reality.

Occupiable Space. Created from Abstractions of Composite Drawing/ Model by Makenzie Leukart at Hobart and William Smith Colleges.

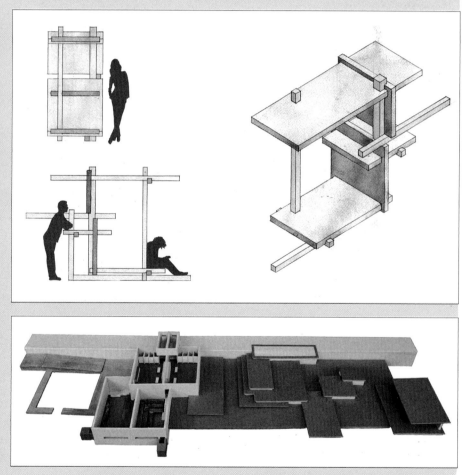

Harbor Front Cultural Arena, Copenhagen, Denmark. Studio Project by Makenzie Leukart at Columbia University.

At Columbia University, you are pursuing a joint degree master of architecture and master of historic preservation; why historic preservation, and does it complement/contrast architecture?

❯ At Columbia, I am pursuing two master degrees, one in historic preservation and one in architecture. This program of study will take me approximately four years to complete. I am often asked why I chose to do both historic preservation and architecture simultaneously, and it is both a simple and a difficult question for me to answer. From my perspective and focus, the two coexist, and it did not make sense to consider one without the other. I grew up spending summers at a historic family home in Connecticut, and the history was always an important aspect. I learned to appreciate the practicality and thoughtfulness of the design of the house built by my great-great grandfather. By combining history and architecture, new design thoughts are often born. Successful application of the thought processes and practices used in the past can be difficult to achieve in modern design, but the end results can be phenomenal. Buildings are not static; they are in constant evolution. If we continue with the razing of structures that seem to be out of date, we are simply being wasteful and perpetuating a cycle of thought that has raised so many issues on all levels.

During your undergraduate studies, you had the opportunity to study abroad through the Danish Institute for Study Abroad. Please describe this experience and how it has proved valuable to your education.

❯ It was the best experience of my life. I chose the Danish Institute for Study (DIS) Abroad in Copenhagen because the program gave me the opportunity to explore sustainability from the Danish perspective, take a design studio with active architects, and widen my perspective on the role architecture plays in society. The experience of taking design studios and seminars from practicing Danish architects was amazing. Through my explorations of Denmark and the other countries I adventured to during my semester abroad, I discovered many things about myself and my perspective on architecture. Being truly independent will do that to you. I returned back to school in the United States with a new sense of purpose and a new level of drive. The opportunity to spend time in so many wonderful and unique places like Denmark, France, Germany, the Netherlands, Sweden, and Iceland made me realize that they all have their own outlook on the world. I saw many amazing things in the built world in many different countries, and this experience drove me to push myself even further.

You had the opportunity to serve as a teaching assistant (TA)/studio critic in your senior year at Hobart and William Smith Colleges. Please describe this experience and how it was to be on the other "side" of teaching.

❯ Being a TA for two studios in the spring of my senior year was definitely a highlight of my four years at HWS. I had some teaching experience during high school and was eager to get back into it and see how it had changed now that I had all this new perspective and knowledge. I found that through teaching and critiquing I developed better relationships with my professors and gained a better understanding of their goals and teaching philosophies. I also learned the importance of different thought processes and interpretations. Helping and guiding my classmates throughout the semester on various projects was extremely fulfilling and created even stronger friendships. In the future, I hope to be able to teach again, ideally in a similar environment as HWS.

You cofounded the AIAS chapter at Hobart and William Smith Colleges. Why, and what is leadership from your experiences?

❯ When I began at HWS there was not a strong student architecture organization. By my sophomore year, prompted by a professor, I teamed up with a fellow classmate and set out to create a student group that would strengthen the community as well as offer experiences and connections that were not necessarily available through the department. AIAS was the perfect cohesion of all of our goals for the group; we established HWS as an official chapter. We ran many successful programs in the next three years, most of which are now staples of the academic year.

For me, leadership is closer to the role of mediator than anything else. At HWS, I saw my purpose as a facilitator of ideas and projects and worked as the ambassador of the student interests to the professors, school administration, and community at large.

What has been your greatest challenge as an architecture student?

❯ Sometimes I get in my own way with a design. Whether it is stopping myself from letting my imagination run its full course or being reluctant to try something outside my comfort zone, I can be my own worst enemy. Trusting myself and the abilities and skills I have gained throughout my education can be very difficult at times, but I am lucky that I am supported by and rely upon a wonderful group of friends, professors, and family.

What is the most/least satisfying part of being an architecture student?

❯ The most satisfying part of being an architecture student is the bonds I have formed with so many other students throughout the country. I've become part of this elite community where everyone has something different to offer and it is a good and accepted thing. It's also that thrill of coming up with a new idea and becoming so engrossed in it that you totally lose track of time.

The least satisfying part can be dealing with the bureaucracy that surrounds architecture; they do not make anything easy for you. It can be a struggle to work through it all.

What do you hope to be doing 5 to 10 years after graduation with regard to your career?

❯ I hope to pursue a career in adaptive reuse. Melding the old and new together with interventions that are functional, economical, and sustainable and not sacrificing the historic integrity of the structure is my favorite aspect of design. At this point, I would love to stay in New York City for at least a few years after I obtain my graduate degrees from Columbia, and then who knows!

Who or what experience has been a major influence on your career?

❯ My grandfather. No matter what I am doing, design related or not, I always think of him. I spent so many summers following him around as he lovingly fixed things in his thoughtful and precise way; I learned the value of ingenuity, integrity, and laughter. With every design decision I make, I always say to myself, "Would Papa like this?" He is a subconscious guide as well as a direct influence on almost everything in my life.

Paths to an Accredited Degree

Before selecting an architecture program, you need to understand the different paths to obtaining an NAAB (www.naab.org)-accredited degree. Because there is more than one path, this may be confusing. To become an architect, you will need to set an educational goal to obtain a professional architecture degree accredited by the NAAB.

The NAAB accredits three different professional degrees: (1) the five-year bachelor of architecture (B.Arch.); (2) the master of architecture (M.Arch.), which can accomplished by first pursuing a four-year pre-professional undergraduate architecture degree or a four-year undergraduate degree (B.A./B.S.) in a field other than architecture; and (3) the doctor of architecture (D.Arch.), available only at the University of Hawaii.

While your eventual goal will be to obtain a NAAB-accredited professional degree, you may wish to consider starting your path at a community college or an institution offering only a four-year degree in architecture. Some community college programs have articulation agreements with programs at four-year institutions, allowing a seamless transition. Further still, you can pursue an undergraduate degree in any discipline related or not to architecture.

BACHELOR OF ARCHITECTURE (B.ARCH.)

The bachelor of architecture is an undergraduate five-year degree for students coming directly from high school. It is the oldest professional degree offered at the university level in the United States. Some schools, including Drexel University, offer the B.Arch., but completing the degree may take more than five years because of work (cooperative education) programs that are required.

At most schools, enrolled students begin intensive architectural studies in the first semester and continue for the duration of the program. If you are highly confident in your choice of architecture as your academic major, pursuing a B.Arch. may be the ideal choice. If, however, you think you may not ultimately choose architecture, the five-year program is not forgiving, meaning that changing majors is difficult. Slightly more than 50 programs offer the B.Arch in the United States.

Recently, some programs offer an NAAB-accredited non-baccalaureate master of architecture degree; in some cases, these programs transitioned from a B. Arch. to this "new" M.Arch. While parallel to the B.Arch., these M.Arch. degrees may require an additional summer or semester of study resulting in either five-plus or five-and-a-half years. Some institutions may also provide an undergraduate pre-professional degree after four years. For more details, contact each institution.

PRE-PROFESSIONAL BACHELOR OF SCIENCE (B.S.) AND MASTER OF ARCHITECTURE (M.ARCH.)

Known as a 4 + 2, this path to the accredited degree involves first obtaining a pre-professional architecture bachelor of science (B.S.) degree followed by the professional master of architecture (M.Arch.). Pre-professional degrees are four-year degrees that prepare candidates for pursuing a professional degree. These degrees may have different actual titles—bachelor of science (B.S.) in architecture, bachelor of science in architectural studies (B.S.A.S.), bachelor of arts (B.A.) in architecture, bachelor of environmental design (B.E.D.), bachelor of fine arts (B.F.A.), or bachelor of architectural studies (B.A.S.).

The amount of architectural coursework in these pre-professional programs varies from school to school and determines the length of time required to complete further professional architectural studies, the M.Arch. Most pre-professional degrees are within universities that also offer the professional M.Arch. degree; however, others are offered within four-year liberal arts institutions. Your undergraduate degree may dictate the eventual length of your graduate program. Some graduate programs may be three years in length even though you have a pre-professional degree, although you may receive advanced standing or course waivers. Contact each graduate program for more details.

Another viable option for this particular route is to begin your studies at a community college. Often, the first two years of a B.S. degree are predominantly general education courses that can be taken at a community college. It is important, however, to be in touch with the institution at which you plan to continue your studies about what courses to take and when to apply. Depending on the institution, it may be worth transferring early rather than receiving an associate's degree from the community college.

Note that if you graduate with the pre-professional degree only, you will not be eligible to become licensed in most states. Therefore, if you desire to be a licensed architect, you should continue your studies and pursue the professional M.Arch. degree program. There are a few states in which you can pursue licensure with a pre-professional undergraduate degree, but you would not be able to obtain the National Council of Architectural Registration Boards (NCARB) certificate (see Chapter 3) necessary for reciprocal licensure.

The professional M.Arch. is a graduate-level degree that typically lasts 2–3 years and offers a comprehensive professional education. The combination of the B.S. degree and the M.Arch. offers flexibility, as you can choose to take any number of years off to gain experience between the two degrees. Plus, you may choose to attend a different institution for your graduate studies. Of the institutions offering an accredited degree in architecture, slightly more than 100 offer the professional architecture accredited M.Arch.

A handful of schools offer an M.Arch. lasting less than two years that follows a pre-professional undergraduate degree. However, these degree programs may be limited to candidates from the same institution. For example, the Catholic University of America (CUA) offers a master of architecture with advanced standing (one-and-a-half years) for select individuals who graduate with a B.S. in architecture from CUA, but those with a B.S. in architecture from other institutions must take two years to complete the master of architecture. At other institutions, the M.Arch. may be less than two years in length because of a switch in the nomenclature of their accredited degree from B.Arch. to M.Arch., but it may require either intersessions or summer sessions.

Finally, a few institutions that offer the M.Arch. for individuals with the pre-professional architecture degree will require three years of study; these include most of the elite institutions, but candidates may be eligible for some advanced standing.

UNDERGRADUATE DEGREES (B.A./B.S.) IN FIELDS OTHER THAN ARCHITECTURE AND MASTER OF ARCHITECTURE (M.ARCH.)

A professional master of architecture program is available for candidates with an undergraduate degree in a field other than architecture. It offers a comprehensive professional education. Depending on the institution, this accredited M.Arch. will require between three and four years of study to complete. Some institutions require that calculus, physics, and freehand drawing be taken prior to enrollment. Depending on your educational background, you may need to fulfill these prerequisites. Of the institutions offering degree programs in architecture, over 60 offer the M.Arch.

Some of these programs have the student begin course work in the summer before the first semester, while others may require full-time study during a later summer semester. Be sure to explore the curricular differences among the programs you are considering.

DOCTOR OF ARCHITECTURE (D.ARCH.)

As a professional degree, the doctor of architecture (D.Arch.) is currently available only at the University of Hawaii. The program consists of a four-year pre-professional degree plus three years of graduate study. Those holding a non-pre-professional degree may require three-and-a-half years of graduate study to complete the D.Arch. The D.Arch. is unique in that it allows the graduate to fulfill the educational requirements for taking the licensing exam, whereas the post-professional doctoral degrees do not.

The University of Hawaii also offers the only dual degree program with an international partner. Students with a pre-professional or professional architecture degree may enter into the three-year graduate program. After a year of residency in Shanghai and successful completion of the second year at Tongji University, the students qualify for a master of architecture from Tongji accredited by the National Board of Architectural Accreditation (NBAA). After successful completion of the third year in Hawaii, the students qualify for the D.Arch. accredited by NAAB.

JOINT DEGREES

If you wish to broaden your education beyond the professional master of architecture degree, consider a joint degree if offered at your chosen institution. Not all but many institutions offer a joint degree with the professional master of architecture. For example, some programs offer the following graduate degrees: planning, business administration, urban design, landscape architecture, history of architecture, historic preservation, real estate, and construction management. More unique offerings include master of architecture/master of social work at Washington University; master of architecture and MS in critical, curatorial, and conceptual practices in architecture at Columbia University; master of architecture/master of science in civil engineering–structures at the University of Illinois at Urbana-Champaign; and master of architecture/master of environmental management at Yale University.

POST-PROFESSIONAL DEGREES

Besides offering professional degree programs, slightly more than half of the institutions offer post-professional degree programs intended for study as an advanced degree after the professional accredited degree. Although these degrees have many different titles (master of science in architecture, master of science in building design, master of urban design, etc.), they all allow candidates to focus on a particular field of study—for example, urban design, building technology, architectural theory, computer-aided design, housing, historic preservation, sustainable design, or tall buildings. The typical candidate pursues this degree after working within the profession for a few years. In addition, a handful of institutions offer a doctor of philosophy (Ph.D.) for those with the master of architecture.

If you have the professional bachelor of architecture, you may wish to consider pursuing the post-professional master degree if you have an interest in teaching within an architecture program. Most architecture programs require a master degree, either the professional or post-professional, as the minimum terminal degree for faculty. However, you may be able to teach as an adjunct faculty with the bachelor of architecture.

Also, you may be able to earn IDP elective hours by pursuing a post-professional degree. For more details, visit NCARB (www.ncarb.org) and search for advanced degree.

Decision-Making Process

Regardless of the architecture degree you may pursue, how do you select an architecture program? After learning about the many degree programs, choosing among them may seem a daunting task; over 125 institutions in the United States and Canada offer professional architecture degree programs. However, if you analyze the criteria that are most important, you can quickly narrow your search and manage this process.

Consider that your formal education in architecture is only one-third of the path to architectural licensure. There are three Es to complete before becoming an architect: (1) education—a professional NAAB-accredited degree (Canadian Architectural Certification Board [CACB-CCCA] in Canada), (2) experience—fulfilling the requirements of the Intern Development Program (IDP), and (3) examination—satisfactorily passing the Architect Registration Examination (ARE).

When choosing the institution where you will pursue your architecture degree, strongly consider the following:

- Ensure that you eventually pursue the accredited degree program. Degree programs are accredited by the NAAB (or the CACB-CCCA in Canada), not the institution itself. (For a current list of institutions offering accredited programs, see Appendix B.)

- Be sure to understand the possible paths to obtaining your professional architecture degree: (1) bachelor of architecture; (2) master of architecture, following a pre-professional architecture degree or a degree from another discipline; and (3) doctor of architecture. Each path has advantages and limitations. Consider which is best suited for you, which will help narrow your choices.

- Identify the typical coursework offered in most, if not all, architecture programs: design studio, structures, systems, graphics/drawing, architectural history, general education, computer, site, professional practice, programming, and architecture electives.

You know the degree paths, the list of architectural programs, and the courses offered, but what is most important to you? Think about the criteria listed in the following sections in the categories You, Institution, and Architecture Program. Take time to think about answers to the questions posed and write them down.

By going through this process, you will be better matched with your eventual college choice and more confident in your decision. As you develop criteria on which to base your decision, certain degree programs and universities will surface as logical choices.

National Museum of Canada, Ottawa, Canada. Architect: Moshe Safdie.
PHOTOGRAPHER: RALPH BENNETT.

YOU

Consider the following attributes prior to selecting a school and an architecture program:

Level of confidence: What is your confidence level in becoming an architect? Do you want options as you progress through college, or do you want to dive right into architecture?

For example, if you are not completely confident in becoming an architect, you may consider a program that offers the pre-professional four-year bachelor of science; this way you can begin to explore architectural studies but not in full force, as in a professional B.Arch. program.

Personality type: What type of person are you? Will you feel more comfortable at a large school or a small school? This is a difficult criterion to nail down but also a critical one. Ask yourself, "Will I be comfortable here?"

Proximity to home: How close do you wish to be to home with respect to miles or time? Closeness to home is typically a top reason for selecting a school. If it is important to you, draw a circle on a map around your hometown indicating your desired distance from home.

What schools are inside the circle you have drawn? However, challenge that notion and select the school that is best for you regardless of its location. You should consider each of the over 125 accredited architecture programs. Narrow the choices later based on other criteria.

Budget: Do you have a specific budget for college? Obviously, with college costs increasing at a rate greater than inflation, cost is an important criterion. However, recognize that your college education is an investment in your future. Remember, once you have your education, no one can take it away.

INSTITUTION

Attributes to consider when selecting an institution include:

Type of school: While most individuals refer to all post–high school institutions as colleges, there are different types from which to choose. Most probably consider the university, typically a cluster of colleges under a single administration. However, just as possible is a four-year college, which is usually smaller and places less emphasis on research. Other choices include an institute of technology or polytechnic institute; these focus primarily on engineering and the sciences. Another choice is a two-year college or community college—a viable option, but one that will require transferring to an accredited program to complete your undergraduate degree.

Locale: Where is the institution located? Is it in an urban or a rural setting or somewhere in between? To what extent is the location of a program important to you? Architecture programs located in cities such as New York, Chicago, or Philadelphia consider this urban location an asset, as it gives proximity to architecture to be studied and to architects and other professionals.

Institution size: How many students attend the institution? What is the faculty-to-student ratio for courses, both in the major and in other fields? How much do class and institution size matter to you? For example, a small number of architecture students may be an advantage of a small school, but a larger institution may have more robust resources to offer.

Public versus private: Is the school private or public? Public institutions tend to be less expensive than private institutions because of the support they receive from the state, but they may have higher student enrollments. For international and other out-of-state students, tuition differences between public and private schools may be insignificant.

Cost: What is the overall cost of tuition and fees, room and board, and other expenses? Be careful about using cost as the primary criterion for your initial selection. Cost is and always will be an important consideration, but do not eliminate an institution because of the advertised tuition rate alone. Be sure to obtain complete cost information that includes tuition and fees, room and board, books and supplies, travel, and personal expenses.

Financial aid: What amount of financial aid will you receive in the form of grants, scholarships, and loans? Financial aid should be an important consideration, especially at the beginning of the search process. Realize that at a given institution, a large percentage of students receive financial aid. Some schools have full-tuition scholarships that save you as much as $100,000. You will never be eligible for such scholarships if you do not apply to or consider these schools. Also, do not only consider financial aid upon entry to the program; ask what financial aid is available for upper-class students. Many programs award scholarships on a merit basis.

ARCHITECTURE PROGRAM

Because you will spend the largest portion of your college career within the architecture program you attend, consider the following factors as you make your decision:

Degree: What professional architecture degree programs are offered? Does the school have minors or joint degrees with other disciplines? The type of degree program varies from institution to institution. Many academic units have joint degrees with engineering, business, urban planning, and others. These opportunities may be attractive to you but not available at all schools.

Academic structure: Where is the architecture degree program housed within the institution? Is it within its own college, school, or department? Is it with other departments in a school/college of engineering, art, design, or other discipline? The location of the architecture program within the university can have an impact on its culture.

During my graduate studies at Arizona State University, the School of Architecture was housed in the College of Environmental Design. Besides architecture, the college offered degree programs in interior design, industrial design, and landscape architecture. We had the chance to study in close proximity to students who would eventually be our professional peers in the work force. In addition, courses in these other programs were easily available to us as electives.

LEE W. WALDREP, Ph.D.

Philosophy/approach: What is the philosophy of the academic unit and of particular faculty? Some schools are technically oriented, while others are design oriented. Does the school lean in one direction more than the other? What is the mission statement of the architecture program? The approach of the programs you consider should be in concert with your own ideas of architecture. Learn about these differences in approach and decide which fits you. Following is a mission statement of an architecture program:

> *Prepare students for professional leadership and lifelong learning in architecture, urbanism, and related fields.*

Reputation/tradition: How long has the program been in existence? What is the reputation of the school among architecture professionals? Reputation is difficult to measure. Decide how important reputation is to you. Ask architects in the profession what they know of the school. If possible, contact alumni or current students to obtain their perspective.

Accreditation: What is the program's current term of accreditation? Even though it may be the full term of accreditation, what was the outcome of the last accreditation visit? When was the last visit? If the program is fully accredited, accreditation may not be a strong criterion for you, but the program's Architecture Program Report (APR) and last Visiting Team Report (VTR) may be helpful in providing you insight on the program.

Enrollment: How many students are in the architecture program or in each academic class? Just as institution size can affect your decision, so can the enrollment of the program itself. Consider the overall enrollment of the program and the number of students in each graduating class as well as the student-faculty ratio for architecture courses, especially the studio courses. The number of students in a program could be a reason to strongly consider or not consider a particular school.

Academic resources: What studio space is available to students? What other spaces or resources exist for students—resource center (library), shop, computer labs, digital fabrication lab? Because you will be provided a personal workspace in a studio, the quality of the facilities must be considered—more so than for other majors. The culture of the studio and access to it can directly affect your choice. What are the hours of the studio? Investigate the other facilities—shop, architecture library, and computer labs.

Special programs: What opportunities beyond the classroom does the architecture program offer its students? Lecture series? Study-abroad programs? Joint degree programs? Minors? Experienced-based programs (co-ops, internships, preceptorships)? What special enrichment programs appeal to you? Do you wish to study abroad during college? If so, attending a program with a study-abroad program might be essential. How about a lecture series? Although not a formal part of the academic coursework, an engaging lecture series can be a plus.

Faculty: Who are the faculty? How many are pure academicians versus practicing architects? Are they new to the profession or seasoned faculty? What is the diversity of the faculty? Faculty brings academic courses to life. Read the faculty biographies and seek to attend a class or meet a faculty member when you visit the school. Do the faculty seem like they would inspire you, motivate you, help you learn? Pay attention to how many faculty members are practitioners first and educators second. What difference does that make in the quality of teaching?

Student body: Who are the students? Where are they from? What are the demographics of the student body (gender, age, ethnicity, etc.)? In searching for a graduate program, consider the educational backgrounds of your future classmates. What proportion are international students, and from what countries do they come? Attending a program with international students can enhance your architectural education. You will spend a great deal of time with your fellow students, and you should be comfortable with them. Consider that many institutions have more than one architecture degree program, which means you may interact with students in degree programs other than your own.

Career programs: What programs/resources are in place to assist you in gaining direct experience in the field? Cooperative education? Internships? Exposure to practicing architects? What programs are in place to assist you in gaining direct experience in the field during summers or after graduation? How does the program connect with the professional community and its alumni? Some schools, including the University of Cincinnati; Drexel University; University of Detroit Mercy; and Boston Architectural College, have cooperative education programs that require students to work in the profession while in school.

Postgraduate plans: What happens to the school's graduates? Where are they employed? How long did it take them to find a job? For those who graduate with the pre-professional degree in architecture, do the graduates continue with the master of architecture degree? If so, what institutions do they attend? Do they continue at the same institution at which they obtained their undergraduate degree? Ask the career center for the annual report on graduates, or obtain the names of recent alumni from the alumni office and contact them.

Duomo, Florence, Italy. PHOTOGRAPHER: MICHAEL A. AMBROSE.

Resources

The following are resources to assist you in your decision-making process.

PROMOTIONAL MATERIALS, VIDEOS, CATALOGS, AND WEBSITES

The first resource you are likely to receive from any school is the promotional materials that accompany the application for admission. Be sure to contact the architecture program as well as the central university admissions office. In some cases, the program provides additional information or materials. All of these materials are helpful in learning more about the university and its architecture program; however, recognize that they are designed to persuade you to select the institution. Review the materials alongside materials not produced by the program or visit the campus to see for yourself.

GUIDE TO ARCHITECTURE SCHOOLS/ARCHSchools.org

Published by the Association of Collegiate Schools of Architecture (ACSA), the Guide to Architecture Schools is a valuable resource for researching programs. Its primary content is a compilation of two-page descriptions of the over 100 institutions offering professional degree programs in architecture.

ACSA launched a companion, online version (archschools.org) to the Guide to Architecture Schools, providing the same information as the book but with the added ability to search the institutions and programs by a number of different criteria, including location (school, state, region), degree, population (female, minority, international, and out of state), curriculum (related disciplines and specialization), and financial factors (scholarships, tuition, residence, and degree level). While both resources provide valuable information, recognize that the programs themselves write and report the information.

CAREER DAYS IN ARCHITECTURE

While many high schools host annual college fairs, these events do not focus specifically on the discipline of architecture. However, there are a few annual events that do.

Typically held each October, the New England Career Day in Architecture is a great opportunity to learn more about a career in architecture by interacting with professionals; attending workshops on selecting a school, career options, and financing your education; and meeting with admissions representatives from over 35 programs. For more information, contact the Boston Society of Architects (BSA) (architects.org).

Another event is the Chicago Architecture–Design College Day (CADCD) (chicagocareerday. org) also held in October. Similar to the event in Boston, the CADCD attracts close to 50 programs interested in both high school students and college students interested in architecture. A third similar event is 2B an Architect sponsored by the AIA Dallas.

Held during AIAS Forum over the winter holiday break, AIAS hosts the College and Career Expo (archcareers.org) connecting students with architecture programs.

CAMPUS VISITS/OPEN HOUSES

A very helpful resource is the campus visit. Campus visits are an absolute must, especially for your top choices. When arranging one, consider spending the night with a current student to get an inside feeling about the institution. If possible, request that you stay with an architecture student. In addition, visit with a faculty member or administrator within the architecture program, ask for a tour of the facilities of the program, and attend a class.

In the fall, most schools host open houses as an opportunity for prospective students to meet with faculty and students and to learn more about curricular opportunities. While these are excellent opportunities, recognize that they present the campus at its best. In addition to these planned events, visit unannounced to see the campus, including the design studios, in its normal setting. Many graduate programs in architecture host an open house in the fall for prospective candidates and a parallel one in the spring for admitted candidates. Take advantage of these opportunities to learn more about a program and make an impression.

In the spring, schools again host open houses, but they are reserved for admitted students. Visit again if your schedule allows, but sometimes visiting on your schedule may be more helpful.

ADMISSIONS COUNSELOR/ADMINISTRATOR

As you narrow your choices, one of the best resources is an admissions counselor or an administrator (director, advisor, or faculty member) from the architecture program. Remember, the task of these individuals is to assist you in learning more about their university and the architecture program. Develop a personal relationship with them to obtain the information you need to make an informed decision. Do not hesitate to keep in touch with them throughout the admissions process.

STUDENTS, FACULTY, ALUMNI, AND ARCHITECTS

An often neglected but important resource is conversations with individuals associated with the architecture program—students, faculty, and alumni. During campus visits, ask for an opportunity to speak with students and faculty. Request the names of a few alumni in your area, both recent and older graduates, to ask their impressions. Finally, seek out architects in your area and ask them their opinions about the schools you are considering for admission. If you are unable to visit a program, request the email addresses of students or recent alumni to ask questions.

NATIONAL ARCHITECTURAL ACCREDITING BOARD (NAAB)

The NAAB is the sole agency that accredits architecture programs in the United States. Their website (www.naab.org) provides a simple search for accredited architecture programs by degree program, state, or region. Each listing provides contact information for the program as well as details on the program's accreditation.

ARCHITECTURE PROGRAM REPORT (APR)/VISITING TEAM REPORT (VTR)

As part of the accreditation process administered by the NAAB, a team representing the profession, educators, regulators, and architecture students visits each program in architecture every eight years, assuming that it has received a full term of accreditation. As part of the accreditation process, each institution prepares a related document called the *Architecture Program Report* (APR). The APR can be an excellent resource as you make your decision. It provides details of the program and describes the institutional context and resources; the document is public information and available from the academic unit on request. It may be too long for the institution to send to you, but it should be available in the library of the program or may be listed online.

Another useful document, the *Visiting Team Report* (VTR), also should be available to you upon request. The VTR conveys the visiting team's assessment of the program's educational quality as measured by the students' performance and the overall learning environment. It includes documentation of the program's noteworthy qualities, its deficiencies, and concerns about the program's future performance.

While all this information may be overwhelming, these documents may be helpful to consider because they provide both an overview of the program from the academic unit itself and a review of the program by an outside group.

RANKING OF ARCHITECTURE PROGRAMS

While rankings are a popular method of assistance in selecting an architecture program, be cautious. Do you know what criteria the book or magazine article uses when ranking programs? Are the criteria used important to you? You should use your own set of highly subjective criteria when determining which program is best for you. Consider that none of the associations involved with architectural education attempt or advocate the rating of architecture programs, beyond their term of accreditation. Qualities that make a school good for one student may not work that way for another. You should consider a variety of factors in making your choice among schools.

Although few would argue that certain programs, particularly those at the Ivy League schools, are excellent, the fact is that if a degree program is accredited by the NAAB it is valid for you to consider.

One resource, DesignIntelligence (di.net), attempts to assess the best architecture schools each year by asking practitioners to comment on how recent graduates from different schools fare in the marketplace. This report provides valuable information but also urges critical evaluation of the research results.

Application Process

Within this next section, please pay attention to the narrative that is for you depending on if you are applying from high school, transfer, or to graduate studies.

After you narrow your choices and receive application materials, the next step is to complete the applications of the institutions to which you have chosen by the stated deadlines. Be cognizant of these deadlines, as many universities have set earlier and earlier deadlines within the academic calendar; some deadlines are as early as November 1.

Also, remember that the purpose of the admissions process is to select highly talented, diverse individuals who will succeed in that program. Institutions use the application materials—application, statement, transcripts, portfolio, test scores, and recommendations—to measure performance to date and project future performance. Schools want to know about you as a person; contact the school directly for more insight on what you can do to maximize your application for admission.

APPLICATION

At first, you might think that applications are designed to be complex and difficult, but if you simply read the instructions and review what is being asked, completing the application is easy. In most cases, the application is a series of questions related to you and your background. Do not make it difficult! If you do not understand an aspect of the application, contact the admissions office for clarification. Now, most universities use online applications. To ease the process, print out the application and complete them by hand first to ensure accuracy when you submit them online.

APPLICATION ESSAY/PERSONAL STATEMENT

As part of the application, you will be asked to write an application essay or personal statement. These personal expressions are the perfect opportunity to showcase your talents and creativity while effectively communicating who you are, what interests you, and why.

For undergraduate applicants, you may have a choice of topics. For example, applicants to Carnegie Mellon University may write on one of these topics:

- Evaluate a significant experience or achievement that has special meaning to you.
- Discuss some issue of personal, local, or national concern and its importance and relevance to you.
- Indicate a person who has had significant influence on you, and describe the influence.

For graduate applicants, the personal statement is an integral part of your application. Rather than a topic, most graduate programs request a statement describing your background, interest in architecture, and how the institution will assist in fulfilling your goal of becoming an architect. Most will have a word limit, so be sure to check. In authoring your personal statement, be sure to start early.

RESEARCHING A GRADUATE PROGRAM

MICHELLE A. RINEHART, Ed.D.

Assistant Dean for Academic Affairs and Outreach
Georgia Institute of Technology

One of the most helpful tools is to write your own statement about architecture. Initially, it will be an important way for you to hone your list of schools; in the longer term, it can be the "bones" for your personal statement. Consider the following: (1) why are you studying architecture; (2) what kind of architect/designer do you aspire to be; (3) what architectural (and related) skills have you already gained; (4) what additional skill sets do you still need/desire; and (5) what environment do you want to be in as you study architecture (e.g., geographic region, city size, available facilities/amenities, social community, etc.).

When narrowing your choices, you should use the Web to see student work and learn more about the faculty, but you should also visit the campus. You should ask your own professors and members of your local design community for recommendations. If you are considering graduate school at your own institution, be sure to ask yourself whether you have learned all that you can or whether there is still knowledge to be gained.

The majority of students will narrow their list without even contacting the schools, only reaching out once they have been accepted. One of the best ways of narrowing your list is by using the schools as resources, delving deeper than the information available on the Web.

Key questions you should ask include:

- Given my educational experiences, where and how will I be placed in your program?
- Will I need to provide syllabi for my previous coursework?
- Are there required courses that I need before attending?
- What financial aid and assistantship opportunities available?
- When was your last NAAB accreditation visit, and is it possible to obtain a copy of the VTR?

Also, ask for the contact information for a few graduate students who are able to answer questions about the program from a student perspective. Asking questions early helps you to narrow your list, but also lets the schools know that you are interested in their program and are thoughtful about your graduate education.

While the amount of research may seem heavy, it will make the rest of the application process go much more smoothly. You will have a draft of your personal statement that you can begin to tailor to each of your schools, and you will have a lot of your questions already answered by the time you are admitted (when you will likely be bogged down with end-of-the-semester deadlines). More information means a more informed decision in the end.

Royal Library, Danish Ministry of Culture, Copenhagen, Denmark. Architect: Schmidt, Hammer & Lassen. PHOTOGRAPHER: GRACE H. KIM, AIA.

TEST SCORES

SAT/ACT: Not all but most institutions will have you take the standardized SAT or ACT. Which test you take depends on the region of the country you live in. Some students perform better on one than on the other; for this reason, consider taking both. Many institutions use these test scores as an indicator of your probable success in college, so you will want to do your absolute best. Some people, however, are not good test takers. If your results are not at the level required for a particular institution, discuss them with the admissions office.

GRE: If you are applying as a graduate candidate, you may be required to submit Graduate Record Examination (GRE) scores with your graduate program application. Institutions vary in how much weight they give to these scores. Study hard and take the practice test. You may consider taking the GRE while you are still an undergraduate in anticipation of pursuing graduate studies. Most schools accept scores even if they are a few years old.

TRANSCRIPTS

All institutions to which you apply will require that transcripts be submitted. The admissions reviewers will, of course, look at your overall grade point average; however, just as important are trends in your academic record. If there is something in your academic background that is less than flattering, feel free to include a letter explaining the circumstances surrounding the situation.

PORTFOLIO

Unlike other majors, undergraduate architecture programs may require a portfolio; this is especially true for bachelor of architecture degree programs. All graduate architecture programs will require a portfolio. Requiring a portfolio does not mean you have to be a talented architect prior to admission. Rather, the portfolio demonstrates your level of creativity and commitment to architecture.

> Portfolios take an unexpectedly large amount of time. Universities expect
> high quality portfolios made with high quality software programs—and no
> two sets of requirements were the same.
>
> Also, do not seek a "correct" way to put together your portfolio ...
> because there is not one. Include a cover page and captions, and then
> the rest is up to you. One school might want your portfolio to tell a story
> and include lots of white space, while another asks for one piece per
> page with no unused space.
>
> ROBYN PAYNE, University of Illinois at Urbana-Champaign

What is a portfolio? For admission purposes, it is a compilation of creative work you have done on your own or as part of a class. It may include freehand drawings, poetry, photographs, or photographs of three-dimensional models or work. A portfolio is a means used by the admissions office to determine technical skills, creative ability, motivation, and originality.

> The portfolio is a creative act, showing your skills and imagination, but it
> is also an act of communication and a tool for self-promotion.
>
> HAROLD LINTON, Portfolio Design, portfoliodesign.com[1]

If you are applying as an undergraduate, gain a better understanding of what to include by contacting the admissions office. Despite the temptation, it is typically recommended not to include any drafting or computer-aided design (CAD) work; again, check with the individual school for exact requirements. As a few programs have very specific requirements on the portfolio, be sure to follow directions; Cooper Union does not require a portfolio, but asks candidates to complete a home test that includes drawing requirements.

Probably more so than when applying from high school, the portfolio is an important criterion when applying to a graduate program. If you background is not in architecture, do not worry about including architectural work, but rather include creative works—painting, studio art, photography, drawing furniture design, and so on. Completing a portfolio is a good reason to take an art or drawing course prior to applying.

When applying to a graduate program with an undergraduate degree in architecture, you must be your own critic to determine what work to include. Again, follow the requirements of the institution to which you are applying. Some graduate programs may limit the physical dimensions and the number of pages; very few programs including University of California at Berkeley now allow the submission of digital portfolios but most still require a true portfolio.

Actually, your portfolio is more than just a collection of your creative work; it is an opportunity to show your design skills through its layout, organization, and format. How the portfolio is done says much about you as a future architect. Bottom line: solicit feedback on your portfolio from classmates, faculty, and the institution to which you are applying.

RECOMMENDATIONS

Most admissions offices require evaluations from counselors or teachers (high school students) and faculty or employers (graduate students) to aid them in making their decision.

Counselor or teacher: The application package typically includes an evaluation form for counselors or teachers to complete. For many high schools, this is the last step, and the counselor will forward your application, high school transcripts, and the evaluation form to the college or university.

Faculty or employer: Applicants to graduate programs must supply letters of recommendation as part of the application. While most programs allow current or former employers to submit a letter on your behalf, you are far better off obtaining letters from your undergraduate faculty. This may be difficult if you have been out of school for a few years, but it is worth the time to track them down. In all cases, the individuals should know you fairly well, particularly your academic abilities.

Most schools enclose a checklist with the application materials asking for an evaluation on specific personal qualities such as:

Clarity of goals for graduate study

Potential for graduate study

Intellectual ability

Analytical ability

Ability to work independently

Ability to work with others

Oral expression in English

Written expression in English

Teaching potential

Research potential

While many architecture programs have moved to accepting recommendations via an online system, they will still accept letters written on the letterhead of the recommender.

Now you know about selecting an architecture program. From the degree programs to the resources available, you have the information you need to make an informed choice. But another important aspect is determining how you will pay for your studies.

SCHOLARSHIPS/FELLOWSHIPS/COMPETITIONS

Once you have made an informed choice on where to pursue your architecture degree, an additional criterion to consider is your financial resources to pay for tuition, fees, and other related expenses; more than ever, cost is one of the leading factors in determining where to attend school. But to the extent possible, do not let your financial resources limit your choices. Work hard to secure funding to make your number one choice a reality.

Aside from need-based financial aid, there is an abundance of scholarships/grants available from companies, organizations/associations, and universities. To start, search the Web. Next, contact your institution of choice to fully understand what is available; be in touch with both the university and academic unit. Also, discuss what scholarships are available to incoming students and inquire about possible scholarships available in future semesters.

One source for scholarships is the American Institute of Architects (AIA). The AIA, through its local components, provides scholarships to architecture students in a professional degree program accredited by NAAB (www.aia.org). Other scholarships/fellowship programs available include the Richard Morris Hunt Fellowship and the RTKL Traveling Fellowships administered by the AIA, and the Rotch Travelling Scholarship administered by the Boston Society of Architects. Other companies and groups have established scholarship programs that benefit architecture students. Again, simply search the Web and ask faculty within your program for ideas.

If you are applying to architecture programs from high school, please recognize that most aid available will come from the university; however, this is not always the case. For example, the College of Architecture at Illinois Institute of Technology (IIT) offers a single five-year full-tuition scholarship named the Crown Scholarship for candidates entering their bachelor of architecture. Most architecture programs provide scholarships to upper-level undergraduate students or those participating in study-abroad programs. Besides the centralized financial aid office, ask questions of your academic unit.

As a graduate student, learn the process of applying for merit-based scholarships, grants, fellowships, and assistantships from your programs of choice. Typically, there are more funds available to graduate students. One source worth pursuing is graduate assistantships because they provide opportunities to teach or develop research skills in addition to providing additional financial benefits beyond the stipend; for some public institutions, assistantships provide tuition remission and provide tuition at the in-state rate for out-of-state students.

Another source of possible funds is design competitions; each academic year the Association of Collegiate Schools of Architecture (ACSA), the American Institute of Architecture Students (AIAS), and other organizations host design competitions open to architecture students that provide prize money and public recognition.

In addition to scholarships/fellowships targeted at students, there are others available when you graduate and begin your architectural career. Again, search the Web, but possibilities include the following: SOM Foundation Traveling Fellowship, Steedman Fellowship in Architecture, Moshe Safdie & Associates Research Fellowship, AIA/NAC Jason Pettigrew ARE Scholarship, Frederick P. Rose Architectural Fellowship, and the prestigious Rome Prize.

Integrating Practice with the Academy

CLARK E. LLEWELLYN, AIA, NCARB

Director of Global Track and Professor, School of Architecture

University of Hawaii at Mānoa

Honolulu, Hawaii

Why and how did you become an architect?

❯ When I was in sixth grade, each student was asked to write on a piece of paper what they "wanted to be." I wanted to write "veterinarian," but I was not sure of the spelling, so I wrote down "architect." My decision was made.

Throughout junior high school I read the writings of Frank Lloyd Wright and managed to visit some of his buildings. Moving to Japan for my last two years of high school, I was amazed, awed, and inspired by traditional Japanese architecture. I would often escape from the dramatic collage of Tokyo and find refuge within rural shrines or temples. While in Japan I attended the 1964 Olympics and, like many Olympics, architecture played an important role. It was through the works of Kenzo Tange that I generated an interest in contemporary architecture that extended beyond Wright. The subtlety, power, and beauty of architecture entered my soul during those years in Japan.

However, my high school counselor was more objective. Because I had not taken any art classes, he did not believe architecture should be my major and "guided" me into engineering. I entered my first year of community college majoring in engineering. Within months I considered joining the military instead of being an engineer. I then contacted an architect inquiring if not having an art background should prevent me from being an architect. Based on his advice, I changed majors and followed my heart . . . something I still believe in.

Why and how did you decide on which school to attend for your architecture degree? What degree(s) do you possess?

❯ My father was in the United States Air Force, and I graduated from an American military high school near Tokyo. After graduation, I returned to my state of residence so I could afford an education. With two schools to choose from, I chose the one farthest away from family and overcast days (not necessarily good advice, but at 18 that was my rationale). Because of the remote location of Washington State University (WSU), upon arrival I planned to transfer after my first year. While disappointed upon my arrival, I grew to admire the location and found WSU to be an exciting program in a very special place. Though I had a relatively difficult start, I managed to graduate with the five-year bachelor of architecture with distinction.

Though I considered waiting until after I completed my professional internship to attend graduate school, I was "counseled" by numerous faculty at WSU to apply immediately after graduation. Unlike my high school counselor, they knew my heart and encouraged me to apply to programs that were previously out of reach (both financially and academically).

I considered graduate programs internationally (AA in London) and within the United States. With more forethought than five years earlier, I decided not to apply to any West Coast schools and narrowed my applications to Harvard and the University of Pennsylvania. I applied to Harvard because of the richness of resources, reputation, recommendations of WSU faculty, and a wide range of available ideologies and electives. Conversely, I applied to the studio of master architect, educator, and philosopher Louis Kahn at the University of Pennsylvania. When I was accepted to both programs, I chose the Graduate School of Design at Harvard. Though I received multiple acceptances, Harvard was my first choice. The education was worth every dollar spent, and the experience was priceless. I was in the first class to occupy Gund Hall. It was a very interesting year. I received my master of architecture from Harvard and, because of the education I received, I have never stopped learning.

Why did you choose to attend Harvard University to pursue your post-professional master of architecture? What was your particular focus or interest?

❯ I chose Harvard University because it did *not* have a particular focus or interest. It provided the most outstanding resources for learning within the world. With the combined resources of Harvard and MIT

(two miles away), not one program could compete for quality of faculty, library, or breadth of programs. Gund Hall was a new building in 1972, and it was an exciting place to learn. It seemed to be a place where the student rather than the school or faculty could set the direction. I had already been through a structured undergraduate program and sought a resource. I was not disappointed. I tried to take advantage of the resources available. I took courses in development, structures, theory, and design at Harvard. I also took courses in building materials, construction law, and planning (with Kevin Lynch) at MIT. Werner Seligman and Shadrack Woods taught me the "why" of architecture that I had missed so much in my undergraduate education.

In retrospect, receiving my first professional degree from Washington State University and my master's degree at Harvard was ideal for my needs. I could not have asked for a better and more appropriate education.

Whipple Ridge, Private Residence, Big Sky, Montana. Architect: Llewellyn Architects. PHOTOGRAPHER: CLARK E. LLEWELLYN, AIA.

Whipple Ridge, Private Residence, Big Sky, Montana. Architect: Llewellyn Architects. PHOTOGRAPHER: CLARK E. LLEWELLYN, AIA.

Llewellyn Residence, Three Forks, Montana. Architect: Llewellyn Architects. PHOTOGRAPHER: CLARK E. LLEWELLYN, AIA.

What has been your greatest challenge as an architect/faculty member?

❭As an architect, my greatest challenge is the ability to create and build work that I feel capable of producing. As a faculty member, my greatest challenge is to eliminate student biases.

How does teaching architecture differ from practicing architecture?

❭Teaching is inspiring or guiding others to value learning. Therefore, I often do not consider myself a teacher. The knowledge I impart, in general, is past knowledge. As an educator (versus teacher), I am responsible for inspiring students to look toward an unknown future. They must take risks that cannot take place in practice. They must imagine beyond what is historically possible.

My practice, however, must make the future part of our history. What I imagine must be built through construction means and tools that are usually historically based. Though I may attempt to create new techniques, forms, construction, processes, and the like, they are all based on historical realms of possibility.

Why did you make this career choice to become involved with education for your professional career?

❯I became involved in education through of a series of events that were not fully planned.

After becoming a licensed architect in 1975 while practicing in Portland, Oregon, I decided to open my own firm. Because I had grown up in a military household and moved throughout my life, I did not have many connections from which to establish a client base. Therefore, I believed that if I returned to Washington State University and taught for a few years that I could move to an urban center, practice architecture, and teach part-time to provide income while establishing an office. My mistake was underestimating how much I would like teaching. However, because I also enjoyed practice, I did both. Doing both full-time requires much more than 40 hours a week.

My heart tells me that I am first an architect, second a university professor, and third an administrator.

While at University of Hawaii Mānoa, you have been developing a new Global Track | China Focus between the University of Hawaii and Tongji University in China; why is such a program being developed and how will it benefit the students?

❯Archawai'i is initiating its exciting new Global Track | China Focus, a truly unique experience, which will present students with the ability to study in the United States and China, and to receive a National Board of Architectural Accreditation (NBAA)-accredited master of architecture degree from the College of Architecture and Urban Planning at Tongji University in Shanghai along with an NAAB-accredited doctor of architecture from the School of Architecture at the University of Hawaii Mānoa. Nowhere else in the world can a student enroll in a single track and graduate with two accredited degrees from the world's two largest construction economies. The school considers such innovation the wave of the future in architectural education and is breaking ground by being in the lead.

Throughout your career, you have been involved with the AIA. Why is this important for you as an architect?

❯I have been an active member of the American Institute of Architects for about as long as I can remember. As a student, I was active within the AIAS; after graduation, I was an associate member; and then I became a full member after gaining licensure in 1975.

There are a number of reasons for my involvement over the decades. The first reason is that I believe the profession should have a stronger and more effective voice. As much as one may find frustration with a professional organization because of its general promotion of "status quo," I believe the way to make effective and long-range change is through the American Institute of Architects. I have found the American Institute of Architects to be a place where one can actually make a difference if you get involved. Therefore, I am.

The second reason I am a member of the AIA is the people I have met over the years. I served seven years on the board of directors in Montana, driving almost 1,000 miles to meetings, so I met people who share a similar commitment to vision. They are valued allies and become valued friends.

The third reason is that I am an architect, educator, and administrator. Therefore, I work with students, faculty, and architects in training on a daily basis. These groups are part of our profession but have been historically underrepresented within the AIA community. Because I also practice architecture, I hope to help bridge the gap that often exists between the constituent groups.

The final reason I belong is that I feel a responsibility to be a member. I have used the AIA contracts for decades, benefited from their national and state lobbying efforts, handed AIA scholarships to students, benefited from their educational programs, and seen national advertising supporting the need for architects. Even if I had done nothing as an AIA member, I feel as though I have benefited from the organization and its volunteer membership. I have a sense of debt and obligation that must be paid in order for me to practice and teach within the profession I so much enjoy being a part of.

Who or what experience has been a major influence on your career?

❯Robert M. Ford III, FAIA, has had the greatest influence on my career. I first met him as a profes-

sor at Washington State University, where we had many discussions that lasted well into the night. We later taught together at WSU, at Mississippi State University, and at a private architecture program in Portland, Oregon. He mentored me through learning, teaching, and much of life. One other person who had a major influence on my career is my wife, Beverly. She encouraged me to apply for tenure when I did not believe in such appointments and then to apply for director when I thought otherwise. She has supported my practice, both in times of growth and recession. People have had, by far, the greatest influence on my career.

However, I cannot leave this section without having noted the influences of places. I remember the very first time I walked into the Pantheon in Rome. I was awestruck. Since then, other particular places have influenced me. These include the Alhambra, the ruins in Tikal, the Great Pyramids, and indigenous villages in Greece, Italy, Portugal, Turkey, Ecuador, the Middle East, and Asia. I have also been influenced and inspired by the rural West with the power of its landscape and architecture that has attempted to respond.

Second Generation

ELSA REIFSTECK

Bachelor of Architectural Studies Graduate

University of Illinois at Urbana-Champaign

Champaign, Illinois

Why did you become an architect?

❯I have always been interested in buildings and
the experience of spaces, but I was not sure if
architecture was the right path for me. It was not
until I started my first studio class that I realized my true passion for design. Architecture
combines practicality and creativity unlike any
other profession. It is a chance to be innovative
and challenge the limits. Even though it is a lot
of hard work, I thoroughly enjoy the work I do
in studio and it is something I want to do for the
rest of my life.

*Why did you decide to choose the University of
Illinois at Urbana-Champaign? What degree(s) do
you possess?*

❯Attending the University of Illinois was an easy
choice for me. The collegiate atmosphere of the
campus was exactly what I was looking for, and I
knew that the architecture program would provide
me a well-rounded education and prepare me for
life after college. I liked that it integrated structured classes into the curriculum as well as design.
However, what really sold me on the University of
Illinois was the full academic-year study-abroad
program in Versailles, France. I recently graduated
with my bachelor of science in architectural studies
and am very happy with my decision to attend the
University of Illinois.

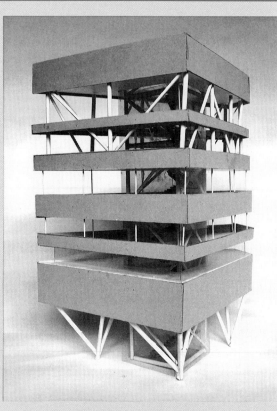

Figure Constructif. Studio Project with French
Students by Elsa Reifsteck, University of Illinois at
Urbana-Champaign.

*During your undergraduate studies, you had the
opportunity to study abroad for a full academic
year in Versailles, France. Please describe this
experience and how it has proved valuable to your
education.*

❯Studying abroad in France is the best decision I
have ever made. It is one thing to study about great
architecture through a textbook, but it is entirely
different to actually experience the buildings yourself. I have learned to not only see buildings but to

analyze and truly understand their purpose and meaning. Experiencing a new culture and working with architecture students from around the world has been eye-opening and extremely rewarding. My design and sketching skills have vastly improved as well as my knowledge of architecture history. For this rigorous academic program, studying abroad for a full academic year was completely necessary. I was able to take the same amount of classes as I would have in the United States as well as travel all around Europe. I would definitely recommend studying abroad in college.

▶ Greek Church Tower, Paros, Greece. Watercolor by Elsa Reifsteck, University of Illinois at Urbana-Champaign.

▼ Pantheon, Rome, Italy. Sketch and Analysis by Elsa Reifsteck, University of Illinois at Urbana-Champaign.

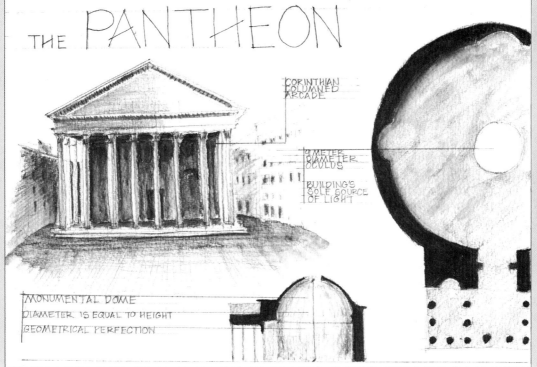

THE PANTHEON

CORINTHIAN COLUMNED ARCADE

9 METER DIAMETER OCULUS

BUILDING'S SOLE SOURCE OF LIGHT

MONUMENTAL DOME
DIAMETER IS EQUAL TO HEIGHT
GEOMETRICAL PERFECTION

What are your initial thoughts about the pursuit of graduate studies?

❯I plan to attend graduate school right after my degree. It is a huge goal of mine to become a licensed architect, and I fear that if I take time off before grad school, I may never go back to obtain my master of architecture.

During your studies, you served as an intern at an architectural firm. Please describe this experience and how it has proved valuable to your education.

❯Having a summer internship opened my eyes to the real practice of architecture. Being in an office taught me skills that I could not have learned in school. It was valuable to experience the process of designing an actual building for real clients. My internship also made me aware of the business side of architecture. A firm owner spends just as much time running their business as they do designing.

What has been your greatest challenge as an architecture student?

❯My greatest challenge as an architecture student has been learning to take criticism. After working for hours on an idea, it is hard to hear someone tell you that it's not good enough. But criticism is a major aspect of architecture. It pushes you to do better and eventually produce your best work. It is important to not take criticism in a negative way, but use it as a tool to improve.

What is the most/least satisfying part of being an architecture student?

❯The most satisfying part of being an architecture student is producing work that I am genuinely proud of. It is nice to look back at previous projects and to truly be impressed by what I have created.

The least satisfying part of being an architecture student is the feeling of being in constant competition to produce the best design. In some cases, this is good because it pushes you to do better, but you're usually competing with some of your closest friends. I think it is wise to not view your fellow students as the competition but as people you can learn from. I find that I learn the most by exchanging ideas with my friends.

What do you hope to be doing 5 to 10 years after graduation with regard to your career?

❯In 5 to 10 years after graduating with my undergraduate degree, I hope to have my graduate degree and be a licensed architect. I also hope to be working in an architectural office and making my way up the corporate ladder because eventually I would like to own my own firm.

Who or what experience has been a major influence on your career?

❯My biggest influence is my father. He is a successful architect and a fantastic role model. From a young age, he taught me to notice and appreciate architecture in a unique way. It was he who inspired me to become an architect, and I can only hope to be as hard working and dedicated as him.

Architectural Designer/Artist

SARAH STEIN, LEED AP BD+C

Architectural Designer

Lee Scolnick Architects & Design Partnership

New York, NY

Why did you become an architect?

❯My motives for joining the profession were somewhat vague. I wanted to use my artistic skills while still challenging myself with problems bigger than I. After nine years of involvement in the field, I recognize my initial motives to be stronger and clearer than ever; I remain within the field because of my passion for creative problem solving.

Why did you decide to choose the school that you did—the University of Maryland?

❯From my undergraduate studies, my decision was based on the variety of opportunities presented: close to a major city, large student body, and an opportunity to run track and field, one of my other passions, while also pursuing architecture.

As a graduate student, I wanted to work with a faculty that would foster growth while also allowing me to "design my own education."

Prior to your master of architecture, you worked at Wiencek & Associates Architects, an architectural firm in Washington, DC; please describe your duties and how that experience has benefited your graduate studies.

❯The experience matured me beyond any previous academic endeavor. I entered the profession barely using AutoCAD and left having worked as a project manager (small-scale projects), construction administrator, and Leadership in Energy and Environmental Design (LEED) consultant. I became proficient in Revit, gained my LEED AP+ certificate, completed my IDP, and gave several public presentations on behalf of the firm. I was fortunate to have, with a few hard knocks, the encouragement and freedom from the directors to gain so much experience. There is a confidence that comes from the surprise of exceeding one's own expectations; I surprised myself and decided to apply my new skill and understanding to a different medium, graduate school.

In the past, you have traveled to Rome (Italy) and Turkey. What did you do on these visits, and why were they important?

❯I have spent several summers in Italy over the past six years, having worked as a nanny for the first summer. That was probably the most unexpected, fearful, and wonderful experience of my life. That summer evolved into a journey through Reggio Emilia, Milan, and Florence, after I left the nanny job to work as a barista. The following summers, I visited for reasons more architectural in nature. I interned at a small firm in Rome, took classes at a local institute, and toured different cities while cataloguing my experiences and capturing the various cityscapes.

But I will never forget that first visit when I arrived by train in Reggio Emilia, so intimidated by the unfamiliarity, and starting lugging my giant suitcase right over the tracks. I have never felt so horrified as when the train official barreled toward me incredulously, screaming out Italian curses and directives; I thought, "That's it, I've been discovered. I guess it's time to go home…." But I didn't go home; I stayed on and gained so many brilliant experiences that have made me the person I am today.

Streets & Plazas. Summer Travel Sketches, Rome, Italy, by Sarah Stein, University of Maryland.

Churches. Summer Travel Sketches, Rome, Italy, by Sarah Stein, University of Maryland.

I spent two months in Bodrum, Turkey, directly following my graduate degree. I had an opportunity to live and work with a Turkish architect, Faruk Yorgancioglu, and his family. The project included 11-plus vacation homes located on an incredible topographic site overlooking the Aegean Sea. It was a unique opportunity to work one-on-one with a very talented architect. I look forward to seeing the completed work.

During your graduate studies, you served as a teaching assistant (TA) for an undergraduate design studio. Please share your experiences as a TA and how it has benefited your own design approach.

❯First of all, it gave me a completely new perspective on my own education and the nature of the student-critic relationship. I realized that while I was to guide and direct the student, I also had to leave room for his/her own discoveries. It also trained me to follow a thought/idea through completion and find ways to both support and confer a particular viewpoint.

Please outline what LEED AP BD+C is and why you pursued this credential?

❯LEED is an accreditation by U.S. Green Building Council. It is a "green" rating system, which has now unfolded into other sustainable ventures, including neighborhood development and others. During my time at Wiencek, there was a lot of encouragement to pursue various credentials. LEED is particularly important in this jurisdiction because DC building code requires schools, public institutions, and I believe the category is expanding, to fulfill a minimum standard of LEED performance. We designed a lot of affordable housing, which gains government grants by fulfilling LEED-comparable green standards. The knowledge is beyond useful, and just a small piece of the issues that confront, not just the building industry, the world today.

What has been your greatest challenge as an architecture student?

❯I told myself not to take architecture studio too seriously during my graduate studies. It is so easy to become weighed down by external pressures. Luckily, this studio group is really supportive; there is a healthy level of competition and an overall spirit of growth. But I am constantly reminding myself that this is my education, and I am here to satisfy my own curiosities and achieve the goals I have set for myself.

What is the most/least satisfying part of being an architecture student?

❯The most satisfying part of architectural academia is the thrill of presenting a design. It is essentially a puzzle that has to be pieced together with images, video, words, and confidence, not to mention that the backbone of the idea should be a solid one. The test of success is watching the reactions of the jury. Within the profession, the public review is less of a performance and more of a business interaction,

Kiplin Hall Herb Garden. Design Studio Project, North Yorkshire, England, by Sarah Stein, University of Maryland

though I have experienced moments where that level of engagement is reached.

The least satisfying part of being a student is that you cannot "put your pencil down" and walk away from it at the end of the day. You could rework a design problem endlessly, finding new solutions from different perspectives. That ability to constantly regenerate is also what makes designing so attractive.

What do you hope to be doing 5 to 10 years after graduation with regard to your career?

❯I wish to become licensed and work within a firm for a while. Eventually, I would like to start a business of my own, whether architectural or more broad-based design, but I would like to gain more from the firm dynamic before branching off.

Who or what experience has been a major influence on your career?

❯That is a hard question. In terms of people, my parents and siblings have always encouraged my artistic ventures and made me think that I might, in fact, have something special to offer the field of design. In terms of experience, I am like a sponge, and *experience* itself is important.

I have finally realized that whatever I expose myself to, place-people-ideas, will become part of my creative toolkit; that recognition really expands design possibilities for my future.

Where Dreams Have No End

ELIZABETH WEINTRAUB

Bachelor of Architecture Candidate

New York Institute of Technology

Queens, New York

Why did you become an architect?

❯I have been saying I wanted to become an architect since I was 10 years old. I never really knew why until now. I was always able to remember the layout of any building I was in and I rarely got lost. Growing up, I was very much into art, especially crafting. I would always put most of my effort into doing homework that involved working with my hands, like dioramas or art homework, instead of any other "important" homework, such as reading or math.

When I finally attended high school, I was able to take more serious art classes. Our art department was very extensive, ranging from fine arts to technical arts, as well as performing arts. I took as many classes as I could, including life drawing, graphic design, art history, computer-aided design, and of course architectural drawing. I also took an intro to sociology class, and loved it. It was one of the most interesting classes I have ever taken, even including my college career.

But if it were not for my freshman art teacher, I would not have had the courage to apply to architecture school. He brought out the passion for the arts that I had for so long and inspired me to work harder than I ever thought I could. When I started NYIT, my safe school, I thought it was going to be just like regular school. Fortunately, I was wrong

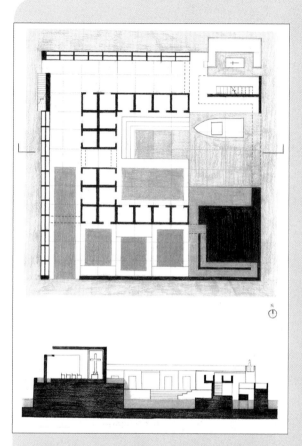

Island Cemetery for Architects. Sketch Design by Elizabeth Weintraub During Study-Abroad Program in Venice, Italy, at New York Institute of Technology.

because I fell in love with the architecture program. Now that I am almost graduating, I honestly do not see myself doing anything else. This is the one field I know that I can excel in and actually make a difference in this world.

Why did you decide to choose the New York Institute of Technology? What degree(s)/minor do you possess? Why did you choose to study the bachelor of architecture degree?

❯I started the bachelor of architecture at NYIT the fall semester after I graduated high school. I wanted

to stay home, so I applied to numerous schools within New York City. The problem was I was not really sure if I was fully committed to studying architecture. I was somewhat leaning toward interior design or graphic design as well. The two strong candidates in the end were Parsons and NYIT. I really wanted to go to Parsons because it was an art school, but I chose NYIT over Parsons because NYIT had the professional degree and the school is a really short drive away from my house. I am so thankful I chose NYIT because the program is excellent. I have made a lot of awesome friends here, and the faculty is great. I am very happy with my choice.

During your undergraduate studies, you had the opportunity to study abroad in Italy. Please describe this experience and how it has proved valuable to your education.

❯Studying abroad in Italy was my most life-changing experience. I never actually wanted to study abroad before college because I was always afraid of being away from home for an extended amount of time. I was interested in participating in a study-abroad program here because all of them were architecture programs, which meant I would be getting studio credit, and they were only five weeks long.

I really wanted to study abroad in Italy, and the director of the Italy program, who was my studio professor at the time, encouraged me to apply. So I applied and I was admitted. I was so excited but extremely nervous at the same time because I did not know anyone. Fortunately, my partner and I instantly clicked, and I got along with the rest of the 10 students on the trip. I got to climb my favorite historical piece of architecture, the dome of the Florence Cathedral. I saw many beautiful churches and other historical buildings. It is definitely more incredible seeing these places in person, as opposed

New York School of Dance. Studio Project by Elizabeth Weintraub at New York Institute of Technology.

New York School of Dance. Studio Project by Elizabeth Weintraub at New York Institute of Technology.

to in a textbook or online. It is amazing to see these magnificent buildings that were built hundreds of years ago, all by hand. They are perfect. We immediately assimilated ourselves right into the culture.

This trip really boosted my confidence because I learned that I can actually live and work on my own in another country for an extended amount of time. I learned that I can collaborate with other people and to produce a desired end product. I also realized that I cannot let fear hold me back from anything. I learned more about myself than I did about architecture.

You had the opportunity to serve as a teaching assistant for Design Fundamentals. Please describe this experience and how it was to be on the other "side" of teaching.

❯I want to thank all of my professors for all of their amazing work because teaching is one of the hardest things anyone can do. It is even harder teaching freshman students design because they are not used to thinking like architects yet. The most difficult task of teaching a freshman design class is teaching them to see the world differently. You have to learn how to really see space in a broader sense early on, and I mean the first few weeks of school. Unfortunately, those who eventually start to think differently will either understand by the end of the semester or never will. It is hard to work with the students who just do not get it. It was really difficult understanding what the students were thinking. Some students are clearer about intent and ideas than others. Eventually, you will start to understand how each student thinks, and they all think differently. I would definitely recommend that every architecture student try this in their last couple of years of school. It is always refreshing to go back to the first design studios, even if it is just for a visit. Also, it is really interesting seeing different design processes. It is amazing how every student thinks completely different and that every project will be completely unique because of it. It was really rewarding to find out at the end of the semester that I was really helpful. I am glad that I was able to mentor them and can continue to mentor them throughout their college careers.

You served as AIAS chapter president at NYIT. How has this experience been helpful in preparing for your career?

❯I have been involved in AIAS since I started at NYIT, but serving as president of an organization like this is definitely one of the hardest things you can ever do. The problem is that you really have to motivate your executive board because no one is getting paid to run this organization. It is hard to convince people to take time out of their busy schedules to make sure things are getting done. It is an incredible feeling because this entire organization on a national level is student run. If it were not for students like me out there who really put the effort into this organization, it would not exist.

I wanted to be president because I want this profession to get better each day. I want the students in my chapter to be motivated and put in 110 percent into their work. I also want them to see that architecture is not just about getting your design work done. There are many other great things architects can do, like charity work and networking with professionals. Being president of this chapter has definitely opened many doors for me in terms of networking. However, it put the entire profession in perspective for me. Every individual who studies architecture contributes to this growing field, whether it is from a local level to a national level. I learned that you can do anything you set your mind to. I never thought I would be elected to lead a chapter of a national organization. It has helped me learn how to delegate tasks, manage my time better, and step up and voice my opinion for something I believe in.

Between your third and fourth years, you served as an intern at an architectural firm. Please describe this experience and how it has proved valuable to your education.

❯In summer 2011, I worked full-time for a small firm, Philip Toscano Architects, in Brooklyn, as an intern. The firm takes on a wide variety of types of jobs. It was one of the greatest experiences of my college career because I was not doing what I have heard interns usually do, like scan old drawings or get coffee for everyone. I was exposed to many different things while I was there. I always walked around the firm and checked out what everyone was working on. One guy would be working on a reflected ceiling plan for a sprinkler job, while the guy next to me was working on a façade job to prepare for landmarks. I also filed paperwork and learned about the Department of Buildings. I worked on more jobs than I can count and went out in the field numerous times, but there were three big jobs that I got to work on extensively.

I learned the most from these three jobs while working at this firm. The first project I worked on was retrofitting an old concrete storage shell into a bar in Brooklyn. The second project was a new apartment building in downtown Brooklyn, a few blocks away from the water. I got to work one-on-one with the client as well. The third project was the biggest of them all, a new large warehouse in Queens. This experience was extremely valuable because I got to learn about a whole new side of the architecture I have never really seen before. In school, they teach you how to design buildings, but most of the time they cannot exist in reality. You can only learn the technical construction of physical structures and how the business works in a firm like this. I am so thankful to have the experience of working at this firm because I was exposed to an area of the field that is extremely important.

What has been your greatest challenge as an architecture student?

❭My greatest challenge as an architecture student has been realizing the fact that I am growing up and I have a lot to learn. This field is very difficult because architecture is also a lifestyle and can be considered a men's sport. Pretty soon, I will not have the security of knowing that I will definitely be working when I graduate. Students do not realize how great they have it because as long as they get their work done and pass, they are secured another semester

in that school. But for those entering the real world, securing a position is not guaranteed.

What is the most/least satisfying part of being an architecture student?

❭The most satisfying part of being an architecture student is the end-of-semester presentation. I feel amazing seeing all of my hard work pinned up on the wall, with my model next to it. It is an amazing feeling knowing that with all those hours you put into your work, such as detailed drawings and hand renderings, you were able to create a great project in such a short amount of time. The least satisfying part of being an architecture student is the lack of sleep. It is very unhealthy both mentally and physically because you find yourself working extensively on design work. It can drive you crazy, but you can also get really sick. I have had my fair share of illnesses, as well as anxiety attacks just trying to finish all of my work.

What do you hope to be doing 5 to 10 years after graduation with regard to your career?

❭The first thing I want to do after I graduate is to get my license as soon as possible. I want to work full-time and finish documenting all of my internship hours. I also want to take my exams as soon as I graduate because I am not a very good test taker. My goal is to complete this within three years of graduating. After that, I do not know yet. I do not know if I want to go to graduate school yet because I do not want to go unless I want to specialize in something. Right now I want to work for a multidisciplinary firm that does not specialize in anything because I want to be exposed to as much of the field as possible. My ultimate career goal is to be as well rounded as possible.

Who or what experience has been a major influence on your career?

❭The greatest influence on my career was definitely my high school art teacher, Mr. Leonard Antinori.

My parents were very supportive of my decisions to pursue a creative profession, but Mr. Antinori changed my whole perspective on school and the arts. Before I met him, I did not put any effort into any of my work at school, and becoming an architect seemed out of my reach. He was a very demanding teacher. He taught me that in order to have good work in the end, you have to produce as much as you can in a short amount of time, and you have to put all of your effort into everything you do. You have to think about every move you make and have a specific intent, a clear reason behind every decision you make. This whole mentality carried throughout my college career to where I am today. I will present work to someone only if it is the best quality I produce. I would rather present a client nothing than something that does not show my full potential. Along with my parents, he taught me to be honest, deliberate, and different. If it were not for Mr. Antinori and my parents, I would not be where I am today. I really appreciate everything that they have done for me, and I would never let any of them down.

You Are an Architecture Student

Congratulations! You are now an architecture student and embarking on the first and most critical phase of becoming an architect. To place your education in context, you should become familiar with the conditions for accreditation (naab.org), including the Student Performance Criteria set by the NAAB (see the sidebar "Student Performance—Educational Realms and Student Performance Criteria."

Remember that most states require you to obtain a professional degree accredited by the NAAB to become a licensed architect. What is architectural accreditation? The NAAB provides the answer:

> Architectural accreditation is the primary means by which programs assure quality to students and the public. Accredited status is a signal to students and the public that an institution or program meets at least minimal standards for its faculty, curriculum, student services, and libraries. The accrediting process is intended to verify that each accredited program substantially meets those standards that, as a whole, comprise an appropriate education for an architect. Since most state registration boards in the United States require any applicant for licensure to have graduated from an NAAB-accredited program, obtaining such a degree is an essential aspect of preparing for the professional practice of architecture.[2]

Through the accreditation process, the NAAB dictates to the architecture programs what must be taught, but it does not dictate *how* they are to be taught. This is why not all architecture programs have the same curriculum. The differences among them may be confusing, but they also allow you to find the program that will suit you best.

STUDENT PERFORMANCE — EDUCATIONAL REALMS AND STUDENT PERFORMANCE CRITERIA[3]

The accredited degree program must demonstrate that each graduate possesses the knowledge and skills defined by the criteria below. The knowledge and skills defined here represent those required to prepare graduates for the pathway to internship, examination and licensure, or to engage in related fields. The program must provide student work as evidence that its graduates have satisfied each criterion.

The criteria encompass two levels of accomplishment[a]:

- **Understanding**—The capacity to classify, compare, summarize, explain and/or interpret information.

- **Ability**—Proficiency in using specific information to accomplish a task, correctly selecting the appropriate information, and accurately applying it to the solution of a specific problem, while also distinguishing the effects of its implementation.

II.1.1 STUDENT PERFORMANCE CRITERIA (SPC):

The NAAB establishes SPC to help accredited degree programs prepare students for the profession while encouraging educational practices suited to the individual degree program. The SPC are organized into realms to more easily understand the relationships between individual criteria.

Realm A: Critical Thinking and Representation:

Graduates from NAAB-accredited programs must be able to build abstract relationships and understand the impact of ideas based on the research and analysis of multiple theoretical, social, political, economic, cultural and environmental contexts. This includes using a diverse range of media to think about and convey architectural ideas including writing, investigative skills, speaking, drawing and model making.

STUDENT LEARNING ASPIRATIONS FOR THIS REALM INCLUDE:

- Being broadly educated.
- Valuing lifelong inquisitiveness.
- Communicating graphically in a range of media.
- Assessing evidence.
- Comprehending people, place, and context.
- Recognizing the disparate needs of client, community, and society.

[a]See also L.W. Anderson & D.R. Krathwold, Eds. *Taxonomy for Learning, Teaching and Assessing: A Revision of Bloom's Taxonomy of Educational Objectives. (New York; Longman 2001).*

A.1   Professional Communication Skills: *Ability* to write and speak effectively and use appropriate representational media both with peers and with the general public.

A.2   Design Thinking Skills: *Ability* to raise clear and precise questions, use abstract ideas to interpret information, consider diverse points of view, reach well-reasoned conclusions, and test alternative outcomes against relevant criteria and standards.

A.3   Investigative Skills: *Ability* to gather, assess, record, and comparatively evaluate relevant information and performance in order to support conclusions related to a specific project or assignment.

A.4   Architectural Design Skills: *Ability* to effectively use basic formal, organizational and environmental principles and the capacity of each to inform two- and three-dimensional design.

A.5   Ordering Systems: *Ability* to apply the fundamentals of both natural and formal ordering systems and the capacity of each to inform two- and three-dimensional design.

A.6   Use of Precedents: *Ability* to examine and comprehend the fundamental principles present in relevant precedents and to make informed choices regarding the incorporation of such principles into architecture and urban design projects.

A.7   History and Culture: *Understanding* of the parallel and divergent histories of architecture and the cultural norms of a variety of indigenous, vernacular, local, regional, settings in terms of their political, economic, social, and technological factors.

A.8   Cultural Diversity and Social Equity: *Understanding* of the diverse needs, values, behavioral norms, physical abilities, and social and spatial patterns that characterize different cultures and individuals and the responsibility of the architect to ensure equity of access to buildings and structures.

Realm B: Building Practices, Technical Skills and Knowledge:

Graduates from NAAB-accredited programs must be able to comprehend the technical aspects of design, systems and materials, and be able to apply that comprehension to architectural solutions. Additionally the impact of such decisions on the environment must be well considered.

STUDENT LEARNING ASPIRATIONS FOR THIS REALM INCLUDE:

- Creating building designs with well-integrated systems.
- Comprehending constructability.
- Integrating the principles of environmental stewardship.
- Conveying technical information accurately.

B.1   Pre-Design: *Ability* to prepare a comprehensive program for an architectural project, which must include an assessment of client and user needs, an inventory of spaces and their requirements, an analysis of site conditions (including existing buildings), a review of the relevant building codes and standards, including relevant sustainability requirements, and assessment of their implications for the project, and a definition of site selection and design assessment criteria.

B.2   Site Design: *Ability* to respond to site characteristics including urban context and developmental patterning, historical fabric, soil, topography, climate, building orientation, and watershed in the development of a project design.

B.3. Codes and Regulations: *Ability* to design sites, facilities and systems consistent with the principles of life-safety standards, accessibility standards, and other codes and regulations.

B.4   Technical Documentation: *Ability* to make technically clear drawings, prepare outline specifications, and construct models illustrating and identifying the assembly of materials, systems, and components appropriate for a building design.

B.5   Structural Systems: *Ability* to demonstrate the basic principles of structural systems and their ability to withstand gravity, seismic, and lateral forces, as well as the selection and application of the appropriate structural system."

B.6   Environmental Systems: *Understanding* the principles of environmental systems' design, how systems can vary by geographic region, and the tools used for performance assessment. This must include active and passive heating and cooling, indoor air quality, solar systems, lighting systems, and acoustics.

B.7   Building Envelope Systems and Assemblies: *Understanding* of the basic principles involved in the appropriate selection and application of building envelope systems relative to fundamental performance, aesthetics, moisture transfer, durability, and energy and material resources.

B.8   Building Materials and Assemblies: *Understanding* of the basic principles utilized in the appropriate selection of interior and exterior construction materials, finishes, products, components and assemblies based on their inherent performance including environmental impact and reuse.

B.9   Building Service Systems: *Understanding* of the basic principles and appropriate application and performance of building service systems including mechanical, plumbing, electrical, communication, vertical transportation security, and fire protection systems.

B.10. Financial Considerations: *Understanding* of the fundamentals of building costs, which must include project financing methods and feasibility, construction cost estimating, construction scheduling, operational costs, and life-cycle costs.

Realm C: Integrated Architectural Solutions:

Graduates from NAAB-accredited programs must be able to synthesize a wide range of variables into an integrated design solution. This realm demonstrates the integrative thinking that shapes complex design and technical solutions.

STUDENT LEARNING ASPIRATIONS IN THIS REALM INCLUDE:

- Synthesizing variables from diverse and complex systems into an integrated architectural solution.

- Respond to environmental stewardship goals across multiple systems for an integrated solution.

- Evaluating options and reconciling the implications of design decisions across systems and scales.

C.1 Integrative Design: *Ability* to make design decisions within a complex architectural project while demonstrating broad integration and consideration of environmental stewardship, technical documentation, accessibility, site conditions, life safety, environmental systems, structural systems, and building envelope systems and assemblies.

C.2 Evaluation and Decision Making: *Ability* to demonstrate the skills associated with making integrated decisions across multiple systems and variables in the completion of a design project. This includes problem identification, setting evaluative criteria, analyzing solutions, and predicting the effectiveness of implementation.

Realm D: Professional Practice.

Graduates from NAAB-accredited programs must understand business principles for the practice of architecture, including management, advocacy, and acting legally, ethically and critically for the good of the client, society and the public.

STUDENT LEARNING ASPIRATIONS FOR THIS REALM INCLUDE:

- Comprehending the business of architecture and construction.

- Discerning the valuable roles and key players in related disciplines.

- Understanding a professional code of ethics, as well as legal and professional responsibilities.

D.1 Stakeholder Roles: In Architecture: *Understanding* of the relationship between the client, contractor, architect and other key stakeholders such as user groups and the community, in the design of the built environment. Understanding the responsibilities of the architect to reconcile the needs of those stakeholders

D.2 Project Management: *Understanding* of the methods for selecting consultants and assembling teams, identifying work plans, project schedules and time requirements, and recommending project delivery methods.

D.3 Business Practices: *Understanding* of the basic principles of business practices within the firm including financial management and business planning, marketing, business organization, and entrepreneurialism.

D.4 Legal Responsibilities: *Understanding* the architect's responsibility to the public and the client as determined by regulations and legal considerations involving the practice of architecture and professional service contracts.

D.5 Professional Ethics: *Understanding* of the ethical issues involved in the exercise of professional judgment in architectural design and practice, and understanding the role of the AIA Code of Ethics in defining professional conduct.

Note: The Student Performance Criteria listed here are pending final approval in July 2014; for the final list of SPC, visit www.naab.org.

Sainte Marie de La Tourette, Éveux, France. Architect: Le Corbusier. PHOTOGRAPHER: DANA TAYLOR.

COURSES

Regardless of which program and institution you select to pursue your architecture degree, the courses offered are similar. A typical sequence includes the following: general education, design, history and theory, technology, professional practice, and electives.

Each architecture program will require courses in *general education*—English, humanities, mathematics and science, and social sciences. While you may not enjoy these required courses, realize that they will connect to your architectural studies. To the extent your curriculum provides, always choose courses that are of interest to you.

As you will quickly learn, *design* is the heart of each architecture curriculum. Once in the studio sequence of a degree program, you will be taking design studio each semester, usually for four to six credits. Design studio may meet between 8 and 12 hours with the designated faculty and countless hours outside of class. Projects may begin in the abstract and deal with basic skill development, but they will quickly progress in scale and complexity.

Faculty members provide the program or space requirements of a given building project. From there, students individually develop solutions to the problem and present the results to faculty and classmates. This final presentation, called a *review*, is the culmination of hours of hard work. Comments are provided to the student on the finished project. Just as important as the product is the process. You will learn not only from the studio faculty but also from your fellow students.

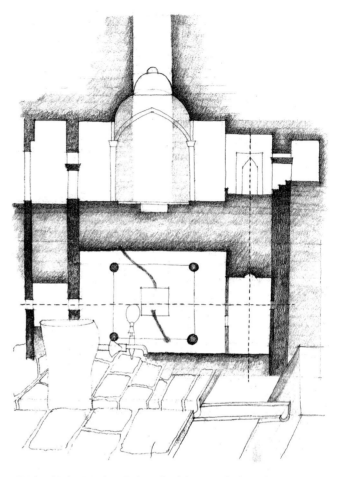

Ertokus Medresi, Atabey, Turkey. Sketch by Hannah Irby at the Catholic University of America.

Design courses are central to an architectural education, but what is studio? More than simply a place to work, the studio is where design happens. A central aspect of an architectural education, the studio is the place to work and more. The studio becomes an extension of the curriculum as you combine what you learn from your architecture courses and apply that knowledge to your design work.

As part of your studio course, you will learn architecture in varying methods as described in the following material. At the beginning of a studio project, you, along with your classmates, may do research on the project and site, and perform a precedent analysis. You may take a field trip to the proposed site. The professor may lecture on aspects of the project as you begin the design process. You will work on design during class time and participate in desk critiques or individual time with the professor to discuss your design and ideas. Depending on the length of the project, there may be pin-ups or interim critiques with your entire studio and professor or subsets of your studio classmates. Eventually, at the end, you participate in the charrette, an intensive burst of energy to complete the project before the stated deadline. Finally, there is the final review or critique, which involves outside faculty or visitors from off-campus.

A vital aspect of the design studio and an architectural education is learning through criticism. Brian Kelly, AIA, director of the architecture program and associate professor at the University of Maryland, offers the following:

The development of a rigorous design process governed by critical thinking is a central component of architectural education and an essential tool for successful professional practice. Design studios utilize critical review, debate, and consultation with faculty and professional guests to engage a wide range of issues central to the making of architecture. This engagement between students and their critics takes place in a public arena where students can learn from discussions of their own work and that of their peers.

For some, the public nature of critique is challenging. Beginning students have been known to mistake comments about their design work as praise of their individual character. "Professor Smith likes me and therefore is always enthusiastic about my work." Likewise, others have confused critical comments focused on the work with evaluation of personal attributes. "Professor Jones has it in for me and always trashes my work." Both of these positions are naïve appraisals of the role of criticism. Criticism is not personal.

The role of criticism is to improve students' design processes and thereby lead the way to a higher quality of architecture. Criticism is not simply a matter of "I like it" or "I dislike it." Criticism involves illuminating the principles on which design work is based and evaluating the rational application of those principles. Simply put, criticism is about the work and the process by which the work was conceptualized. It is not about the individual. The goal of criticism is to enable the student to become a competent critic. Both self-criticism and critique of others is an essential tool for architects in practice.

BRIAN KELLY, University of Maryland

VM Houses, Copenhagen, Denmark. Architect: JDS Architects and Bjarke Ingels Group. PHOTOGRAPHER: DANA TAYLOR.

All architecture programs require courses in *history and theory* to address values, concepts, and methods. Most curriculums offer courses that provide an understanding of both Western and non-Western traditions across the ages, from ancient Greek architecture to the modern day. In addition, more focused history courses may be required or offered as electives.

Technology covers structures and environmental systems. Each program teaches these courses differently, but structures will involve basic statics and strength of materials—wood, steel, timber, and masonry. Courses in environmental systems cover HVAC (heating, ventilating, and air conditioning), plumbing, lighting, and acoustics. Most programs also have courses in construction materials and methods. All of these courses, required by most programs, are taught with the idea that you will integrate what you learn to your design studio.

All programs offer coursework in *professional* practice addressing the legal aspects of architecture, contracts, ethics, leadership roles, and business issues.

In addition, all programs provide a wide array of *electives* (see the sidebar "Architecture Electives: A Sample"). These may include courses in computer applications, advanced technology, history and theory, urban design, and so on. Some programs permit or require students to take elective courses outside the major in areas such as art, business, or engineering.

ARCHITECTURE ELECTIVES: A SAMPLE

Architect as Developer

Methods in Architectural Design

Biomorphic Design

History of the City

Kahn: Theory of Tectonics

Advanced Freehand Perspective Drawing

The Ideologies of Architecture Theory: The Situations of Theory and the Syntax of History
Beyond Postmodern Urbanism

The Cultural Landscape: The Grand Canyon

Finding Purpose: Survival in Design

International Boulevard: The Analysis of Everything Else

Architecture and Corporate Culture

The City Theoretically Considered

Introduction to Crime Prevention through Environmental Design

Understanding Clients and Users: Methods for Programming and Evaluation

Traditions of Architectural Practice

Design in the Digital Age

Critical Positions in Architectural Design

The Bone Studio 2: Experimental Concrete Architecture

Digital Fabrications

Legal Aspects of Design Practice

Methods of Presentation, Representation, and Re-Presentation

Seminar in Architectural Philosophy

Issues in Sustainability

TOOLS

Aside from courses, an element of an architectural education is the tools. Unlike those in other majors who have textbooks, architecture students have tools. In fact, while architecture students will need to purchase some textbooks, they will need to purchase these tools. Included are the tools of the profession: t-square, drawing board, scale, triangles, leadholders with various leads

(2H, H, B, 2B), sharpener, erasers, erasing shield, compass, X-Acto knife with blades, circles template, brush, lamp, push pins, and drafting tape or dots. For now, these tools may not be familiar, but they soon will be. Many programs, through their AIAS chapter, sell toolkits with the items just mentioned plus more. It is well worth the money to purchase such a kit to save time and hassles.

Also, consider obtaining a laptop computer, tablet, and music-playing device with headphones. In recent years, more and more programs are requiring laptops as part of attendance. Regardless, all students are now entering colleges with a laptop or desktop computer. Talk with upperclass students and the program to learn about which platform (Macintosh or PC) is the best. You will want headphones to listen to your favorite music but also to eliminate the distracting noise in the studio.

Again, check with the students about software to have loaded; technology is changing quickly, but you will want AutoCAD, SketchUp, Adobe Creative Suite (Photoshop, Illustrator, InDesign, and others), and software for building information modeling (Revit, Graphisoft, and others). Of course, will probably want Microsoft Office (Word, Excel, Powerpoint) and other software that make you more efficient. In the past few years, more and more students are starting college with tablets and smartphone apps that can help you in your studies.

Academic Enrichment

Beyond the required coursework outlined in the preceding section for a particular degree in architecture, you can enrich your academic experience in many other ways, if you choose.

OFF-CAMPUS PROGRAMS (STUDY ABROAD)

Many architecture programs offer the opportunity to study abroad. Some architecture programs, including the University of Notre Dame and Syracuse University, actually require study abroad. Other programs offer foreign study as an option. Such programs may occur during the summer or be for an entire semester. Some students may also choose to study at another institution abroad for a full academic year. Regardless, you are strongly encouraged to study abroad during your academic tenure. In fact, faculty will say that you should make it mandatory for yourself. Money is typically an obstacle for some students, but most programs offer scholarships. Remember, once you graduate and enter the workforce, you may not have the same opportunity to travel.

INDEPENDENT STUDY

Most institutions have a mechanism that allows you to develop an independent study under the direction of a faculty member. (This is rarely undertaken before the upper years of a curriculum.)

The independent study allows you to focus on a chosen topic not typically offered at your school.

Throughout my architectural education, I realized I also had a strong interest in marketing and business in the context of architecture. Because Maryland did not offer a course that addressed this interest, I developed an independent study to understand marketing as a discipline and how it relates to architecture. The course consisted of researching marketing and marketing in architecture by visiting and interviewing two architecture firms of different sizes. Pursuing the independent study was one of my most rewarding experiences in college. It allowed me to work closely with a faculty member, focus on my interests relating to architecture, and start to understand potential career opportunities for my future.

JESSICA LEONARD, University of Maryland

MINORS/CERTIFICATES

If you have an interest in an academic subject other than architecture, consider completing a minor. An academic minor typically requires no fewer than 15 to 18 credits of coursework, shows structure and coherence, and contains some upper-level courses. Also, students who declare and complete an approved academic minor may receive a notation on their transcript.

At the graduate level, certificate programs exist. Parallel in concept to academic minors, certificate programs allow you to gain specific knowledge in an area outside of, but still related to, your degree program.Certificate programs include the following: historic preservation, sustainable urbanism, urban design, museum studies, and design computing.

DOUBLE MAJOR/DEGREES/JOINT DEGREES

For some, a double major/degree/joint degree may be an option. Depending on the institution, you may be able to pursue a double major or degree at the undergraduate level or a joint degree at the graduate level. Because of the time demands of an architectural curriculum, this choice may be difficult at the undergraduate level. A second major or degree would typically require you to complete the academic requirements of two-degree programs. If you are interested, consult the undergraduate catalog.

At the graduate level, many institutions have established dual-degree options with the master of architecture. For example, the School of Architecture at the University of Illinois at Urbana-Champaign offers a joint master of architecture/master of business administration (MBA), allowing you to graduate with both degrees in less time than if you were to pursue each on its own.

LECTURE SERIES/EXHIBITS/ REVIEWS

Most if not all architecture programs sponsor a lecture series during the semester. The architecture program will host series of lectures given by practitioners, faculty from other programs, or other professionals, designed to increase the discourse within the school. On occasion, invited lecturers include well-known "star" architects. You should make every effort to attend these lectures to expand your architectural experience. In addition, many programs sponsor more informal brown-bag lectures at lunchtime that feature faculty and, sometimes, students. You can also attend lectures sponsored

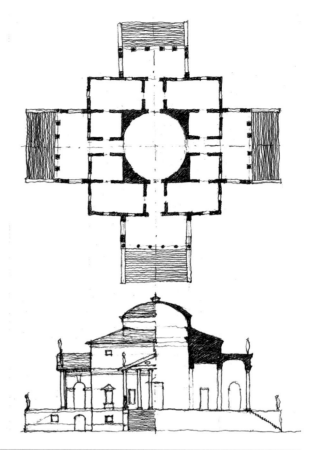

▶Villa Rotunda, Vicenza, Italy, Study-Abroad Program. Sketch by Margaret Deleeuw at University of Maryland.

▼Villa Rotunda, Vicenza, Italy. Architect: Palladio. PHOTOGRAPHER: R. LINDLEY VANN.

by nearby schools and chapters of the American Institute of Architects or other institutions. For example, students in architecture programs in the Washington, DC, region frequently attend lectures at the National Building Museum or other cultural institutions because of the close proximity.

Aside from the lecture series, some architecture programs may sponsor exhibits in a gallery within their facility; these exhibitions may be a part of a traveling exhibition from an outside sponsor or be a show of student or faculty work. These exhibits are an excellent way to observe and learn from others, either professionals or fellow students.

Finally, attend reviews at the end of the semester to see students' presentations of their work and hear feedback from the faculty or visiting guests. The semester-ending reviews are very instructional in many different ways—you can see firsthand the final presentation drawings and models done by the students, hear their oral presentations, and learn from the critiques from the visiting reviewers.

COMMUNITY SERVICE

A recent opportunity provided by many architecture programs is community service programs. Many institutions participate in Habitat for Humanity International, an organization that works to build or renovate homes for the inadequately sheltered in the United States and in 20 countries around the world, while others assist area schoolchildren through tutoring programs. These programs provide you with an opportunity to give back to the community while developing skills.

A relatively new community service program is Freedom by Design™, sponsored by the American Institute of Architecture Students (AIAS). Freedom by Design[4] utilizes the talents of architecture students to radically impact the lives of disabled individuals in their community through modest design and construction solutions. Each year, over 50 AIAS chapters throughout the country work on projects to enhance the lives of individuals.

Many architecture programs, along with their students, assisted in various ways in the city of New Orleans, Louisiana, and the surrounding region after Hurricane Katrina in 2005. Other organizations that provide opportunities for you to develop your community service as an architect or after graduation include AmeriCorps, Peace Corps, Design Corps, The Mad Housers, Inc., Architecture for Humanity, and Public Architecture. For example, Public Architecture challenges architects to pledge 1 percent of their time to pro bono service to nonprofits organizations in need of design services.

Architecture in the Schools, a program led by local chapters of the AIA, matches volunteer architects with public school teachers to enrich the learning experience of children. To test your own architectural knowledge, volunteer to bring architectural concepts to life in any subject area in grades K–12. The bottom line: become involved with community service during both your education and your professional career.

MENTORING

Throughout the history of the architecture profession, mentoring has played a role. Architects mentor and guide their apprentices on the path to becoming an architect. Some schools have both formal and informal mentoring programs to connect you with mentors. One such program is the Mentoring Program of the Architecture Program at the University of Minnesota, the self-proclaimed largest in the nation, which matches students with area architects.

Regardless of whether your school sponsors a mentoring program, seek out a mentor from whom you can gain insight and wisdom. Your mentor could be a student further along in the program, a faculty member, or a local architect. Also, consider serving as a mentor to a student earlier in the program than you. In this way, you are involved with laddering mentoring—receiving mentoring from someone further along than you and providing mentoring to someone earlier in their career than you. Mentoring does not end when you finish your formal education; in fact, it should continue throughout your career.

STUDENT ORGANIZATIONS

Become involved with your architectural education by joining one of the student organizations within your university. First, membership in any student organization is a way to develop friendships and leadership abilities, and to have fun. Second, seek involvement with one of the architectural student organizations, the largest of which is the AIAS.

AIAS (aias.org) operates at both the national and local levels. Located in Washington, DC, the national office sponsors student design competitions, an annual meeting (Forum) and Quad Conferences during the academic years, and leadership training for chapter presidents. It publishes a magazine, *Crit*, and serves as one of the collateral organizations representing architecture students to the profession. Most programs in architecture have a local chapter of the AIAS that provides varied opportunities, including social and networking ones, and connections to the profession.

The National Organization of Minority Architects (NOMA noma.net) is a national professional association of minority architects that has chapters at over 20 architecture schools. Like AIAS, student chapters of the NOMA organize to connect architecture students with each other as well as architects in the profession. In addition, the NOMA has as its mission "the building of a strong national organization, strong chapters, and strong members for the purpose of minimizing the effect of racism in our profession."

Other student organizations include Arquitectos (for Latino students); Students for Congress for New Urbanism (CNU); Alpha Rho Chi, the fraternity for architecture; and Tau Sigma Delta, the national collegiate honor society. In addition, you may also find others unique to your institution. Also, investigate the value of involvement with student government or committees of your academic unit.

Conclusion

Now that you know how to prepare for an architectural education, select an architecture program based on your criteria, and live the life of an architecture student, consider the following steps of maximizing your education as described by Brian Kelly, AIA, director of the architecture program and associate professor at the University of Maryland:

1. Take charge of your time; you are responsible for your educational experience.

2. Work in the studio.

3. Get to know your peers and faculty.

4. Study abroad; step outside the box.

5. Take time for yourself; your health is paramount.

An Addiction to Rome

BRIAN KELLY, AIA

Associate Professor/Director–Architecture Program

University of Maryland

College Park, Maryland

Why did you become an architect?

❯ I have always been fond of drawing. When I was a child, my mother did not want me to watch too much television, so she made a deal that I could watch TV if I did something else, too. Drawing was natural! So I would watch, say, a science fiction movie, and while it was under way I would be drawing plans and sections of the spacecraft in the film. Instead of my being a passive observer to the programming, I became an interactive player and would even speculate about what might beyond the control room of the spacecraft. Or I would discover spatial errors in how the movie portrayed the organization of compartments in the craft's design. In school, I enjoyed history, science, to a lesser

extent mathematics, and of course art classes. I do not really know how I came to understand that architecture would satisfy my career desires, but I do remember informing my parents that I would become an architect somewhere around sixth grade. I am not sure what they thought about it, but they did encourage me to follow my dream.

Why did you decide to choose the schools you did—University of Notre Dame and Cornell University? What degree(s) do you possess?

❯ I selected the University of Notre Dame because it had a mandatory junior year abroad in Rome, Italy. As a high school senior, I was not really quite sure what Rome was all about, but I knew it would have important lessons for a young architect. Now as a somewhat older architect who continues to regularly return to Rome, I can certainly say that my gut reading on the importance of Rome was right. After Notre Dame, I practiced in Chicago for several years before returning to graduate school at Cornell University. I selected Cornell because

Castel Sant'angelo, Rome, Italy. Watercolor: Brian Kelly, AIA.

I was interested in the writings of Colin Rowe, who at that time taught the urban design studio there. Since my undergraduate degree was a bachelor of architecture, the post-professional degree at Cornell allowed me to specialize in how large groups of buildings come together to make cities or large institutions within the landscape.

What are your primary responsibilities and duties as a faculty member/director of a program in architecture?

❯ I oversee our pre-professional, accredited professional, and post-professional degree programs. I work primarily with faculty members to develop our vision, mission, and goals; lead the design and implementation of our curriculum; hire part-time faculty colleagues; oversee the admissions, scholarship, and graduate assistant programs; develop recruitment and retention strategies; work closely with our advising staff; and serve as a liaison to alumni, the profession, and other schools of architecture. Most of what I do as the director requires me to use my architectural education to be an effective leader, collaborator, and communicator.

In 2010, you launched Lines of Inquiry, a traveling exhibit of your freehand drawings; why is freehand drawing important in architecture given this age of digital representation?

❯ I cannot imagine architecture without freehand drawing. Drawing is at the foundation of seeing. If you do not draw something, chances are you did not see it. Le Corbusier's observations on drawing are thought provoking, "The camera is for idlers ... To draw oneself, to trace the lines, handle the volumes, organize the surface, ...and all this means first to look, and then to observe and finally perhaps to discover ...and then the inspiration may come." With all but the most astute photographers, the camera turns us into passive observers. Drawing brings you into active encounters with architecture, urbanism, and landscape, while snapping a picture for most of us places us in the role of being a passive observer. "Drawing is *retarditaire*," you might say, "in an age of digital media!"

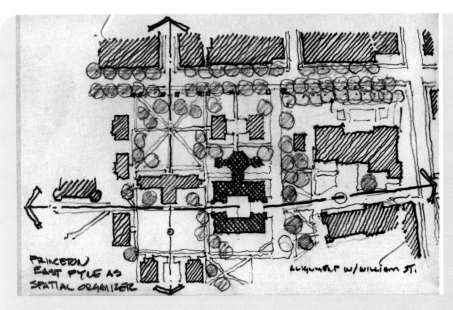

PRINCETON
EAST PYLE AS
SPATIAL ORGANIZER

ALIGNMENT W/ WILLIAM ST.

Sketch Plan of
Princeton University
Campus, Princeton,
New Jersey. Drawing:
Brian Kelly, AIA.

Roman Forum,
Rome, Italy. Drawing:
Brian Kelly, AIA.

One need only to look at the shift from the graphical user interface (GUI) supported by traditional computers (keyboard, mouse, etc.) to the human user interface (HUI) supported on tablets, smartphones, and other devices to understand the transformation in digital technology that is underway. Drawing is fundamental—from the cave drawings of Lascaux made over 17,000 years ago to the magical possibilities you can discover on your iPad, this form of communication is here to stay. So, okay, you can stick to your GUI, but beware that others will have a tremendous advantage as we move beyond computers being controlled exclusively by descendants of typewriters and electronic rodents. Oh, and what is more, in GUI, you do not draw, you model at best. It uses another portion of the brain. Drawing exercises the right brain, the qualitative and creative center of our minds. GUI is better suited to left brain numerical and quantitate thought. So drawing enabled by HUI will enable us to better access our creative selves.

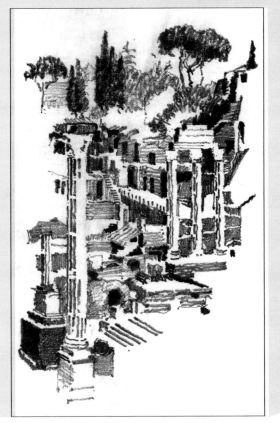

During your professional career, you have done work in urban design and campus planning. What is urban design, and why is it important for an architect?

❯ I operate under the conviction that the highest and noblest task that an architect can do is to make the world a better place through design. If my designs succeed at the expense of their contexts, that is, if my building is interesting but it does not contribute well to the setting, then I have failed.

Urban design teaches us to think about the relationship between an individual act of building and the community of ideas embedded in a particular context albeit an open landscape or a city. Buildings and their contexts go hand-in-hand. I have found that my study of urban design led me to rethink how buildings should behave in context of other buildings, landscapes, and cities. This idea also has a dimension of sustainability embedded within it, in that many settlement patterns (particularly our American penchant for suburban sprawl) contribute negatively to the creation of a sustainable future for us all.

Urban design and campus planning (a subset of urban design) ask questions about how groups of buildings work together in service of a greater whole. More compact, walkable, and ecologically responsive cities consume less land, encourage us to leave the car at home, and mitigate the negative effects of human settlement on ecosystems. Obviously, questions of sustainable design have a profound impact on the manner in which we might design cities and campuses.

How does your work as a faculty member inform your architecture and vice versa?

❯ Since my practice nowadays is limited exclusively to campus planning, I have found that I can easily move back and forth between the world of univer-

sity leadership and my colleagues in architectural practice. I am an academic insider in that I really do know what faculty members do, what role a provost plays, and how trustees influence (for better or worse) the development of architectural ideas.

A dear friend of mine, an architect and principal of a respected firm that works in academic contexts, once asked me, "What do you do in the time that you are not actually teaching?" At first, I was astonished. Here was a successful architect in a practice with lots of university clients, who despite years of engagement in this arena really didn't know the daily routine of a faculty member. Then I thought about it some more and realized that if you have not been a faculty member, you can only know just so much about how what we do. I am sure that I could ask a similarly naïve question about what architecture firm principals really do when they are not designing. On second thought, I think I can give a pretty good answer to that question.

But here is what I like about college campuses and designing for them. Universities are brokers of meaning. The campus, like the institution, should be a meaningful place. I like campus planning because you can talk about how the institutional history and ethos of an institution is reflected in its strategic plan, its business plan, its curricular models, and indeed in its physical plan. College campuses are like books—you can read the institutional values simply by walking around them. Each campus tells an exciting story, and for me it is thrilling to have an opportunity to help write another chapter.

What has been your greatest challenge as an architect/faculty member?

❯ I try to split my time between being a faculty member, an architect, and an administrator. Time is the single most valuable thing we have at our disposal. This is a very hard concept for young folks to grasp, but in reality time is the most important asset that we have. We need to use it wisely. Managing my time, knowing when I have to get things done to satisfy my duties as a teacher, designer, and director, is a tremendous challenge.

Who or what experience has been a major influence on your career?

❯Three colleagues/teachers were greatly influential on my development. On the third day of classes at Notre Dame, in my freshman year, Steven Hurtt lectured to us. He talked about how architecture was a medium for communicating intellectual ideas. I was hooked. He was my first role model. Steven later became my dean at the University of Maryland, and we continue to be good friends.

In graduate school, I studied with Colin Rowe. Colin was a formidable figure in architectural and urban history, theory, and criticism. His teaching methodology could be characterized as unconventional at best. He preferred long sessions around his dining room table to actual time in studio or in class. The methodology was one that descended from the Oxford Dons of the nineteenth and early twentieth century—tutorial.

The final influence was Tom Schumacher, whom I taught with at Maryland until his untimely death in 2009. Tom, like Colin Rowe, had the gift of total recall. I used to say that you could sneak up behind Tom in Rome, put a sack over his head, put him into the trunk of an Alpha Romeo, drive several times around the city, pull him out of the trunk, remove the hood, and without missing a beat, he would start talking. "Well that façade is attributed to Giulio Romano, but the top floors on the right were added later by someone else. Did you know that Biscotti's famous film Il Notte del Giorno was filmed right here? That man's suit is a mock Armani; I think he just buys the labels and has them sewn into cheaper cuts. Oh you can get the second-best pizza in Rome in that restaurant there...." And he would go on and on.

The thing that all three had in common was a love of Rome. Steve introduced me to it as my first teacher, Colin taught me how to spar with it to extract meaning, and for several summers I taught there with Tom. Not bad, huh?

Designing for Business

JORDAN BUCKNER

Master of Architecture/Master of Business Administration Graduate

University of Illinois at Urbana-Champaign

Champaign, Illinois

Why did you become an architect?

❯I have an innate curiosity with the world around me. This led toward a profession through which I can manipulate the environment I inhabit. Through architecture I can study human psychology and create environments that support and enhance the lives of those around me.

Lemp Brewery Urban Design. Studio Project: Jordan Buckner.

Why did you decide to choose the schools that you did—the University of Michigan and University of Illinois at Urbana-Champaign? What degree(s) do you possess and are you pursuing?

❯I chose my educational path to maximize my exposure to both design and business. I received my bachelor of science in architecture at the University of Michigan with a focus on design. I recently graduated with a dual master of business administration and master of architecture from the University of Illinois Urbana-Champaign. The program at Illinois encourages students to pursue multiple degrees and makes it easy to take classes from different colleges.

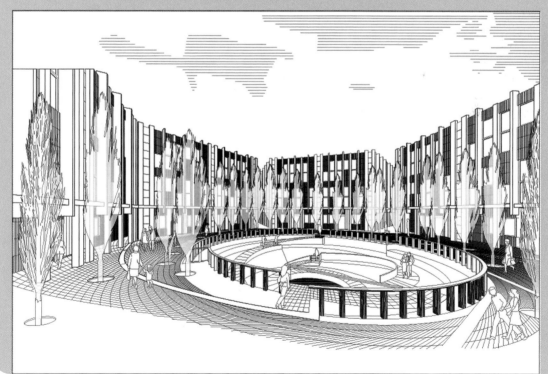

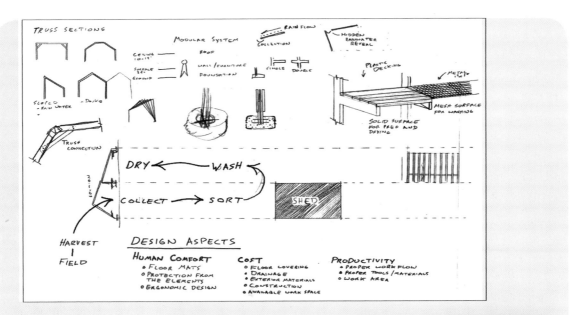

▲ Student Sustainable Farm Design Build, Champaign, Illinois.

▶ Student Sustainable Farm Design Build, Champaign, Illinois. PHOTOGRAPHER: JORDAN BUCKNER.

Why are you pursuing two graduate degrees—master of architecture and master of business administration—during your graduate studies?

〉 I believe that the design and business worlds have much to learn from each other regarding how to approach and solve problems. I am interested in understanding this relationship to find mutual benefits for each.

As part of your graduate studies, you had the unique opportunity to participate in a design-build studio. Please provide the details and explain what you learned through the experience.

〉 The design-build experience allowed me to incorporate my architecture and business experience in creating a project that was functional and creative. The project was to design a multi-functional structure for a Sustainable Student Farm on campus. Our team was responsible for the research, design, construction, and project management over the course of six months. Because of my experience in business, I led the financial and management aspects while coordinating between the design team and client. Through this experience I gained valuable insights on project coordination among designers, managers, and clients.

You have also served as a teaching assistant for an introductory architecture course. Again, what have you learned from this experience?

❭ Serving as a teaching assistant was a rewarding and challenging experience. I was able to give back by teaching young, aspiring architecture students. In addition, I was challenged at managing a class of 200 students by preparing and presenting lectures, creating exam questions, and designing assignments and projects.

How much of your studio work is done by hand versus digital technology?

❭ Architecture necessitates a variety of tools including both hand and digital technology. Each is beneficial for completing different tasks, and best used in conjunction. Hand drawings allow for a quick expression of ideas in the beginning phases of design. Digital technology is great at creating precision drawings and representing space three-dimensionally. Any successful designer must learn how to use each of these tools equally.

What has been your greatest challenge as an architecture student?

❭ My greatest challenge is wanting to do so much with my design projects but not having enough time to fully realize ideas. I am always amazed at the research and conclusions I find from architecture, and realize that the creative process never ends.

What is the most/least satisfying part of being an architecture student?

❭ The most satisfying part of being an architecture student is being able to turn my own ideas and creations into projects. Working on self-driven projects is the most fulfilling aspect of architecture. The least satisfying part of being an architecture student has to be the long hours that are sometimes required to finish projects. Fortunately, I love working on my design projects and am willing to spend however much time is required to finish them.

What do you hope to be doing 5 to 10 years after graduation with regard to your career?

❭ My exploration of design and business has led me to the field of innovation consulting, which involves the use of design thinking in problems solving. I plan to help businesses redesign their product and service offerings starting with a humanistic design approach that incorporates creative business practices.

Who or what experience has been a major influence on your career?

❭ The major influence on my career has been my father and mother, both entrepreneurs who have taught me that pursing my passion would breed excellence, and excellence would result in fortune.

The Student Voice

DANIELLE MITCHELL

Bachelor of Architecture Candidate

Pennsylvania State University

University Park, Pennsylvania

Why did you become an architect?

❯My passion for drawing, building, and creating began at a very young age. I wanted to go into a profession where I could continue to do what I loved while making a positive impact on society. I chose to become an architect in order to turn my visions into a reality. As an architect, I hope to use the creativity I have always expressed and turn it into something tangible and valuable. I chose the path to become an architect in hope that my designs will someday influence a person's experience of the built space.

Why did you decide to choose Pennsylvania State University (PSU)? What degree do you possess?

❯I chose the bachelor of architecture degree at Penn State for a number of reasons. Once I realized that I wanted become an architect, I knew that I wanted to attend an accredited, five-year bachelor of architecture program allowing me to sit for my

architectural license upon graduation. I also lived in the Philadelphia suburbs, therefore Penn State was close to home, making my parents happy and comfortable with my decision as well.

Penn State gave me the best of both worlds with a small, personalized architecture school experience inside a 40,000-student, football-crazed, and school-spirited university. It excited me to be a part of the energized atmosphere at Penn State while exposing myself to the diverse school of many disciplines and interests. I wanted to have a multitude of opportunities presented to me during my collegiate experience, and Penn State offered just that.

Although Penn State was always a strong contender, I truly made my decision when I attended the Architecture Summer Camp at Penn State. It was one week of living life like an architecture student (or so I thought) as we worked in the beautiful new studio building, went on construction site tours of buildings on campus, used the digital fabrication technologies, and jumped right into the design process. I absolutely loved my experience at the camp, and after that week in the summer before my senior year of high school, I determined that architecture at Penn State was the right fit for me.

Arcosanti, Mayer, Arizona. Architect: Paolo Soleri.

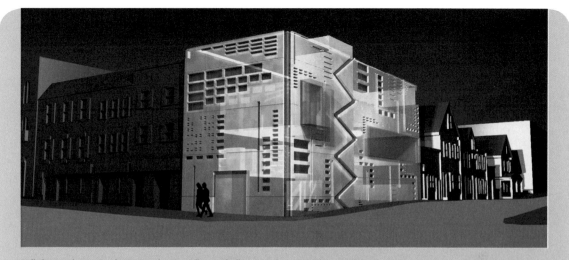

Bellefonte Library. Studio Project by Danielle Mitchell, Pennsylvania State University.

Why did you choose to study the bachelor of architecture degree?

❯I chose to study architecture because my love of art and design. In deciding my career path, I wanted to continue to do what I loved while having a practical application and purpose to my profession. My objective was to apply my talents and interests in art to a pragmatic use. In high school, my geometry teacher and art teacher both suggested architecture to me as I began to think about college and career options. As I started to look into it, I really enjoyed the hands-on and interactive aspects of architecture and realized it was a field in which I could continue to use my creativity and self-expression.

You served as AIAS NE quad director and AIAS chapter president for two years at PSU. How is this experience helpful in preparing for your career?

❯As I stepped into these leadership positions, I was faced head-on with a true challenge. The experience motivated me to grow and mature as an individual and professional, as I needed to quickly learn how to be a leader to my peers, a representative student voice in my school and community, and how to manage and operate a real organization.

Serving in these positions helped me to define my interests and passions. I realized how much I enjoy collaboration, community service and engagement, and mentoring. Serving as a leader with AIAS took me out of my sheltered studio environment and allowed me to see the bigger picture of architecture and education through the varied perspectives of students from across the nation. By the exchange of experiences, ideas, and opinions I saw the importance of advocacy and relevance within our profession.

One of the most crucial skills I acquired through these positions was confidence. As a professional, you must have the confidence to strongly conduct yourself in a business setting. You must have the confidence to talk freely among your peers and clients, engaging in professional, casual, and entertaining conversation. You must also be confident in your abilities as a designer and leader in order for others to believe in and rely on you.

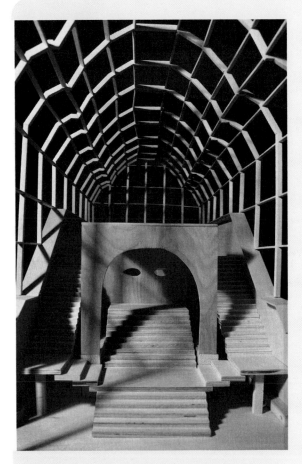

Room for a Machine. Studio Project by Danielle Mitchell, Pennsylvania State University.

Based on your experiences, what is leadership, and why is it important as an architect?

〉 Leadership is taking ownership of your ideas and goals and moving them forward. When ambitions are shared among a group of people, it is critical to be a leader in the facilitation of the goals and in securing their accomplishment. Leadership is making intelligent decisions for the benefit of a whole, giving others confidence in you and your visions. This allows others to support and follow your direction.

As architects, we interact in a collaborative work environment where it is essential to be a leader among the group in order to create order, gain the support of your team, and follow through with the design process. In my experience, I have seen great work accomplished by a large whole through the leadership of a select few. These leaders motivated their peers and stimulated engagement and excitement to work toward a cause they believed in. It is imperative to have leaders that will enlist the support needed to carry out a project, new idea, or full-scale building.

What aspect of architecture are you most interested in?

〉 I am most interested in how architecture affects the community. I am interested in architects as social and cultural innovators. I believe that architects have great potential to define community needs and helps to achieve goals through the built environment. Architecture has the ability to influence the way a society functions and develops, making it a very powerful tool in determining our future.

What has been your greatest challenge as an architecture student?

〉 As most architecture students will attest, the greatest challenge is finding a balance among your many demands. As an architecture student, your core studio classes require an incredible amount of energy, time, and dedication and can easily become all-consuming. The demands of your architecture studio class can strain you in your other classes, social life, and sleep schedule. It is very difficult to find a balance among the many things you are interested in and want to accomplish in your college career. The balance is different for every architecture student and may take some time to find. You must determine what your priorities are and set both goals and limits for yourself in order to find this balance.

For me, I had the most difficulty balancing my time and energy between my architecture studio classes and my role as AIAS chapter president and Northeast quadrant director. Both studio and AIAS were very important to me and I wanted to excel in both areas. I quickly realized that I had to make strong decisions and sacrifices to hold a balance between the two while juggling other interests and activities. Although this proved to be very difficult for me, I believe the strain was well worth it in the end.

What is the most/least satisfying part of being an architecture student?

〉 The most satisfying part of being an architecture student is seeing the progress you have made as a designer in a short period of time. Looking back on the work that you have accomplished is incredibly satisfying and rewarding and makes the stress and long hours you've endured well worthwhile . In reviewing your architectural design work, it is very satisfying to see the transition and improvement you have made in each project that you complete. As an architecture student, there is a high expectation set; when you are able to achieve and surpass those expectations, your work and effort is well worth it in the end. The education you receive is visually evident in your work and you are able to see tangible results of your dedication and energy.

The least satisfying part is taking criticism on work in which you have poured your heart and soul. All architectural designs can be improved, and all critiques of your work will find an aspect of your work that could have been better executed. At times, it can be disappointing to hear this criticism, but this constructive analysis is meant to help you improve as a designer and ultimately benefit you and your education.

What do you hope to be doing 5 to 10 years after graduation with regard to your career?

〉 I greatly value of the voice of the architect. In 5 to 10 years after graduation, I would like to hold on to this value. After serving on the AIAS board of directors, I would like to become involved in the actions and activities of the other architecture collateral organizations. I hope to one day serve on a NAAB Accreditation Team, involve myself in the National Associate Committee as an associate member of the AIA, and once I become a licensed architect, I would like to engage in the Young Architects Forum of the AIA.

My first priority upon graduation is to obtain my architectural license. I wish to work at a firm that will help me to pursue my goals and provide me experience necessary for the Intern Development Program. Once I have learned through experience and developed my skills, I would love to start my own firm to carry out personally desired projects. Through architecture, I would like to make a difference and an impact for my clients and community.

Who or what experience has been a major influence on your career?

〉 The largest influence on my education and career has been my experience with the AIAS. The best thing I did upon entering college was joining AIAS and actively engaging in the organization from the start. As a freshman, being a part of the AIAS gave me an upperclassman mentor, fun architectural activities to be a part of, new friends throughout the major, and networking opportunities with our local AIA. Through this experience, I learned about the profession from a different perspective than my professors or studio classes could offer me.

Jumping into a leadership position influenced me even more. Being chapter president during my sophomore and junior year at Penn State was incredibly rewarding. I witnessed changes made in our school from student advocating and saw the morale and excitement within the student body grow as more and more people wanted to get involved with student activities, community engagement, and professional networking. This inspired and motivated me to work for what I believe in.

Matthew Barstow, the 2012–2013 AIAS national president, significantly influenced my career as well. Matt sought me out and encouraged me to serve as the AIAS Northeast quadrant director. He was a great mentor and helped me to grow into the leadership position. Without his encouragement and support, I would not have been exposed to the many opportunities I was offered as a quadrant director. The amazing experience I have had with the AIAS is truly irreplaceable.

Becoming a Positive Influence

JENNIFER PENNER

Master of Architecture Graduate

University of New Mexico

Regional Associate Director

AIA Western Mountain Regional Director

Albuquerque, New Mexico

Why and how did you become an architect?

❯When I was in first grade playing with Legos with my brother, we were having so much fun I told him that I wished I could build when I grew up. He told me that it was an architect. From that moment on I was driven to become an architect. All through elementary school to high school my mom would tell me that architecture was a competitive field and I needed to earn good grades because my employer would look all the way back to my kindergarten report card. I laugh about it now, but I understand what she was trying to do. I am very thankful to have had this advantage growing up.

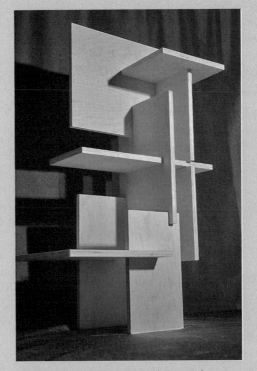

Flat Pack: Plant Stand for a Bromeliad. Jennifer Penner at the University of New Mexico.

Why and how did you decide on the University of New Mexico to attend for your architecture degree? What degree(s) do you possess?

❯I received both my bachelor of arts in architecture (undergraduate) and master of architecture (graduate) from the University of New Mexico (UNM). When deciding where to attend college, my decision was an easy choice. I lived in a suburb of Albuquerque, New Mexico, the home of the University of New Mexico, the only architecture program in the state. Also, my decision was easy because I was awarded the Legislative Lottery Scholarship, a state-sponsored scholarship program funded by proceeds from the New Mexico Lottery.

You worked in the profession between your undergraduate and graduate degrees; how did that change your experience in the graduate program?

❯Before returning to UNM for my graduate degree, I took a three-year break from school to gain valuable experience in an architecture firm. While working, I completed most of the IDP, which helped me when I reentered the academic world. Because I was able to draw on what I had learned in the office in regards to clients, city planning officials, project drawings, and coordination, my studio projects had a much more grounded approach. Conversely, this also weighed on my creativity as I fought to imagine designs without budgets and near-limitless possibilities.

What has been your greatest challenge as an architectural intern/student?

❯As an intern, my greatest challenge has been in understanding my role on an architectural project. I have the energy that wants to take on an entire project and run the show, but my lack of experience prevents it. I can only gain experience from completing the everyday tasks of a project and logging time in the categories in the IDP. In other words, my greatest challenge has been the capacity for patience. My greatest challenge as a student, though, has been time management. The projects given to students are very demanding but completely achievable with self-discipline and rigor.

What are your 5-year and 10-year career goals relative to architecture?

❯My 5-year goal includes passing the ARE and working on meaningful projects. I want my work to impact communities for the greater good. My 10-year goals are to lead project teams on environmentally responsible designs, teach at the high school or college level, and always remain in a position that aids in the development of architectural interns.

Presently, you serve as auxiliary IDP coordinator and the regional associate director for the AIA Western Mountain Region. How did you become involved with these experiences, and how do they contribute to your career as an architect?

❯I have had the good fortune of a spectacular mentor, Tina M. Reames of Cherry/See/Reames Architects, PC. She has been an active and positive influence in my life; by her example, I have developed a side of me that could have gone uncultivated. She serves as the state IDP coordinator for New Mexico and therefore is always seeking avenues of getting intern information out to the architecture community. Because of her, I learned of the annual IDP Coordinators Conference being held in Chicago in 2007 that I attended on behalf of my firm at the time. At the conference, I became an auxiliary coordinator, and after displaying my passion for helping fellow interns, I was invited to sit on the board of AIA New Mexico as the associate director.

▶The Uptown Cityscaper: Sustainable Horizontal Skyscaper. Studio Design by Jennifer Penner at the University of New Mexico.

▼ Celebration of Water: a Pocket Park with Water Feature, Therapeutic Bathhouse, Laundry, and Teahouse. Studio Design Site Plan by Jennifer Penner at the University of New Mexico.

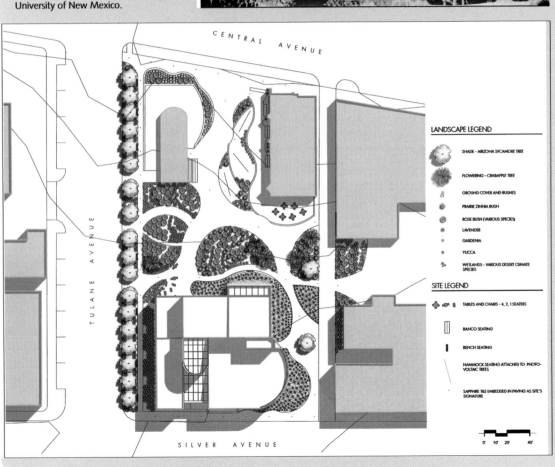

LANDSCAPE LEGEND

SHADE - ARIZONA SYCAMORE TREE

FLOWERING - CRABAPPLE TREE

GROUND COVER AND BUSHES

PRAIRIE ZINNIA BUSH

ROSE BUSH (VARIOUS SPECIES)

LAVENDER

GARDENIA

YUCCA

WETLANDS - VARIOUS DESERT CLIMATE SPECIES

SITE LEGEND

TABLES AND CHAIRS - 4, 2, 1 SEATERS

BANCO SEATING

BENCH SEATING

HAMMOCK SEATING ATTACHED TO PHOTO-VOLTAIC TREES

SAPPHIRE TILE EMBEDDED IN PAVING AS SITE'S SIGNATURE

CENTRAL AVENUE

TULANE AVENUE

SILVER AVENUE

0'   10'   20'   40'

From there I moved up to my current position as the regional associate director for the AIA Western Mountain Region. I have taken these positions as opportunities to meet architects and professionals from around the country with a range of backgrounds in order to gain valuable insight on their experiences and opinions on architecture. Through my service to my fellow intern architects I have been able to get a better understanding of what it's like in different parts of the country, and it is most encouraging to find that we are all going through much of the same thing.

What is the most/least satisfying part of your career as an architect?

❯ The most satisfying aspect is being a part of such an exciting and relevant profession. Take, for example, the history of architecture; it goes back to the beginning of time as man sought shelter, and it developed over thousands of years to what we see today. The buildings we live and learn in are all the physical representation of creativity realized, and they affect us ecologically. As the world becomes more environmentally conscious and demands performance from the built surroundings, it is the architect who has the skills and expertise to lead this revolution. I am honored to be a part of it all.

The least satisfying part of my architectural journey thus far has been balancing technology with learning how to put a building together. It is so easy to get caught up in the intricacies of a software program and become an expert in 3D modeling or parametrics and lose the grasp of learning how to build a real building. It is necessary to question every decision that is made in the design of a building and press the architect to teach you what they know. This is what internship really is.

Who or what experience has been a major influence on your career?

❯ During my senior year at UNM, I was invited by the construction administration department at UNM to attend the Western Mountain Region ASC-AGC Design/Build Competition. In this competition a team is presented with a project at 6:00 a.m. The entire construction project and architectural design drawings are due by midnight of the same day. I was the "architect" in charge of the design and construction documents.

This competition was a major influence on my career because I gained so much respect for my team members. Prior to the competition, I never knew the tasks a contractor has to perform for a project. During the competition, I was able to display the vital role an architect plays in the design process and gain the respect of each of my team members. Our team took second place, and up until that year UNM had never placed in the Design/Build Competition.

NOTES

1. Harold Linton, "Portfolio Design." Retrieved August 21, 2013, from portfoliodesign.com.
2. NAAB, retrieved August 31, 2013, from www.naab.org.
3. NAAB, *NAAB Conditions for Accreditation for Professional Degree Programs in Architecture* (Washington, DC: National Architectural Accrediting Board, 2014).
4. AIAS, retrieved August 31, 2013, from www.aias.org.

❸ The Experience of an Architect

"I hear and I forget. I see and I remember. I do and I understand."

CONFUCIUS (551 BC–479 BC)

EXPERIENCE IS THE SECOND REQUIREMENT for becoming an architect. In most states, candidates satisfy the formal requirement for experience by participating in and completing the Intern Development Program (IDP), a program of the profession. However, early exposure to the profession through the experiential programs often offered through your institution is important. These programs may consist of shadowing an architect before you begin your formal education, a credit-bearing internship while in school, a career-related summer position in an architecture firm, or your first full-time position in an architecture firm. In all cases, you should seek opportunities for experience.

The authors of *Building Community: A New Future for Architecture Education and Practice*[1] recommend that schools, practitioners, and local and national architecture organizations collaborate to increase the availability, information about, and incentives for students to gain work experience during school. Because the five collateral organizations commissioned this report, there is substantial consensus within the profession that gaining experience while an architecture student is valuable.

But the question is how? How do you, as a student of architecture, obtain a position when you have no experience? This is a classic Catch-22; you need experience to gain a position and a position to gain experience.

◀ Armada Housing, s'Hertogenbosch, Netherlands. Architect: Building Design Partnership (BDP). PHOTOGRAPHER: GRACE H. KIM, AIA.

What is experience? The dictionary defines experience as follows:

> n. 1: the accumulation of knowledge or skill that results from direct participation in events or activities; 2: the content of direct observation or participation in an event[2]

Thus, to become an architect, it is important for you to participate directly in the profession—to observe or participate in architecture, an architectural firm, or your education. As you begin your studies, check with your school to determine if it has programs to assist you in gaining experience. Even if it does not, you still gain experience as you work in the design studio and other courses.

Gaining Experience as a Student

SHADOW

One effective way to learn about the profession is to shadow an architect through a typical day of activities. Obviously, this is a short-lived experience, but it should be easy to accomplish. Many architects are more than willing to help the next generation in this way. Also, some high schools have a career program involving shadowing to expose their students to career fields. Any opportunity to interact with an architect, however briefly, can help you understand the profession. For referrals to architects in your area, contact the local chapter of the American Institute of Architects (AIA).

VOLUNTEER

Volunteering is a common way to gain experience. After shadowing an architect, you could request an opportunity to volunteer in the firm for a short period. A number of nonprofit organizations have formal programs that can help you find a firm at which to volunteer.

RESEARCH WITH FACULTY

Another opportunity for college students is a research experience with a faculty member. Approach a faculty member with teaching or research interests parallel to yours. Specifically, ask if you may assist in some manner with his or her research or writing efforts. This kind of experience may lead to further opportunities, both during college and after. Research with a faculty may continue as an independent study or actually being hired by the faculty. Also, the faculty member may be willing to write a letter of recommendation.

EXTERNSHIP

Sometimes considered a mini-internship, an externship provides students the opportunity to explore a specific career path, gain marketable experience, and make professional connections by working with professional alumni for an abbreviated period, usually a week during the winter or spring breaks. In many cases, schools match students with alumni, but they may also make connections with other area professionals.

Getty Center, Los Angeles. Architect: Richard Meier. PHOTOGRAPHER: R. LINDLEY VANN.

The School of Architecture at the University of Virginia sponsors one of the largest externship programs in the country. Held during the winter break, the program provides students an opportunity to shadow an architect—typically an alumnus—in their workplace for a week. More than 125 students have this professional experience each year. The University of Michigan does a parallel program, Spring Break Internships, but it is held during the spring break. Through an unpaid weeklong internship, architecture students have an opportunity to learn more about the practice of architecture within firms throughout the United States.

INTERNSHIP

The formal training required for licensure as an architect is typically referred to as an internship, but some institutions sponsor an internship program for students. The purpose of an internship is to provide the student with work experience for an extended period, usually a semester. In some cases, the internship earns academic credit. The position may be unpaid because it involves a large learning component; to the extent possible, avoid unpaid internships; however, you will need to make the decision on the experience gained versus the wages not earned.

At Massachusetts Institute of Technology (MIT), the internship program helps students gain experience, improve practical skills, and be involved with real projects and practice during their Independent Activities Period, typically three weeks in January. Interns work full time for three-and-a-half weeks in small, medium, and large firms or in public or nonprofit agencies, and they receive six units of academic credit. In preparation for the program, students are expected to attend three meetings during the semester before the experience.

At the University of Texas at Austin, the Professional Residency Program allows students at the advanced levels of architectural design to serve an internship under the supervision of a registered architect in a selected architectural firm. The seven-month internship spans a semester and the preceding or following summer. Students can earn academic credit for the experience by extensive documentation of their work and may receive a modest stipend while in residency. Each year, the program involves no more than 30 students, both undergraduate and graduate students, in two sessions, January–July and June–December. Students are placed in firms in Texas, throughout the United States, and other countries.

COOPERATIVE EDUCATION

Cooperative education combines classroom learning with productive work experience in a field related to a student's academic or career goals, achieved through a partnership of students, educational institutions, and employers. While details differ from school to school, some have established programs based on the idea of cooperative education.

The Boston Architectural College (BAC) has one of the most distinctive approaches to educating future architects in the entire country.

> The professional degree programs feature the model of concurrent learning: working in approved, paid, supervised positions in design firms during the day—the "practice" component of the curriculum— while studying several evenings a week at the BAC—the "academic" component of the curriculum. Although each component has a sequence of its own, the two are designed to be concurrent, allowing progress in one to facilitate learning in the other.
>
> BAC CATALOG[3]

Required for all students in the School of Architecture and Interior Design at the University of Cincinnati, the Professional Practice Program gives students selected practical experience purposefully mingled with a gradually expanding academic background. The program consists of three-and-a-half months of carefully planned professional practice assignments alternating with three-month study periods. For students in architecture, the year-round schedule allows for five semesters of experience while obtaining a six-year bachelor of architecture degree. Through the Professional Practice Program, students obtain firsthand knowledge of professional practices, expectancies, and opportunities. At the same time, they benefit from a realistic test of their career interests and aptitudes. Finally, as graduates, their experience makes them valuable to employers and increases their qualifications for responsible career opportunities.

Established in 1994, the cooperative education program for students in the School of Architecture at the University of Arkansas is designed to allow students to work for a full academic year (9 to 15 months) in an architecture firm after the third year. Initiated by the faculty, the program presently has students working throughout the state and the country.

PRECEPTORSHIP

Somewhat parallel to cooperative education, a preceptorship is another program implemented by architecture programs to provide students with experience. As part of their bachelor of architecture, the School of Architecture at Rice University provides a yearlong practicum between the fourth and fifth years of the program. During the spring of their fourth year, students apply to serve their preceptorship in a number of firms throughout the United States. Another architecture program, Judson University, also provides a professional experience (preceptorship) to its students as part of their master of architecture.

CAREER-RELATED EXPERIENCE

Perhaps the most popular way to gain experience while in school is simply to obtain a position in a firm either part-time while in school or full-time during the summer. While not a formal program like an internship or cooperative education, a career-related experience can be just as valuable, although perhaps more difficult to obtain.

Learn how either your academic unit or the career center of the institution publicizes positions for students. Most will post positions with area firms, sponsor annual career fairs to connect students with firms, or host firms who interview on campus. But do not simply wait for firms to advertise positions; instead, be proactive and contact firms in which you are interested with your credentials.

Gaining experience while in school makes you more marketable to prospective employers upon graduation. In addition, the experience may count toward IDP if it meets certain requirements. For graduates of the BAC, completing the degree usually coincides with taking the Architect Registration Exam (ARE) because students work full time while attending school. Note that in a recent survey of interns and young architects, almost half indicated that they had gained practical experience while in school.

Gaining Experience as an Emerging Professional

FULL-TIME POSITIONS

Upon graduation with your architecture degree, the true challenge begins—gaining experience as an emerging professional or, more accurately, securing a full-time position with an architecture firm. Searching for a full-time position on your path to becoming an architect is important but not always easy. Of course, if you have had the opportunity to gain experience while in school, your prospects for a full-time position may be improved.

First, the firm for which you worked while a student may be in a position to continue your employment full time; next, if not, they may be able to refer you to other firms that are hiring. Finally, new firms you approach for a possible position will likely be more willing to hire you because you have experience; thus, it is valuable to gain experience prior to graduation.

Regardless of whether you gain experience in school, you will need to work in certain settings as outlined by IDP (discussed later in this chapter) to gain experience as you begin your career in architecture. Ideally, you will need to work under the supervision of an architect, however, IDP allows a few exceptions. Also, be cognizant for whom you work, as the firm will impact your career trajectory.

More on your career/job searching later, but take care in your search for an employer. Not only are they supportive of IDP, but will you develop as a professional there.

VOLUNTEER

Aside from a full-time position, another means to gain experience is to volunteer. By contributing your talents in support of an organized activity or a specific organization, you can gain experience in leadership and services, one of the experience settings of IDP.[4] For purposes of IDP, your volunteer time does not need to relate to architecture, but it can. Contributing your time could speed the time in which you complete the IDP, but if you are not yet employed, you can still develop your skills as an architect.

DESIGN COMPETITIONS

Design competitions are another vehicle to develop your skills and gain experience. Again, IDP allows you to earn experience when entering a design competition under the supervision of your mentor and meeting certain requirements. Regardless of the IDP credit, entering a design competition allows you to "design" when you may not have the same opportunity in a firm soon out of school.

MENTORING

Mentoring was a part of the architectural profession long before licensure and IDP; years ago, an aspiring architect (apprentice) would work for a master architect until the architect felt the apprentice was ready to be on his/her own. For different reasons, many emerging professionals do not have a mentor, but you are encouraged to secure a mentor—someone outside the firm for which you work to provide professional support and guidance as you progress through your career.

PROFESSIONAL ASSOCIATIONS

Did you join student clubs when you were in high school or college? If so, you already know the value of membership in an organization; if not, consider joining now as you embark on your career. By design, professional associations help with your career; regardless of the particular association, each host programming (professional and social) along with conferences and other professional development to advance your career.

Perhaps the most known professional association in architecture is the American Institute of Architects (AIA). With the AIA, you may become involved directly after school as an "Associate" member; they even provide free membership upon your graduation. In addition, the AIA supports emerging professionals through a number of initiatives.

Aside from the AIA, there are many other associations (see Appendix A), but others more directly connected with architecture include the National Organization of Minority Architects (NOMA), Society of American Registered Architects (SARA), and Arquitectos. While most associations are national in scope, some are either regional or local; for example, a very active local group is CWA, Chicago Women in Architecture (www.cwarch.org).

For networking purposes, connecting to the profession, and gaining experience, strongly consider joining one or more professional associations. But do not just join; become engaged with the planning and implementing of the association; what better way to gain experience in areas that you may not be able to gain with your employer.

What Do You Look for When Hiring a New Designer?

❭I look for a strong portfolio of work.

Thomas Fowler IV, AIA, NCARB, DPACSA Professor and Director, Community Interdisciplinary Design Studio (CIDS), California Polytechnic State University—San Luis Obispo

❭I look for communication skills, both verbal and graphic. I look for confidence, a broad range of skills, and team spirit. I look for evidence of volunteerism and leadership.

Grace H. Kim, AIA, Principal, Schemata Workshop, Inc.

❭I look for an excellent listener who has experience designing and planning buildings for the environment I work in.

H. Alan Brangman, AIA, Vice President of Facilities, Real Estate Auxiliary Services, University of Delaware

❭I do not hire yet, but I would look for design partners who are the whole package. In other words, they can think big, speak knowledgably to clients, and have the ability to get into the nitty-gritty of the tools we use every day.

Rosannah B. Sandoval, AIA, Designer II, Perkins + Will

❭I look for incredible talent and ambition and for the ability to listen and to work with our team.

William J. Carpenter, Ph.D., FAIA, Protfessor, Southern Polytechnic State University; President, Lightroom

❭I look for someone who is motivated, eager, and not afraid to get their hands dirty and is also not afraid to ask questions. The best architects ask the best questions. They must be able to communicate well and speak to the power of their ideas. They need to have a vision but still show humility. They need to be able to demonstrate that they can work with others in a positive and collaborative manner.

Robert D. Fox, AIA, IIDA, Principal, FOX Architects

❭Professionalism (organizational and communication skills), how do the individuals pursue their work, interest, design capability or potential, and computer literacy with hand sketching/drawing as a bonus. Broad design perspective. Level of artistry and craft in presentation.

Mary Kay Lanzillotta, FAIA, Partner, Hartman-Cox Architects

What Do You Look for When Hiring a New Designer? (Continued)

❯ First and foremost, I am looking for someone who embraces the collaborative, evolving nature of the process. Good design is iterative, so a person must be able to take criticism from team members, embrace change rapidly, and always be searching for ways to improve the project.

Cody Bornsheuer, Associate AIA, LEED AP BD+C, Architectural Designer, Dewberry Architects, Inc.

❯ Because young practitioners often have a considerable wealth of knowledge in digital technology that can be useful to the development of a practice, I recruit individuals with expertise in a range of digital tools who also have excellent visual, oral, and written communication skills because they add value to the firm.

Kathryn T. Prigmore, FAIA, Senior Project Manager, HDR Architecture, Inc.

❯ Someone who has strong personal skills to deal with other employees and clients, possesses the fundamentals needed to be an architect such as drawing, drafting, and CAD, but most important, a well-rounded individual.

John W. Myefski, AIA, Principal, Myefski Architects, Inc.

❯ I looked for well-rounded individuals who were interested in contributing to a firm. I appreciated those who conveyed that they were just beginning their careers yet were ready to work hard and learn from others. I was definitely not interested in individuals who stated that they were seeking employment with a firm because of how it would help them—business hires are not altruistic acts and to convey a primary concern for your personal goals doesn't relay a good message about your work attitude. Also, I was not interested in those

St. Bartholomew Catholic Church, Columbus, Indiana. Architect: Ratio Architects. PHOTOGRAPHER: SUSAN HANES.

who thought of themselves as "only" designers. If you are a good designer, you should be able to bring that perspective to any role in practice, as the work needs quality design at every opportunity. Writing and spelling are as important as design—I have typically found that students who organize thoughts well can do so in any medium.

Karen Cordes Spence, Ph.D., AIA, LEED AP, Associate Professor, Drury University

❭ People hire people, not portfolios. While excellence in design work is necessary, it is irrelevant if you cannot clearly articulate the details of your exploration or demonstrate the value of your design solution. Good designers have the ability to provide value, to communicate a clear and compelling design vision that directly addresses the needs of a client.

Also, architecture is a team sport. Compelling design ideas are great, but it is equally important to demonstrate your cultural fit with the organization you wish to join, and to articulate your x-factor, the unique value that you bring to the team.

Andrew Caruso, AIA, LEED AP BD+C, CDT, Head of Intern Development and Academic Outreach, Gensler

❭ Passion and commitment to the profession. A desire to learn and work collaboratively. We seek out bright, motivated individuals who take problem solving seriously. The hard skills required such as rendering and drafting are secondary to their attitude, but we would not hire someone without a strong portfolio showing graphic sophistication.

Lynsey J. G. Sorrell, AIA, LEED AP, Principal Perimeter Architects

❭ It is a given that the individual must possess the basic technical skills in and innate capacity for design. What is more intriguing to me is a team player—someone who gathers inspiration from others and strives to achieve a feeling of synergy with the team. Having a good work ethic, a strong under-

standing of building materials and methods, and an interest in business practices is a plus as well.

Kevin Sneed, AIA, IIDA, NOMA, LEED AP BD+C, Partner/ Senior Director of Architecture, OTJ Architects, LLC

❭ In emerging professionals, including those just out of school, we look for strong hand-drawing and sketching skills, strong computer aptitude, a spark of design inspiration and understanding in the portfolio, and an eager enthusiasm and openness to a variety of experiences. Good communication skills, a great attitude, and positive personality are essential—the technical skills can be taught at work, but these cannot.

The ability to solve design problems through sketching solutions in real time with the client is a key differentiator in our services. Also critical, our designers must have an aptitude for and willingness to use a computer.

Carolyn G. Jones, AIA, Principal, Mulvanny G2

❭ The best designers have an open mind and a desire to learn. There are constantly new technologies, theories, and ideas circling the world, and I think that the best architects take what we have learned from the past and use new technology and innovation to make something better. The designers I look up to most are always drawing, thinking, learning, and problem solving.

Amanda Strawitch, Level 1 Architect, Design Collective

❭ We look for different attributes for different skill positions. Not everyone is destined to be a designer, nor should we all. There are many rewarding ways to find your voice in this amazing profession.

For a designer specifically, we most often look for a special combination of passion, confidence, talent, and attitude. We want our designers to have a fire in the belly for architecture, and this can trump portfolio. As we work in collaborative teams throughout design, we want designers who are passionate about design, who communicate ideas effectively, and whose attitude plays well with others.

We look for designers who engage and inspire.

Shannon Kraus, FAIA, MBA, Principal and Senior Vice-President, HKS Architects

❯A designer needs to have a thought process unlike the typical individual. A continuous reply of "what if we do this?" should be the ingrained attitude for any designer or design challenge. An individual who is

Jay Pritzker Pavilion, Chicago, Illinois. Architect: Frank Gehry. PHOTOGRAPHER: LEE W. WALDREP, Ph.D.

a quick learner is ideal due to the rapidly changing technologies and products in the profession.

Kathy Denise Dixon, AIA, NOMA, Associate Principal, Arel Architects, Inc.

❯In addition to being skilled communicators and critical thinkers, I have noticed that the most successful individuals I have recommended have throughout their educational career developed a strong design process that directs them in both the analysis and solution of problems. The able designer needs to be able to think quickly on her or his feet while skillfully representing ideas in visual and verbal media.

Brian Kelly, AIA, Associate Professor and Director, Architecture Program, University of Maryland

❯Practical views on how space is used, drive to pursue their own ideas while continuing to learn from new experiences, and impeccable organizational skills.

Megan S. Chusid, AIA, Manager of Facilities and Office Services, Solomon R. Guggenheim Museum and Foundation

❯When I am hiring new designers, I am looking to see if the individuals present themselves clearly and confidently and can articulate design concepts. I look to see if they present themselves professionally and if they have a personality and attitude that will fit in with our organization.

Sean M. Stadler, AIA, LEED AP, Design Principal, WDG Architecture, PLLC

❯I look for people who will integrate well into the culture of the office or fill a void we are currently missing. Technical skills can be taught, and there is a technical learning curve in every position, but if you don't have a personality that is going to work well with those whom you interface with, it is going to be hard to enjoy doing your work and therefore contribute to the team.

Ashley W. Clark, Associate AIA, LEED AP, SMPS, Marketing Manager, LandDesign

❯ What is most important is having passion for what they are doing. If the person exhibits a real passion for their work, this excites the interview team. I can see passion in the work as well, so displaying work examples that successfully exhibit ideas and resolving these ideas into buildings is paramount. At an interview, it is important to express what drives you and how this would be important to the firm.

Joseph Mayo, Intern Architect, Mahlum

❯ Within my architecture firm I lead our consulting practice that is less about drawing and more about facilitating, analyzing, and consensus building. Our consulting practice focuses on workplace strategy, change management, and research. Most of our work is spent convincing people to make major investments in a building and changing the way they work to benefit their organization. To be successful, we have to be able to speak, write, illustrate, and connect with people. We have to be comfortable talking about how our client's business vision and how design can help support that vision. The ability to draw is a "nice to have," but not nearly as important (to my group) as the ability to communicate ideas.

Leigh Stringer, LEED AP, Senior Vice President, HOK

❯ I look at how the applicant lives. I get nervous whenever I get an applicant that has wild theoretical visions for how others should live but cannot imagine a similar world in which they themselves would reside. Next up would be the ability to draw and paint what they see. This is the most tangible sign that they are careful observers how others behave, conduct commerce, and interact with one another. Finally is communication. Our art is as much science as it is storytelling.

Joseph Nickol, AICP, LEED AP BD+C, Urbanist, Urban Design Associates

❯ It lies in the "other."
Beyond the specific skill sets of technical and building proficiency of the position, we seek out the other latent passions that a person may have that would be influential to the project at hand. We have hired designers with backgrounds in social work in LGBTQ communities, graphic design, and anthropology that have been a compliment to our skills and made the project process more robust and enjoyable.

Katherine Darnstadt, AIA LEED AP BD+C, Founder and Principal Architect, Latent Design

❯ I recommend you have a concise and informative single-page resume and a single-page sample of work sent as a PDF with a brief, yet thoughtful, cover letter. I remind candidates that the people who review these packages have very little time to do so and they appreciate brevity. Beyond the application package, I tend to favor candidates who are able to convey their creativity, demonstrate diverse experience in the field, and show community involvement. Verbal communication and computer skills are important as well, especially computer modeling and rendering capabilities in today's marketplace. Personality is a factor in decision making as well. Some people are better suited for certain office environments, while others might flourish in different environments. It is very useful for candidates to learn as much as they can about an office, organization, or agency before applying for a position.

Kimberly Dowdell, Project Manager/Director of Marketing, Levien & Company

Explore; Ask for What You Want; Look for Mentors

BETH KALIN

Job Captain

Gensler

Minneapolis, MN

Why and how did you become an architect?

❯ Somewhere around fifth grade I knew I wanted to be an architect. An architecture elective at my middle school, led by our art teacher, was my first semiformal introduction to the field, including drafting and modeling. Growing up in a metropolitan suburb bordered by new developments also

▼ Sagrada Familia, Study Abroad Sketch by Elizabeth Kalin at Illinois Institute of Technology.

helped. My father, an engineer with an interest in architecture, and I would often bike around construction sites, wandering through partially built wood-framed homes, trying to guess the function of each room. Our family also frequented the Parade of Homes, a biannual builders' showcase in the Twin Cities. Collecting floor plans and sketching "dream homes" became hobbies.

Shadowing real architects solidified my desire to become a professional and pursue this field. Both my middle and high school encouraged shadowing and gave students extra credit for participating. Luckily, a friend's father was a residential architect, so following him around was my first shadowing experience, and the scale models and large mock-ups stoked my curiosity. Later, my high school paired me up with a woman who owned a small firm with her husband. I spent a full day with her and was itching to go to college by the end of it. So many aspects of the career appealed to me—the design challenges, the teamwork, the interactions with consultants and various user groups, the hands-on aspect of making models, and, most important, the variety of work. If you can, try to explore what piques your interest at the big picture scale but also through a practical, realistic lens, too. Shadowing is a great tool to better understand the day-to-day life of an architect or any other professional.

Why and how did you decide on which school to attend for your architecture degree? What degree(s) do you possess?

❯ Investigating architecture school options began my junior year of high school. Immediately, the five-year professional bachelor of architecture program seemed best suited to my interests, as their coursework typically began with a design studio from the

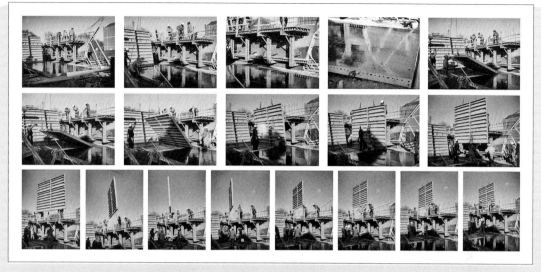

SOS Children's Villages, Lavezzorio Community Center, Chicago, Illinois. Architect: Studio Gang Architects. PHOTOGRAPHER: ELIZABETH KALIN, STUDIO GANG ARCHITECTS.

very first semester. Pratt Institute offers a pre-college summer program that I was fortunate enough to attend prior to my senior year in high school. During my senior year, after several visits to schools and interviews, and receiving information on scholarships at the schools to which I had applied, I decided to attend Illinois Institute of Technology (IIT) to obtain a five-year professional bachelor of architecture degree. Crown Hall was a huge draw, the faculty and program was a huge draw, being in the city of Chicago was a huge draw. I graduated with high honors and a minor in computers, which makes me sound ancient. During my five years, I spent a semester in Paris through the IIT Study-Abroad program and loved every minute of it.

Why did you pursue the additional degree, master of design science, at the University of Sydney? What was your emphasis, and what was it like to study in another country?

❭ Graduate school was always something I was interested in, but not necessarily committed to during my early working years. A professor I had at IIT recommended working a few years before heading back to school, and while I ended up waiting almost eight years to go back, I think it was really great advice and worked well for me. I care deeply about sustainable design, and while I was getting to apply it in bits in pieces at work prior to grad school, as time went by I was feeling less fulfilled with the work I was doing. There are several countries that are ahead of the United States in terms of really embracing sustainable design, and Australia is definitely one of them. I had also just felt an intuitive pull, which kept growing stronger, to visit Australia and reconsider graduate school. The University of Sydney had a program that was short but full of classes that fit exactly what I was looking for, I had a lot of freedom in choosing electives, and the application process couldn't be easier—no GRE, no portfolio required.

It was an incredible experience and I could go on at great length about all the reasons I had an amazing time studying in Sydney. Living abroad can be a really enriching experience that gives one totally new perspective on many aspects of life and work, and a chance to reflect and reset the course your life. I *highly* recommend studying abroad while in school and, based on my experience, also recommend considering a foreign degree. While I am not necessarily drawing on what I learned there every day now that I am back in the United States and working again, it has given me the foundation I desired and a sense of expertise that will be useful for the rest of my career. I also made incredible friends who are now scattered all over the world, which I am grateful for.

Having a plan or a goal is never a bad thing, and I think it's good to set up a framework for yourself professionally, but it is also important to go with the flow and be resilient with wherever your path leads. It is absolutely crucial to listen to your intuition. There are many tangents that start with an architectural education, and only you know what your most successful, fulfilling professional path will be.

What has been your greatest challenge as an architect thus far?

❭ Finding balance! I know many of my peers also wrestle with how much time to spend at work versus time to take for yourself, spend with loved ones, volunteer, enter competitions. There is so much for us to do as architects, I still find it difficult at times to draw the line between what must get done and what I want to get done to fully express an idea.

The difference between being a full-time architecture student and being a full-time architectural intern is quite significant. I knew this adjustment was coming, and I felt I had prepared for it with my experiences working in offices over summer and winter breaks. It was something I struggled with most during my first full-time experience after graduation. The firm I worked for had a clear hierarchical system, and I clearly fell into the lowest

level. Of course, everyone has to start somewhere, but at that firm in particular, I did not feel like I was asked to contribute anything personally design-wise and often felt I filled a role that so many know as the CAD monkey.

Enjoy every minute of being a student because it is such a personal, selfish, and indulgent time. You are the client as well as the architect. The constraints on projects are relatively small. You, as the head designer, are free to take design ideas and run with them. No budgets to agonize over!

Being in school is like testing the waters, and at work you have to dive right in. Many components of the realities of practice are never touched on in school, and I've felt a range of emotions while dealing with them on the job, from frustration to excitement. The learning never stops, which is part of the beauty of our profession. Don't let the vast abyss of things yet to learn/experience overwhelm you—you will take in what you need to as each project moves forward.

I also recommend being vocal about the experiences you want to obtain as in intern. When I started at Studio Gang, I made it clear that I needed construction administration experience to complete the Intern Development Program (IDP) and was put on a job that began construction a year later. Following a building from construction documents through completion and the grand opening celebration has by far been the most rewarding part of my career. It was an uphill battle at many points along the way, but we have been fortunate to receive a number of significant awards for the project, and though completing the project alone was incredibly satisfying, the recognition is certainly an added bonus.

Keep up with the IDP paperwork as well. In a previous edition, I mentioned that I hoped by the third edition of this book, I would be licensed. At

SOS Children's Villages, Lavezzorio Community Center, Chicago, Illinois. Architect: Studio Gang Architects. PHOTOGRAPHER: STEVE HALL, HEDRICH BLESSING.

the time of publishing, I have taken and passed one of the seven Architectural Registration Exams. It has been an incredibly supportive environment at Gensler, and I am very fortunate that our firm pays for study courses and exams. I have taken advantage and completed study courses through the AIA MN chapter, which have helped motivate me to work on this part of my journey to become licensed. I think it helps having some experience under my belt, but on the other hand, making time to study never gets easier, especially as one takes on more responsibilities at work, so get those AREs out of the way a few years out of school if you can.

What are your primary responsibilities and duties?

❱ My role parallels that of a project architect, but I am not licensed (yet), so job captain is my current title and I help design, draw, manage consultants, and run construction administration for projects within our office. Working at Gensler in Minneapolis has been a really interesting, rewarding experience. As a whole, we are one of the largest firms in the world, but our office of 12 feels like its own family with endless resources to draw from. It has been really great to partner with offices in other cities and collaborate

with people from all over the firm, which I personally have gotten to do on several projects already, and I've only been with the firm a year and a half.

Gensler also runs a very savvy business, like no other architecture firm I have experienced or heard about. During the second month, we had a lunch presentation about the business of design. I really respect that not only do we hold ourselves to high design standards but also management values meeting high business standards, too. Among my classmates and friends, it is the only firm I am aware of that pays architects for overtime, even if you are a salary employee. Every additional hour I work shows up in my paycheck.

I really love pulling together a thorough drawing set and seeing a project through construction to its grand opening celebration. I never imagined I would end up at a firm that is more known for its interior work, but it's been fun to see multiple projects completed in a year, instead of always working a project that can extend over four or five years or longer. Solving puzzles has always been fun, and at work I do that all the time, coordinating structure, ducts, lighting, and sprinkler lines to figure out what ceiling height is possible in a space, for example. Being able to think in three dimensions and sketch your way through problems with a pencil is also incredibly useful. New software and technology is important to know and keep up with, but nothing beats a pencil and some scratch paper.

It is very important to find a firm that is a good fit for both you and the firm. At my very first summer job I heard encouragement from more than one person about switching majors "while it is still easy." Being an architect is not for everyone, and certainly every firm is a different little world of its own; part of the challenge is finding one that is a match for you.

Please also look for mentors and never be afraid to ask for help, either. There is so much to learn in this profession, and it's a waste if you don't use those around you with more experience (read: mistakes from which they learned quite a bit) to help catapult your growth as a designer to a higher level. I feel very fortunate to have the support of a handful of amazing mentors, some of which appeared in my life at the right time and others that I had to more actively seek out.

Hands-on Architecture

TANYA ALLY
Architectural Staff
Bonstra I Haresign Architects
Washington, DC

Why did you become an architect?

❯ I have not always known I wanted to pursue architecture; I always knew what I *did not* want to pursue. Architecture appealed to me in my late teens, and I felt it was the perfect balance between art and techniques. I had no idea how vast the profession is, and now that I know, I am even more content that I have chosen this path. It is a great way to be many things all at once, and I think it is a very fulfilling career.

Why did you decide to choose the school that you did—the University of Tennessee—to attend for your architecture degree(s)? What degrees to you possess?

❯ It was an easy decision for me. I grew up in East Tennessee, and luckily the University of Tennessee, in such close proximity to my hometown, has an ac-

Sketch of The Temple de la Sagrada Familia, Barcelona, Spain. Architect: Antonio Gaudi.

credited, five-year bachelor of architecture program that I attended. I completed this program, received my B.Arch. and also continued my foreign language education, receiving a French minor. The University of Tennessee had many assets at our disposal and I took advantage of everything I could—great faculty, study-abroad programs (I went twice), teaching assistant positions, and summer courses, among others.

During school, you participated in "Living Light," the entry to the DOE Solar Decathlon from the University of Tennessee. What was your involvement, and how did you benefit from the experience?

❯ I was very fortunate to have been in the studio that did the preliminary design for submission into the 2011 Solar Decathlon. I watched the house take shape and evolve from a parti to a livable, breathable house that seamlessly meshed all the design components, and concepts, to form "Living Light."

This was the only experience, as a student, that I received where a project I had worked on was actually built. The realization of a project at such a young age, and so early in one's career, is extremely valuable. We also worked alongside students and professionals of other disciplines in order to bring this project to fruition. Educating each other on our respective areas of expertise, and understanding how each discipline had a place in the overall design, allowed this project to succeed. This collaboration was one of the best exercises in coordinating, networking, and building relationships that I experienced during my undergraduate career.

What are your primary responsibilities and duties?

❯ At this stage in my career, my primary responsibility is to utilize my resources and take advantage of a steep learning curve that takes place at the start of one's career. This is the best time to learn quickly and directly apply new knowledge. I feel that this is the

best way to be an asset to my firm, as well as further my own expertise as I move forward in my career.

What has been your greatest challenge as an intern thus far?

❯ The greatest challenge that I have faced as an intern is *actually* learning what it means to be an architect. It was a difficult adjustment in the beginning; and one that is hard to prepare for. I am learning so much every day and will continue to do so throughout my career.

❯ What is the most satisfying part of a career as an architect?

Educating others who are unfamiliar with our profession is probably the most satisfying thing, in my opinion. Explaining to others how good design can change the world, and educating them about the broader role of architects. It's not just about putting a building together; it is about a concept, an idea, making a statement …

What are your 5-year and 10-year career goals relative to architecture?

❯ My 5-year goal is to become a licensed architect. I am currently enrolled in the Intern Development Program (IDP), and I am working toward fulfilling my hours at my current firm, as well as studying for the Architecture Registration Exam (ARE). My future goals are much broader—to stay in touch with the design community through traveling, design competitions, and photography. I hope to have a robust portfolio by the end of my career; to do this, I must accomplish just as much in my personal life as I will have accomplished at work.

Who or what experience has been a major influence on your career?

❯ I have had several exceptional mentors throughout my life, some of whom are in the field of architecture

◄Living Light, University of Tennessee, U.S. Department of Energy Solar Decathlon 2011, Washington DC, September 23, 2011. PHOTOGRAPHER: DIANE BOSSART. PHOTO © DIANE BOSSART.

▼Sketch of an old theatre in Segunto, a small town in Spain.

and others who are not. I think there are important lessons to be learned from people in unrelated fields as well—I once worked for an electrical engineer who also did design work, albeit a very different type of design work, and I learned important lessons about scale, craft, and problem solving, just as I do in my own field. If you make the most of every situation, there are always lessons to be learned that can be applied in differing contexts and situations.

My most influential experiences are my travels. Experiencing different cultures, cities, and parks has exposed me to so much material that I am constantly reflecting on, consciously or subconsciously, in my work. They have helped me realize that architecture and design is a universal language; buildings are historical markers that tell the story of a time and a place long after the people who have lived there are around to tell it themselves. Architecture is symbolic; history can be absorbed just by walking through city centers and downtowns. To realize the world around us and to understand its progression is beautiful.

It Is All About the Clients

CODY BORNSHEUER, ASSOCIATE AIA, LEED AP BD+C

Architectural Designer
Dewberry Architects, Inc.
Peoria, Illinois

Why did you become an architect?

❯ A lot of architects around my age will give you the same answer: Legos. It was no different for me. Growing up, I was always up to my elbows in little plastic bricks, driving my parents crazy with the sounds of me rustling through some giant tub in our basement, searching for the right piece. I have always had a fascination with how things go together. As I began to study architecture, I became even more fascinated with the idea of crafting environments to serve some societal need. I love working with people to figure out what they need and how I can best deliver it to them.

Why did you decide to choose the school that you did—the University of Illinois at Urbana-Champaign—to attend for your architecture degree(s)? What degrees to you possess?

❯ Growing up in Central Illinois, I was always a lifelong Illini fan. Regardless of my chosen field, I was going to be an Illini, and in fact I did not even apply to a "safety" school. It was Champaign or bust for me! After earning my BS in architectural studies, I was still so in love with the Champaign-Urbana community that I knew I wanted to stay for my master of architecture. I could have gone elsewhere, but Champaign was home.

What are your primary responsibilities and duties?

❯ I am primarily involved on the front end of a project, working closely with our business develop-

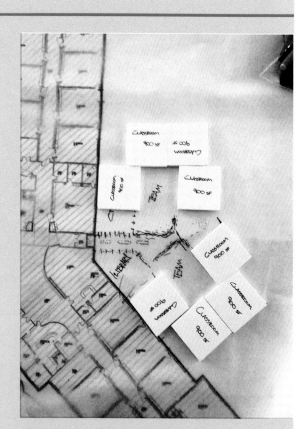

Elementary School Addition Study, Dunlap, Illinois. Architect: Dewberry Architects, Inc. PHOTOGRAPHER: CODY BORNSHEUER.

ment director and office design director to pursue work and prepare for interviews, often as part of the "interview team" as project designer. After we have been awarded a project, I will work with our clients through programming and concept design, and then provide design leadership to our team as the project progresses.

As project designer, I outlay the overall direction for a project; developing plans, elevations, and important sections for the building, preliminary code research, material and production selections, and

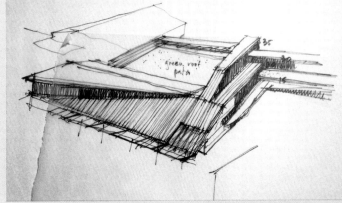

◄ Health and Human Performance Center Study, Wisconsin. Architect: Dewberry Architects, Inc. PHOTOGRAPHER: CODY BORNSHEUER.

▼ Lombard Junior High School Renovation, Galesburg, Illinois. Architect: Dewberry Architects, Inc. PHOTOGRAPHER: CODY BORNSHEUER.

working with our interior designers to select finishes, colors, etc. Throughout the project, I will give periodic presentations back to the client to review the progress and incorporate any changes they may need. Typically, once a job moves into construction documents, I will take a reduced role as I begin to transition to the next job.

Aside from project responsibilities, I am also relied upon to be our "special projects guy." Awards submittals, conference presentation materials, banners, public outreach events, and basically anything else our design director needs … I enjoy a lot of variety in my day-to-day.

What has been your greatest challenge as an intern thus far?

❯ My biggest challenge thus far has been getting the "well-rounded" experience. It is less a result of being an intern as much as it is being a project designer. Because I often transition away from projects as they near construction, I haven't had the field experience needed to complete my IDP requirements. The trade-off, however, is that I have spent a great deal of time learning the business side of architecture, including marketing and business development and working directly with our clients.

From the perspective of an emerging professional, can you describe the Intern Development Program (IDP) and the Architect Registration Examination (ARE)?

❯ The IDP and ARE have immense value to the emerging professional. The structure of both ensures a diverse experience, ensuring that a person gets proper experience on all sides of the profession to discover what they enjoy, and imbues them with the requisite knowledge to be a capable architect.

What is the most/least satisfying part of a career as an architect?

❯ The most satisfying part of my job is that feeling of accomplishment when I have worked with a group to find consensus on a direction for a project. In one specific example, I worked on a school project that had a "design committee" composed of 50-some teachers, parents, administrators, and community members. At the start of our first meeting, one of the committee members was very vocal in his opposition to the process being undertaken and the general direction of the project. By the start of our second meeting, he had become one of our biggest supporters.

I do not know that there really is a "least satisfying" part of my career. I derive great satisfaction from my chosen profession and view every challenge as a new opportunity for growth. I am one of those lucky persons that loves what I do and cannot really picture myself doing anything else.

What are your 5-year and 10-year career goals relative to architecture?

❯ Within 5 years, I hope to move into a lead design position, taking on more clients independently, and perhaps overseeing a younger group of project designers. Within 10 years, I would like to be an office studio leader or design director, overseeing and leading the efforts of many projects. However, both of these goals are secondary to my desire to continue to provide my clients with responsible, high-quality architecture that exceeds their highest expectations.

Who or what experience has been a major influence on your career?

❯ I have had a number of people that have influenced my career thus far. As a graduate student, I took a course on research methods with Professors James Anderson and John Stallmeyer. During the course, I spent a portion of my time observing and interviewing people, which gave me a chance to begin to understand how to really listen to people and read between the lines. In addition, my first design director placed heavy emphasis on client focus and taught me to understand the "pulse" of the group to whom I was presenting, to understand the unspoken and lead the group in the direction in which they want to go.

Breaking into the Profession

ALLISON WILSON
Intern Architect
Ayers Saint Gross
Baltimore, Maryland

Why did you decide to become an architect?

❯ My grandfather built birdhouses, model ships, boats, and planes all through my childhood, and playing in his workshop is one of my favorite memories. We'd make cities from his cutoff scraps, and he'd take me to the craft shop to buy little trees and people to populate our cities. Those really simple acts of making stayed with me and with some guidance from my parents I went into college as an architecture major and never looked back. In school, I loved that studying architecture also meant that I got to study sociology and physics and history; that I didn't have to choose one discipline in a silo that would separate me from all other kinds of knowledge.

The same way that having a tangible product when I finished making cities with my grandfather mesmerized me as a kid came back in a big way when I started having presentable work and finished buildings that I could walk around in. I am absolutely addicted to watching a building change from a set of thought sketches on paper to a three-dimensional reality. I decided to become an architect because that process of thinking and making makes me happy.

Why did you choose to pursue the 4+2 year master of architecture program at the University of Maryland? What degree(s) do you possess?

❯ While I love learning, thinking, and talking about architecture, there are many other disciplines that also interest me. Being in a four+two program let me explore other academic programs and celebrate my varied interests. Aside from

Machu Picchu, Peru.
PHOTOGRAPHER:
JENNIFER KOZICKI.

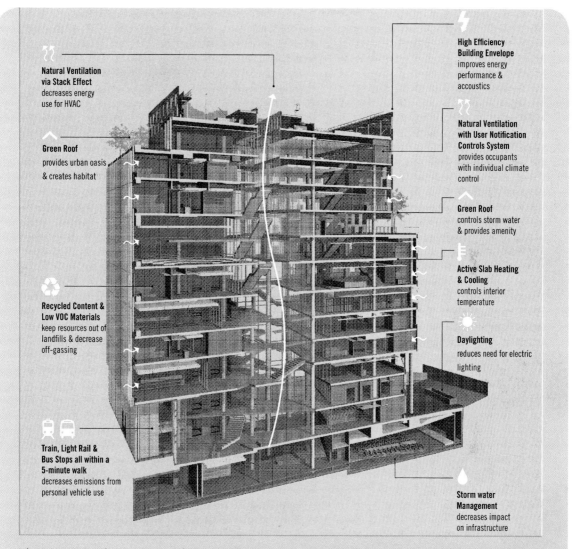

Natural Ventilation via Stack Effect
decreases energy use for HVAC

Green Roof
provides urban oasis & creates habitat

Recycled Content & Low VOC Materials
keep resources out of landfills & decrease off-gassing

Train, Light Rail & Bus Stops all within a 5-minute walk
decreases emissions from personal vehicle use

High Efficiency Building Envelope
improves energy performance & accoustics

Natural Ventilation with User Notification Controls System
provides occupants with individual climate control

Green Roof
controls storm water & provides amenity

Active Slab Heating & Cooling
controls interior temperature

Daylighting
reduces need for electric lighting

Storm water Management
decreases impact on infrastructure

John & Frances Angelos Law Center, Baltimore, Maryland. Architect: Ayers Saint Gross and Behnisch Architekten. GRAPHIC: AYERS SAINT GROSS.

my bachelor of science in architecture, I finished undergrad with a minor in English and an undergraduate team research thesis about a local immigrant community. Having experiences outside of architecture with non-architects helps me become a better designer because it gives me a broader range of experiences for inspiration and keeps me grounded.

Maryland provided me all the opportunities of going to a big state school with a sports teams, a large alumni network, affordability, and a great location. It also provided me a tight-knit School of Architecture community that I felt very at home in. I enjoyed having the best of both worlds and stayed at Maryland for graduate school, where I earned a master of architecture degree.

You have had many opportunities to study abroad during your studies. How were these experiences valuable to your education?

❯ Studying abroad opened the door, literally, to a much larger world for me. These experiences allowed me to explore the architectural values of other cultures and provided me the opportunity to learn a great deal in a short amount of time.

Architecture is for everyone, and while big design moves are incredibly important, at some point architecture is about crafting places that help people live a higher quality of life. I couldn't make the kinds of buildings I want to bring into the world without constantly growing my knowledge of how other people live, work, and play. Studying abroad helped me be more aware of what kinds of questions are necessary in a collaborative and inclusive design process and what kinds of design strategies cross cultural and historical boundaries.

Everyone should study abroad at some point, regardless of discipline, but especially in architecture. There is much to gain from understanding why a culture creates the built environment it does.

In 2011, you served as a team leader for WaterShed, the University of Maryland's winning entry to the U.S. Department of Energy's Solar Decathlon 2011; can you describe that experience, and how has your involvement influenced your professional career?

❯ WaterShed has been the most pivotal part of my academic and professional development. I got involved with the team at the beginning of the Solar Decathlon process as a graduate student at Maryland and quickly became committed to and passionate about the work we were doing as a team. I helped develop our schematic design package,

write our specifications for design development and construction documents, build the house, craft our communications package, raise funding, and tell our story to the 20,000 people who visited WaterShed on the National Mall.

There is nothing more empowering than realizing you have had a valuable experience that puts you in a position to educate the public and change the way people view and use our built environment. The people who came to hear WaterShed's story came from all walks of life with similar questions: How do I live more sustainability? Can I do any of what you're talking about in my own home? How much does it cost to live like this? It's enlightening to realize that because of the experiences I had with WaterShed, I can answer those questions.

WaterShed also helped me earn my current professional position. We pitched WaterShed to Ayers Saint Gross, a Baltimore-based design firm, looking for sponsorship. After the meeting, Ayers Saint Gross agreed to financially support WaterShed and its mission of educating the public about the relationship between buildings and the environment and simultaneously decided to craft a position for me that would allow me to finish my commitment to WaterShed through the Solar Decathlon six months after I finished graduate school and start my professional career. Ayers Saint Gross realized that I was learning things through WaterShed that I could never learn as effectively in an office and that supporting me in gaining that knowledge would ultimately make me a better practitioner for them. It's a phenomenal group of people to work with, and when I go to the office every day, I'm always learning something new.

◀ Interior, WaterShed, University of Maryland,
U.S. Department of Energy Solar Decathlon
2011, Washington DC, September 23, 2011.
PHOTOGRAPHER: JIM TETRO/U.S. DEPARTMENT OF
ENERGY SOLAR DECATHLON.

▼ Exterior, WaterShed, University of Maryland,
U.S. Department of Energy Solar Decathlon
2011, Washington DC, September 23, 2011.
PHOTOGRAPHER: JIM TETRO/U.S. DEPARTMENT OF
ENERGY SOLAR DECATHLON.

What has been your greatest challenge as an intern architect?

❯ My greatest challenge is figuring out what I want to be when I grow up. It is entirely true that that more I learn the less I know, and the more I discover about architecture the more paths I realize are open to me. While my title might not be student anymore, I'm still learning constantly. I hope I never stop being a student in that sense; I always want my knowledge to be growing.

What is the most satisfying part of being an architect?

❯ The most satisfying part of being an architect is that moment in construction where the drawings come to life. All of a sudden this building that's been on paper becomes a three-dimensional reality that can be touched and experienced. I always thought there was such great discovery happening in the design process, and there is, but it can't hold a candle to all the things that get discovered as the building starts to take on three dimensions. The details come to life, the materials become tangible, and the spirit of the place starts to exist in a way that it just can't on paper.

What do you hope to be doing 5 to 10 years after graduation with regard to your career?

❯ I hope 5 to 10 years after graduation I'm still as fired up about learning and practicing my craft as I am today. Like I said, I learn something new almost every day and I don't expect that to change any time soon. I'm working toward licensure now by concurrently completing my IDP hours and the ARE; with any luck I'll be through both in the next couple of years.

Who or what experience has been a major influence on your career?

❯ WaterShed was absolutely the most influential experience I have ever had. The adventures I had as a part of that team have shaped me personally and professionally in ways I am still discovering, and I'm absurdly grateful to have been in the right place at the right time to take advantage of all the opportunities WaterShed offered me. Our team is a passionate community of practitioners who believe in the power of design to create a more sustainable future, and our friendships and camaraderie enrich my personal and professional experiences constantly.

To specifically name a few, faculty leaders Amy Gardner, Brian Grieb, and Brittany Williams have been phenomenal mentors. As I started working, their guidance and willingness to share their experiences have helped me transition from a student to a professional and have helped me get comfortable with the ambiguity that comes with being an emerging professional. It's not just more experienced architects that I look to as mentors, though; my peers David Daily and Scott Tjaden are equally responsible for crafting me into this hybrid professional I'm becoming. David and Scott taught me to be multilingual. I am not a designer who prides herself on being conversant with other designers; I am a collaborator who is happiest when I am talking environmental science with ecology specialists and systems design with engineers. I like sitting in the gray area between disciplines, and while my degrees may say architecture and my license will eventually be in architecture, I hope I never forget that the best place to be is connecting the dots between all the different players that craft the built environment.

Force by Fire

JENNIFER TAYLOR

National Vice President
American Institute of Architecture Students
Washington, DC

Why did you become an architect?

❯As a high school student, my passion and primary form of expression was art. In making college visits, I was urged to try forms of engineering; however, I did not feel that this would allow my passion for art to continue. It was not until I visited the architecture program at Tuskegee University that I actually had a formal introduction to architecture.

Unlike many in my first-year class, I found a passion and a form of art to which I had never before been introduced. Architecture was physical and had the capability of impacting a community and even a country as a whole. It allowed me to grow as a leader and impact the community on a larger level through my artwork.

Why did you decide to choose Tuskegee University? What degree(s) do you possess?

❯In a sense, you can say I am a Tuskegee "baby." My father graduated from Tuskegee. I remember being as young as 10 years old sitting across from the student section wishing I could scream the chants that the big kids were screaming.

My mother felt that exposure to multiple college settings was important in making my college decision. Both of my parents saw fit for me to visit any school of interest; however, Tuskegee's legacy and welcoming atmosphere always stuck with me.

It was never my goal to travel far from home during undergraduate studies, and a smaller university

Landscape–Acrylic. Painting by Jennifer Taylor at Tuskegee University.

seemed to fit my college setting preference. These factors easily allowed me to narrow my decisions between the two accredited architecture programs within Alabama. After a tour of the architecture program at Tuskegee University, I sealed the deal and accepted a full academic and athletic scholarship. I received the bachelor of architecture degree.

During your summers, you had the opportunity to work in three different architecture firms. Please describe these experiences, and explain to what extent they were helpful in your studies.

❯My first internship was with Goodwyn, Mills & Cawood, Inc. in Montgomery, Alabama (summer

NORTH

Maxwell Boulevard. Development Proposal Studio Project by Jennifer Taylor at Tuskegee University.

2009). The focus of Goodwyn, Mills & Cawood was commercial projects. Although I did not know architecture programs such as AutoCAD, SketchUp, and Revit, I was able to participate in design charrettes and daily tasks around the office such as as-built measurements and observation. My mentor offered a clear explanation of how projects get started and the process it takes to create ideas during the preliminary and schematic design stages.

My second internship was with Merrick and Company, Duluth, Georgia (summer 2012). This experience was completely opposite of my first experience because Merrick focused on government-based work. I found these project types were predetermined and limited in design opportunities since the buildings were required to be uniformed to match the base at which they were designed for. This was also a great learning experience because it offered an alternative look on architectural design.

My most recent internship was with Sherlock, Smith & Adams, Inc. in Montgomery, Alabama (November 2012–May 2013). I was brought on as intern to assist in registering Leadership in Energy and Environmental Design (LEED)

projects under my mentor. My daily task usually include project registry through LEED online by filling out LEED templates, assisting in calculation, and project team meetings.

What has been your greatest challenge as an architecture student?

❭ Throughout my education, my greatest challenge has been securing internships from summer to summer and gaining the professional development I need to be fully aware of profession. During my first internship at Goodwyn, Mills & Cawood, the economy impacted the rate at which architecture students in my area were being hired. I became distraught that I would not receive another internship for the remaining years I had left before graduation. The following two summers were spent working positions that were not architecture related; however, after attending the Career Track presentations led by Lee W. Waldrep, Ph.D., at the AIAS Grassroots Leadership Conference, I had a new perspective on the internship search. The information and tools we received were great ideas, and I took it upon myself to make it my top priority to have an internship, which turned into my position at Merrick and Company in summer 2012.

How have you become a leader during your undergraduate studies? In what organizations have you developed your leadership skills?

❭ During my first three years as an undergraduate student consisted of leadership through the university softball team. I had never really been the type of leader who led by voice, but rather actions. When games got tough, my performance always encouraged my fellow teammates, as I was the pitcher on the softball team.

In my fourth year, I became the president of the AIAS Tuskegee Chapter. What I thought would be just a position and a few meetings ended up turning my chapter and department around. I learned a tremendous amount about myself from this position. It also allowed me to plan events that gave hope to the student body through mentorship, networking, and internship opportunities.

For the first time, I attended national AIAS and NOMAS (National Organization of Minority Architects) conferences and noticed that there were other students out there who had the same passion as I did. National leaders started to take notice and sought me out at me as a prominent leader with the full capability to inspire and make change on both a local and national level. At that point my leadership grew from the local level to a national level. I was a part of the AIA Diversity and Inclusion Ambassador Program, AIA Council of Emerging Professionals, and student representative for the Tuskegee Architecture and Construction Alumni Association.

If you had asked me three years ago if I would have considered running for the national vice president of the AIAS, my answer probably would have been no. I honestly could not see myself possibly going for something as big as a national position. My primary goal when entering AIAS leadership was to get my local AIAS chapter on track and meeting student needs on a local level

Although local-level leadership is still my passion, AIAS as a national organization has given me the opportunity to become a spokesman on behalf of architecture students around the country. I look forward to the year ahead because it is truly an honor and an amazing opportunity.

What is the most/least satisfying part of being an architecture student?

❭ The most satisfying part of being an architecture student is the impact you can make on a community and the people affected. As an undergraduate student, I participated in Habitat for Humanity and design charrettes that literally gave life back to the people affected by the design and construction. Each of these community service activities made a lasting impact on the way I viewed architecture and its contribution to communities.

The least satisfying part of architecture is the time that it can take away from family and friends. Many times, I would return home for Thanksgiving, Christmas, and spring break just to find myself meeting a deadline for studio when I returned from school. The amount of time architecture takes often drains students to the point where some change their major.

What do you hope to be doing 5 to 10 years after graduation with regard to your career?

❭ Within 5 to 10 years, I will have gained my architecture license and will work for a firm specializing on commercial projects that impact the pride and attitudes of the community. I will also seek to obtain a master's degree in an architecture-related field in hopes to return back to the academic realm, impacting students' lives. Aside from the architectural profession, I would like to continue mentoring undergraduate students who participate in leadership roles pertaining to student organization involvement.

Landscape. Hand-Drawn Perspective by Jennifer Taylor at Tuskegee University.

According to the Directory of African American Architects (http://blackarch.uc.edu), there are about 300 female African American architects. As a graduating female African American with a degree in architecture, what are you thoughts on diversity in architecture?

❯ Personally, I feel obligated to obtain licensure and become a part of the growing number of female African American architects. By becoming an architect, I can add one more inspirational voice to all women and African Americans who wish to pursue architecture as a career.

Students of diverse backgrounds may become discouraged by the low percentages that represent their race in architecture. Because of this, some students and professionals find inspiration from others in organizations such as the National Organization of Minority Architects.

Students often learn from and relate better to fellow students than teachers. In the same way, people often learn and relate better to those who are most like themselves and have experienced similar things. One of my mentors, an African American woman, shared a story with me reflecting on an instance during undergraduate studies when a professor approached her to suggest changing her major on the first day of class when no assignment had been given and there was clearly no measure of potential. I find stories such as this one inspirational and encouraging; obstacles can be overcome.

Numbers will never lie, and as long as there are great marginal differences in numbers, the profession will never be as diverse as it should be. In a sense, diversity must become a mindset, and inclusion must become a living verb in order to learn from and celebrate contributions and impact everyone can have on the profession. The architectural profession, its organizations, and even educational settings must also set a standard of universality, appealing to all instead of a certain demographic.

Who or what experience has been a major influence on your career?

❯ Many individuals have influenced and watched over me throughout my career; however, two in particular have contributed to my overall success as a graduating senior. Vaughn Horn, AIA, NOMA, LEED AP (Tuskegee faculty, AIAS advisor, and 2012 AIAS Educator Honor Award) pushed me not only in the classroom but to excel through leadership in AIAS. Most notably, he believed in

me when I doubted my own ability to run for AIAS national vice president.

In the professional realm, Shavon Charlot, AIA, LEED AP BD+C, an African American architect and associate of Sherlock, Smith & Adams, Inc., became my mentor shortly after we met at the AIAS 2011 Career Fair at Auburn. Since then, Shavon has been a tremendous help with my goals as an architecture student and my pursuit of becoming a LEED Green Associate. Her dedication has shown me that there are architects out there who are willing to go the extra mile to ensure they set a great example for students pursuing architecture degrees and licensure. The fact that she is an African American woman who passed the license exam in six months is even more enlightening and inspiring. Many of the goals I set are because of her.

Architects as Public Artists

ROSANNAH B. SANDOVAL, AIA
Designer II
Perkins + Will
San Francisco, California

Why and how did you become an architect?

❯ Since I can remember, I cared about built things and the way light falls—about color and shapes and simplicity. Before I knew of "architecture" in the formal sense, I was drawn to the action of making and realizing ideas through materials. This is what sparked my passion, but what has kept me going is the impact that these elements can have on the user. It is this interaction and social dynamic that draws my exploration.

Why and how did you decide on which school to attend for your architecture degree? What degree(s) do you possess?

❯ My father was a pilot in the Air Force, and moving all over the country gave me a wide cultural perspective and a huge appreciation for context. I began architecture school in Alabama and finished in San Francisco at 18 years old. I chose Auburn University because of the Rural Studio, and family circumstances led to my transfer to California College of the Arts (CCA) in the third year. After obtaining my undergraduate degree, my goal was to gain professional experience and achieve licensure before returning to graduate school.

Wise people in my path advised me that in doing so, I would gain more out of the graduate-level experience and also have a nice shift back to conceptual thinking after a few years in practice. I have chosen to pursue a master of Architecture (post-professional) at Cooper Union because the Irwin S. Chanin School of Architecture embraces this

fundamental value—the exercise of individual creativity within a willing community is a profoundly social act. New York is my new laboratory for testing ideas and pushing boundaries through art in the form of buildings and the lives of the people who interact with them.

What was your experience at Auburn University and the Rural Studio? How did it differ from California College of the Arts?

❯ At Auburn, learning to be a citizen architect was one of the most valuable experiences in my education. Before a designer can propose a relevant concept, one must submerse into the context, be a participant in the community, and intimately appreciate the tools available to test ideas. The studios I took at CCA focused on context and process. I enjoyed the more theoretical approach and found my own expression in weaving big ideas with clear purpose.

◀Branching Systems: Architectural Prototypes. RENDERING BY ROSANNAH B. SANDOVAL AT CALIFORNIA COLLEGE OF THE ARTS.

▼Rural Studio—Second-Year House, Mason's Bend, Alabama. Studio Project by Rosannah B. Sandoval at Auburn University.

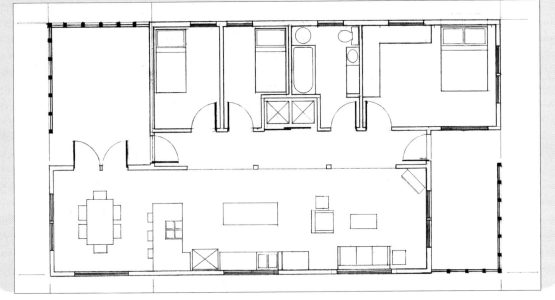

Calexico West Land Port of Entry, Calexico, California. Architect: Perkins + Will. MODEL RENDERING COURTESY OF PERKINS + WILL.

During your studies, you had the opportunity to travel abroad to Switzerland, Mexico, and Peru; describe these experiences and how they were helpful in your architectural studies.

❯ Travel is perhaps the best educational experience one can have. I recognized this early on and signed up for every opportunity available while as an undergraduate student. These studios always connected with a local university and embedded the project with an existing urban ecosystem. This took the notion of "Citizen Architect" to a whole new level for me. It is a very humbling experience to be in a place completely unfamiliar and as a designer, to be expected to propose an idea. It requires a great deal of observation and empathy—essential to creating architecture. Through my study abroad to Peru, I met my husband.

At 23, you are the youngest licensed architect in the AIA; how did you accomplish licensure at such a young age, and what does this mean to you?

❯ Licensure for me meant that I can be entrusted with the basic responsibilities of architecture—a milestone for obtaining the standard of the pro-

fession. My aim is to go above and beyond that standard, so right out of school I put my focus on becoming a sponge in the professional studio to absorb all the information I could to make that happen. And so I did. The process took over three years, and while it was tough to balance with work and life in general, it was so worth it. I think this accomplishment ties to a notion of self-investment and not letting standards get in the way of greatness. Getting licensed for me was proving to myself that I can do this and that my value to society starts here—a foundation that I can build upon.

What has been your greatest challenge as an architect thus far in your career?

❯ As I am still early in my career, I have faced similar challenges as my peers in this historically traditional profession. As a female architect, I think my generation has benefited greatly from the pioneers in our industry who have opened many doors for strong and talented female architects to become thought leaders in our industry. The struggle I face is staying true to myself, taking risks, and always questioning the problem.

Jones Neighborhood Nexus, San Francisco, California. Architect: Perkins + Will. STREET MURAL COURTESY OF PERKINS + WILL.

How do you use your advanced skills in 3D visualization and rapid prototyping? How are these skills changing the way architecture is practiced?

❯ The architectural design process is a constantly changing landscape shaped by tools that are available. Those who can fluidly work between these mediums are going to be more valuable in the future. The profession has been slow to adapt, since we have been building for thousands of years and these tools are relatively new. But as designers who grew up with touch screens and cloud computing become the leaders in our profession, I believe the landscape will drastically shift again and the language of communication will be more universal. What is crucial to point out: from the pencil to iPad to scripting—each of these are tools, meant to enable the designer to communicate ideas. Rather than allow the tool to create the design, the designer must edit the outcome.

What is the most satisfying part of your career as an architect?

❯ The thread that is common in all my studies is the emphasis on the people who inhabit the spaces we create. An architecture of responsiveness is more relevant to society than an experiment in formal expression. Formal beauty is even more exquisite when it is grown out of a feedback with the collective while gracefully reacting to individual factors. I have synthesized that architecture is in the beauty of clear ideas manifest in the spatial arrangement of the environment. The glorious intersection of design and humanity is the nexus that takes architecture beyond pure artistry of built form into the realm of social impact.

What are your 5-year and 10-year career goals relative to architecture?

❯ I hope my career will take me to uncharted territories. I imagine that will be hard in a field so defined and well trotted. Technology will always be a changing factor, and I want to leverage design technology as a catalyst for social change in urban environments. For the next year of graduate school I hope to immerse myself in design research and set up the focus for the next chapter in my career. A strong goal is to set something in motion that will long outlast me.

A.R.C.H.I.T.E.C.T.

By applying the skills you have learned as an architecture student to gaining experience, you will be able to design your own career rather than just letting it happen. Be creative in organizing your search for prospective employers. While not guaranteed, the following ideas, spelling the word architect, will assist you in gaining experience.

ASSESSMENT

The first step in gaining experience involves assessing yourself. Assess what aspect of architecture inspires you: programming, design, interior architecture, construction management, and so on. What do you want to do in an architecture firm? What are you able to offer a prospective employer? Ask yourself, "Why should this firm hire me?" Constantly evaluate your interests, abilities, and values and how they match those of your current or a prospective employer.

RESEARCH

Research is critical. What positions in an architecture firm can best utilize your skills and knowledge? What employers have such positions? Do not limit your search to the architecture profession; the best employment opportunities may be with an interior design firm, a construction firm, a government agency, a corporation, or an engineering firm. Again, be creative in your search.

CONNECTIONS

Connections are crucial to success. Regardless of the discipline, over 60 percent of all positions are obtained through networking. Consider adding no less than 10 names to your network monthly. Be sure to attend local AIA meetings, where you will meet architects in area firms. Listen. Learn. Talk. Remember, every conversation is a possible lead. The more ears and eyes you have looking out for the positions you want, the more likely it is that options will materialize.

The most effective method of learning of opportunities is networking, but most people, especially students, do not know what this is. Simply put, networking is informing people around you of your intent to gain experience and asking if they know of leads for you. In a school setting, you may network with classmates, professors, and staff. You may also approach guest lecturers or architects on your reviews. Ask if they hire students for the summer or for part-time positions. They may not be immediately responsive, so politely ask for a business card so you can follow up.

New sources available online to make connections include social media websites Facebook (www.facebook.com) and LinkedIn (www.linkedin.com). First, subscribe to these social media websites, but use them in strictly a professional, business-like manner. Once you have added your profile, you can search for individuals who have a connection to someone you are searching for. With LinkedIn, you can search by industry, school attended, or company to connect with future contacts.

HELP

You can get help with your search from a variety of sources. A good place to start is the university career center; a career counselor can help you target your job search. Along with the national AIA (http://careercenter.aia.org), many local AIA chapters post positions on the Web or allow you to post your resume. Public libraries are another valuable resource. You should also seek support from others, especially family and friends; talking to them can be a big boost to your job search.

Most architecture programs post positions that announce regional employment opportunities on an online system. When seeking students to perform entry-level tasks, many firms send schools a position announcement outlining job duties and responsibilities, qualifications, and contact information. Do not limit yourself to your own institution, especially if you wish to relocate.

If you determine that you either need or want to work part time while in school, use these postings as a first step to learn of opportunities, but do not stop there. Contact the local AIA chapter to learn if they accept listings from area firms. Some local AIA chapters collect resumes from individuals seeking employment and allow firms to review them.

INTERIM POSITIONS

If you are unable to secure your ideal position for the summer or after graduation, consider an *interim position* to develop skills and gain experience. An interim position provides you with related experience, but is only a stopgap solution; you have no intention of staying permanently. Ideally, interim jobs allow you to continue your search, network with a wide variety of people, and build up your skills.

TOOLS

Your resume, ability to write cover letters, portfolio, and ability to interview are critical to the job search. They are important tools for communicating yourself to potential employers. Are your tools in top form?

If not, practice your interviewing skills, rework your resume, or have someone critique your portfolio.

- *Resume:* As in any discipline, a resume is essential when conducting a search for experience. Keep your resume simple and straightforward. Provide information from your background and experiences that demonstrates your abilities. Do not be afraid to include skills learned from studio or other classroom projects under a section entitled "Course Projects." If you have not worked formally in an architectural office, promote your drawing, modeling or building, and design skills learned in studio.

    You can add graphics to your resume. With the ease of scanning drawings and using graphic publishing software, placing an image on your resume can be powerful; however, exercise caution, as the image may make reading the resume difficult. Rather than including graphics on your resume, you could create a one-page portfolio, sometimes referred to as a "viewsheet."

- *Cover letters:* Just as critical and often treated as an afterthought compared to resumes, cover letters are in fact your introduction to the prospective employer. Most cover letters consist of three paragraphs: The first introduces you and explains the purpose of the letter; the second sells your skill set and makes the case that you are a match for the employer, and the third provides the terms of follow-up. Be sure to address the letter to an individual, not "Dear Sir/ Madam." If you do not know the name of an individual, take the time to contact the firm and ask. Be persistent if the firm is reluctant to provide this information.

Finally, remember that the purpose of the resume and cover letter is to obtain an interview!

- *Portfolio:* Perhaps your portfolio is most important. As architecture is a visual discipline, the portfolio is a direct link between the employer and your skills. For this reason, you should provide images that demonstrate all of your architectural skills—drafting, model building, drawing, design, and so on. Also provide drawings from the beginning of one project's design process to the end. In other words, do not include only finished end-of-project drawings. The sequential drawings allow the employer to see your thought process as it relates to a design problem.

- *Interviewing:* Good interviewing skills can make the difference between receiving an offer and not. Prepare for an interview by researching the firm. Think what questions might be asked of you and what questions you might ask of the interviewer. Ideally, practice prior to your interview with a roommate, colleague, or friend.

EXPERIENCE

At this point in your career, you may feel you have little experience. However, keep in mind that in many cases employers are hiring your *potential*. If you do not have adequate experience, consider trying one of the following to obtain the necessary experience: part-time work, volunteer work, informal experiences, or temporary work. As a caution, do not work for free to gain experience.

COMMITMENT

Searching for a position that will give you experience can be a full-time task. Although you are busy with school commitments, you should devote every possible minute to your search; doing so will pay off. However, as with any project, break your job search down into smaller, manageable parts. Finalize your resume, research five firms, and contact three colleagues, instead of being paralyzed by the scope of the entire job search. If you have not already done so, start your search now! Do not wait until next week, next month, or your last semester of school.

EPIC Miami Hotel, Miami, Florida. Architect: Luis Revuelta. PHOTOGRAPHER: LEE W. WALDREP, Ph.D.

TRANSITION

Realize that you are going through a major life transition—that of entering the profession of architecture. Recognize that all aspects of your life will be affected. Summer vacations are a luxury of the past. Financial adjustments are necessary as you begin to receive a salary and acquire new expenses.

The job market may be challenging; therefore, be assertive, learn the search process, and do not fear rejection. Searching for a position is a skill you will use throughout your life.

> The answer, in a nutshell, is:
> Thru your research
> And then thru your contacts.
>
> RICHARD N. BOLLES

Moving toward Licensure

> Transition: n. The process or an instance of changing from one form, state, activity, or place to another. Passage from one form, state, activity, or place to another.[5]

Entry into the real world should be a time of excitement, enthusiasm, and exploration. For the time being, school is over and it is finally time for you to apply the knowledge and insights you acquired during all those hours of studio. A yearly salary ensures financial independence. All kinds of doors are opening, presenting a world of opportunities.

This transition from the world of education to your first career position is dramatic and perhaps challenging. Most college graduates are not fully prepared for the magnitude of the transitions and adjustments that must be made on virtually all fronts and are unaware of the consequences of not making these adjustments in a mature and speedy manner.

What a shock it can be when you, a new graduate, drop to the bottom rung of the career ladder. Just as a new college student has to learn the ropes of the new environment, the recent graduate starting a career position faces a whole new world. The challenges include maintaining a budget, dealing with your personal life, and adjusting to your first career position. The difficulty is that the real world is less tolerant of mistakes, offers less time and flexibility for adjustment, and demands performance for the pay it offers.

INTERN DEVELOPMENT PROGRAM (IDP)

Established jointly by the American Institute of Architects (AIA) and the National Council of Architectural Registration Boards (NCARB) in the late 1970s, the Intern Development Program (IDP) is designed to ease the transition from academia to the profession. In becoming an architect, the IDP is an essential step. All jurisdictions require a structured internship for a period of time as their training requirement, and most have adopted the IDP as the training requirement necessary for licensure. Become aware of IDP early in your academic career.

> Intern Development Program (IDP) identifies the comprehensive experience that is essential for competent practice; it is structured to prepare you to practice architecture independently upon initial registration.
>
> IDP GUIDELINES, DECEMBER 2013[6]

In 2010, the NCARB transitioned to IDP 2.0 to ensure that interns acquire the comprehensive training that is essential for competent practice and make reporting experience easier. To fully complete the IDP, the intern must complete a total of 5,600 hours across four experience categories and 17 experience areas. If working full time, you could complete the requirements for IDP in slightly less than three years; however, according to the NCARB in its annual publication, *NCARB by the Numbers 2013*, the mean time to complete the IDP is 5.33 years.[7] For the most up-to-date information on the IDP, visit the NCARB website (www.ncarb.org/idp).

The foundation of the program is the requirements for experience areas.

1. Category 1: Pre-Design
2. Category 2: Design
3. Category 3: Project Management
4. Category 4: Practice Management

Each of these experience categories is divided into experience areas (see the sidebar "Intern Development Program (IDP) Experience Categories and Areas").

You earn experience under the direct supervision of a qualified professional. The IDP Guidelines provides a detailed definition of each experience category and area as well as the IDP tasks and knowledge/skills that you should be able to perform at the completion of the internship phase of your career.

Just as critical are the experience settings in which you can gain experience. Experience Setting A: Practice of Architecture is the one experience setting with no limit as to the number of hours working under the direct supervision of a licensed architect. Experience Setting O: Other Work Settings has a maximum and includes working in an organization whose practice does not encompass the comprehensive practice of architecture, working for a firm outside the United States or Canada, gaining experience related to architecture under a registered engineer or registered landscape architect; for more details, review the *IDP Guidelines.*

A new development within the IDP is academic internships. An academic internship is any internship that is integrated into an academic program, whether it is a requirement or an elective. If it includes experience in Experience Setting A or O, it may earn credit for the IDP while earning academic credit at the same time.

Experience Setting S: Supplemental Experience allows opportunities to earn experience outside a traditional work setting. Also, many of the supplemental experience opportunities may be completed whether employed or not. Examples of Supplemental Experience include (1) Leadership and Service, (2) Community-Based Design Center, (3) CSI Certification Programs, (4) Design Competitions, (5) Emerging Professional's Companion (EPC; discussed later in this chapter), and (6) Site Visit with Mentor.

An integral part of the IDP is the mentorship system. Within the IDP, you have access to two individuals who assist you with your work experience and career plans. The supervisor is typically your immediate supervisor in your place of employment, while your mentor is an architect outside your firm with whom you meet periodically to discuss your career path.

As part of the IDP, the intern is solely responsible for maintaining a continuous record of experience using the electronic Experience Verification Reporting system (e-EVR) to enhance the delivery of reports by interns. The report identifies areas where experience has been acquired. For supervisors, it is an assessment and personnel management tool; for state registration boards, it is verified evidence of compliance with the IDP training requirements. Also, the NCARB has established the six-month rule that requires interns to submit their experience in reporting periods of no longer than six months and within two months of completion of each period.

Updated in 2013, the Emerging Professional Companion (EPC)[8] (http://epcompanion.org) is an online professional development tool for interns on their path to licensure. Intended as a means for interns to earn IDP credit, the EPC is broken into chapters that parallel the experience areas of the IDP. Other resources available to assist in you navigating the IDP are both the state and educator IDP coordinator, both of whom are available to answer questions on the program and connect you with possible mentors.

In a recent discussion with an intern-architect a few years out of school, she confessed that while architecture school prepared her to think and design, it did not sufficiently prepare her to work in an architectural office. She further admitted that the IDP, with its experience areas, simply lists what you need to do. Asked for advice to give current students of architecture, she replied, "Take a chance, take a risk, and enroll in the IDP now while you are still in school."

Regardless of your academic level, take the first step to learning about the IDP by contacting the NCARB to request an information packet and apply online to begin an NCARB Council Record. Begin the transition now; do not wait until graduation.

ARCHITECT REGISTRATION EXAMINATION (ARE)

Developed and administered by the NCARB, the last step in becoming an architect is taking and passing the Architect Registration Examination (ARE). It is an essential step in becoming an architect, as every U.S. jurisdiction requires interns to pass the ARE to satisfy its examination requirements. Its purpose is "to determine if an applicant has the minimum knowledge, skills, and abilities to practice architecture independently while safeguarding the public health, safety, and welfare." It does not measure whether you are a good architect but rather your ability to practice architecture.

INTERN DEVELOPMENT PROGRAM (IDP) EXPERIENCE CATEGORIES AND AREAS

CATEGORY 1: PRE-DESIGN (260)[a]

Programming (80): The process of discovering the owner/client's requirements and desires for a project and setting them down in written, numerical, and graphic form.

Site and Building Analysis (80): Involves research and evaluation of a project's context and may include site and building evaluation, land planning or design, and urban planning.

Project Cost and Feasibility (40): Analyze and/or establish project costs relative to project conditions and owner's budget

Planning and Zoning Regulations (60): Evaluate, reconcile, and coordinate applicable regulatory requirements and professional design standards.

CATEGORY 2: DESIGN (2,600)

Schematic Design (320): Involves the development of graphic and written conceptual design solutions for the owner/client's approval.

Engineering Systems (360): Involves selecting and specifying structural, mechanical, electrical, and other systems, and integrating them into the building design. These systems are normally designed by consultants in accordance with the client's needs.

Construction Cost (120): Involves estimating the probable construction cost of a project.

Codes and Regulations (120): Involves evaluating a specific project in the context of relevant local, state, and federal regulations that protect public health, safety, and welfare.

Design Development (320): During design development, a project's schematic design is refined, including designing details and selecting materials. This step occurs after the owner/client approves the schematic design.

Construction Documents (1,200): Includes the written and graphic instructions used for construction of the project. These documents must be accurate, consistent, complete, and understandable.

Material Selection and Specification (160): The analysis and selection of building materials and systems for a project. The materials specified for a particular project communicate the requirements and quality expected during construction. Specifications are included in a project manual that is used during bidding and construction.

CATEGORY 3: PROJECT MANAGEMENT (720)

Bidding and Contract Negotiation (120): Involves the establishment and administration of the bidding process, issuing of addenda, evaluation of proposed substitutions, review of the bidder qualifications, analysis of bids, and selection of the contractor(s).

Construction Administration (240): Tasks carried out in the architect's office include facilitating project communication, maintaining project records, reviewing and certifying amounts due contractors, and preparing change orders.

Construction Phase—Observation (120): Tasks carried out in the field include observing construction for conformity with drawings and specifications and reviewing and certifying amounts due to contractors.

General Project Management (240): Includes planning, organizing, and staffing; budgeting and scheduling; leading and managing the project team; documenting key project information; and monitoring quality assurance.

CATEGORY 4: PRACTICE MANAGEMENT (160)

Business Operations (80): Involves allocation and administration of office resources to support the goals of the firm.

Leadership and Service (80): These tasks will increase your understanding of the people and forces that shape society, as well as augment your professional knowledge and leadership skills. Interns will find that voluntary participation in professional and community activities enhances their professional development. Community service does not have to be limited to architecture-related activities for volunteers to accrue these benefits.

[a]Numbers in parentheses refer to minimum hours of experience required; total IDP training units required equals 5,600.

Source: National Council of Architectural Registration Boards, *Intern Development Program Guidelines*, pp. 12, 22–32, December 2013.

Since 1997, candidates have taken the ARE exclusively by computer for all divisions. This newer format generates a more comprehensive and efficient exam that more accurately measures a candidate's ability in a shorter period than traditional methods. In addition, the automated exam allows for more frequent and flexible testing opportunities, a more relaxed testing environment, faster score reporting, and greater testing security.

A more recent development is that not quite half the states allow early eligibility for the ARE. While it varies by jurisdiction, candidates enrolled in the IDP can take divisions of the ARE prior to the completion of the IDP; in many cases, the candidate must have completed the National Architectural Accrediting Board (NAAB)-accredited degree. Be sure to check with the NCARB and your state registration board for exact requirements, but early eligibility will reduce the time it takes to complete both the IDP and the ARE. However, note that you will not be licensed as an architect until both are completed.

Under the terms of the rolling clock, candidates for the ARE must pass all of the divisions within five years. The five-year time limit begins on the date when the first passed division is administered. By virtue of this rule, candidates will need to be more diligent in scheduling the exam.

Old South Church in Boston, Architects: Charles Amos Cummings and Willard T. Sears. PHOTOGRAPHER: LEE W. WALDREP, Ph.D.

ARE 4.0 consists of the following seven divisions:

Programming Planning and Practice

Site Planning and Design

Building Design and Construction Systems

Schematic Design

Structural Systems

Building Systems

Construction Documents & Services

To begin, read the ARE Guidelines available from the NCARB (http://ncarb.org/are); aside from the guidelines, the website has detailed ARE study aids, including sample multiple-choice questions, one passing and one failing solution for each sample vignette, and a list of references for further study. Also, download the practice software used by the ARE. The NCARB also publishes the pass rates by division and by NAAB-accredited programs of architecture.

Launching in late 2016, the NCARB has plans for the ARE (ARE 5.0), namely, new question types, elimination of computer-aided design (CAD) software, and increased agility and efficiency. The new divisions will be as follows:

Practice Management

Project Management

Programming and Analysis

Project Planning and Design

Project Development and Documentation

Construction and Evaluation

NCARB CERTIFICATE

Once licensed as an architect, you may wish to become licensed in additional states. To do so, consider obtaining an NCARB certificate to facilitate licensure in other states, a process known as reciprocity. The first step is to establish an NCARB Council Record, which you would have done for initial registration. Once you complete the requirements for the NCARB certificate—earning an NAAB- or Canadian Architectural Certification Board (CACB)-accredited degree, fulfilling the requirements of the IDP, and passing the seven divisions of the ARE—you can apply for registration from other states as needed to practice architecture. Based on the most recent NCARB survey of registered architects, on average, architects are registered in two jurisdictions. There are 121,535 reciprocal (out-of-state) registrants and 227,382 total registrations in the United States.

Conclusion

As you have learned, experience is a vital step in becoming an architect. Begin to gain experience in the profession as soon as possible by shadowing an architect in high school, completing an internship, or pursuing a summer position while in college. In addition, your experience after you complete your professional degree will play an important role in your future career. Choose wisely.

Baptism by Fire

ROBERT D. ROUBIK, AIA, LEED AP

Project Architect

Antunovich Associates Architects and Planners

Chicago, Illinois

Why and how did you become an architect?

❯ Growing up, I had an affinity for art and I was very detail oriented. I liked to draw and was an avid model builder. My friends and I used to build model rockets, and I took great care in the craftsmanship of each model and would spend hours meticulously refining their construction. I was equally concerned about how the collection was presented in my room, as each model rocket was hung from the ceiling in a location based on the proportions of the overall collection.

When I went to college, I started out in the College of Engineering and transferred into the Architecture School a year later—not necessarily because I wanted to be an architect, but because I knew that I did not want to be an engineer. At that time, I was still uncertain about what career I wanted to pursue. However, when I took my first architectural studio course, one of the first principles that the instructor taught us was the importance of presentation, proportion, and attention to detail in architecture. It was almost like a light bulb went on, and it seemed like a natural fit for me. It was soon apparent that architecture was the direction that my career should be headed.

Catholic Theological Union, Chicago. Architect: Antunovich Associates Architects and Planners. PHOTOGRAPHER: SEBASTIAN RUT.

Why and how did you decide on which schools to attend for your architecture degrees? What degree(s) do you possess?

❭ My home state university, the University of Colorado at Boulder (CU), is a very well respected public university that has one of the most beautiful campuses in the country. For these reasons, in addition to receiving in-state tuition, I had always planned to attend CU. It was here that I received a bachelor of environmental design with an emphasis in architecture. After I finished my pre-professional degree at CU, I decided that I wanted to pursue my professional degree at a school that had very different strengths. I also wanted to study in an urban center, since I was aware that most architectural graduates ended up practicing in close proximity to where they attended school—and cities offered more opportunities for architects.

Although I had visited Chicago only a few times in my life, I knew that it had a great architectural history and tradition. In addition, my father was originally from Chicago, and moving there would give me the opportunity to reconnect with some family that I did not know very well. I applied and was fortunate enough to receive a scholarship that allowed me to attend the Illinois Institute of Technology (IIT). While I did not know a great deal about the school prior to attending, I was aware of the legacy of Mies van der Rohe and had studied Crown Hall in my architectural history courses at CU. At IIT, I received my master of architecture degree.

With over 10 years of experience in the discipline, how will your career continue to progress, and what do you foresee as challenges moving forward?

❭ I will continue to work on increasingly more complex projects while helping my office transition to the use of BIM (building information modeling) to design and document them. My career progression will include the expansion of my leadership role— not only on the individual projects themselves but within our office as a whole. A big challenge for me will continue to be finding a balance between my professional and personal lives, which includes raising two small children with my wife.

Catholic Theological Union, Chicago. Illinois. Architect: Antunovich Associates Architects and Planners. RENDERING COURTESY OF ANTUNOVICH ASSOCIATES.

What has been your greatest challenge as an architect?

❭ During a stretch of about 18 months from 2001 to 2002, I experienced my first economic downturn as an architect. The office where I was working, which six months earlier had been bustling with activity and more work than we could handle, suddenly did not have enough work to sustain the current staff. In that time period, I witnessed five rounds of layoffs and a 40 percent reduction in staff. It was very disheartening to watch qualified and capable colleagues lose their jobs. This made for an uneasy working environment—since it was never clear when another round of layoffs would occur and who would be targeted. I have since experienced another economic cycle and was much better prepared for the layoffs that accompanied the resulting downturn.

Why did you pursue becoming a LEED AP Professional?

❭ As an architect, I feel that it is our responsibility to do our part to help the environment by designing energy-efficient buildings. In addition, with the advancement of energy codes, sustainable design is going to evolve from an ethical decision to a legal obligation.

What are your primary responsibilities and duties as a project architect?

❭ Currently, I am the project architect for a new School of Music on the DePaul University Lincoln Park campus. I have been involved with the project since conceptual design and will continue to develop and document the design through the permitting, bidding, and construction phases. I supervise several staff architects assigned to the project and am the primary point of contact with both the owner and contractor. I also lead the coordination effort among members of our extensive consultant team.

What is the most/least satisfying part of your career as an architect?

❭ The most satisfying part of being an architect is seeing our work get built. The process of designing a building can be an arduous, painstaking, stressful

DePaul University School of Music, Chicago, Illinois. Architect: Antunovich Associates Architects and Planners.
PHOTOGRAPHER: SEBASTIAN RUT.

one—and what makes it all worthwhile is to see the tangible fruits of our labor.

The least satisfying part of being an architect is the compensation. Although it is improving, the pay is not always commensurate with the time, responsibility, and stress that are an integral part of an architect's daily work life.

Who or what experience has been a major influence on your career?

❯ The most influential experience of my career so far has been my first project functioning in the role of project architect (PA). I had been working as a staff architect on a team of four on the schematic design of an institutional project called the Catholic Theological Union (CTU). A staff architect typically works on the design and documentation of individual components of a building, but ultimately the PA leads the team and is responsible for all drawing issues and construction administration.

About midway through the permit process, the PA for the project left the firm to pursue other opportunities and my boss asked me to be the lead. Suddenly, I was thrust into an unfamiliar role, with responsibilities that were new to me. It was "baptism by fire." Somehow, I got through it and completed the project—which turned out to be very successful in terms of client satisfaction, budget, and schedule. The time period from when I took over as PA to the completion of construction was about two years—and it was the most stressful time in my professional life. However, I have no regrets, as the CTU experience enabled me to gain the experience and confidence necessary for helping me to grow as an architect.

Learning How the Real World Works

AMANDA STRAWITCH

Level 1 Architect

Design Collective, Inc.

Baltimore, Maryland

Why did you become an architect?

❯ In high school, I took an architectural drafting class with a free-thinking teacher that I really admired. Instead of listening to him lecture for an hour, we were sketching ideas and building models. As an academically oriented student who always thought inside the box, I was pushed by him to look at the world in a new way and solve problems that I had never encountered in my other classes. I saw a career in architecture as a chance for me to be creative, fully engaged, and critically thinking—all things I knew I wanted in my future profession. Three people in that small class went into architecture and several became engineers—the sign of an inspiring teacher!

Why did you decide to choose the school that you did—the University of Maryland? What degree do you possess?

❯ I have a bachelor of science in architecture from the University of Maryland. Maryland seemed like a great choice because it provided me with the best of both worlds—a large state university with endless opportunities and a small school of architecture with intimate class sizes. The University of Maryland is also well known for having great tuition, and I knew that saving money in tuition would allow me to pursue other things, like study abroad.

In school, you studied abroad in Italy; how did this experience prove valuable to your education?

❯ Some of my favorite classes in college were architectural history classes—history seemed to make more sense when in the context of architecture. When I heard about the archaeological dig in Stabia, I immediately signed up. I cannot honestly say that this trip helped me in my studio architec-

McDonogh School (Allan, Burck, and Lyle Buildings). Owings Mills, Maryland. Architect: Design Collective, Inc. WATERCOLOR RENDERING: STEWART WHITE, DESIGN COLLECTIVE, INC.

ture classes, but it was so enriching in other ways. We found hundreds of Roman artifacts, roamed the streets of Pompeii, and met a bunch of amazing people in the process. It was a great cultural experience for me and gave my life a bit more perspective.

Why did you choose to enter the work force after your undergraduate degree instead of directly attending a graduate program? When do you plan to continue your studies?

❭ This was a very difficult decision for me since many of my peers continued on to graduate school, and I questioned my decision frequently. I was worried about finding a job since a BS in architecture is not very competitive.

During my senior year, I talked to many graduate students at Maryland, and several who went directly to graduate school said that they were burnt out and tired of school. After much thought, I decided that I would gain more out of my graduate degree program if I had some time off to breathe and was ready and excited to go back to school. Having a few years of work under my belt will hopefully make some classes go more smoothly, too. I also considered the fact that working first would allow me to take out fewer loans and not start my adult life in debt. I plan to apply to graduate programs within the next two years, but am also aware that life has a mind of its own. It feels great to have some flexibility.

In your position at Design Collective, Inc., what are your primary responsibilities and duties?

❭ My responsibilities vary greatly depending on the scale of the project on which I am working. On some of the smaller projects, I have had the opportunity to contribute to the floor plans and design of the building, as well as develop renderings of both interior and exterior design options. On larger projects, I support the design team by drawing

Orthopaedic Associates of Central Maryland. Catonsville, Maryland. Architect: Design Collective, Inc. RENDERING: AMANDA STRAWITCH, DESIGN COLLECTIVE, INC.

section and plan details, creating needed schedules, and coordinating with consultants.

As one who recently graduated, what has been your greatest challenge thus far as an intern?

❭ As someone who feels like a very competent and confident person, it has been a challenge to enter a firm of over 70 bright and talented designers and have the least experience. As the youngest person in the office, it is sometimes hard to feel confident when you know you have no experience in what you're doing every day. I have worked at Design Collective, Inc. for just over seven months now, and that fear of making a mistake is slowly subsiding as I realize that's part of the learning process. I know that I offer a different skill set than some of my more experienced peers, and that is the skill of using new technology to speed up the design and documentation process.

What is the most/least satisfying part of a career as an architect?

❯ As part of the generation that entered the field during the housing crisis, the least satisfying aspects of a career in architecture are obvious—hours are long, jobs are scarce, budgets are low and restrict design, and compensation for your contributions are limited. The most satisfying parts of architecture are working with other people to create something that satisfies a need and seeing it built. Through school, travel, and my first position, I have been exposed to many great buildings to study and learn from. I have also found the amount I learn every day to be very rewarding. Within just a few months, I already have a much better idea of how a building is put together and the various steps and people involved in the process.

What are your 5-year and 10-year career goals relative to architecture?

❯ In the next 5 years, I want to obtain my master of architecture degree or one in a related field and begin the ARE. Within 10 years, I hope to be an integral member of a firm who is able to influence the design and technologies used in projects. I also hope to travel the world and study the architecture and lifestyle of other countries.

I see many possibilities with my degree at this point. The field of architecture is changing so much and niches in adaptive reuse and green building have formed and will become larger parts of the profession. As a very goal-oriented person, it is odd for me to have such nonspecific goals right now, but I just feel like I have so many options and all the time in the world to choose my path.

Who or what experience has been a major influence on your career?

❯ I lucked into the most influential experience of my life. When I was in high school, my mom became friends with a coworker whose father was the president of an architecture firm. Because she knew

Rudy's Café, Robert H. Smith School of Business, University of Maryland. College Park, Maryland. Architect: Design Collective, Inc. WATERCOLOR RENDERING: STEWART WHITE, DESIGN COLLECTIVE, INC.

I was interested in the profession but knew little about it, she helped me set up an appointment. One day after school, I went with her to visit the firm and was in awe. The models, drawings, and office space inspired me to pursue architecture in college.

Throughout all of college, I had the goal of working for this firm that first inspired me to become an architect, and I am very pleased to say that this firm was Design Collective, Inc. It feels great to be a part of the team now.

Architecture as an Art and Science

AMY PERENCHIO, AIA, LEED AP BD+C
Associate
ZGF Architects, LLP
Portland, Oregon

Why did you become an architect?

❭ I came to architecture in the second year of my university career because my first major, physics, did not provide the kind of creative outlet I needed. I had friends in the architecture program and thought their assignments looked like a ton of fun. I have found that architecture is the perfect opportunity to combine art and science, and to think creativity and logically to solve problems.

Why did you decide to choose the schools that you did—Washington State University and University of Oregon—to attend for your architecture degree(s)? What degrees do you possess? Why did you attend different institutions for your degrees?

❭ I chose Washington State University because it provides a high-quality and well-rounded education. My parents and grandparents are also alumni, so you could say it was an easy choice.

I chose to attend another university for graduate studies because I wanted to broaden my educa-

Arc de Triomphe, Paris, France. Architect: Jean Chalgrin. PHOTOGRAPHER: AMY PERENCHIO.

tion. I attended the University of Oregon's Portland Program because it was complementary to my experience at Washington State University. At the time, the master of architecture program had a focus on urban architecture (design and planning) and sustainability—both of which were topics I wanted to study in more depth.

Villa Savoye, Poissy, France.
Architect: Le Corbusier.
PHOTOGRAPHER: AMY
PERENCHIO.

Why did you choose to pursue the 4+2 year master of architecture degree?

❯ I switched majors into architecture at a university that only offered a four+two-year track. Instead of transferring to a five-year bachelor of architecture program elsewhere, I decided to stay in the pre-professional program and pursue my master of architecture afterward.

Currently, you serve as a director on the National Architectural Accrediting Board; from your perspective, what is accreditation, and why is it important for students to know about it?

❯ Accreditation is a quality assurance process. It ensures that students graduate with a minimum required knowledge set to become an architect. Accreditation is important for students to know about because it directly impacts them. In most jurisdictions, an NAAB-accredited degree is a pre-requisite for licensure.

What has been your greatest challenge as an architect thus far?

❯ My greatest challenge as an architect thus far has been appreciating a work-life balance. I absolutely love what I do for a living. Finding ways to comple-ment my career with other fun things outside of ar-chitecture has been a big challenge but also the most rewarding experience I've had as an intern. Allowing myself to enjoy time outside of the office has allowed me to live more fully, lower my stress, and perform at a much higher level when I am at work.

What is the most satisfying part of a career as an architect?

❯ The most satisfying part of a career as an architect is that our ideas and hard work manifest themselves in reality. The Emery, a mixed-use residential build-ing in the South Waterfront of Portland, is the first project on which I have participated in the design process from start to finish. It is currently under construction, and each time I see it, I am amazed at how the walls and spaces we conceived of become tangible objects. Most of the spaces are just as I had imagined they would be, and others become a lesson for future projects. Being able to physically inhabit a space that I have designed and drawn is an amaz-ingly rewarding and learning experience.

What are your 5-year and 10-year career goals relative to architecture?

❯ In my career thus far, I have made the right deci-sions at critical junctures that have landed me where

◄ The Emery, Portland, Oregon. Architect: ZGF Architects, LLP. RENDERING: ZGF ARCHITECTS, LLP.

▼ The Emery, Portland, Oregon. Architect: ZGF Architects, LLP. PHOTOGRAPHER: AMY PERENCHIO.

I am today. I have general ideas of what I would like in my career, but I won't limit them to a time frame. For instance, I know that I want to be in a firm-wide management role, to be a meaningful mentor and someone who helps others excel in their architectural careers—but whether these are 2 or 10 years in my future is not known yet.

Who or what experience has been a major influence on your career?

❯ My experience on the National AIAS and NAAB boards has shaped me personally and professionally in more ways than I can list here. Through my involvement in both organizations, I have been able to grow my perspective and gain a new appreciation for the profession.

Gene Sandoval, my mentor and Partner at ZGF, has been a major influence on my career. His careful prodding and expectation for high design thinking has significantly impacted my growth. From him, I have learned that buildings, like stories, need to be crafted with the utmost care.

Realizing a Vision

JESSICA L. LEONARD, ASSOCIATE AIA, LEED AP BD+C

Associate, Campus Planner/Intern Architect
Ayer Saint Gross Architects and Planners
Baltimore, Maryland

Why and how did you become an architect?

❯ My father is a landscape architect so I have always been surrounded by design. When I was a senior in high school, I was on a bus to a soccer game and looked out the window and saw a historic building with a beautiful courtyard. I decided that day that I wanted to create places like that. I now look at "becoming an architect" as a way to create beautiful, socially responsible places for people—architects are able to help people make their vision a reality. I believe we can be a voice and provide a vision for communities that otherwise wouldn't be heard.

Why and how did you decide on which school to attend for your architecture degree? What degree(s) do you possess?

❯ I received a bachelor of science in architecture and a master of architecture from the University of Maryland (UMD), College Park. When choosing a school for my undergraduate architecture education, I knew I wanted to attend a four-year program (four+two) in order to have a balanced liberal arts and architecture education. In addition to having a strong architecture program, it was important for me to be at a university that offered a wide variety of extracurricular activities and programs. UMD had the benefit of being a large institution with a small architecture program. The intimate academic experience and one-on-one relationships with faculty provided the ideal learning environment. The relationships with faculty, focus on urban design, and the school's proximity to Baltimore and DC (physical and professional) prompted me to stay at Maryland for my graduate studies.

Glass Museum, Section Model by Jessica Leonard at the University of Maryland.

Reestablishing Community: A Renewed Village Center for Edmondson Village, Baltimore, Maryland. Thesis by Jessica Leonard at the University of Maryland

What led you to pursue an urban design certificate? How does your work with ASG incorporate urban design?

❭ It became clear to me by the end of my undergraduate education that my interest and skills were in large-scale design—understanding a site, transportation, access, program, and schematic design from a 20,000-foot view compared to the ground. Pursuing the urban design certificate allowed me to take focused classes outside of architecture to expand my knowledge of community design and understanding the relationship between people and architecture. Most of all, taking the urban design certificate and working on my thesis gave me the technical skills and knowledge to design and plan in the urban environment.

Working in the planning studio at ASG requires me to understand a large site (campus) from 20,000 feet in the air. While not all of the projects that I

work on are in an urban setting, the same principles of analysis and design apply. It is necessary to understand circulation patterns (both vehicular and pedestrian), the open space network, land use, constraints, and opportunities when you are designing in any environment or at any scale. The classes I took at UMD to obtain the urban design certificate led me to focus on this level of analysis in greater detail, which has resulted in a natural transition into planning at ASG.

What are your primary responsibilities and duties?

❭ In the past few years, my career focus has been on bridging the gap between planning and architecture. I still work on various aspects of planning, including area plans, land use studies, campus zoning, impact analysis, transportation, public/ private development, and demographic and economic studies, but there is a greater focus on space planning, programming, and migration studies. The scale of these projects can be from 20,000 feet in the air down to analyzing and documenting a single room and its equipment. Helping an institution better understand how they currently use their space and how it can be used more efficiently in the future is an exciting part of what I do. These studies often become the pre-planning work for a building project, which can quickly move into the programming and schematic design phase.

What has been your greatest challenge as an intern thus far?

❯ Balance. Advancing in your career is exciting but comes with new challenges. Since I love what I do, it is easy to get absorbed in projects and deadlines.

I have to remember to make time for the other things I am passionate about, both personally and professionally.

Also, the path to licensure is not easy. It requires focus, discipline, and advocating for yourself. ASG is a great firm that encourages its employees to get licensed and provides resources to help with the process. In the first few years at ASG, I was able to complete my IDP by regularly meeting with project managers and the leadership of the firm to ensure that I was getting the experience I needed. I am currently in the middle of taking my AREs and hope to complete them in the next two years. Finding the time to study has been the most challenging part of the process so far, but I believe the reward of licensure is worth it!

Loyola University Maryland Master Plan, Baltimore, Maryland. Architect: Ayers Saint Gross Architects and Planners. PLAN GRAPHIC BY AYERS SAINT GROSS ARCHITECTS AND PLANNERS.

Donnelly Hall, Loyola University Maryland, Baltimore, Maryland. Architect: Ayers Saint Gross Architects and Planners. PHOTOGRAPHER: TOM HOLDSWORTH PHOTOGRAPHY. © 2011 TOM HOLDWORTH.

What are your 5-year and 10-year career goals relative to architecture?

❯ I was fortunate to be promoted to an associate at ASG in less than five years. In the next two years I hope to finish my remaining ARE exams and become a licensed architect. I want continue to gain project management experience and learn more about the "business of architecture." Professionally, it is important for me to stay active in the Baltimore community and larger architecture community. Taking leadership roles in local design, transportation, and planning initiatives as well as mentoring future designers (high school and college students) are important goals for my career.

What is the most/least satisfying part of your career as an architect?

❯ The most satisfying part of being an architect is helping people realize their vision. As architects and planners, we get to be advocates for our clients and help bring their ideas into a reality. Finding ways to communicate complicated information to diverse audiences is both challenging and rewarding. I am always pushing myself to develop better graphics and presentations. Having a career that I thoroughly enjoy and keeps challenging me is very satisfying.

Working in the planning studio allows me to travel to colleges, universities, and institutions around the country—being around an intellectual environment and seeing so many diverse places is definitely a highlight of my job. Plus, I get to work with great colleagues and clients, which is a great bonus!

Who or what experience has been a major influence on your career?

❯ There have been many people and experiences that have influenced my career and helped me reach my goals, but two major influences were the faculty and my assistantship at Maryland and my current boss and mentors.

Throughout my education I was fortunate to have faculty that encouraged me to explore my interests and highlighted my strengths (even when I didn't realize them). I had an assistantship as an academic advisor and recruitment chair. Through that experience, I had constant interaction with people, gave presentations to large and small groups, and helped create and pull together marketing materials for the school. I never realized until I started working how

important that experience was. I developed communication skills and a comfort level speaking in front of people that has been a huge advantage in my career.

Now, as a professional, I realize the importance of surrounding yourself with supportive, inspiring, and creative people. I am fortunate to have a great mentor and boss who inspire me each day. Working with them has accelerated my professional growth and helped me focus on my future career goals.

A Practice of Involvement and Research

JOSEPH MAYO
Intern Architect
Mahlum
Seattle, Washington

Why did you become an architect?

❯ For me, becoming an architect seemed like the best way to create positive change in my city and my world. Architects have a very tangible impact on our environment, and this was appealing to me. Simply, I wanted to create places that could improve the world around me. I also have been an avid sketcher since childhood, drawn to art and graphic design, so architecture seemed like a logical path. My family also thought that architecture would be a good career choice, so I finally decided to listen to them for a change.

Why did you choose the school that you did to attend for your architecture degree? What degrees do you possess?

❯ I have a three-year master of architecture. I chose to study at the University of Oregon because I felt connected to the Pacific Northwest and wanted to

study in a place that would connect design with the physical landscape I loved so much. I had attended the University of Washington for my undergraduate degree in communications and wanted to stay in the Pacific Northwest for graduate studies. Because a part of my family is from Eugene, Oregon, attending school there felt like a homecoming of sorts, and it also allowed me to stay in the Northwest, be at a different school, and be enrolled in a professional degree program. Also, the University of Oregon was well known for combining architecture with research in sustainability and passive design, which further inspired me to attend school here.

With a previous degree in communications, what prompted you to pursue architecture?

❯ As an undergraduate, I was torn between choosing a degree in writing and in visual arts, both of which I loved. Specifically, I considered either journalism or graphic design. However, I knew that I did not really want to be a newspaper reporter, and I thought that a degree in graphic design would not be marketable. In retrospect, both of these instincts were wrong,

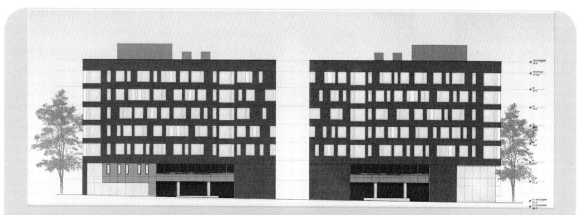

Cedar Apartments Elevation, Seattle, Washington. Architect: Mahlum. PHOTOGRAPHER: MAHLUM.

but nevertheless I chose communications because it seemed to offer the potential for combination of the written word and visual communications.

This combination of the two things I loved was very appealing to me. After graduation, I felt like my degree did not provide me with tangible skills, so I started my own personal journey to gather as many "real-world" skills as possible. It was this process of learning more about myself and my own interests that pushed me to architecture. Serving on two Americorps service terms also influenced my decision for architecture, which seemed like a continuation of the environmental and social responsibility I learned while participating in these volunteer service roles. The process of choosing architecture was part of a long personal discovery process that came to fruition from real-world work experience and personal contemplation, rather than an "aha" moment.

What are your primary responsibilities as an intern architect at Mahlum?

❭ My primary responsibilities at Mahlum are mixed and based on project needs. Therefore, my duties often change and I am called upon for a variety of tasks. At the start of projects, I am often involved in proposals for graphic support and conceptual digital modeling and diagrams as well as building physical models. However, I generally stay on projects from start to finish, providing me experience with all phases of the design and construction process. As a project progresses, I am often involved with daylight and sun-shading studies, CAD documentation, and some consultant coordination. Visualization remains one of my primary responsibilities throughout a project. Demonstrating curiosity and passion for a particular aspect of the architectural workflow is a good way to gain more exposure. I find that curiosity and passion are key for growth in the field and demonstrating capacity for leadership within the firm.

Since graduation, you had the opportunity to study abroad thanks to an AIA Seattle Emerging Professionals Travel Scholarship; can you provide details to this experience, and how it has helped your career?

❭ The Seattle AIA Travel Scholarship has helped my career in countless ways. For the scholarship I traveled through Canada and Europe to study new trends in timber architecture, manufacturing, and

Poplar Hall Elevation,
Seattle, Washington.
Architect: Mahlum.
PHOTOGRAPHER:
MAHLUM.

engineering. The AIA provided a legitimacy to the study, and through this I was able to meet several of the most important international leaders in this bourgeoning field.

Many of these ideas and ways of building are simply not present in the United States. From this travel I was able to take these fresh ideas back to Seattle and present them to the Seattle design community, furthering the dialogue on design and sustainability in the city. My travels also led to presenting my research to members of the Seattle City Council and the creation of a new City Task Force investigating the building code implications of new wood building techniques. Connecting advances in architecture with city policy and code jurisdiction demonstrated that architects can take leadership positions on issues beyond the bounds of the traditional office environment and affect our built environment on a larger scale than simply one building, one client at a time.

As an emerging professional, you serve as the Pacific and Northwest RAD (regional associate director) for the AIA; how did you become involved with the AIA, and why is it important for your career?

❯ Being involved in the AIA is less about career advancement and more about personal responsibility and service to the profession. The AIA provides a venue for critical discussion about the profession, critique, and dialogue on what the future face of the profession should be. There are many important yet exceedingly difficult questions about the architectural profession and the architect's greater role in society that cannot be answered individually in offices, but must instead be discussed by architects as a collective group. The AIA is the place where this can happen—where we can come together as colleagues, not competitors, and advance the profession as a whole. I got involved with the AIA first through the travel scholarship, which exposed me to the AIA and opened my eyes to the good work my local AIA

Seattle component was doing. A principal at my firm also encouraged me to get involved, and I am grateful for this gentle push because involvement has created many new connections and given me a greater sense of fulfillment in my own work.

What has been your greatest challenge as an intern thus far?

❯ I recently read an article describing the "glacial pace" of career advancement in architecture. I found this to ring true, and I think my greatest challenge has related to gaining more responsibility at work and being exposed to more aspects of the profession, such as the interview process, client relations, billing, and so on. There are many good reasons for this, such as the incredible complexities, time constraints, and liability within the profession. Gaining the whole spectrum of skills an architect needs is a lifelong pursuit, so it makes sense that career advancement is slow. However, the architecture office should take an active role in building skills and career advancement through mentorship and apprenticeship. By looking ahead and actively training younger pro-

fessionals, offices will build a critical base of experience that will be crucial to the overall success of the profession in the coming years.

From the perspective of an emerging professional, can you describe the Intern Development Program (IDP) and the Architect Registration Examination (ARE)? Where are you in the process of becoming licensed?

❯ IDP is set up to maintain competency and legitimacy of the architectural profession. Completion of the program is a supposed benchmark for competency and one's ability to manage the design, life safety, and business aspects of the practice of architecture. The program is highly formalized and rigid and focuses on creating a certain mold for architects with little concern for nontraditional career paths and experience that does not directly fall into the IDP's defined categories.

I have completed IDP, but have not yet started taking the ARE. Instead, I have found more value in independent research and sharing this research at local conventions and universities. Unfortunately,

Secondary School, Klaus, Austria. Architect: Dietrich Untertrifaller. PHOTOGRAPHER: JOSEPH MAYO.

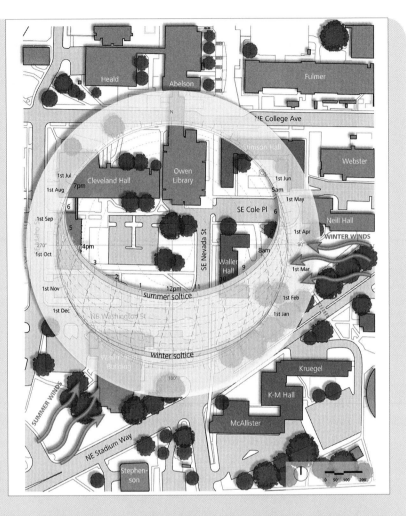

Waller Hall Solar Diagram,
Seattle, Washington.
Architect: Mahlum.
PHOTOGRAPHER: MAHLUM.

this architectural research does not count toward my completion of the program. This is the problem with the IDP—it dictates that there is only one way to become an "architect," yet in practice there is a huge variety of different types of architects and different paths to competency. Rethinking the licensure track for architects is a hot topic, and I hope we will see positive changes in the future.

What is the most/least satisfying part of a career as an architect?

❯ The most satisfying part of architecture is that it touches all aspects of our lives and has such poten-

tial to make not only individual lives better but the whole planet and environment better. There are few other professions that touch so many people and have such huge capacity for change. This, of course, is a huge responsibility, and architects often work enormous hours—well beyond our billable time—to meet this (sometimes overwhelming) responsibility. Because our clients and the public at large have little knowledge of what architects actually do, we are not well valued, and thus our fees are likely lower than they should be. This means that, as a profession, we do not make a lot of money, yet work incredibly hard and long hours. On top of this are the ever-growing complexities of the work that leads to "glacial" career advancement. However, the collaborative nature of architecture, problem solving, research opportunities, and design makes it one of the most personally fulfilling careers, despite all the disadvantages.

What are your 5-year and 10-year career goals relative to architecture?

❭ Certainly within the next 5 years I desire to be licensed. This is currently one of my biggest goals. I am also in the process of writing a book on architecture and hope to have this published within the next 5 years. On a larger time frame, I have many goals, but am not sure which ones I will ultimately pursue. I would like to learn more about the money side of architecture in terms of fees, pro formas, development potential, construction costs, and

management. However, I would like to also become more skilled in building enclosure issues and environmental design. Finally, I would like to better integrate the practice of architecture with the act of making (using computer numerical control [CNC] machines, 3D printing, etc.).

Who or what experience has been a major influence on your career?

❭ A trip to Europe during architecture school certainly influenced my understanding of architecture, and I would emphasize the value of travel in anyone's architectural education. There are several people in my office who also are major influences. I am constantly amazed by their skill and prowess in design and architecture, and this is really what keeps me pushing forward, striving to somehow be as good as they are.

Optimist

LAUREN PASION
Architectural Designer
Studio E Architects
San Diego, California

Why did you become an architect?

❭ I want to become an architect because it is the best means to contribute to my community, culture, and future. The influence and potential impact one can make with architecture is exponential. I am an optimist.

Why did you decide to choose the school that you did—NewSchool of Architecture + Design (NSAD)? What degree do you possess?

❭ I chose NewSchool of Architecture + Design because it is an accredited architecture program, which is the first step to licensure. I possess a bachelor of architecture (B.Arch.), the five-year accredited professional degree.

In school and entering your professional career, you have held a number of leadership positions; for you, what is leadership, and why might it be important for architects?

❭ Yes, I have held a number of positions at the local and state levels. Leadership is a way of exercising my democratic right and having a voice. These positions keep me informed and active in the decisions that affect me and my employers and ultimately the direction of the profession.

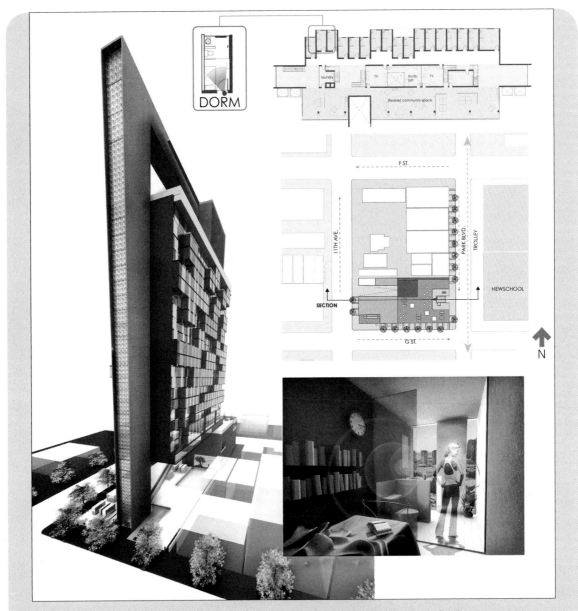

Transitional Boundaries: An Urban Residence Hall. Studio Project by Lauren Pasion at NewSchool of Architecture & Design.

As regional associate director with the AIA California Council, how have you benefited from this involvement? Also, what are the issues facing emerging professionals?

❯ As regional associate director, I have gained invaluable insight to structure and complexities of our profession. I have been given opportunities to be involved in critical conversations and decisions, which I would have otherwise not encountered. I have also met amazing people and created lifelong relationships.

Issues emerging professionals are facing today include:

- Student debt relief.
- Connections with academia and institutions.
- Unpaid internships.
- Intern Development Program.
- Architect Registration Examination.

In your position at Studio E Architects, what are your primary responsibilities and duties?

❭ My responsibilities include assisting the project manager with deliverables to the client, consultants, and review authorities. I primarily work in Revit to coordinate design decisions and create construction documents. We also provide graphic representations, such as renderings, and assure compliance with established client standards, in addition to planning, zoning, and code regulations.

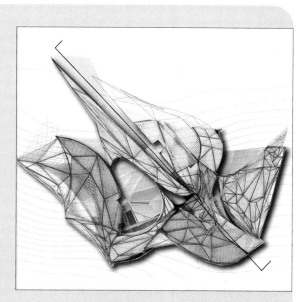

Interstitial "C." Museum of Contemporary Conflict by Lauren Pasion at NewSchool of Architecture & Design.

I.D.E.A. District. Studio Project by Lauren Pasion at NewSchool of Architecture & Design.

EAST VILLAGE GREEN

e.v.g.   bus rapid transit   e.v.g.

As one who recently graduated, what has been your greatest challenge thus far as an intern?

> Since graduation, the most challenging task has been studying for the ARE. It has been difficult finding the time and support for studying while transitioning to a full-time position. It has also been very costly.

As an emerging professional, can you describe the Intern Development Program (IDP) and the Architect Registration Examination (ARE)? Where are you in the process of becoming an architect?

> IDP is a great tool for emerging professionals, although it is often perceived as an obstacle. The IDP ensures that an emerging professional experiences the diverse responsibilities of an architect and is provided a comprehensive understanding of the process. Without the IDP, emerging professionals can be easily pigeonholed into drafting.

What is the most/least satisfying part of a career as an architect?

> The most satisfying part of my career is the ability to experience a space that I had a part in creating. The least satisfying part of my career is defending it.

What are your 5-year and 10-year career goals relative to architecture?

> Within 5 years, I wish to be licensed; within 10 years, I hope to have direct relationships with clients and have my own practice.

Who or what experience has been a major influence on your career?

> My leadership roles have greatly shaped my view on architecture. I also contribute my success to my studio mates and colleagues, whom I have learned a great deal from.

Building Better Architects

ANDREW CARUSO, AIA, NCARB, LEED AP BD+C, CDT
Firmwide Head of Intern Development and Academic Outreach
Gensler
Washington, DC

What degree(s) do you possess?

> I completed the five-year professional bachelor of architecture (B.Arch.). Many students ask me whether they should pursue the B.Arch or the two-to three-year master of architecture (following a four-year undergraduate degree). There is no right or wrong answer, but the five-year B.Arch allowed me to pursue licensure as quickly as possible while preserving my ability to study other fields during graduate study. Since I knew I wanted to be an architect, but ultimately wanted to build a career outside of traditional practice, this was the best option.

As firmwide head of intern development and academic outreach, what are your primary responsibilities and duties in your firm?

> Gensler believes that having the industry's best talent is central to creating work that redefines what is possible through the power of design. As part of the firm's Talent Development team, I provide leadership, strategy, and oversight for early-career talent initiatives across the global footprint of Gensler. This includes developing and leading a

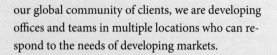

Gensler Intern Program: Tool + Guidelines for Intern Programming, January 2013, Gensler.

program portfolio focused on early-career talent acquisition, professional development and licensure, academic outreach, student internships, scholarships, and global talent exchange programs.

You recently relocated to Shanghai, China, for an assignment abroad. What were your responsibilities while there?

❭ The industry is rapidly globalizing. Gensler is regularly engaged with clients and communities around the world, working in over 90 countries across six continents every year. As part of serving

Historic Housing and Street, Xidi Village, Anhui Provence, China. PHOTOGRAPHER: ANDREW CARUSO.

our global community of clients, we are developing offices and teams in multiple locations who can respond to the needs of developing markets.

In 2012, I was asked to relocate to our Asia market to provide specialized focus on the development of talent strategies across our offices in Japan, China, Singapore, South Korea, Thailand, and India. Through an immersive experience with our staff in these locations, we were able to build an infrastructure to support talent recruitment, retention, assessment, professional development and licensure, leadership development, talent exchange, and cross-cultural training. These issues will be key to the future growth of our Asia region.

Given your position at Gensler, please provide insight on how emerging professionals (interns) can best take advantage of their early years in the profession.

❭ First, every day presents a learning opportunity. Making the most of your early years in the profession is a careful balance of being open to new experiences, but also clearly communicating your

Adapted Housing, South Bund Historic District, Shanghai, China. PHOTOGRAPHER: ANDREW CARUSO.

interests and passions. All firms are not equal; be sure to find the company that best fits your unique design point of view. This makes it much easier to align your own professional development goals with the goals of the company, the key to creating career-changing opportunities.

Second, get involved in your community. There are many opportunities to give back as an emerging architect to the place in which you are building your career. Engaging your community will enrich the skills and perspective you bring to your firm and allow you to build relationships that one day may lead to new clients and design opportunities for your design practice.

Third, become licensed! The road to registration is long and challenging. It is never too early to start, and it is important to capture every possible opportunity and training hour as part of your progress toward fulfilling your licensure requirements. Focusing on a plan to pace yourself through the internship and examination experience will help you be successful and will also positively contribute to building your level of expertise in the workplace.

In addition, you are a featured contributor to "Inside the Design Mind," a column of the National Building Museum and Metropolis magazine. How did you obtain this opportunity, and why is it important in your career?

❯ I enjoy writing and actively look for ways to maintain that practice within the industry. During the early years of my career, I delivered a large amount of public speaking and publishing about issues in the industry. These opportunities allowed me to frame a point of view about our profession, and more broadly, about talent in the creative industries. This point of view ultimately inspired "Inside the Design Mind."

Simultaneous to developing the framework for the column, I recognized an opportunity for the content I was generating to advance the mission and reach of my colleagues' businesses. It was a natural fit for the National Building Museum and Metropolis magazine to partner on this project, and in fact it was the first time they had entered a media partnership. The column now reaches thousands of readers each time it's published, and has been reprinted around the world by *ArchDaily, World Architecture News*, and even the *Huffington Post*.

What I have taken away from this experience is that it's important to develop and maintain a unique perspective in our industry, and to actively seek out opportunities where a point of view can enrich the efforts of others. That's when industry-changing collaborations begin.

What has been your greatest challenge as an architect?

❯ My greatest challenge as an architect has been helping the profession to move and change at pace with contemporary society. Much of traditional practice focuses on a delivery model rooted in the early twentieth-century American context. Clients, projects, and cities have radically changed, and the profession is trying to adapt. Great clients help to push us in new directions and modes of practice. But architects must also take hold of reframing the value of design thinking to a broader array of today's issues. Entering the profession at this particular moment—a time of great change and uncertainty—is both a tremendous challenge and opportunity.

What are your career goals for the next 5 to 10 years?

❯ Clearly, the challenges of the built environment are growing. Whether it is the unprecedented urbanization of the world's population, global environmental imperatives, or the call to make our cities more adaptive and inclusive, there are significant opportunities to make positive change as an architect. My passions and interests have always been at a scale larger than specific buildings. I like to explore the economic, social, and political systems that drive the built environment. Integrating and innovating these key factors—ecology, transportation, public health, tourism, and other major urban drivers—will likely be my future focus.

What is the most satisfying part of being an architect?

❯ You never forget the experience of stepping into a space that you've designed for the first time. Seeing and *feeling* a building come to life from lines on paper to steel beams and walls is life changing. It makes you realize how much responsibility you have as an architect, but how rewarding it can be to create space for people. And construction always has its fair share of surprises. The collaborative process of putting buildings together and tackling unforeseen challenges underscores the team-oriented approach required for successful architecture. It's

these moments when creativity meets reality that I always find the most interesting.

Who or what experience has been a major influence on your career?

❯ Design education truly reoriented the way I saw the world. It provided a new framework to explore, question, and hypothesize about the environment around me. This encouragement to ask questions, challenge perspectives, and find comfort in uncertainty have developed into life skills that apply to more than just design exercises.

These skills came into sharp focus during my time spent living and working in Asia. While I have had previous experience working with cultures around the world, the opportunity to live and work in an emerging market for an extended period of time has given me new insights on the true challenges of globalization. Whether understanding the realities of practice in a developing country or trying to provide training that bridges cultural and educational differences, each experience has added depth and dimension to my view of the profession's future. The opportunities and needs for cross-cultural partnerships are abundant, and the impacts are profound.

NOTES

1. Ernest L. Boyer and Lee D. Mitgang, *Building Community: A New Future for Architecture Education and Practice* (Princeton, NJ: Carnegie Foundation for the Advancement of Teaching, 1996), 117.
2. *The American Heritage Dictionary* (Boston: Houghton Mifflin, 2000).
3. Boston Architectural Center, www.the-bac.edu. Retrieved August 31, 2013.
4. NCARB, *Intern Development Program Guidelines* (Washington, DC: NCARB, 2013), 14.
5. *American Heritage Dictionary.* (2000).
6. *Intern Development Program Guidelines,* p. 2.
7. NCARB, *NCARB by the Numbers* (Washington, DC: NCARB, 2013).
8. Emerging Professional Companions, www.epcompanion.org. Retrieved August 31, 2013.

4 The Careers of an Architect

Architects are broadly qualified to practice in a wide variety of roles and settings within the architecture profession and building enterprise.

DAVID HAVILAND, HON. AIA

The building of a career is quite as difficult a problem as the building of a house, yet few ever sit down with pencil and paper, with expert information and counsel, to plan a working career and deal with the life problem scientifically, as they would deal with the problem of building a house, taking the advice of an architect to help them.

FRANK PARSONS[1]

AS PARSONS STATES IN THE PRECEDING QUOTATION, the building of a career—the process of career development—is a difficult but important task, yet he also notes that few individuals prepare for their careers in a thoughtful, careful, and deliberate manner. Instead, many often fall into a career, while others make random career choices that show little commitment to their occupation, often leading to dissatisfaction.

Career Designing

Regardless of where you are along the path to becoming an architect—completing your architectural education, gaining experience in an architecture firm, or in the process of taking the Architect Registration Exam (ARE), you should pursue deliberate career designing to maximize career success.

You may argue that a career is not something you create or plan, that it just happens. However, as with architectural projects, careers should be carefully planned. In many ways, designing a career is parallel to designing a building. Programming, schematic design, design development, working drawings, and construction are replaced in the career development process with assessing, exploring, decision making, and planning.

ASSESSING

Know thyself.

INSCRIPTION OVER THE ORACLE AT DELPHI, GREECE

When an architect designs a project, what is typically the first step in the process? Most likely, programming. As William Pena points out in *Problem Seeking,*[2] the main idea behind programming is the search for sufficient information, to clarify, understand, and state the problem. In a similar manner, when designing your career, the process begins with assessing.

Assessing is learning about yourself. Assess where you want to be; analyze what is important to you, your abilities, the work you would like to do, and your strengths and weaknesses. Just as programming assists the architect in understanding a particular design problem, assessment helps determine what you want from your career. This ongoing process must be reiterated throughout your entire career. The details of assessment include values, interests, and skills. But what exactly are values, interests, and skills, and how do you determine them?

Values

Values are feelings, attitudes, and beliefs you hold close to your heart. They reflect what is important to you; they tell you what you should or should not do. Work values are the enduring dimensions or aspects of our work that you regard as important sources of satisfaction. Values traditionally held in high esteem by architects include creativity, recognition, variety, independence, and responsibility.

As a quick inventory, circle which of the following you value in the work you do:

- Social contributions
- Creativity
- Excitement
- Working alone/with others
- Monetary reward
- Competition
- Change and variety
- Independence

- Intellectual challenge

- Physical challenge

- Fast pace

- Security

- Responsibility

- Making decisions

- Power and authority

- Spiritual/Transpersonal

- Gaining knowledge

- Recognition

Your responses provide insight on a career path within the profession. For example, if contributions to society are valued most highly, you might look for opportunities for work in public interest design.

Interests

Interests are those ideas, events, and activities that stimulate your enthusiasm; they are reflected in choices you make about how you spend your time. In simplest terms, interests are activities you enjoy doing. Typically, architects have a breadth of interests because the field of architecture encompasses artistic, scientific, and technical aspects. Architects enjoy being involved in all phases of the creative process—from original conceptualization to a tangible finished product.[3]

To determine your interests, for an entire month note what you most and least enjoy doing each day. At the end of the month, summarize and categorize the preferences you have recorded. Here is another method; in 10 minutes of continuous writing, never removing your pen from the paper or your fingers from the keyboard, answer the question: *What do I like to do when I am not working?*

Career development theory dictates that your career path follow your interests; if you do, you will see success.

Skills

Unlike values and interests, skills or abilities can be learned. There are three types of skills—functional, self-management, and special knowledge. Having a functional skill means being able to perform some specific type of activity, action, or operation with a good deal of proficiency; according to the Bureau of Labor Statistics, an architect needs the following skills: analytical, communication, creativity, critical thinking, organizational, technical, and visualization. In contrast, self-management skills are your specific behavioral responses or character traits such as eagerness, initiative, or dependability. Finally, special knowledge skills are what you have learned and what you know.

The importance of knowing your skills is echoed by Richard Bolles in his book *The Quick Job-Hunting Map*[4]: "You must know, for now and all the future, not only what skills you have, but more importantly, what skills you have and enjoy." With respect to skills, think back over the past five years. What were your five most satisfying accomplishments? Next to each, list the skills or abilities that enabled you to succeed. Similarly, review your failures to determine traits or deficiencies you want to overcome.

A variety of techniques may be used to conduct an assessment. The few listed here are simply to get you started; others include writing an autobiography and undertaking empirical inventories or a psychological assessment with the assistance of a career counselor. Regardless of the method you choose, only you can best determine what skills you have acquired and enjoy using; the issues, ideas, problems, organizations that interest you; and the values that you care about for your life and career.

EXPLORING

Students spend four or more years learning how to dig data out of the library and other sources, but it rarely occurs to them that they should also apply some of the same new-found research skills to their own benefit—to looking up information on companies, types of professions, sections of the country that might interest them.

ALBERT SHAPERO

Schematic design follows programming in the design process. Schematic design generates alternative solutions; its goal is to establish general characteristics of the design including scale, form, estimated costs, and the general image of the building, the size and organization of spaces. Additionally, schematic design identifies major issues and makes initial decisions that serve as the basis of subsequent stages.

Even if you already have chosen architecture as a career, it is still a valuable and necessary process. Instead of exploring careers, you can explore firms, possible career paths within architecture, and other areas that impact your architectural path; understanding exploring will help you be flexible and adaptable when needed due to the economy or other legitimate reasons.

How do you explore? In *Career Planning Today*,[5] the author describes a systematic process that includes collecting, evaluating, integrating, and deciding. Following these four steps guarantees the highest possible level of career awareness.

To begin, collect career information from a variety of sources, both people and publications. Conduct an *information interview*—interviewing someone to obtain information. Individuals to interview might include a senior partner in a local firm, a faculty member, a classmate or colleague, or a mentor. Other ways to explore are through attending lectures sponsored by the local American Institute of Architects (AIA) chapter or a university, volunteering time through local AIA commit-

HSB Twisting Torso, Malmo,
Sweden. Architect: Santiago
Calatrava. PHOTOGRAPHER:
GRACE H. KIM, AIA.

tee or other organizations of interest, becoming involved with a mentor program, and observing or
shadowing someone for a day.

As Shapero states, you should use your research skills to access any and all information
you need on a career. Visit your university career center or local public library and inquire about
the following publications: *The Dictionary of Occupational Titles* (DOT), *Occupational Outlook
Handbook* (OOH), *Guide to Occupational Exploration* (GOE), and *What Color Is Your Parachute?*
Ask a reference librarian to identify other resources that you might find valuable. In addition, investigate resources at your local AIA chapter or the library/resource center at area architecture program. Other resources to access include the Web and professional associations (see Appendix A).

DECISION MAKING

What most people want out of life, more than anything else, is the opportunity to make choices.

DAVID P. CAMPBELL

The heart of the design process is design development. Similarly, decision making is the heart of the career designing process. Design development describes the specific character and intent of the entire project; it further refines the schematic design and defines the alternatives. Decision making means selecting alternatives and evaluating them against a predetermined set of criteria.

How do you make decisions? Do you let others decide for you? Do you rely on gut-level reactions? Or do you follow a planned strategy of weighing alternatives? Whatever your method of deciding, you should to be aware of it. While some decisions can be made at the drop of a hat, others, including career designing, require more thought.

For demonstration purposes, review the following architectural application of the decision-making process.

Decision Making

Decision-Making Model	Architectural Application
1) Identify the decision to be made	Need or desire for new space or building.
2) Gather information	Develop a building program (budget, style, size, room, specification, layout).
3) Identify alternatives	Develop alternative schematic designs, incorporating the program.
4) Weigh evidence	Evaluate schematic designs as they meet determined needs, preferences.
5) Choose among the alternatives	Select the design that best captures ideals.
6) Take action	Draw construction documents; develop timetable; break ground; begin construction activity; architectural "punch list."
7) Review decision and consequences.	Long-range evaluation may identify need for major building renovation for reuse.

Decision making can be difficult and time consuming, but knowing that the quality of decisions is affected by the information used to make them, you will quickly realize that making informed decisions is an important skill to learn.

Both exploring and decision making are critical steps in successful career designing. Do not wait to begin this important process; instead, take this information and build your future with career designing.

PLANNING

If you do not have plans for your life, someone else does.

ANTHONY ROBBINS

Planning is bringing the future into the present so that we can do something about it now.

ALAN LAKEIN

"Cheshire-Puss," ... said Alice, "would you tell me, please which way I ought to go from here?"

"That depends a good deal on where you want to get to," said the Cat.

"I don't much care where...." said Alice.

"Then it doesn't matter which way you go," said the Cat.

LEWIS CARROLL, *ALICE IN WONDERLAND*

You may wonder why a quote from a popular children's book. If you look closer, you realize that half of reaching your destination is knowing the direction in which you wish to head. Planning is key to fulfilling your career goals.

After the owner/client and architect decide upon a design for a potential building, the next step is the development of plans. These plans—construction documents, specifications, and schedules—all play an important role in realizing the design. In a similar way, planning, as part of the career designing process, ensures that a successful career will be realized.

In its simplest form, planning is the bridge from dreams to action; it is merely an intention to take an action by a certain time. At its fullest, planning is creating a mission statement, developing career goals, and preparing action plans.

But what is a mission statement, goals, or action plans?

In his book *Seven Habits of Highly Effective People,*[6] author Stephen Covey states that a mission statement focuses on what you want to be (character) and to do (contributions and achievements) and on the values or principles on which being and doing are based. To start the planning process, draft your mission statement by asking yourself: "What do I want to be? What do I want to do? What are my career aspirations?"

After you have crafted your mission statement, the next step is to develop goals that will lead to its fulfillment. Goals are future-oriented statements of purpose and direction to be accomplished within a specified time frame. They are steppingstones in achieving long-range aims and should be specific and measurable. Write down your goals. It has been said that the difference between a wish and a goal is that a goal is written down.

I desire to act in a manner that brings out the best in me and those important to me— especially when it might be most justifiable to act otherwise.

Once you establish your goals, you are ready to develop the action plan that will help you accomplish them. Action plans are steps on the path toward your goals; they are steppingstones in achieving related short-range intentions. Look at your accomplished goals. What steps must you take to accomplish them? As with career goals, write down your action plan, including specific completion dates.

The final step in planning is to review your action plans and goals regularly. Cross out the goals you have accomplished and revise, add to, or delete others. Be honest with yourself. Are you still committed to achieving your goals? You can change them, but remember that the magic road to achievement is *persistence.* Abandon goals only if they have lost meaning for you—not because they are tough or you have suffered a setback.

Now, you understand the career designing process: assessing, exploring, decision making, and planning, you can implement it. As you progress through your professional career, you will realize that this process is never-ending and cyclical. As soon as you have secured an ideal position in a firm, you will wish to assess your new life situation and make adjustments to your career design accordingly. In addition, consider the following:

Petajavesi Old Church, Petajavesi, Finland. PHOTOGRAPHER: TED SHELTON, AIA.

You know the story of the three brick masons. When the first man was asked what he was building, he answered gruffly, without even raising his eyes from his work, "I am laying bricks." The second man replied, "I am building a wall." But the third man said enthusiastically and with obvious pride, "I am building a cathedral."

MARGARET STEVENS

In your future career, will you lay bricks, build a wall, or build a cathedral? Regardless of your answer, designing your career is one of the most important tasks during your lifetime. Yet if career designing is so important, why do most people spend so little time on it? Think about it!

Succeeding in the Built Environment

H. ALAN BRANGMAN, AIA
Vice President of Facilities
Real Estate and Auxiliary Services
University of Delaware
Newark, Delaware

Why and how did you become an architect?

❯ I became an architect because I have always had a fascination with building things.

Why and how did you decide on which school to attend for your architecture degree? What degree(s) do you possess?

❯ I initially went to the University of New Hampshire to study civil engineering. At the beginning of my sophomore year, I met an art professor who had been a former instructor at Cornell University. He suggested that I transfer to Cornell. My degree is the bachelor of architecture.

What has been your greatest challenge as an architect?

❯ My greatest challenge as an architect has been and continues to be convincing other professionals that architects are capable of doing much more than just architecture.

How is working as a university architect different from the more traditional role of an architect?

❯ My job responsibilities are more in line with those of a principal in a real estate development firm. I am responsible not only for the hiring and oversight of design and planning consultants, providing program, planning, and design oversight for all university facilities, but also for all real estate–related matters.

You have worked as a university architect at Georgetown University, the University of Delaware, and Howard University; how have your responsibilities changed with each position?

❯ My responsibilities at the various universities that I have worked for have been generally the same when it comes to oversight of the design and planning world. By that I mean each campus has provided me with an opportunity to oversee and manage the design and planning of not only new projects but also over any renovations that needed to occur on campus, both large and small in scale. The one change from campus to campus is that of real estate oversight. At the University of Delaware I have a colleague who was responsible for real estate. The other major change in responsibility is that at Howard I was also responsible to Facilities Management, Auxiliary Services (dining services, mail services, bookstore), Transportation and Parking Services, the Office of Sustainability, and Environmental Health & Safety. So my field of influence has widened with my latest change in jobs. I am now back at the University of Delaware and responsible for all the disciplines that I had oversight for at Howard.

How and why did you pursue what might be considered a nontraditional career path as opposed to a more traditional one?

❯ Initially, I did so because I had an interest in something more than just designing buildings. I spent nine years with the Oliver T. Carr Company, a real estate development company in Washington, DC. That opportunity opened my eyes to the breadth of the built environment and provided me with a much more global perspective on place making.

McDonough School of Business, Georgetown University, Washington, DC. Architect: Goody, Clancy.

During your career, you worked in the Design Arts program for the National Endowment for the Arts, an independent agency of the federal government. Can you describe your role in this agency?

❯ I was the deputy director of the Design Arts program. The program was primarily responsible for grant making and supporting initiatives to spread the word about the benefits of good design. The initiatives that I enjoyed the most were:

- Mayors Institute on City Design—a series of national and regional forums dedicated to improving the understanding of the design of American cities through a forum that brought together of mayors and urban design professionals.
- Your Town—Designing Its Future—regional workshops geared to teaching the importance of design to those who can influence and make decisions about the way rural communities will look and work in the future.

- Design for Housing Initiative—a national workshop dedicated to bringing together representatives from the housing delivery system to spur a better understanding of "Good Design" and its application to affordable housing.
- Presidential Design Awards—an honor award program done in conjunction with the White House, given every four years by the president to projects that came about as a result of federal involvement.

The first three initiatives were partnered with universities that had schools of design such as the University of Virginia, MIT, University of Minnesota, Tulane, UC Berkeley, Georgia Tech, and University of Maryland. These initiatives were typically run as a three-day seminar and not only involved decision makers like mayors, in the case of the Mayors Institute, but also involved nationally renowned design professionals, planners, landscape architects, real estate developers, economists, sociologists, and educators.

◀ Residence Halls, Howard University, Washington, DC. Architect: McKissack & McKissack.

▼ SW Quadrangle, Georgetown University, Washington, DC. Architect: Robert A. M. Stern/EYP. PHOTOGRAPHER: H. ALAN BRANGMAN, AIA.

Why did you pursue the additional credentials of a real estate development primer certificate at Harvard Graduate School of Design and Wharton School of Business?

❭ When I started my career in real estate development, I had been counseled to consider obtaining an MBA. At the time, I did not want to commit the time required to return to graduate school. Besides, the president of the firm did not have a business degree and seemed to be doing quite fine. I decided to pursue the path of learning through experience. Besides, I had been schooled as an architect, and architects are taught to solve problems. I was able to manage any of the issues or problems that were part of my job responsibilities quite well. After having gotten a few years under my belt, I took the primer courses as a way of confirming what I had learned. It worked.

What is the most/least satisfying part of your job?

❭ The least satisfying aspect of my current job is the pace at which things are accomplished in an academic environment—very slowly. Entrepreneurship is not something that is typically associated with academia.

Who or what experience has been a major influence on your career?

❭ Bob Smith, AIA, associate principal, RTKL, was very influential in encouraging me in 1979 to look to real estate development as a possible career to pursue.

Oliver T. Carr, Jr., The Oliver T. Carr Company, was a mentor in my early years, through my employment at Carr. He provided me with the opportunity to preside over 5 million gross square feet of commercial development in downtown Washington, DC.

Advocate for Architecture

MURRYE BERNARD, ASSOCIATE AIA, LEED AP
Managing Editor
Contract **Magazine**
New York, New York

Why did you pursue architecture?

❭ When I was 12, I came down with mono and was confined to the couch for a few weeks. Bored with daytime TV, I began watching the construction of the house next door. I quickly became enthralled, and once I recovered, I spent every day after school exploring the site and drafting plans. As it turns out, those plans were off by a few hundred square feet, but my future career path was set in stone, so to speak.

Why did you choose to attend the University of Arkansas? What degree do you possess?

❭ B.Arch. The University of Arkansas offered me a scholarship on top of what was already an affordable education, but it happened that the Fay Jones School

of Architecture is an excellent program that employs some amazing professors. Though my school's name carries less weight than some, I am proud of my state university education. And to be honest, I was also wooed by the potential to study in Rome.

How did your time in Rome shape the direction of your career?

❭ The semester I spent in Rome was my first experience living in a large city, and it crystallized my desire to move to New York City eventually (it took me a couple of years after college to save the money and work up the nerve, but I've been here for almost

Sketch of Tarquinia, Tarquinia, Italy.

Sketch of Piazza Navona, Rome, Italy.

Arkansas Studies Institute, Little Rock, Arkansas. Architect: Polk Stanley Wilcox Architects. RENDERING COURTESY OF POLK STANLEY WILCOX ARCHITECTS.

seven years now). Also, the act of sketching almost every day in Rome taught me a new way of looking at buildings, spaces, and cities. I don't sketch much anymore, but I like to believe that I approach each writing or editing assignment with that same critical eye.

Upon graduation, you interned in a firm; what were your responsibilities, and how was the experience different than your studies?

❯ I completed the typical, mundane tasks of internship: door schedules, bathroom elevations, and picking up red marks until my eyes crossed. But my firm did provide me with a well-rounded experience including opportunities to sketch and design, attend client meetings, and visit job sites. I was also thrilled to finally have some free time after the intensity of architecture school, which I devoted to my then hobby, writing.

Why and how did you transition from working architecture to writing?

❯ Though I will always love architecture, I quickly realized that I had no desire to move up through the ranks of a firm or start my own, and ultimately I was better suited as an advocate for the profession. I began my writing and editing career by moonlighting for several years before I chose to become a freelancer. My first assignment came about when the American Institute of Architects (AIA) National Associates Committee (NAC) invited me to edit their newsletter, *AssociateNews*. After I moved to New York, I began building connections with editors and accomplished the milestone of publishing my first article in print.

As a writer, you have authored articles on the topics of architecture and design for print publications, and websites, including **Architect, Architectural Record, Contract** *magazine,* **Design Bureau, Eco-Structure,** *and* **USA Today***; how is writing the same as/different from architecture?*

❯ When designing a building, you must analyze the site and develop a program before you even start sketching. It's much the same with writing; I spend most of my time researching and gathering information. Just as a building design must go through many iterations before it reaches its final state, my first draft becomes unrecognizable as I edit, edit again, and then edit some more. And nothing is more satisfying than seeing the finished product, whether a completed building or, for me, a published piece.

Aside from writing, you are still pursuing your architectural license, having completed some of the ARE; why pursue licensure when your passion is writing?

❯ While I have no plans to practice in the traditional sense, I've always maintained the goal of becoming a licensed architect, but it probably sounds a little masochistic to take seven tests when there is no pressure or obvious reward. However, I survived five years of architecture school and faithfully logged all of my IDP hours as an intern, so why not complete the process? Being licensed will only give me credibility and enhance my byline, plus it will also help me to better communicate with architects about their work.

You recently became managing editor of Contract *magazine. Why did you choose to join the staff of a publication?*

❯ I enjoyed the freedom that comes with being a freelancer, but it has long been a goal of mine to work on staff as an editor. I have written for *Contract* on a freelance basis for the past year and a half, so I had become very familiar with the publication, which made for a natural transition. I am honored to join the team, and I look forward to helping shape the magazine and impart inspiration and knowledge to design professionals. I might not become an architect in the traditional sense, but I am using my architecture education and background to contribute in my own unique way.

Pinch Me!

MEGAN S. CHUSID, AIA

Associate Director, Facilities and Office Services

Solomon R. Guggenheim Museum & Foundation

New York, New York

Why did you become an architect?

❯ My passion was always in photography, and growing up I spent hours hidden away in a dark room learning how to carefully develop negatives and prints. Contrast and the timing and precision needed for the chemicals and the exposures were a technical science for me that I greatly enjoyed. My career choice made a turn when my mother urged me to choose a more formal profession. Architecture was the creative and technical career choice, and photography will always be a hobby.

Why did you decide to choose Syracuse University? What degree(s) do you possess?

❯ My high school guidance counselor handed me a compact pamphlet of architecture schools, and after reviewing them, I applied only to NAAB-accredited programs. I narrowed down my acceptances according to the following criteria: proximity to home (New York City), the school's ranking in the United States, and scholarship opportunities.

I received a five-year bachelor of architecture from the School of Architecture at Syracuse University.

Jose E. Serrano Center for Global Conservation Wildlife Conservation Society, Bronx Zoo, Bronx, New York. Architect: FXFowle, Contractor: Richter+Ratner Contracting Corp. PHOTO COURTESY OF RICHTER+RATNER CONTRACTING CORP.

In your position as manager of facilities and office services, what are your primary responsibilities and duties? Please describe a typical day.

❯ My primary responsibility at the Guggenheim is to serve as the property administrator for all owned and leased properties in the New York area. In addition, I manage the department that provides all of the office services required within and between all of the properties.

A typical day includes meetings ranging from discussions about capital projects to logistics of upcoming art exhibitions. Besides the typical maintenance and repair issues that arrive throughout the day, I spend a great deal of time meeting with various departments within the museum to better understand the ever-changing staffing and space

requirements. No two days are ever alike, and every day I find out new things about the museum.

Please share what it is like to work in/with the iconic structure, the Solomon R. Guggenheim Museum designed by Frank Lloyd Wright.

❯ Working in and with one of the most iconic pieces of architecture in the world is like having a "pinch me" moment every time I walk in the door. My favorite part of my job is the small periods of time when I get to research the original materials and construction details. When I look through shop drawings and submittals, I am either reviewing 1956–1959 documents that are carefully stored in a controlled environment or requesting archive documents that were personally signed by FLW.

◀Exterior of the Solomon R. Guggenheim Museum, New York, New York. Architect: Frank Lloyd Wright. PHOTOGRAPHER: DAVID HEALD © THE SOLOMON GUGGENHEIM FOUNDATION, NEW YORK.

▼Construction of the Solomon R. Guggenheim Museum, 1956–1959, New York, New York. Architect: Frank Lloyd Wright. PHOTOGRAPHER: WILLIAM H. SHORT © THE SOLOMON GUGGENHEIM FOUNDATION, NEW YORK.

Previously, you worked as a project manager for a traditional architecture firm and director of operations for a construction management firm. How were these two positions the same/different?

❯ The two positions utilized and honed very different skills. Working at a traditional firm, I learned how to put together a proper set of construction documents for a building as well as the skills for effectively managing a project from conception and zoning feasibility through final construction. In my role at Richter + Ratner, I was able to sit on the other side of the table at a boutique construction management company, where I learned the construction side of getting things built as well as the business side of running a company.

What has been your greatest challenge as an architect?

❯ Mainstream society, outside of the architecture, engineering, construction, and real estate industries, and in some cases, the art world, don't necessarily understand the full meaning of what architects can do and what they contribute to society.

What is the most/least satisfying part of being an architect?

❯ Taking the Architect Registration Exam (ARE) is the least satisfying part of becoming an architect,

but the day you receive your final PASS letter is the most satisfying.

Who or what experience has been a major influence on your career?

❯ *Who* comes down to my first boss, my mother, from whom I learned project management, working with clients, seeing all possibilities, and practicality.

What experience could be more influential than being an architect working in and getting to care for one of the most famous pieces of architecture in the world?

Adapt, Grow, Prosper

JOSEPH NICKOL, AICP, LEED AP BD+C
Urbanist
Urban Design Associates
Pittsburgh, Pennsylvania

Why did you initially pursue architecture?

❯ Oddly enough, I chose architecture to build stadia and airports. They always seemed to me (in my child mind) as quite simply the coolest (therefore the most important) building types.

Why did you decide to choose the school you did—the University of Notre Dame? What degree(s) do you possess?

❯ Notre Dame is one of the few schools that use classical architecture as a vehicle for building

a rock-solid basis for building design. Even as a young person, this resonated with me at a basic, intuitive level. I distinctly remember thinking that I could go there to get a practical education based in reality. Looking back, it is strange to see how avant-garde it was and to think that tradition was the key to learning how we might build new.

As the project manager of Urban Design Associates, what are your primary responsibilities and duties? Please describe a typical day.

❯ Although I was raised a detail guy, I now am hyper-specialized in being a generalist. I lead a diverse team of creative types that include architects, planners, landscape architects, artists, engineers, economists, developers, and graphic designers. My chief role, beyond management of people, is to

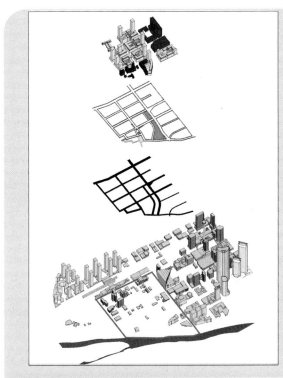

focus the efforts of the team on reaching our objectives in the most ethical, responsible, practical, and economical fashion, while never losing sight of both our own and our patron/client/customer's aspirations, hopes, and goals.

In 2010, you cofounded www.Street-Sense.org; what is its focus and why did you start it?

❭ A colleague of mine left Pittsburgh about a year beforehand. We always maintained a strong friendship and correspondence (mostly through email and phone calls) about what we were seeing around us. These conversations slowly evolved into an online platform for sharing our conversation with

◀ Calgary East Village, Calgary, Alberta, Canada. Architect: Urban Design Associates.

▼ Calgary East Village, Calgary, Alberta, Canada. Architect: Urban Design Associates.

a much broader audience. Street-Sense is now a multidisciplinary look at the challenges and opportunities that our cities, towns, and countrysides are facing.

It is based on the principle that the design of our environments cannot be left simply to architects and engineers. On the contrary, what is around us is a product of every discipline working, or not working, together to create the most practical response to the needs of a society. Our open panel of contributors includes architects, urbanists, economists, developers, financiers, lawyers, and engineers. The goal is to make connections where there often is none. By making uncommon links we arrive at commonsense solutions to adapt, grow, and prosper in an ever-evolving world. Our approach relies on the principles of thrift ("that which cause a ramifying series of solutions"—Wendell Berry).

Since launching, we have begun our most important initiative to date in uncovering what have come to be called Investment-Ready Places. These are the towns and cities dotting our country that are large enough to matter and small enough to attract meaningful change. Their return to a strong and robust form will be among our generation's greatest opportunities.

How and why did you pursue what might be considered a career path beyond architecture?

❯ The reason is probably equal parts interests and need. I had always thought of building in terms of assemblage. What are the relationships between seemingly unrelated subjects? How does the way we organize ourselves in the landscape and in cities affect our ability to adapt to an unpredictable world or come together to celebrate traditions and living? How do buildings come together in a way that is understandable to someone who does not easily read plans, elevations, or sections? And so it is that I came to love urbanism as the melding together of such a diverse array of overlapping influences.

But there was also a market need that fueled a basic entrepreneurial spirit within. Even in school I could see how the myopia in which many in the field looked at their responsibilities was causing widespread unintended consequences that could not be adequately addressed in single-building programs. This is not to say that building architects, draftsmen, and civil engineers do not have a role. They are critical and indisposable. The trick—and the need—is in finding creative and supportive means to pull it all together to create vibrant, magical places that endure.

What has been your greatest challenge during your professional career?

❯ Dealing with the loss of trust in those that used to rule the building site: the foreman, craftsman, artisans, and empiricists. For example, the Golden Gate Bridge was built off a drawing set of less than a hundred sheets because everyone from the chief engineers to the welder had a skill that could reasonably be expected to perform. My parents' house built in 2007 (one built in a traditional vernacular with little complexity), on the other hand, took at least as many sheets as the far more complex bridge. This is unsustainable. Finding the balance of what should be set on the drafting table (or computer) and what should or could be determined by those in the field is our challenge and a fantastic opportunity to collaborate.

BUILDING TYPES

URBAN RESIDENTIAL A

Building Type Criteria

Lot Size (L)		Min.	Max.
(L1)	Lot width (feet)	80	300
(L2)	Lot depth (feet)	40	200
(L3)	Lot area (square feet)	3,200	60,000
(L3)	Lot area (acres)	.07	1.4

Setbacks and Build-to Zone (S)		Min.	Max.
(S1)	Front setback (feet)	0	15
(S2)	Side yard (feet)	5	25
(S3)	Side street setback on corner lots (feet)	0	15
(S4)	Build-to zone depth (feet)	5	10
(S5)	Main body facade % in build-to zone	50	100
(S6)	Front Parking setback (feet)	30	Varies

Main Body Specifications (B)		Min.	Max.
(B1)	Main body width (feet)	60	230
(B2)	Main body depth (feet)	30	65
(B3)	Main body area (square feet)	2,600	60,000
(B4)	Height (number of stories)	2	4.5
(B5)	Ground storey height (feet floor-to-floor)	14	20
(B6)	Upper storey height (feet floor-to-floor)	11	12

Massing & Composition (M)		
(M1)	Roof pitch range	3:12 to 14:12
(M2)	Flat roofs permitted	Yes
(M3)	Green roofs permitted	Yes
(M4)	Bay width range (% of width)	10 to 50
(M5)	Minimum ground storey transparency (% of street-facing facade)	50
(M6)	Minimum upper storey transparency (% of street-facing facade)	30
(M7)	Maximum distance between street-facing building entrances (feet)	80

Use and Density (U)		
(U1)	Ground storey permitted uses	Residential, Commercial
(U2)	Upper storey permitted uses	Residential

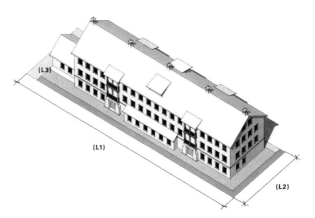

General lot dimensions (L)

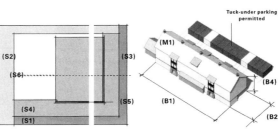

Setbacks and build-to zone on in-line and corner lots (S)

Main body specifications (B) & massing (M)

Permitted Transect Zones

T1	T2	T3	T4
Not Permitted	Conditional	Permitted	Permitted

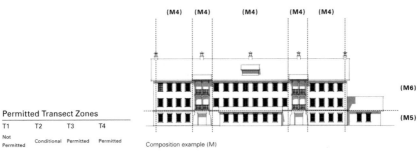

Composition example (M)

Great Pond Village, Windsor, Connecticut. Architect: Urban Design Associates.

DRAFT | 6 MAY 2011

URBAN RESIDENTIAL B

Building Type Criteria

Lot Size (L)

		Min.	Max.
(L1)	Lot width (feet)	80	100
(L2)	Lot depth (feet)	110	200
(L3)	Lot area (square feet)	9000	15000
(L3)	Lot area (acres)	0.20	0.35

Setbacks and Build-to Zone (S)

		Min.	Max.
(S1)	Front setback (feet)	5	25
(S2)	Side yard (feet)	5	20
(S3)	Side street setback on corner lots (feet)	5	25
(S4)	Build-to zone depth (feet)	5	10
(S5)	Main body facade % in build-to zone	50	100
(S6)	Front Parking setback (feet from front facade)	20	n/a

Main Body Specifications (B)

		Min.	Max.
(B1)	Main body width (feet)	50	70
(B2)	Main body depth (feet)	30	50
(B3)	Main body area (square feet)	3,750	14,000
(B4)	Height (number of stories)	2.5	4
(B5)	Ground storey height (feet floor-to-floor)	10	n/a
(B6)	Upper storey height (feet floor-to-floor)	9	n/a

Massing & Composition (M)

(M1)	Roof pitch range	4:12 to 14:12
(M2)	Flat roofs permitted	Yes
(M3)	Green roofs permitted	Yes
(M4)	Bay width range (% of width)	20 to 50
(M5)	Minimum ground storey transparency (% of street-facing facade)	40
(M6)	Minimum upper storey transparency (% of street-facing facade)	30
(M7)	Maximum distance between street-facing building entrances (feet)	150

Use and Density (U)

(U1)	Ground storey permitted uses	Residential
(U2)	Upper storey permitted uses	Residential

Permitted Transect Zones

T1	T2	T3	T4
Not Permitted	Permitted	Permitted	Permitted

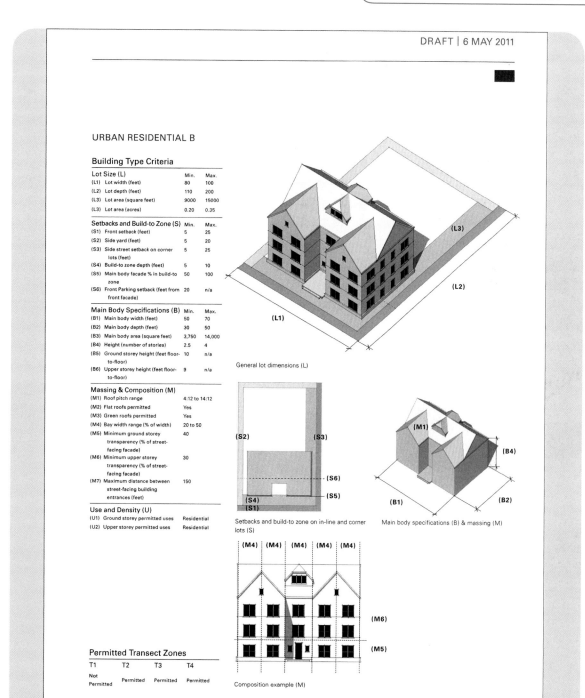

General lot dimensions (L)

Setbacks and build-to zone on in-line and corner lots (S)

Main body specifications (B) & massing (M)

Composition example (M)

What is the most/least satisfying part of your position/career?

❭ The most satisfying part is solving problems in a practical and beautiful way with the clients and customers at our side and the builders in the room. The least satisfying is how easily this can get short-cutted out of the design process.

Who or what experience has been a major influence on your career?

❭ Katrina, the 2008 recession, and living in the neighborhoods of Pittsburgh all taught me lessons too important to be ignored. Jane Jacobs, William Whyte, Wendell Berry, Nassim Teleb, Ray Gindroz, Andres Duany, and Richard Florida have all been key to understanding the power of observation to drive design responses. I am very fortunate to have a talented team at Urban Design Associates, a creative group of friends interested in everything from fly fishing to macroeconomics, and an amazing wife and family that helps make sense of it all.

Do you still consider yourself as an architect?

❭ Now more than ever.

Perception Architect

ASHLEY W. CLARK, ASSOCIATE AIA, LEED AP, SMPS
Marketing Manager
LandDesign
Charlotte, North Carolina

Why did you become an architect?

❭ I often describe my arrival at architecture school as a complete accident. Architecture was barely on my radar by my senior year of high school, but be-cause of my interest in design and communications my calculus teacher encouraged me to look into it. After spending a day in a multidisciplinary firm, I decided to apply to a few programs. I was lucky to be accepted in late spring to the architecture pro-gram at University of North Carolina at Charlotte (UNCC).

Why did you decide to choose the school, University of North Carolina at Charlotte? What degree(s) do you possess?

❭ This was the only architecture program I was accepted into, and I liked UNCC because it was a growing campus offering larger university ame-nities, but with a modest architecture program. Coming from a small town and high school, this was comfortable to me. I received my bachelor of arts in architecture and bachelor of architecture from UNC Charlotte, as it was a five+one under-graduate program.

In your position as marketing manager, what are your primary responsibilities and duties? Please describe a typical day.

❭ My primary responsibilities include tracking opportunities to pursue, managing our proposal

Middleton Place Plantation. Precedent Sketches of Thesis Project by Ashley Clark at University of North Carolina at Charlotte.

process, making contacts with potential clients and consultants, ensuring our written and graphic marketing collateral is up to date, and seeking public relation opportunities for our firm. I am also working with our creative and technical staff to manage our website and social media efforts. My schedule is typically anything but consistent, which is part of what keeps things interesting. I am always keeping a balance between meeting firm deadlines, fulfilling a number of requests from various parties and finding time to ensure my head is up and looking at what is coming next.

How and why did you pursue what might be considered a career path beyond architecture? Do you still wish to become a licensed architect?

❯ I am currently taking the ARE and plan to become licensed. I believe that if I continue in a role within a A/E/C firm where I am involved in marketing, having my license gives me credibility and more options long term.

I feel that marketing is much more aligned with my skills and interests, and see myself being most successful and satisfied long term by sticking with a career that is focused on communicating the value of design. During school, I would often stop working on the design of my projects so that I could focus more on my presentation and drawings. I just felt that if I had a well-laid-out presentation and was confident in what I was talking about, that I would have a better review. I believe it was this approach that was largely responsible for my receipt of the College of Architecture's Book Award for Representation upon graduation and an early indicator of where my professional career was headed.

For the past few years, you have been in leadership positions for the National Associates Committee of the AIA. What are the challenges facing emerging professionals in the profession?

❯ There are several easy ones we can all agree are present issues: the recovering economy, the lack of retiring partners resulting in stagnant leadership and opportunity within firms, changing technology and how architects best leverage our skills to make a positive difference … I could go on. But one problem I think needs more attention is defining what it means to practice architecture. While I am one who believes that career paths beyond traditional practive are one of the attributes of our education, many continue to focus on the fact that fewer graduates are pursuing traditional practice. While much of the dialogue

WEST | EAST ELEVATION . 2   SCALE: 1/4" = 1'-0"

WEST | EAST ELEVATION . 1   SCALE: 1/4" = 1'-0"

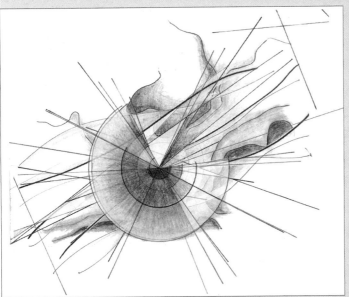

▲ Residing Respectfully: an Ecological Retreat on Kiawah Island. Elevations of Thesis Project by Ashley Clark at University of North Carolina at Charlotte.

◀ Residing Respectfully: an Ecological Retreat on Kiawah Island. Thesis Phenomenological Diagram by Ashley Clark at University of North Carolina at Charlotte.

about this focuses on whether licensure is too hard, or needs to be more accessible, I often if we are focusing on the right piece of the conversation. I support efforts to make the ARE more accessible to graduates but I also think we need to be focused on how the professional can be more collaborative both within the A/E/C industry, and within society. I think this provides the greatest opportunity to architects in sharing the value of design and increasing our value.

Also, what is leadership and how has it benefitted your career path?

❯ I think that leadership is sticking to what you believe, even if it means being different. I do not tend to think of myself as a leader, but when I think about the leadership positions I have held, I believe I ended up in them because I stuck to certain principals that were important to me, rather than trying to blend into the crowd. These opportunities have enabled me to develop an extensive network of mentors and friends who have become an amazing resource to me both personally and professionally. It has also helped me develop valuable skills and perspective that has contributed to my career in ways a traditional internship would not have.

Previously, you worked as an intern architect within an architecture firm. How were these positions the same/different than your current one?

❯ As someone who tends to be a big picture thinker, what I have found to be most exciting about working in marketing is the opportunity to contribute to higher-level conversations about strategy and opportunity for the firm, rather than focusing on sole projects. Much of the work requires similar skills; creative thinking, collaboration, and the management of expectations, but applying them to a different set of problems.

From a compensation standpoint, marketing positions typically provide higher salaries than working as an intern. Considering the number of conversations happening within the profession regarding the value of design thinking, it has been frustrating to learn how little value is placed on the contributions of interns. I actually had an architect tell me one time that he was thinking of hiring two architecture interns to help with marketing efforts, since he could pay them both what he was paying his former marketing director. I was glad to learn at a later time that he did not do so, but it was a perfect example of why I believe so many graduates consider applying their skills elsewhere.

What skills did you gain from your architectural education, or working in the architecture industry, that have contributed to success in your current position?

❯ Regardless of what I end up doing in my career, my architecture education will remain invaluable. The perspective you build, the processes you learn and the critical thinking and problem-solving abilities are applicable in so many ways. I have had many firm partners and principals tell me how much they appreciate their marking team but wish they better understood the industry and what clients are looking for. Because of my education, training, and passion for sharing the value of design, marketing in the A/E/C industry really is a great niche for me.

What has been your greatest challenge as an architect?

❯ Despite the incredible opportunities I have had as a young woman in the field of architecture and design, which has in no doubt been due to the sacrifice and hardships of many women in the profession before me, I have been subject to discrimination and discouraged from pursuing my interests. Although enrollment in our schools is an indicator of progress we are still not where we should be to make architecture a desirable option for many women. This is a multi-faceted problem of personal versus professional goals, firm cultures, societal pressures and job demands, which I believe are in great part circumstantial and tough to tackle with widespread effort. But even though it has not been at the forefront of the issues I have advocated for through my leadership roles, I have hoped that my involvement at the national level has provided a fresh perspective of what it means to be an architect today.

Architect, Connector, Change Agent

KIMBERLY DOWDELL

Project Manager/Director of Marketing

Levien & Company

New York, New York

Why and how did you become an architect?

❭ I decided to enter the profession because of my interest in playing a key role in urban redevelopment in my hometown, Detroit. I made this decision when I was 11 years old and I have been working towards that goal ever since. I enrolled in a high school with an emphasis on the arts and I went to one of the highest-ranked architecture programs in the nation—Cornell University. After my architecture degree, I worked for the federal government and then gained experience in the private sector to complete my internship (IDP) requirements.

Why and how did you decide on which school to attend for your architecture degree? What degree(s) do you possess?

❭ I earned a bachelor of architecture from Cornell University in 2006. I selected Cornell because of its outstanding reputation as well as the opportunity to be exposed to a world away from home (but not too far) to gain a new perspective. Another key component of my decision to select Cornell was the breadth of course offerings in virtually every subject matter. The College of Architecture, Art and Planning (AAP) is one of seven academically diverse colleges within the university. I appreciated the opportunity to take classes in all of the colleges to benefit from a well-rounded educational experience at a world-class institution.

Middle Collegiate Church Façade and Accessibility Improvements Project, New York, New York. Architect: Rosen Johnson Architects; Project Manager: Levien & Company. PHOTOGRAPHER: KIMBERLY DOWDELL.

What has been your greatest challenge as an architect?

❭ My greatest challenge has been finding my way back to do the work that prompted my interest in architecture initially—revitalizing Detroit. The issues facing Detroit currently are vast and far beyond the scope of design. While design can play a pivotal role in revitalizing the city, there is much to be done from a political, social, and economic standpoint in order to provide a platform for physical improvements.

One of the benefits of my secondary career training in marketing and business development is the opportunity to better understand relationship building and the power of creating a strong network. The most important asset of a change agent is having the ability to connect people, ideas, and resources to create positive results. While it is incredibly challenging to improve complex urban problems as an architect without a client to pay the bills, it is my hope that some of my other skills and resources will enable me to have a vital impact on Detroit and other places that struggle with similar issues.

For you, how has it been being a minority female in a predominantly male white profession?

❯ I have found the profession to be more welcoming than not. I realize that has not always been the case for women of color in architecture, but I have to be honest and say that I have had an exceptional experience. Those who have come before me, such as the legendary Norma Merrick Sklarek, have blazed a phenomenal trail that was not particularly easy at times. I deeply appreciate the barriers that she and so many others have overcome to allow me to have better opportunities in this profession.

I owe part of my positive professional experiences to my involvement with the National Organization of Minority Architects (NOMA). From the beginning of my engagement with NOMA as a third-year student, I have had access to the best mentors and advocates a young architect could ask for. Most of my employment opportunities have been a direct result of my NOMA network. Another important aspect of my positive experience in the profession has been the Cornell network and reputation, which is incredibly beneficial.

In addition to Cornell and NOMA, I have been fortunate to have great mentors and advocates in the workplace—representing both genders and a variety of backgrounds. In general, I believe that the key to minimizing feelings of disadvantage is building a strong support system that can help shield you from some of the unfortunate things that happen in such a challenging profession. This statement applies to any person of any ethnic background or social status. Further, as the beneficiary of so many great mentors, I feel that it is my duty to mentor younger architects who are entering the profession, helping them to build their networks and have positive experiences as well.

In 2005, you cofounded the SEED (Social, Economic, Environmental Design) Network (www.seed-network.org); what is it, and why was it important to create?

❯ SEED (Social, Economic, Environmental Design) is a network, a tool and a certification system created to address "Triple Bottom Line" issues during the development process. SEED's mission is to "advance the right of every person to live in a socially, economically and environmentally healthy community." SEED was important to create because it provides designers, developers, and community leaders a framework with which to think critically about the holistic well-being of a place and it provides resources that allow good work to be measured, recognized, celebrated, and incentivized.

Here is the SEED background story: I was interning at the General Services Administration (GSA), in the Office of the Chief Architect during the summer of 2005, just before my final year of architecture school. My supervisor was Steve Lewis, AIA, a dear friend and mentor. Steve handed me a copy of *Metropolis* and suggested that I take a look. Immediately, I was drawn into the article written by Lance Hosey entitled "The Ethics of Brick." It addressed the triple bottom line, with a particular

▶ Military Park Revitalization Project, Newark, New Jersey. Design Team: Birdsall Services Group, H3 Hardy Collaboration Architecture, Hackett Landscape Design, Domingo Gonzalez Associates; Redevelopers: Biederman Redevelopment Ventures; Project Managers: Levien & Company. PHOTOGRAPHER: KIMBERLY DOWDELL.

▼ Military Park Revitalization Project, Newark, New Jersey. Design Team: Birdsall Services Group, H3 Hardy Collaboration Architecture, Hackett Landscape Design, Domingo Gonzalez Associates; Redevelopers: Biederman Redevelopment Ventures; Project Managers: Levien & Company. PHOTOGRAPHER: KIMBERLY DOWDELL.

focus on social equity. As I read Hosey's article and reminisced on my experience of growing up in Detroit, I had an epiphany, and I saw a solution. The U.S. Green Building Council had created a new rating system called Leadership in Energy and Environmental Design or LEED.

After reading the article, the concept of augmenting LEED with a social focus in the development realm emerged. I simply suggested to Steve there should be something like LEED for social issues, and we could call it "SEED." At that moment, SEED was born and has received the support of countless individuals and organizations since 2005. Design Corps, led by Bryan Bell, has been the primary steward of SEED's development over the past several years. Due to the dedicated work of many, SEED is now poised to become the common standard to guide, evaluate, and measure the social, economic and environmental impact of design projects.

What led you to enter real estate development? And how is what you do different than an architect?

❯ I was recruited to join Levien & Company by the firm's president and founder, Kenneth Levien, FAIA. He and I had a brief introductory discussion at a networking event, and he was impressed by the fact that while I was trained as an architect, I had taken on a marketing, communications, and business development role at HOK New York. Mr. Levien invited me to consider leaving HOK to pursue a leadership role in marketing at his real estate project management firm. Being an architect himself, he understood my request to have a dual role that encompassed both marketing and project management. Mr. Levien offered me the dual position and I am now gratefully learning about the practice of project management and owner representation in addition to bringing in new business.

The primary difference between project management and architecture is perspective (no pun intended). Having sat on both sides of the table, I understand that architects are looking out for the client's best interests chiefly from a programming, functionality, and aesthetic perspective. Project managers are looking out for the client's best interests from an overall project budget, schedule, and quality-of-work point of view. As project managers (who also happen to be architects), we respect the role and expertise of the architects on our projects. Our job is to ensure that the architects, contractors, and all of the consultants on a building project collaborate successfully as a team to meet the client's objectives.

What are your primary responsibilities and duties?

❯ At Levien & Company, I am primarily responsible for marketing, business development, public relations, and ensuring that our 20-person staff is fully engaged in great projects in and around New York City. Our practice manages building projects for a lot of major independent schools, religious institutions, museums, workplaces, service organizations, residential buildings, theaters, and urban landscapes. I gather intelligence about new opportunities and pursuing the work that our talented staff members enjoy managing.

My other role is to serve as a project manager for two projects where I work closely with a senior project manager at Levien. Together, we are working on a small renovation project for a historic church in Manhattan and a six-acre park revitalization project in the heart of Downtown Newark. I am learning about the development process from the owner's perspective, which has been incredibly enlightening. We organize, manage, and document all aspects of the assignment on behalf of our clients to ensure that the project remains on target from a budget, schedule, and quality standpoint.

What is the most/least satisfying part of career as an architect?

❯ The path toward licensure has been the most disappointing and challenging aspect of the profession. I hope the process will improve for future generations of architects because as it stands today, many of my colleagues and I feel that the IDP and ARE are designed to be deterrents to the profession.

To date, the most satisfying work that I've been able to do as an architect has actually been my volunteer work on behalf of NOMA. In 2008, I initiated the First Annual NOMA Service Learning Project in Washington, DC, one day prior to the NOMA Conference.

Since then, NOMA has conducted four additional service projects in the cities where the conferences have been held, including St. Louis, Boston, Atlanta, and Detroit. I have really enjoyed leading the project each year and working closely with the local NOMA chapters to provide a day of service to a community organization in need of design and/or modest constructions services. It has been great to work with local students to provide them with exposure to the projects each year as well.

Also satisfying is my playing a role in the growing movement of Public Interest Design. I have been involved since I cofounded SEED in 2005, and the experience has been incredibly rewarding. When I was employed at HOK, I had a unique opportunity to cofound HOK Impact with another employee, Sarah (Weissman) Dirsa, which sought to promote the pro-bono work done by the firm and to more formally connect all of the employees who were engaged in Public Interest Design work, both on behalf of HOK and privately

Who or what experience has been a major influence on your career?

❯ My overall positive experience in architecture can be attributed to the school that I attended (Cornell), the organizations that I have been involved with (NOMA, AIA, ACE, AREW, etc.), the organizations that I have cofounded (SEED and HOK Impact) and my incredible mentors (Kathy Dixon, Steve Lewis, Alick Dearie, Herman Howard, Barbara Laurie, John Cary, Chris Laul, Ken Levien, and Pamela Holzapfel, among so many others).

In this profession, as with many other aspects of life, the more you put into it, the more you are able to get out of it. Since beginning architecture school in the fall 2001, I have invested my all into this work and I have seen tremendous returns thus far. It is my hope that the best of my experience working in the built environment remains to be seen.

Career Paths

Pursuing architecture prepares you for a vast array of career possibilities. Many of these are within traditional architectural practice, but many are also available in related career fields.

Within the traditional architecture firm, you may obtain a beginning position as an intern and progress to junior designer, project architect, and, eventually, associate or principal. This does not happen overnight; it can take a lifetime. You may pursue your career in a traditional firm regardless of its size—small, medium, or large—or you may choose to work in a different setting such as a private corporation or company; a local, state, or federal government agency; or a university—or, after obtaining your architectural license, you may start your own firm. You must consider which path is best suited for you.

ARCHITECTURAL PRACTICE

How does a career in architecture begin? How does a person progress from graduation to become an architect? Following the AIA Definition of Architect Positions, the path seems linear, progressing from an intern to architect; once licensed (and depending on the firm), the path continues to Architect I (3 to 5 years) and Architect/Designers III (8 to 10 years). From there, the path progresses to project manager, department head or senior manager, junior principal/partner, and concludes with senior principal/partner.

Of course, the path of a career in architecture is not linear; however, it is helpful to understand these titles with the knowledge and responsibility associated with them as outlined in Dana Cuff's *Architecture: The Story of Practice.* Upon entry into the profession, the intern is building upon their educational foundation through practical experience under the supervision of an architect; the intern is tracking their experience in the Intern Development Program (IDP), an essential step in becoming an architect. After becoming licensed, the architect demonstrates competence, gathers responsibility, and gains autonomy, and management tasks. When at the full-fledged stage, the architect is gaining fiscal responsibility on a widening sphere of influence.

The entering graduate does face challenges. Because there is a gap between education and practice, what happens in the studios of schools is much different than the studios of the firms. For this reason, architecture students are strongly encouraged to seek experience in architecture firms during their academic years.

Those seeking licensure will find it essential to secure employment within an architecture firm to gain the necessary experience under the direct supervision of an architect and meet the requirements of the IDP; however, in recognition of opportunities to go beyond traditional practice (such as working under registered professionals in related professions like landscape architecture; or working under an architect outside of a firm setting), interns can gain experience in other work settings.

When seeking employment, you should consider firm size as a factor when considering where to work; in large firms, an intern will be exposed to a broad scale of projects and a full-service firm, but may be limited in their exposure to aspects of practice. In a small firm, the intern may

ARCHITECT POSITIONS

Senior Principal/Partner	Architect/Designer II
Mid-Level Principal/Partner	Architect/Designer I
Junior Principal/Partner	Third-Year Intern
Department Head/Senior Manager	Second-Year Intern
Project Manager	Entry-Level Intern
Senior Architect/Designer	Student
Architect/Designer III	

Source: AIA, *Definition of Architect Positions* (Washington, DC: AIA, 2006).

Milwaukee Art Museum, Milwaukee, Wisconsin. Architect: Santiago Calatrava. PHOTOGRAPHER: LEE W. WALDREP, Ph.D.

see a full spectrum of projects, but the projects may be limiting in scope and size. Where you work at the start of your career can have an impact on your future career trajectory in architecture.

Within what is typically referred to as traditional practice, there are firms that develop specialties. While still architecture firms, these specialties provide opportunities to showcase talent or strong interest. Examples of such specialties include programming, design, specifications, or construction contract administration, or sustainability.

Some firms focus on a particular building types, such as healthcare, religious, justice facilities, housing, interiors, sports facilities, educational, and institutional. One firm, for instance, Animal Arts in Boulder, Colorado, focuses on facilities related to animals, including veterinary hospitals, shelters, and pet resorts. As a specialist in healthcare, an architect can become a certified healthcare architect with the American College of Healthcare Architects (ACHA). Certain knowledge communities of the AIA that focus their energies on building types or specialties include Academy of Architecture for Health; Academy of Architecture for Justice; Committee on Architecture for Education; and Interfaith Forum on Religion, Art and Architecture, among others.

Another means to expand a career within the profession is through supplemental architectural services. Because of the recent economic downturn, the AIA created the Supplemental Architectural Services program, a series of detailed essays and slide presentations to offer assistance to architects in expanding their consulting services.

OUTSIDE TRADITIONAL PRACTICE

Beyond traditional practice, architects work in other settings. While no exact statistics are kept, it is estimated that one in five architects work outside private practice.

Corporations and institutions: Do you want to work at McDonald's? It may come as a surprise that McDonald's hires architects, as do many businesses and corporations. Corporate architects may serve as in-house architects, but in most cases they represent the interests of the corporation to the outside architects they hire. Depending on the industry, they may be involved with the all phases of a project.

Government and public agencies: Federal, state, and local governments commission more than one-quarter of construction annually. As such, opportunities exist for architects in public agencies. Many levels of government including the military employ architects. In addition to traditional tasks, architects manage facilities and projects, and oversee construction. Emerging professionals may find it difficult to start a career in a public agency, but such career can be extremely worthwhile. Employers of public architects as represented by the Advisory Group of the Public Architects Committee of the AIA Knowledge Community include the State of Ohio, Texas A&M University, U.S. Army Corps of Engineers, Thomas Jefferson National Lab, the City of Dallas, and the Judicial Council of California.

Education and research: For some architects, a substantial career path is teaching and research. According to the National Architectural Accrediting Board (NAAB), there were over 5,998 faculty members within accredited programs of architecture, many of whom are adjunct faculty. Additionally, with over 300 programs in architectural technology at the community college level, many more opportunities exist for architects to teach at this level. In addition to teaching, architects serving as faculty will pursue research interests to test ideas that connect education and practice. Besides teaching future architects, many faculty members also maintain a practice.

BEYOND ARCHITECTURE

As a profession, architecture offers a myriad of possibilities for rewarding careers.

IRENE DUMAS-TYSON

I am certain that architectural graduates who are in command of the powerful problem defining and problem solving skills of the designer, will be fully capable of designing their own imaginative careers by creating new definitions of meaningful work for architects that are embedded in the social landscape of human activity and life's events.

LESLIE KANES WEISMAN

An architectural education is excellent preparation for many career paths beyond architecture. In fact, the career possibilities with an architectural education are truly limitless. Anecdotal estimates suggest that only one-half of architectural graduates pursue licensure. By applying the ideas listed earlier in "career designing," one can launch a successful career beyond architecture.

Career paths beyond traditional practice tap into the creative-thinking and problem-solving skills developed from an architectural education. The interest in these paths is growing; the results of the most recent AIA/NCARB Internship and Career Survey of interns and emerging professionals indicate that nearly one-fifth of the respondents do not plan on pursuing a traditional career in architecture, although they still plan to obtain their license.

Over the last four years, *Archinect*, an online forum for architecture, has featured over 25 architects who have applied their backgrounds in architecture to other careers fields through its "Working out of the Box" series. While most are still connected to design in some form, the range of career fields is quite diverse: filmmaker, organic farmer, artist, design director at a resort hotel chain, user experience designer, information designer, and design technology consulting. Also, the reasons for pursuing careers beyond architecture are varied and typically not tied to the recent economic downturn.

For his doctoral thesis, Robert Douglas, FAIA, studied nontraditional careers (maverick architects) and found those that he studied credited "design thinking" as helpful in their careers beyond architecture. From his research, architectural graduates and architects pursued careers in law, investment banking and real estate development, computer software, lighting design, film production and set design, cultural policy, architectural criticism and journalism, facilities planning, land planning and management, industrial and product design, arts programming, structural engineering, highway design, public arts installation, architectural photography, painting and sculpture, and clothing design.

An article in a recent issue of *Columns*, the AIA Pittsburgh magazine, entitled "It's a Wonderful Life," highlighted architects who built new careers after first having one as an architect. First, the article outlines the path of actor Jimmy Stewart, who graduated from Princeton University having studied architecture but instead pursued acting (hence the title of the article). Next, it highlights four individuals who after successful careers as architects moved to new careers paths—development, needlepoint (fiber art), community design, and construction supervisor. In each case, they discuss how their education and background in architecture paved the way for their new chosen career.

Related design professional (landscape architecture, interior design, urban design): Given the parallel education of design, it is clear why some architects pursue the related career fields of landscape architecture, interior design, and urban design. Many architects pursue careers in interior architecture or space designing while other pursue the profession of landscape architecture to design outdoor spaces. Others still combine their talents in design to focus on urban design.

Engineering and technical: As architecture is both an art and a science, many architects will pursue careers in engineering or more technical fields. Many with a joint degree in architecture and engineering will pursue civil or structural engineering, but there are other opportunities that exist if there is an interest in the technical side of the profession.

Construction: Because of the connection between design and construction, many architects have pursued careers in construction as construction managers, general contractors, and/or related associates. Architecture firms are expanding their services to include design-build and construction management, bridging the two disciplines together.

Real estate: More recently, more architects have become involved with real estate development, the creation of communities and the repositioning of land or buildings into a higher or better use. For architects wishing to expand their influence on the building process, real estate may be a good fit as it connects multiple disciplines (engineering, architecture, planning, finance, marketing, law, and environmental impact).

Art and design: Because much of what architects do is considered an art, it is no surprise that many architects pursue careers in art and design; this extends from fine arts—painting to applied arts—graphic design and furniture design. Some will determine a way to combine their background in architecture more directly with art while others truly move away from architecture to pursue their art.

Architectural products and services: Perhaps less obvious is careers in architectural products and services; as these manufacturers market and sell their products and services to architects, who better to serve in these positions but those trained as architects. With an interest and talent in sales, opportunities exist for a rewarding and fulfilling career.

Other: Building on the quote from Irene Dumas-Tyson, what are the myriad of possibilities? What career paths are open to architectural graduates, emerging professionals or architects? The true answer is over 25,000 occupations as defined by the Bureau of Labor Statistics that potentially highlight skills and fulfill passion. Truly, the only limitation to possible career paths is one's imagination.

Katherine S. Proctor, FCSI, CDT, AIA, former director of student services at the University of Tennessee, shares her perspective:

For an individual interested in the career of architecture, the possibilities are endless. I have seen students graduate and become registered architects, professional photographers, lawyers, bankers, business owners, interior designers, contractors and artists. The education is so broad with a strong liberal arts base, that it provides a firm foundation for a wide array of exploration. This comes from the content of the curriculums, but also from the methodology. The design studio, which is the core of the curriculum, provides a method to take pieces of intellectual information and apply it within the design process. The movement from thinking to doing is powerful. The ability to integrate hundreds of pieces of information, issues, influences and form and find a solution is a skill that any professional needs to solve problems, whether they are building issues or life issues.

KATHERINE S. PROCTOR, FCSI, CDT, AIA

Notre Dame du Haut, Ronchamp, France. Architect: Le Corbusier. PHOTOGRAPHER: DANA TAYLOR

THE CAREER PATHS OF AN ARCHITECT

ARCHITECTURAL PRACTICE

Draftsperson
Intern
Junior Designer
Model Maker
Principal
Project Architect
Senior Designer
Staff Architect

OUTSIDE TRADITIONAL PRACTICE

Academic Dean/Administrator
Architectural Historian
Corporate Architect
Facilities Architect
Professor
Public Architect
Researcher
University Architect

RELATED DESIGN PROFESSIONAL

Golf Course Architect
Interior Designer
Landscape Architect
Urban Planner

ENGINEERING AND TECHNICAL

Architectural Acoustics
Building Pathologist
Cartographer

Civil Engineer
Computer System Analyst
Construction/Building Inspector
Environmental Planner
Illuminating Engineer
Marine Architect
Structural Engineer

CONSTRUCTION

Carpenter
Construction Manager
Construction Software Designer
Contractor
Design Build
Estimator
Fire Protection Designer
Land Surveyor
Project Manager

REAL ESTATE

Real Estate Agent
Real Estate Developer

ART AND DESIGN

Architectural Illustrator
Architectural Photographer
Art/Creative Director
Artist
Clothing Designer
Exhibit Designer
Filmmaker
Furniture Designer

Graphic Artist/Designer

Industrial/Product Designer

Lighting Designer

Museum Curator

Set Designer

Toy Designer

Web Designer

ARCHITECTURAL PRODUCTS AND SERVICES

Product Manufacturer Representative

Product Sales

OTHER

Architectural Critic

City Manager

Lawyer

Preservationist

Property Assessor

Public Official

Writer

Nascent Practice Models for Social Impact

KATHERINE DARNSTADT, AIA, LEED AP BD+C, NCARB

Founder and Principal Architect

Latent Design

Director

Architecture for Humanity–Chicago

Chicago, Illinois

Why did you become an architect?

❯ I think about this question a great deal and try to always find a better answer.

Sometimes I think it was the years hanging out in the shop and job sites of my father's electrical contracting company on weekends while he worked in the office, or the sophisticated mechanical pencils he would bring home that blew away my yellow,

wooden 2B. Other times I am sure my prior studies in philosophy had some level of influence on me. Maybe it was a naïve but bold desire for equity that needed a profession to be able to manifest itself.

I chose architecture to create a space for everyone.

I created Latent Design because I got laid off from architecture.

I had to decide, very quickly, if I wanted to be an architect or not. I chose the former and over time, have created a demand for the firm that allows it to practice the creation of space at all scales in ways that are sometimes not traditionally architecture.

Why did you decide to choose Illinois Institute of Technology? What degree(s) do you possess?

❯ I graduated from IIT in 2005 with a professional bachelor degree in Architecture. I selected IIT

STEM Bootcamp/Public Workshop, Chicago, Illinois.
PHOTOGRAPHER: LATENT DESIGN.

because of the materials-based program deeply entrenched in a modernist pedagogy that happened to be situated on a campus in a neighborhood undergoing dramatic transition. Studying architecture while witnessing the demolition and creation of architecture and subsequent social upheaval was an important factor in my decision.

Latent Design is a full-service architecture and design collaborative developing innovative solutions to social issues for underrepresented individuals and communities; please outline why the passion for public interest design.

❯ All design is within the public interest.

Whether pro bono, which means "for good," without monetary compensation or $30M museum, the profession has always impacted the public, and architects uniquely think about the public, but it has not been framed that way. While Latent Design may seek to use design as a form of social justice localized within our Chicago communities, what we collectively call good design as architects' impacts individuals through social, environmental, and economic impact. The design we create needs to be sustainable not only in the environmental sense, but viable as a long-term economic driver for a community.

What are your primary responsibilities and duties as founder and principal? Please describe a typical day.

❯ The typical day for Latent Design as a start up architecture firm is about 10 hours long and involves work in every area of the business at all levels. The roles necessary for myself as founder and for the first years the only architect included marketing, accounting, intern, project manager, and principal. Meetings with clients take place, proposals are written, CAD drawings are redlined, and new concepts developed. As the firm is growing, time now includes collaborating with employees and researching storefront office spaces. Each day is rigorous, sometimes uneventful, but always enjoyable.

In addition to your work with Latent Design, you serve as director of Architecture for Humanity–Chicago. What is Architecture for Humanity and what type of work does it perform?

❯ Architecture for Humanity is a nonprofit founded in 1999 by Cameron Sinclair and Kate Stohr to build a more sustainable future using the power of design through a global network of building professionals. The organization has over 50 chapters around the world and I was the Director of the

Fresh Moves Mobile Produce Market, Chicago, Illinois. Architect: Latent Design with Architecture for Humanity Chicago.
PHOTOGRAPHER: MIG ROD.

Chicago Chapter for the past four years. The work performed in the chapter is completed pro bono by an all volunteer team of professionals which ranges from design, development, and small scale construction partnerships on projects that focus on restoring access to public space, affordable housing, critical services, facilities design, and post natural disaster resiliency planning. Since 2009, the Chicago chapter has been able to provide over $1.2M in pro bono services to Chicago and international nonprofits on an average operating budget of less than $2,000.

What has been your greatest challenge as an architect?

❯ Empathetic design, understanding other professions that shape the built environment and their role/influence, examples of firms that utilized these methods currently as inspiration.

What is the most/least satisfying part of being an architect?

❯ The most satisfying part of being an architect is being able to hear the stories behind the organization and people and then manifesting that into a space and place. The biggest challenge, and sometimes least satisfying part of being an architect is trying to incorporate design into advocacy and policy initiatives.

Who or what experience has been a major influence on your career?

❯ Recently, during a community design workshop for a project which was full of the prescribed tools

Jackson Flat, Chicago, Illinois.
Architect: Latent Design.
PHOTOGRAPHER: LATENT
DESIGN.

Jackson Flat, Chicago, Illinois.
Architect: Latent Design.
PHOTOGRAPHER: LATENT DESIGN.

of design workshops of Post-it notes and Sharpie markers, I had a participant come up to me at the end. She thanked me for the time and workshop, but informed me, quite succinctly, that a Post-it Note is not a job. This building I was creating and this process of design I was advocating for needed to create jobs, skills, and economic opportunity.

I thought about this for some time, and since that meeting, I have taken on the model of vertical integration, common in manufacturing, to hire local community members as consultants to our design team to help us define the context of a place more accurately so we can design the context more authentically.

A Creative Career Transformation

ERIC TAYLOR, ASSOCIATE AIA
Photographer
Taylor Design & Photography, Inc.
Fairfax Station, Virginia

Why and how did you become an architect?

❯ I decided on an architectural career to combine my visual/creative side with technical aptitudes. I went to college, worked in intern positions in high school and college to learn about the work world of architecture; during my architectural career I worked

in variety of firms—a three-person design firm to 150-person (Architecture & Engineering) firm.

Why and how did you decide on which school to attend for your architecture degree? What degree(s) do you possess?

❯ I looked for a school that combined a strong design direction with the practical side. I wanted to graduate with practical skills along with design sensibilities. I chose Syracuse University and graduated with a bachelor of architecture degree. I also studied photography as a sideline.

Corporate Interior, Fairfax, Virginia. PHOTOGRAPHER: ERIC TAYLOR, ASSOCIATE AIA. PHOTO© ERICTAYLORPHOTO.COM.

Potomac Tower, Fairfax, Virginia. Architect: I. M. Pei. PHOTOGRAPHER: ERIC TAYLOR, ASSOCIATE AIA. PHOTO © ERICTAYLORPHOTO.COM.

Why and how did you transition from being an architect to an architectural photographer?

❯ I had 17 successful years in architecture, many as a senior project architect and designer. My work included office buildings; commercial, municipal, and educational buildings; and interior design. But I came to a crossroads in my career—I could join another firm, start my own firm, or try something new. I chose something new.

I had always loved photography and had coordinated the photo programs at the firms where I had worked. I realized I could bring something to architectural photography that was unique: a true understanding of architecture from inside the profession. So my new direction was set. Because I lacked some of the technical expertise, I attended photography school to learn about professional lighting and camera systems. I built up a photo portfolio by shooting projects on specification and by photographing the projects of architect friends. Then I got serious about marketing and launched my new career.

How are the two disciplines the same/different?

❯ The skills needed for success in architecture are parallel to those needed for success in architectural photography—ability to communicate visually and verbally, ability to visualize three-dimensionally, ability to distill a set of requirements to their essence, and the ability to arrive at solutions that answer these requirements.

Both disciplines require an attention to detail and the ability to visualize what does not yet exist. The goal of architecture is to arrive at a three-dimensional solution to a complex set of criteria. The goal of architectural photography is to analyze that three-dimensional solution and find a compelling two-dimensional representation of it that explains the three-dimensional reality. While architectural design deals with form, volume, color, texture, perspective, and so on, the essence of photography is light and its effect on the rendering of those design elements. I believe an understanding of design concepts, design elements, and construction methods enhances architectural photography.

When provided a commission, how do you approach the assignment?

❯ First, I meet with client to discuss the scope of the assignment—exteriors, interiors, and/or aerials, quantity of images expected, and so on. Next, we discuss the intended uses of the photography—display prints, award submissions, in-house newsletters, website, and so on; the design concept that the designer wants to be sure is expressed in the photos; the logistics of access to the space, scheduling, budget. From there, I scout the location to assess the equipment needs. Finally, I schedule assistants and do the photography.

What has been your greatest challenge as a photographer?

❯ Predicting the weather! It is difficult to schedule exterior shoots very far in the future since it is weather dependent. Other than that, it has the same challenge as starting any new business: developing a client base. On the technical side, photographing interiors under mixed lighting—daylight, fluorescent, incandescent—was a new challenge. But on the creative side, I feel like I have been preparing for this my whole life.

What is most/least satisfying about your work as a photographer?

❯ Most satisfying is creating dynamic images and having clients excited about them; being involved with a wide diversity of building types, design, and construction; in addition, I no longer have to wait a year or two to see the results of my efforts!

I do miss the complexity of the design problem-solving process, but it is outweighed by the satisfaction I gain from photography.

Do you still consider yourself to be an architect?

❯ Yes, but more now as it influences my photography and my understanding of the buildings and construction that I photograph.

Who or what experience has been a major influence on your career?

❯ In college, I became aware of the value of strong visual presentation. Good design professors required it, and I learned that dynamic graphics and photography were essential tools to explain and ultimately gain the support of others for a design solution. As an architectural photographer, I see myself as an aid to others in their marketing efforts, by providing dynamic images of their design work.

Why still photography versus video or interactive images?

❯ While video allows a broad-sweep understanding of a building or space, I see architectural still photography as visual editing. In this way, still compositions present the built environment in an edited version, so others will see the inherent concept, form, composition, texture, color, balance, and beauty that I see.

Fredericksburg Academy, Fredericksburg, Virginia. Architect: Cooper Carry & Associates. PHOTOGRAPHER: ERIC TAYLOR, ASSOCIATE AIA. PHOTO © ERICTAYLORPHOTO.COM.

Ronald Reagan Washington National Airport, Washington, DC. Architect: Cesar Pelli & Associates. PHOTOGRAPHER: ERIC TAYLOR, ASSOCIATE AIA. PHOTO © ERICTAYLORPHOTO.COM.

Theorizing in Architecture

KAREN CORDES SPENCE, Ph.D., AIA, LEED AP

Associate Professor
Drury University
Springfield, Missouri

Why did you become an architect?

❭ I was interested in architecture because I liked art but wanted to pursue a career other than in the fine arts. I was good at math, so architecture seemed to fit. Once I was in architecture school, it opened my eyes to the built environment and how it shapes our societies and lives. I saw that it can honestly make a difference in the success of a community or the quality of a person's existence. I also enjoyed the challenges of the studio projects and history, theory, and other courses were of great interest to me.

▶ Professor Karen Cordes Spence with Student, Drury University. PHOTOGRAPHER: BRUCE MOORE, AIA, LEED AP.

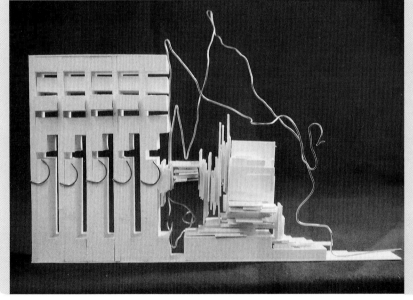

◀ Student Model— First Year Project, Drury University. PHOTOGRAPHER: KAREN CORDES SPENCE, Ph.D.

Why did you decide to choose the school(s) that you did? What degree(s) do you possess? Why did you continue your education and pursue the master of science and doctor of philosophy in architecture?

❯ I attended the Fay Jones School of Architecture at the University of Arkansas for my undergraduate studies because it was my state school and it had a great reputation. After receiving my bachelor of architecture, I moved to Washington, DC, to serve as the AIAS national vice president for a year before working for a large, established firm in that city. After I became licensed, I taught for a year as a visiting professor then pursued graduate work in order to study design further. The master of science from the University of Cincinnati offered a great post-professional program in writing and theory, which were subjects of particular interest. I explored these topics in greater depth with a doctorate in theory and criticism at Texas A&M University. While I love many aspects of architecture, the thinking that supports and drives the activities of design are especially intriguing to me.

As a faculty member that coordinates a first-year studio, how do you teach fundamental design ideas and skills to entering architecture students?

❯ I believe first-year design is the most challenging studio to teach because there are so many things that beginning students must absorb and assimilate, beyond simply adjusting to studio. My overall approach strives to raise their awareness of the variety of ways design can be accomplished as well as introducing many basic strategies and principles that are typically identified in design. My hope is that this enables the students to see a larger framework from which they can identify or devise design

approaches that fit their values and allows them to work on the issues that they feel are critical or are important to them.

I am not particularly interested in indoctrinating students. I refuse to teach only one method of design but instead strive to open the discussion, making the activity of architecture something that is explicit and an inclusive conversation. Within this approach, I focus on teaching the ability to see space instead of form. I believe experience is shaped by the quality of space, making this a most critical consideration of architecture, yet too often students prioritize the form. By introducing ways to see and comprehend space, the design is able to create a stronger experience.

Student Sketch—Study of Space and Light. Drury University.

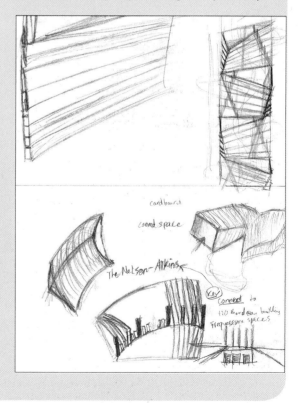

What are your primary responsibilities and duties as a faculty member?

❯ As a faculty member, my primary responsibilities are teaching and advising students, serving the university and community by participating in a number of committees and projects, and continuing my research in theory in order to help illuminate design thinking in the field. Much of this work ties together, as the focus of my research regarding design and theory helps my teaching while my service commitments allow me to apply and test this knowledge. Day to day, I spend the majority of my time striving to teach architecture clearly and effectively, communicating information in ways that help students express their ideas and views as well as possible. Month to month and year to year, I reflect on the teaching, service, and research to see how I can ensure that my efforts have a positive effect. I am a harsh critic of my own work, so I am constantly assessing and revising to make my academic activities better.

How does your work as a faculty member inform your architectural practice and vice versa?

❯ Because my research involves theory and writing rather than building, I have not pursued an active architectural practice while I have been in academia. I would rather do a few things well than many things with mediocrity, and I choose to focus on teaching and writing because I believe I owe that to the students in the theory and studio courses I teach. Some academic positions are well designed for people who teach and practice, yet the areas in which I am engaged are not necessarily areas that need an outlet in the form of building. This is not to say that I have not or do not practice; I have as many years of experience as many of my colleagues and absolutely loved my involvement in the profession. I still enjoy engaging in small projects when time allows.

How does teaching differ from practicing architecture?

❯ For me, teaching and practice are more similar than different. Teaching and practice are alike in that both involve the design of something that is communicated to others. In teaching, there is the need to design how to communicate a body of knowledge to students. In practice, there is the need to design how to communicate ideas or issues about a project to the public. Both require considerable effort in reflecting on the desired outcome of particular actions and critically working to improve them. Teaching and practice differ, as I believe teaching can have a wider influence, impacting many future designers rather than only those individuals who experience a specific building. While the effects of teaching can be argued to be more abstract than that of practice, I believe they can also be seen to be more powerful.

What has been your greatest challenge as an architect or faculty member?

❯ There are always situations that involve obstacles, whether these obstacles are time constraints, budgets, professional requirements, or even experiencing the entrenchment of the profession's dominant social structure. However, I think any good designer learns to see these challenges as a chance to design a way that not only meets but exceeds these parameters. I like to look at apparent limitations and determine how to both abide by and surpass them, designing an even better solution for my activities and career. Everyone has setbacks and rejections, but it is how you learn and continue to raise your own expectations that make these challenges work for you. In this way, I am not sure if I could identify my greatest challenge—instead, it has been a process of continually designing a more effective

Architecture Students Sketching. Crystal Bridge Museum of American Art, Bentonville, Arkansas. Architect: Moshe Safdie.

way to move beyond these supposed limitations and achieve something that is even better.

What is the most/least satisfying part of being an architecture student?

❭ The most satisfying part of being an architecture student is learning about your own values and how they can be identified and expressed to address difficult problems. There is something really powerful in examining what you believe and offering it as a solution that can make the world a better place. It's not about personal expression but about being able to help in some way. The least satisfying part of being an architecture student is the separation from non-architecture students, other classes, and the isolation of the studio. However, I think architecture students today are more involved in campus life than in the past, which is a great development to see occurring.

Who or what experience has been a major influence on your career?

❭ I have been fortunate in that my career has been influenced by an amalgamation of amazing people and experiences. Every institution I have attended has provided a host of great professors and colleagues who are eager to share their wisdom and every firm has included a number of great mentors and coworkers that relay their knowledge about the profession. I remain in contact with many of them. Opportunities have transformed into great experiences that accumulate to provide a background that I feel fortunate to have. Out of all of my influences, the people and places of the Ozarks have been especially powerful in shaping my views and work—the region where I was raised and now live provides a rich and meaningful context that continues to inspire my activities.

The Journey Is the Destination

KEVIN SNEED, AIA, IIDA, NOMA, LEED AP BD+C

Partner/Senior Director of Architecture

OTJ Architects, LLC

Washington, DC

Why did you become an architect?

❯ I had a specific interest in design and drawing at a young age. Early on, my career counselor—my grandmother—introduced me to architecture and how it contributes to the community and its surroundings. She also explained to me how architects had an obligation to participate in the community using the talents they developed at school and in their work. The very notion that architecture provided such a breadth of opportunity for giving back was a major component of what drew me to being an architect.

Why did you decide to choose the school you did—the University of Texas at Arlington? What degree(s) do you possess?

❯ I attended Skyline High School Career Development Center, which is a four-year architecture magnet school program. In part, I followed some of my friends from Skyline when I chose to attend the University of Texas at Arlington (UTA) School of Architecture. I also chose UTA based on its location (specifically, its proximity to my family), and its reputation relative to the other schools of architecture in the southwest region. I graduated with a bachelor of science in architecture, and a minor in art history.

As the partner/senior director of architecture at OTJ Architects, what are your primary responsibilities and duties? Please describe a typical day.

❯ As senior director of architecture, I am responsible for the quality assurance/quality control plan of my office. This entails instituting policies and proce-

American Wind Energy Association, Washington, DC. Architect: OTJ Architects, LLC.

dures to guide projects through all phases of design, into the production of contract documents, and on through construction administration. I organize and execute "lesson learned" presentations that help educate our staff on issues of construction administration practice, current building codes, and permits.

In addition, I also am a team leader on several projects, assisting in overall in project delivery. I participate in my studio's interviews and presentations to clients and brokers, providing technical expertise to assist in winning complex projects. To strengthen existing firm relationships, as a senior-level representative of OTJ Architects, I act as a resource to brokers, developers, and other real estate professionals on issues associated with my particular areas of expertise.

A typical day in my office starts with answering a variety of questions regarding the building codes and/or zoning ordinances before arriving at work. Once in the office, I am bombarded with issues regarding questions from permit expeditors and local permit plan reviewers on projects that are in the permitting review process. I attend construction progress meetings on site, and also prepare for other meetings with clients regarding the programming and design development phases. Explaining to commercial real estate brokers and facility managers the difference between a single-tenant core factor versus a multi-tenant core factor is a common theme. On a good day, I make it back home before my son goes to sleep, and I start the same ritual the following day.

As a co-author of Significant Interiors, can you define "interior architecture" and to what extent architects should know it?

❯ For the book *Significant Interiors* the Interior Architecture Knowledge Community—which is part of the AIA—wanted to have a book that highlighted award-winning designs from the Interiors categories of the AIA National Design Awards within a five-year period. We created the book to

be used as a textbook for schools of both interior design and architecture. The process of participating in the creation of this book made me both realize the extent of the overlap between the architecture and the interiors realm, and to understand the difference between the two disciplines.

The proper use of the term *interior architect* has been debated heavily for the past several years in the architectural industry. It has been used as part of the professional titles and incorporated in the name of school programs and professional offices. I believe the decision is heading into a direction that will require a separation in the practice with respect to both one's training and experience, in order to maintain a high standard of care and service to our clients.

Simply put, my definition of an interior architect is an architect who creates commercial interior spaces. An interior architect has experience in the technical mechanics and systems of the interior built environment as well as knowledge of the health, safety, and welfare concerns specific to the interior environment. Understanding the complexities of an interiors project's interface with the existing building shell's structure and mechanical/electrical/plumbing systems are vital to the completion of a successful project. A subspecialty within the architectural profession, interior architects also have an in-depth understanding of, and experience with, the fine-grained scale and concerns of a project as it interfaces directly with a space's occupants.

During your career, you have been overly involved with both the American Institute of Architects (AIA) and the National Organization of Minority Architects (NOMA); why are you involved, and how has your career benefited?

❯ Due to a past economic recession, I left Texas for the Washington, DC, metropolitan area. I made this change in part knowing that this would present unique opportunities to learn more about the

Global, Washington, DC. Architect: OTJ Architects, LLC.

politics driving the architectural profession. Once I arrived in DC, I wanted to be part of an organization that had colleagues with like minds and similar interests, and would provide me the chance to support my goals of making a difference in my community.

I joined the AIA Northern Virginia Chapter and started as a committee member of the AIA Associate/Young Architects Committee. My participation in that committee consisted of community involvement, encouragement of participation in the architecture registration exam (ARE), tours of construction sites, and recognition of the importance of young architects in design by helping to create the Young Architects awards. One of my favorite community programs was my chapter's ARCHES (Architects in Elementary Schools) program that helps to educate elementary school kids about architecture. During my time with the Associate/Young Architects committee, it was recognized as a model for other Young Architect Committees within the AIA. I also wanted to be involved in increasing minority involvement in the AIA. I accomplished this by first becoming the chair of

the AIA National Minority Resource Committee, and this led to my participation with the National Organization of Minority Architects (NOMA).

The Associate/Young Architects committee was a steppingstone to other opportunities in my chapter—from heading the design awards event, to participation as a board member, to eventual election as president of my chapter. My collective participation with the AIA local, state, and national chapters lead to my becoming the first of two recipients of the AIA National Young Architects Award for my chapter. This recognition of my leadership outside of the workplace also led to opportunities in my professional life and my rise from project manager to a partnership position in my firm.

As a recipient of the DC NOMA Lankford-Giles-Vaughn Minority Architect Award, why is diversity in the profession important? What can the profession do to increase the number of minorities to pursue the profession?

❯ Through my participation with the AIA and NOMA on a local, state, and national level, I became the first recipient of the DC NOMA Lankford-Giles-

Vaughn Minority Architect Award. This award was created to honor current practitioners, while also acknowledging the architectural legacy of Washington, DC's, pioneering African American architects.

In looking back on this legacy, I see a continuing need to devote focused attention toward increasing the diversity of our profession—the job is far from complete. While I have personally committed to add this diversity by increasing awareness of the profession in the minority community, I feel that the profile and presence of the profession in that community is still lagging. The participation and licensure of both women (11 percent) and African Americans (2 percent) in the profession still trails behind what we should reasonably expect to see given the diversity of our society. I believe that in any profession or industry whose membership does not reflect the demographics of its society, there must be a serious problem. The lack of diversity in the architectural profession impedes progress not only in the field but also in society as a whole. As long as this participation in the profession lags, the profession and our society suffer from an ignorance of the unique perspectives, criti-

cisms, and improvements to our built environment minority architects are uniquely poised to provide.

I feel that one of the best ways to improve or increase in diversity in architecture is to start at the elementary and high school level. Particularly because the process of becoming an architect starts so early, so quickly after secondary school, it is important to ensure that minorities within the profession provide children and younger members of society with concrete examples of, and opportunities to interact with, architects who have completed that journey. By providing the younger generation the opportunity to connect directly with a member of the profession, to ask questions about our practice and spark interest in the creation of the built environment, we can make the idea that they, too, can become an architect seem far more of a possible and attainable goal.

What has been your greatest challenge as an architect?

❯ My greatest challenge is balancing my professional life with my family/personal life, and to provide each with the time and effort required to keep both aspects of my life thriving and strong.

National Association of Independent Schools, Washington, DC. Architect: OTJ Architects, LLC.

What is the most/least satisfying part of being an architect?

❭ The most satisfying aspect of being part of the design process is seeing the completion of a project—the excitement of the client moving into the space, as well as my own excitement at seeing plans and sketches become a reality.

Also, as so much of my professional work is involved in mentoring and guiding processes in the office, seeing a young colleague reaching that "I get this" moment from drawing details or hardware schedule from a time that I taught them in the past is very rewarding. I am honored and flattered when I can extend my expertise to someone who needs it.

The least rewarding is seeing clients who are just not willing to open their minds to the architectural process—those who refuse to see the possibilities in a project, to contribute their expertise to it, and sometimes even refuse to allow others to contribute toward leading the project to a successful conclusion.

Who or what experience has been a major influence on your career?

❭ My participation in the American Institute of Architects (AIA), and the International Interior Design Association (IIDA) is a major influence in my career. In addition to providing critical mentoring opportunities, they have helped elevate me to be a leader in the profession.

Citizen Architect

AMANDA HARRELL-SEYBURN, ASSOCIATE AIA

Instructor, School of Planning, Design and Construction

Michigan State University

East Lansing, Michigan

Why did you become an architect?

❭ I love buildings, great and small. I am interested in the structure and design of buildings, from a garden shed to the family house to the state capitol. I want to design them all. Plus, architecture is the ultimate confluence of art and science.

Why did you decide to choose the school that you did to attend for your architecture degree(s)? What degrees do you possess?

❭ The philosophy of the School of Architecture at Andrews University is to practice architecture of real and lasting value while being both socially and environmentally responsible primarily attracted me. The school promotes the craft in architecture throughout the curriculum, training me to design buildings that are dignified, durable, purposeful, and a delight to the senses. My architecture education provided an excellent mix of theory and practice that contribute to my success in architecture.

I have a master of architecture from Andrews University and an undergraduate degree in art history from Kalamazoo College.

With a previous degree in art history, what prompted you to pursue architecture?

❭ Architecture was the natural progression following my studies in art history. Art history is not simply the appreciation of paintings but is the study of society examined through the visual arts in terms

Centsible House, Lansing, Michigan. Design/Watercolor: by Amanda Harrell-Seyburn.

of historical, social, geographical, cultural, psychological, and architectural contexts. Architecture is prominent in the history of art. In fact, while studying art history and curating at the University of London, my interest in architecture grew. As a result, I wrote a thesis examining art and the nature of the buildings in which it is displayed. Eventually, I found myself more interested in the aesthetic and structure of the buildings than the art hanging on the wall. My art history education taught me to think critically, observe carefully, and understand subtle nuances of technique and the impact of light that are abilities that I use every day in my architecture career.

What are your primary responsibilities and duties as a full-time faculty member at Michigan State University?

❯ I am an instructor and a researcher at the School of Planning, Design and Construction. My research is primarily focused on high-performance buildings in the Great Lakes Region. I am a member of the research team at Michigan State University developing and implementing innovative retrofit technologies primarily for cold and mixed-humid climate regions in collaboration with the U.S. Department of Energy's Building America Program. My other work includes green building development research with the Michigan Department of Natural Resources as part of the Sustainable Park Planning Project. I am also collaborating with the Michigan State Housing Development Authority to reimagine the state for the twenty-first century. As an instructor, I teach courses including Integrated Sustainable Built Environment, an interdisciplinary studio course, and 3D Computer Modeling and Structural Systems.

In addition, my portfolio is diverse with experience ranging from single-family home design to award winning master planning. Much of this experience was gained prior to my current position at Michigan State University. I have worked for several small architecture firms doing schematic design and computer modeling. I have also worked for urban planning firms as an urban designer during charrettes and post-production masterplan hand-drawn watercolor renderings.

Aside from being a faculty member, you also serve as architecture critic for the Lansing City Pulse newspaper. How did you obtain this opportunity, and how does it help your architecture career?

❯ A literary critic at the newspaper thought I would be a good addition to the paper and recommended me to the editor. My role began with limited contributions and grew into a weekly column on architecture and urbanism. My writings highlight successes and examine opportunities. The critical examination of architecture in the mid-Michigan region has dramatically expanded my knowledge of architecture in terms of regional aesthetics, materials, and construction practices that, in turn, makes me a better designer and scholar.

Michigan State
Medical Society
Building, East
Lansing, Michigan.
RENDERING:
AMANDA HARRELL-
SEYBURN.

Mixed-Use
Building—Visioning
Project, East Lansing,
Michigan. Design/
Sketch: Amanda
Harrell-Seyburn.

What does it mean to be a citizen architect, and why are you passionate about it?

❯ A citizen architect uses his/her talents and training to contribute meaningfully to the improvement of the community. I believe that architecture is about doing something, not being someone. I translate this philosophy into action currently by providing education to the public through my weekly column, serving on the East Lansing Historic District Commission, and teaching at Michigan State University, a land grant university.

What has been your greatest challenge as an intern thus far?

❯ Most of my current building science research and teaching hours do not qualify for IDP.

From the perspective of an emerging professional, can you describe the Intern Development Program (IDP) and the Architect Registration Examination (ARE)? Where are you in the process of becoming licensed?

❯ The IDP is the second part of the path to becoming an architect. Architects have a huge ethical and professional responsibility to safeguard the health, safety, and welfare of the public. IDP is a process established to ensure that future architects are trained under the tutelage of a licensed architect. Mentorship is crucial at this stage between school and licensure. This model follows the architectural tradition of apprenticeships where senior architects train young architects. IDP can be accomplished in as few as three years or take many years depending on the individual and their career choices.

What is the most/least satisfying part of a career as an architect?

❯ Educating people on the value of architecture, as a designer and a columnist, is the most satisfying part of what I get to do. I also revel in seeing a design go from concept to physical existence.

What is the most surprising part of your career in architecture?

❯ The amount of writing I do is unexpected. In architecture school, I was once told that writing is as important as drawing to an architect. I dismissed the notion but have come to find that I write daily about architecture.

What are your 5-year and 10-year career goals relative to architecture?

❯ I plan to obtain my architectural license within 5 years. In 10 years, I see myself as a leader in the Michigan architecture community, working to raise the profile of the profession and promote the value of design in the Great Lakes region.

Who or what experience has been a major influence on your career?

❯ Architects who are not only practitioners but also teach are my greatest inspiration. There is no greater way to give back to the profession than by educating. I consider the mentor who provides advice and counsel to a young architect, the architect who hires an intern and provides them the opportunity to earn IDP, and the professor who teaches the basics to a student to all be engaged in ensuring the future of architecture. I am shaping my career to encompass practice and scholarship.

Shaping Our Buildings

LEIGH STRINGER, LEED AP

Senior Vice President

HOK

Washington, DC

GlaxoSmithKline, Research Triangle Park, North Carolina. Architect: HOK. PHOTOGRAPHER: ADRIAN WILSON.

Why did you become an architect?

❭ My father was a mathematician (early computer scientist) and my mother was an artist. I became an architect because it came natural to me. I have always worked for architecture firms because I love being around design and every day is challenging. I especially love the social side of architecture—the fact that it's so much about people makes it endlessly fascinating.

Why did you decide to choose Washington University? What degree(s) do you possess?

❭ I have a bachelor of arts with a major in architecture, a master of architecture, and a master of business administration (MBA), all from Washington University in St. Louis. I chose Washington University initially because it was an excellent liberal arts school. I worked for a couple of years and came back because I realized I could pursue architecture and business in three years, and I really loved and continue to love the school. My undergraduate and graduate experiences were very different—different friends, different teachers, and a different level of focus in terms of education.

Why did you pursue the master of business administration, and how has it helped you in the career as an architect?

❭ When I worked as an intern, my first year out of school, I worked for a small firm of highly talented designers who could not run a business to save their lives. I also got exposure to "programming" or pre-design services and realized that I wanted to be more involved in the early part of the design process. I was accepted to the master of architecture program at Washington University without knowing I would get into the business school, but really happy it worked out. I was always the one person in the architecture school having to wear a suit and the only architect in the business school wearing all black.

What is programming/pre-design services? Why and how is it important in architecture?

❯ Before it is determined that a building should be built, there are a number of decisions that must be made with our clients. Can the needs of a client be accommodated within existing facilities? Could moving into a new building be an opportunity to change the way the business operates? Could this be an opportunity to change the way the organization operates to gain efficiencies? What if more people work at home or share office space?

Then, once it is decided that the building is necessary, there are another yet another set of decisions to be made. Where should the facility be located? Should the objective be to centralize or decentralize facilities? Should facilities be leased or is it better for the client to build, operate, or own the facility? Should the building be flexible to accommodate change or highly customized? What methodology should be used to determine the amount of space and technical requirements for the building?

The process of making these early decisions, of narrowing the options and helping a client carefully consider their choices before they design or begin construction is called "programming" or sometimes "pre-design services." In the pre-design phase of a project, it is fairly easy to change direction, consider multiple options, and do so at little cost. Later on, when the construction site is cleared, steel is being welded, and carpet is going down, it is significantly more costly and difficult to change direction. At the beginning of a project, it is very tempting to want to put pen to paper and just start drawing! But the

The Commonwealth Medical College, Scranton, Pennsylvania. Architect: HOK. PHOTOGRAPHER: PAUL WARCHOL.

years have taught us that it is really best to "go slow to go fast" and take the time to put the right structure and parameters on the project up front, before major investments are made and expectations are set. I also refer to this phase as the "credibility phase." When clients see that their architect is taking time to get to know them, to test assumptions and ask good questions, they are establishing their credibility as a professional and as a valued partner.

What has been your greatest challenge as an architect?

❯ The same challenge the planet is facing right now. Learning how to do more with less, and how to differentiate what I do from everyone else so that it is valued. Many architects today complain about how our fees are reducing, how we have to do the job of two people and there are not enough hours in the day. I feel pretty confident that this trend will continue.

My personal (and continuing) challenge is to stay inspired … to set a vision for myself, my team, and our profession.

What is the most/least satisfying part of being an architect?

❯ My life's work has been about helping people understand the impact of space on human behavior and then leveraging space as an instrument for change. Clients tell me that the spaces we design make them more efficient and more effective and increase collaboration and innovation. The connection between buildings and behavior are remarkable and real.

You may have heard the famous quote from Winston Churchill. "We shape our buildings, and afterwards our buildings shape us." Here is the full quote from Churchill:

On the night of May 10, 1941, with one of the last bombs of the last serious raid, our House of Commons was destroyed by the violence of the enemy, and we have now to consider whether we should build it up again, and how, and when.

We shape our buildings, and afterwards our buildings shape us. Having dwelt and served for more than forty years in the late Chamber, and having derived very great pleasure and advantage therefrom, I, naturally, should like to see it restored in all essentials to its old form, convenience and dignity.

At the time, Churchill was speaking to the House of Commons but in the space designed for the House of Lords that day in October 1943. The old House of Commons was being rebuilt in its old form, remaining insufficient to seat all its members. Churchill was against "giving each member a desk to sit at and a lid to bang" because, he explained, the House would be mostly empty most of the time; whereas, at critical votes and moments, it would fill beyond capacity, with members spilling out into the aisles, in his view a suitable "sense of crowd and urgency."

I work with clients to influence the behavior of their organization to become more flexible, agile, connected, and global. Churchill wisely knew that *design matters* and can impact organizations in a meaningful way. Seeing design "work" as it should is one of the most powerful and satisfying moments for me.

Who or what experience has been a major influence on your career?

❯ In 2008, I started a blog called TheGreenWorkplace.com. That blog became a book, and that book became a mulitcity global

Millward Brown Chicago Office, Chicago, Illinois. Architect: HOK. PHOTOGRAPHER: STEVE HALL/HEDRICH BLESSING.

book tour. The process of writing (and lots of speaking!) has helped me to really think through my ideas and give them structure and purpose. I learned, through writing, how important the environment really is to us, our impact on it, and the power we have to improve our planet. I realize that I can make a difference in a way unlike most architects—not just through drawing and designing, but by writing and speaking about trends, ideas, and visions of a better future than today. It has been a powerful and liberating lesson for me. I always thought I had to have my design work published in a fancy architecture magazine to be influential. Turns out that is not the only way. Writing and speaking about design is just as powerful and can have an even further reach.

NOTES

1. Frank Parsons, *Choosing a Vocation* (Boston: Houghton Mifflin Company, 1909).
2. William Pena, *Problem Seeking: An Architectural Programming Primer* (Washington, DC: AIA Press).
3. Richard Beery, "Profile of the Architect: A Psychologist's View." *Review,* Summer 1984, p. 5.
4. Richard Bolles, *The Quick Job-Hunting Map* (Berkeley, CA: Ten Speed Press, 1991).
5. C. Randall Powell, *Career Planning Today* (Dubuque, IA: Kendall/Hunt, 1990), 42.
6. Stephen Covey, *Seven Habits of Highly Effective People* (New York: Fireside, 1989).

5 The Future of the Architecture Profession

The future is not a result of choices among alternative paths offered by the present, but a place that is created—created first in the mind and will, created next in activity. The future is not some place we are going to, but one we are creating. The paths are not to be found, but made, and the activity of making them, changes both the maker and the destination.

JOHN SCHAAR, Futurist

The best way to predict the future is to design it.

BUCKMINSTER FULLER (1895–1983)

HAVE YOU EVER TRIED TO PREDICT THE FUTURE? If not, you might determine that such an exercise is not worthwhile. Although impossible, John Schaar and Buckminster Fuller suggest that the future is to be created or designed. Chapter 4 discussed how career designing helps in launching your career, but what is the future of the architecture profession? To what extent can you prepare for it? How do you prepare for it? How do you create it?

Although it is not the intent of this publication to engage in prognostication, it will provide some topics currently emerging from the profession as it evolves.

◀ Beyeler Foundation Museum, Riehen (Basel), Switzerland. Architect: Renzo Piano. PHOTOGRAPHER: GRACE H. KIM, AIA.

Prior to reviewing the emerging topics, consider what the Institute for the Future (IFTF, www.iftf.org) calls the "ReWorking of Work." Instead of focusing on future occupations or jobs, the IFTF focuses on future work skills.

In the report, *Future Work Skills 2020,*[1] the IFTF outlined 6 drivers of change and 10 future work skills.

6 Drivers of Change

1. Extreme Longevity
2. Rise of Smart Machines and Systems
3. Computational World
4. New Media Ecology
5. Superstructured Organizations
6. Globally Connected World

10 Skills for the Future Workplace

1. *Sense-Making:* Ability to determine the deeper meaning or significance of what is being expressed.
2. *Social Intelligence:* Ability to connect to others in a deep and direct way, to sense and stimulate reactions and desired interactions.
3. *Novel & Adaptive Thinking:* Proficiency at thinking and coming up with solutions and responses beyond that which is rote or rules based.
4. *Cross-Cultural Competency:* Ability to operate in different cultural settings.
5. *Computational Thinking:* Ability to translate vast amounts of data into abstract concepts and to understand data-based reasoning.
6. *New-Media Literacy:* Ability to critically assess and develop content that uses new media forms, and to leverage these media for persuasive communication.
7. *Transdisciplinarity:* Literacy in and ability to understand concepts across multiple disciplines.
8. *Design Mindset:* Ability to represent and develop tasks and work processes for desired outcomes.
9. *Cognitive Load Management:* Ability to discriminate and filter information for importance, and to understand how to maximize cognitive functioning using a variety of tools and techniques.
10. *Virtual Collaboration:* Ability to work productively, drive engagement, and demonstrate presence as a member of a virtual team.

With an architectural education, which of the listed skills have you developed? Of course, the true answer is up for debate, but certainly a degree in architecture will prepare you for the future workplace.

Sustainability

More than 30 years ago, "energy-conscious design"—the use of natural systems to heat and cool buildings—was a hot trend in architecture. Now, it is called *sustainability*. Green architecture goes beyond the use of natural systems; it is changing the process of designing a building, for example, to eliminate the use of fossil fuels, being aware of the building materials we use, and understanding the impact of architecture on the environment. On your path to becoming an architect, you will want to learn more about sustainability.

To that end, you may wish to become a Leadership in Energy and Environmental Design Accredited Professional (LEED AP). As outlined by the Green Building Certification Institute, those credentialed as LEED AP are building-industry professionals who have demonstrated a thorough understanding of green building and the LEED® Green Building Rating System™ developed and maintained by the U.S. Green Building Council (USGBC).[2] More students prior to graduation and recent graduates upon graduation are pursuing LEED AP as a credential to help launch their professional careers.

And, in response to climate change and the fact that the building sector is a major contributor to greenhouse gas emissions, Architecture 2030 (www.architecture2030.org) is an effort to reduce the impact of the building sector by changing the way buildings are planned, designed, and constructed. As a future architect, what will you do between now and the year 2030?

New Technologies/Social Media

SketchUp, smartphones, cloud computing, 3D printing, tablets—you probably know these terms, but seasoned architects may not. Over the past 20 years, technology has played an increasing role within the architecture profession. Because of continued advancements, technology will continue to impact architects and the work they do. The American Institute of Architects (AIA) Technology in Architectural Practice even monitors the development of technology in the profession.

To stay ahead of the technology curve, seek out opportunities to learn how to maximize the technology to your advantage. Certainly, most architecture programs have resources and courses that will assist you but be proactive. All architecture programs have computer labs with the necessary software and output facilities, but more and more are adding digital fabrication facilities. Students can now plot three-dimensional models of their ideas. However, be cautious, as technology will not design buildings; technology is only a tool.

Flickr, Twitter, LinkedIN, Instagram, Pinterest—again, you know what these are, but less than a few years ago, they did not exist. Social media is impacting all of us in different ways; take the initiative to understand these new tools and how you can capitalize on them in your career as an architect. Also, do not forget about blogs and the cloud.

Building Information Modeling (BIM)

Over 30 years ago, it was thought that the advent of computer-aided design (CAD) would eliminate or reduce the need for architects. Of course, the exact opposite happened as CAD and computer technology actually created career opportunities for architects. The practice of architecture was revolutionized as construction drawings were done on the computer, but at the end of the design process. Now, building information modeling (BIM) is the new CAD.

BIM manages the components of building through its life cycle using a three-dimensional, real-time, modeling software. By doing so, it increases productivity during building design and construction. With CAD, the architect would draw a representation of the building on the computer; with BIM, the architect creates a "virtual model" of the building along with all of its components.

Firms are increasingly adopting BIM as part of their architectural practice as well as clients and contractors are demanding it. To be adequately prepared for your future, challenge your architecture program to teach it as part of the curriculum; or learn it on your own. Take the time to learn the software: Autodesk: Revit, Bentley Architecture, Graphisoft: ArchiCAD, Tekla Structures, and Nemetschek N.A. VectorWorks: Architect.

THE FUTURE OF ~~ARCHITECTURE~~ ARCHITECTS

David Zach, Futurist
2011–2013 Public Director, AIA National Board

The future of architects is bigger than architecture. Much bigger! Not only will the skills you gain in architecture school let you do more than just design buildings, they can let you be someone more than just an architect. And if you are particularly imaginative and adventurous, you can design buildings and do other creative work too. *Learning to think like an architect can be learning to design your own future on your own terms.*

Architectural education needs to catch up with the fact that design often ignores boundaries. Design influences everything and the job market for design talent grows continually. This training is more than just knowing how to design buildings; it is a rich paradox of art and science, technical specs and creativity, the measurable and the immeasurable. Keep that paradox at the heart of your education.

Check out the Tumblr list Architects of Other Things (http://architectsofotherthings.tumblr.com). You will find a myriad of non-architects who studied architecture. It is a fascinating roster of actors, musicians, politicians, and even the head of Chrysler—Saad Chehab, who received an architecture degree from University of Detroit–Mercy. Martha Stewart studied architectural history. Weird Al Yankovic has a degree in architecture. Harvey Gantt, a successful architect, also became a successful mayor of Charlotte. These people did not just think outside the box, they think into other boxes. They used their education in architecture to make imaginative connections to make the world better.

Traditional occupational boundaries are expiring and architects must be ready for all sorts of adventures. Along the way, you may have to gently question the size and scope of your own career objectives. Become a peripheral visionary. Do not just pay attention to the center of architecture—watch and learn from what is happening on the edges.

If your school looks at the work of a starchitect, ask about the work by architects of other things. Help make your education fit with the world that is coming, not just reflect the world that was. Learn from everyone. Study entrepreneurs and industrialists, poets and saints, makers and mothers, engineers and artists.

Beware the hardening of categories. Bureaucracy and a rigidity of practice threaten the vitality of architecture. Frank Gehry said, "Our documents have infantilized us." That is not a compliment. The safety of buildings must not be compromised, but too much of a safe career will compromise you and your dreams.

Fight the cheapness that is infecting architecture. Too many new buildings look like technical drawings. If that is all you can do, there's an app for that. These apps should not just take us to a cheaper bottom line; use them to take architecture (and yourself) to a farther, cooler horizon. Never before has so much been available to those with practical imagination. Imagine that!

New Practices

Given the recent past and the projected future, new practice models are emerging. Practitioners from all areas of design including architects are engaging in diverse fields. *Future Practice: Conversations from the Edge of Architecture*, a 2012 book by Rory Hyde,[3] highlights professionals in architecture, policy, activism, design, education, research, history, community engagement, and more, each representing an emergent role for designers/architects to occupy.

So what do you want to do with your architectural education? As outlined in Chapter 4 and by David Zach in this chapter, the only limitation is your imagination and creativity. As an architect, you can pursue the practice that fulfills your definition of the future.

Integrated Project Delivery (IPD)

As outlined in the AIA/AIA California Council guide, *Integrated Project Delivery* (IPD) is a project delivery approach that integrates people, systems, and business structures and practices into a process that collaboratively harnesses the talents and insights of all participants to optimize project results; increases value to the owner; reduces waste; and maximizes efficiency through all phases of design, fabrication, and construction.[4]

The traditional method has the architect work with the client through to construction documents (CDs). At that point, the CDs are put out to bid by general contractors. From there, the architect and client would select a contractor to build the project. In some cases, the bids would come back from the contractors too high for the project budget or errors might be found in the CDs. With IPD, there is collaboration between the architect and contractor; they team up much earlier in the design process to avoid any issues.

Collaboration

During your education in architecture, you may participate in a group design project, but this is rare. Instead, any group projects you have may be for non-design courses or simply to construct a site-context model for a studio project; you will complete most of the projects by yourself. In contrast, almost all projects in practice are the work of a team. Each individual contributes to the overall task.

In practice, teamwork becomes paramount. Compared to BIM and IPD collaboration is even more important. Thus, to adequately prepare for your future as an architect, seek out opportunities that connect you with others in accomplishing a task. Even challenge a professor to assign a group design project. Or team up with a few classmates to enter a design competition to develop teamwork or collaboration skills.

Diversity

Why is diversity important to the future of architecture? It is important because the profession of architecture lacks diversity, especially in the terms of gender and ethnicity (see Chapter 1). More recently, the profession has sought means by which to increase the numbers of women and minorities, but much more still needs to be done. What can you do to encourage others (women and minorities) to become architects?

Aside from demographics, diverse experiences, ideas, and lifestyles are also important. To become a true architect, you should be able to appreciate diversity and understand its meaning from the perspective of design. How can you, as an architect, design a project/building for a client with a viewpoint different from your own?

Globalization

Thanks to globalization, the world is shrinking. As a result, the practice of architecture is becoming more global. More U.S. firms are designing projects around the world; some have offices in Beijing, London, Paris, Dubai, and countries throughout the world. In October 2012, *DesignIntelligence* reported that U.S. architecture firms exported a record $2.02 billion in design services, a growth of slightly over 50 percent over the past four years.[5] More international students are studying architecture at U.S. institutions, while more students from the United States are studying abroad for a semester as part of their curriculum. In addition, U.S. students are obtaining their degrees from international institutions. Opportunities exist, but do due diligence in learning licensure requirements when your education is from another country.

This trend of globalization will continue. If interested, participate in a study abroad program, learn architecture from around the world, and seek possible employment positions in other countries. Working abroad may quite worthwhile but may prove to be more difficult.

Public Interest Design

Public interest design emphasizes the creation or redesign of products, environments, and systems, with a clear human-centered approach, while often likened to the well-established fields of public interest law and public health. As shared on the website by the same name, Public interest design is the next frontier of the sustainability movement.

Many architecture students pursue a career in architecture to serve community; they want to help others and do not pursue it for the stature or money; they specifically state that their career goal is to improve neighborhoods, communities, and cities through design. Why? Does it truly matter? What is important is that these aspiring architects want to change the status quo. They want to give back.

Further proof of such a movement is the popularity of organizations such as Habitat for Humanity International, Architecture for Humanity, Design Corps, and Freedom by Design™, a community service program of the American Institute of Architecture Students (AIAS). Do you wish to be an agent of social change? If so, become involved with an issue that impacts our society. Change the world.

Additional proof is the workshops, training, and conferences on the topic sponsored by Public Interest Design and Design Corps. For example, Cameron Sinclair, founder of Architecture for Humanity, served as one of the keynotes at the AIA 2013 Convention.

Distance Education/Learning

Aside from the preceding subjects, another topic is distance education/learning; this current form of pedagogy is becoming more prevalent. The Boston Architectural College (BAC) launched the first online, minimal-residency distance master of architecture, allowing students in the program to work full time where they live and work while studying through online courses; students need not relocate but do come to Boston for intensive study days at the start of each semester.

As an architect, you may need continuing education to maintain licensure or AIA membership. Instead of attending conferences in person, you can participate via online webinars or listen to available podcasts. Some architecture programs also provide certain continuing education courses online. Remember, one of the ten future work skills is virtual collaboration.

Another recent development in learning is MOOCs—Massive Open Online Courses. As the name implies, MOOCs are online courses designed for large audiences available via the web. While their use for credit is under discussion, e-learning is here; the question is how will it continue to impact your becoming an architect.

The Future

Undoubtedly, terms or issues related to the future have been omitted. If so, it was not done intentionally, but rather because no one can truly predict the future. And finally, to adequately prepare for the future of architecture, consider reading *The Next Architect: A New Twist on the Future of Design* by James P. Cramer and Scott Simpson.[6]

Aside from the trends listed in the sidebar, Cramer and Simpson state that the Next Architect must develop excellent "clientship" skills, the ability to deal effectively with multiple decision makers simultaneously, many of whom have conflicting goals. But how do you develop this new set of workplace skills? Listen!

THE NEXT ARCHITECT: A NEW TWIST ON THE FUTURE OF DESIGN

James P. Cramer and Scott Simpson

TRANSFORMING TRENDS

Integrated, Collaborative Design

Design-Build Dominates

Globalization Comes Home

Talent Shortage

BIM Technology Sets a New Standard

Demographics Are Destiny

Productivity and Performance

The Power of Branding

Fast Architecture

Designing the "Design Experience"

Going Green

Life Cycle Design

High-Definition Value

Strategic Optimism

What Do You See as the Future for the Architecture Profession?

❯It is a guaranteed future; since the beginning of time we have constantly built and rebuilt—this will not change. The future five years is extremely strong for young architects because of the pent-up demand for new buildings caused by the current economic recession.

John W. Myefski, AIA, Principal, Myefski Architects, Inc.

❯The future of the profession is on fire. Students coming out of architecture programs are armed with knowledge in wide-ranging academic subjects and hold critically reviewed problem-solving skills. Architecturally trained professionals facilitate processes, for example: identify and define the problem, design the solution, examine the solution, and bring the necessary parties together for implementation. What better combination in this day in age with the interconnectedness of economics, medicine, and social and political arenas?

Jennifer Penner, M.Arch. Graduate, University of New Mexico, Regional Associate Director, AIA Western Mountain Region

❯Today, I see a lot more globalization and collaboration of the profession. I also see a number of firms growing in size so that they are versed at providing every possible building solution. Design-build is becoming a more desired method for project delivery as well. Public-private partnerships or federal procurement are looking at this as a way to deliver the buildings they need within the time and budget constraints that they have. In projects where we are in a traditional design, bid, build delivery we see the contractor being much more involved earlier in the process to help inform the team of the costs. I also see the advantage of bringing on the subcontractors during the design phase so that sophisticated details can be developed more practically.

Sean M. Stadler, AIA, LEED AP, Design Principal, WDG Architecture, PLLC

❯Builders and architects over the centuries have constantly had to reinvent themselves. Back when HOK started in St. Louis, the founders decided they wanted to "diversify" by specializing in more than one building type. Then they started to diversify by placing an office in Detroit, then San Francisco. It worked pretty well. Now we are in 26 countries across the globe and design just about every building type imaginable. And we do not just design buildings, we design cities, we write software, we complete with consulting companies like IBM and Deloitte. I think sticking with diversity is probably a good thing for HOK and for other firms to do to continue to transform what they do and how they do it. The profession needs this to survive.

We will always need physical buildings to protect us from the elements. That said, there is a convergence or "mash-up" of so many things happening right now from real worlds and virtual worlds to engineering and biology to human factors and humanoid robotics. The future of architects is tethered to the future of all professions, which are in flux and have yet to be defined. I can see the profession "mashing up" with other professions or just as easily splintering off in to several subprofessions.

Leigh Stringer, LEED AP, Senior Vice President, HOK

❯The profession is evolving along with society and learning that in order to satisfy the needs of a rapidly changing world, it must engage the other disciplines on a much deeper level, disciplines including but not limited to psychology, sociology, science, and technology.

Sarah Stein, Architectural Designer, Lee Scolnick Architects & Design Partnership

❯It is a bright future for architects. As inventors and builders, we can help this generation face some of the toughest problems. We need to rethink how

What Do You See as the Future for the Architecture Profession? (Continued)

buildings use resources, house our retiring Baby Boomers, and create a new idea for city growth.

Infrastructure is failing, cities are sprawling and threatened by encroaching waters, and the need for food sources closer to cities is great. Addressing these issues will become the future of the field.

Amanda Strawitch, Level 1 Architect, Design Collective

❯I believe the architecture profession is a career in which you must have a knowledge base of immense breadth in other related trades and professions. Whether it is the understanding of the client's needs, possessing the technical and practical knowledge of a variety of systems and construction types, or the political acuity to explain to a city council on how the design relates to the context of its community, having this diverse talent is what architecture is all about.

Kevin Sneed, AIA, IIDA, NOMA, LEED AP BD+C, Partner / Senior Director of Architecture, OTJ Architects, LLC

❯Architects will be active leaders in their communities, active leaders in the environment and on issues of sustainability, and active leaders in evidence-based design. The profession will welcome all of those that pursue it—that is, become increasingly diverse and culturally rich. Architects do more than design buildings; they build communities. The profession will embrace those individuals who pursue alternative careers, who find themselves on the client side of the table, or who seek to represent architects and communities through public pursuits. The profession will evolve as architects retake more responsibility in the building process and as technologies such as BIM emerge.

Shannon Kraus, FAIA, MBA, Principal and Senior Vice President, HKS Architects

❯Because architecture is so closely knit with other disciplines, I fear that it will one day be conquered, in large part by others in related fields who are not taught design principles and who have not been instructed by other architects to think and react the way that we do. I fear that, eventually, it will become a lost [although not forgotten] art if future generations do not preserve the art of design.

Tanya Ally, Architectural Staff, Bonstra | Haresign Architects

❯The recent economic situation presents a new set of challenges and opportunities for our profession to really understand what "good design" is all about. A well-designed building does not have to be complex, or come with a premium price tag. "Sustainability" does not have to rely solely on expensive systems or next-generation technology. At its core, "good design" is about making well-reasoned, responsible decisions. It is not magic; it is just about understanding people. I believe our current situation will leave a lasting legacy that will define an entire generation of architects that embraces a holistically designed, high-quality, high-value architecture.

As architects, we must acknowledge our connectivity to others; we must know that what we see is often not the entire truth. We must venture beyond our comfortable boundaries into the reality of others.

Kathryn T. Prigmore, FAIA, Senior Project Manager, HDR Architecture, Inc.

❯Within the challenges of the world, there exists the opportunity to transform the world in increasingly meaningful ways that span borders, disciplines, cultures and economies. This is a call to service for future architects.

Andrew Caruso, AIA, LEED AP BD+C, CDT, Head of Intern Development and Academic Outreach, Gensler

❯We are generating knowledge and information at an astonishing rate, beyond what we as individuals can possibly comprehend and it is ever increasing. Specific subject-matter experts will become more and more critical to our ability to execute great design. There will be many more opportunities for architects, should we decide to embrace them.

More and more, architects need to demonstrate excellent leadership skills to successfully navigate the team dynamics and different ideas if they are to maintain any reasonable ability to manage a project. But at the same time they need to be open to new ideas and know how to incorporate them when appropriate.

Robert D. Fox, AIA, IIDA, LEED AP Principal, FOX Architects

❯ The profession will continue to move in an inter-disciplinary direction. Architects will need to place themselves at the forefront of major political, environmental, and social issues and become integral in solving problems (through design and policy).

Jessica L. Leonard, Associate AIA, LEED AP BD+C, Associate, Ayers Saint Gross Architects and Planners

❯ The emergence of new technological advances in software and fabrication is causing an identity crisis for many architects. Recently, architects have become ever more separated from their designs, and I foresee a greater level of involvement through design-build projects as architects regain the means to construct their own designs.

Jordan Buckner, M.Arch./MBA Graduate, University of Illinois at Urbana-Champaign

❯ Architecture is becoming more collaborative and interdisciplinary. Architects need to be more multilingual and conversant not just about design but also about politics, ecology, economics, sociology, and science. We are charged with creating a sustainable built environment. To craft that future we must change the way buildings are conceived, designed, and built and cross-generational and academic-industry boundaries.

Allison Wilson, Intern Architect, Ayers, Saint Gross

Harm Weber Academic Center, Judson University, Elgin, Illinois. Architect: Short and Associates. PHOTOGRAPHER: LEE W. WALDREP, Ph.D.

What Do You See as the Future for the Architecture Profession? (Continued)

❯ In the future, the profession will see more restrictive building and energy codes as well as increased client demands. To meet these challenges, design professionals will need to explore and develop innovative building materials and systems, as well as faster and more efficient methods of documenting designs.

Robert D. Roubik, AIA, LEED AP, Project Architect, Antunovich Associates Architects and Planners

❯ Architecture will be more about retrofitting existing buildings than it will be about creating new in response to societal and environmental concerns. As it becomes increasingly important to limit the human impact on the earth and change decades of unsustainable practices, the profession of architecture will be about helping existing buildings remain relevant into the future.

The traditional practice of architecture is changing. I heard a statistic the other day that for every seven licensed architects at present retiring, only one new architect is licensed. The simple fact is that graduates from architecture school are not pursuing traditional practice in the same numbers as they did in the past. They are engaging in careers beyond the profession, often related to architecture. Thus, the definition of architecture is expanding. It is encompassing a greater skill set than previously defined.

Amanda Harrell-Seyburn, Associate AIA, Instructor, School of Planning, Design and Construction, Michigan State University

❯ The computer is the single most important development in architecture since the widespread use of steel in construction. The ability to quickly modify plans, model them in accurate three-dimensional settings, and produce a highly integrated set of construction documents is a boon to architectural design and to the construction field.

The global pressures that are pushing green design to the forefront will continue to increase, creating high demand for architects who base their practice on green principles. I feel that green design is not a passing style but essential for all design. There is no other choice.

Nathan Kipnis, AIA, Principal, Nathan Kipnis Architects, Inc.

❯ The architecture profession of tomorrow will be almost limitless in the ways that we work. Architects are already taking leadership roles in collaborations with governments, engineers, artists, and communities to tackle problems ranging from poverty to historical preservation. They are designing everything from new materials to revolutionary transportation systems and their work environments range from corporate and government offices to nongovernmental organizations and humanitarian relief agencies. Architects are no longer sitting in offices and waiting for clients to step through the door—they are actively pursuing how design can improve the world. It is an exciting future.

Karen Cordes Spence, Ph.D., AIA, LEED AP, Associate Professor, Drury University

❯ I see more multifunctional architects—architects that possess more skills from across the board to contribute to the future of inhabitable design. I see a collaborative environment in which architects, general contractors, and other influential people work together to create the most optimal design for the client. Design has become and is becoming more integrated, so this type of environment is necessary to produce architecture that will change or enhance the way we live. I see more collaboration between experienced and inexperienced, architecture professionals and non-architecture professionals, all contributing valuable information and solutions. I do not see the architecture profession dissipating—I see it *evolving*.

Anna A. Kissell, M.Arch. Candidate, Boston Architectural College, Associate Manager Environmental Design, Reebok International Inc.

❯Architecture will go down one of two paths: (1) it can increase its relevance in society and therefore enhance the benefits associated with becoming an architect, or (2) it can diminish in relevance and become commoditized, thereby decreasing the appeal of becoming an architect.

At present, we are at a crossroads in the path to relevance or obsolescence. Society does not really understand the value that architects offer. As a profession, we are viewed as more of a luxury than a necessity. If this perception does not change, the design profession will remain undervalued in society. However, if the value proposition of architecture is better articulated and exemplified in society, the profession will flourish. Only time will tell which path will prevail—hopefully, an increase in relevance.

Kimberly Dowdell, Project Manager/Director of Marketing, Levien & Company

❯I was once told that architecture is the caboose of our civilization in that it must respond to the winding path of our environment, economy, and values. As the world shifts from its post–World War II "irrational exuberence" to one that relies on smaller, stronger, and more enduring investments in our towns and cities, architects will have to respond in how they organize their services and how they implement visions for their clients and the clients' customers.

The way in which we practice is evolving as well. We are seeing much more collaboration with other disciplines and professions and equal sharing of credit and blame. Architects and related professions are increasingly being called to be national and world advocates for a number of important issues but, simultaneously, we are all expected to act locally in our own neighborhoods and cities, bringing real value right to our own backyards.

Joseph Nickol, AICP, LEED AP BD+C, Urbanist, Urban Design Associates

❯The urban fabric is completely changing. We are running out of natural resources we use to create energy. As a result, we will be completely changing the process of energy production. We are going to discover new ways to create energy without destroying the environment and the profession is going to change in order to accommodate these needs.

Elizabeth Weintraub, B.Arch. Candidate, New York Institute of Technology

❯The future of the profession will have increased collaboration, additional civic engagement, and a more focused effort in sustainability. With these comes a need for architects to step up and increase their leadership capacity—not only on project teams but also within society as a whole.

Amy Perenchio, Associate AIA, LEED AP BD+C, Architectural Designer, ZGF Architects, LLP

❯There is a strong future for the profession of architecture as long as architects listen to the needs of clients and to the voices of people trained in architecture who do not necessarily practice architecture.

H. Alan Brangman, AIA, Vice President of Facilities, Real Estate Auxiliary Services, University of Delaware

❯The future of architecture is rapidly changing and evolving with new technologies. There is a constant debate as to what the responsibilities of an architect are, especially in the social realm. I see architecture as a profession with the potential to reach into other disciplines and advance society through the built environment.

Danielle Mitchell, B.Arch. Candidate, Pennsylvania State University

❯Most architects can agree that sustainable design is steadily becoming the future of architecture due to the deletion of our environmental resources and the growing recognition among many government agencies and property owners. In order to be more marketable for certain design projects, it is desir-

What Do You See as the Future for the Architecture Profession? (Continued)

able to become a LEED AP and uphold a standard of "designing for the environment." The current economy can no longer allow our buildings to use unnecessary resources with no recollection of how it may affect the environment.

Jennifer Taylor, Vice President, American Institute of Architecture Students

❭The architecture profession remains a fascinating and rewarding career choice despite the biased reporting that one might read in the press. Architectural design does not narrowly focus on the building, but rather it is about a wide range of activities including master planning, interior architecture, sustainable design, site design, integrated project delivery, product design, post-occupancy services, and a host of other activities that will ensure that the profession is vibrant well into the future. However, to survive, the profession must broaden its appeal to women and under-represented groups. Also, the profession needs to expand its clientele to engage a broader constituency than the elite wealthy-class and corporate world that epitomized twentieth-century practice.

Brian Kelly, AIA, Associate Professor and Director, Architecture Program, University of Maryland

❭My hope is that for a whole range of reasons, including technology and environmental responsibility, the profession and the public will develop a better appreciation of history.

Mary Kay Lanzillotta, FAIA, Partner, Hartman-Cox Architects

❭1. Buildings and cities that make our health better and produce more energy than they use. Some day, our cities will be solar and geothermal power plants themselves. We need to see things on a more wholistic scale to do this.

2. The design build movement in architectural education has produced a watershed change. Students

and faculty see the opportunity in connecting designing and making and giving back to society.

3. Digital fabrication and printed buildings will completely change the way we build and the way we design.

William J. Carpenter, Ph.D., FAIA, Professor, Southern Polytechnic State University; President, Lightroom

❭The profession needs to change to continue to be relevant. We have to embrace that design-build work will continue to rise and that learning to partner well with contractors is critical.

To maintain our relevance, architects need to spend less time in our offices and in industry-focused activities and more time out in the world with our communities and activities and groups related to our clients' businesses.

There appears to be a rapid decline in the technical skills and interest of young architects; many newer architects today do not seem as focused on technical detailing. Additionally, as amazing as computers are in revolutionizing architectural design and documentation, it seems they have also contributed to the decline of some of the "craft" of the profession in sketching and problem solving both design and technical issues.

Carolyn G. Jones, AIA, Principal, Mulvanny G2

❭Architects have vision and ideas for positive change and they must take more leadership on these positions in the built environment and be the voice and the face of the built environment. This means showing how good design improves lives and the planet as a whole. The future of the profession must involve a better connection with the public and policy makers to influence important decisions that affect our environment. Expanding the definition of architecture and effectively communicating its importance will be of great importance. Of course, technology will continue to play an increasing role in architecture, but at its root, the profession will remain driven by relationships, ideas, and thoughtfulness.

Joseph Mayo, Intern Architect, Mahlum

❯ Young architects are coming out of school with a renewed interest in craft and the tectonics of construction and with an ever-increasing interest in design-build and creating community. I hope the architectural profession will realize the importance of being generalists and take back the roles and responsibilities that were once integral to doing good architecture.

Grace H. Kim, AIA, Principal, Schemata Workshop, Inc.

❯ Architects are becoming increasingly specialized, which is not necessarily good for the profession as a whole.

Lynsey J. G. Sorrell, AIA, LEED AP, Principal Perimeter Architects

❯ The complex manner in which architecture is conceived and how the mind of an architect processes ideas will become an asset to multiple industries, even those outside of the design world. The critical thinking and strategic planning that guides the process of architecture will become mainstream making the architect an asset in other industries. Branches of government that shape the growth of cities and operations divisions of large corporations are engaging architects in a non traditional way to help shape the focus of their business strategy. Much like how a design decision will affect the way a space or object is utilized, the architect's mind can design the way a business is structured to operate in a more effective and streamlined manner.

Megan S. Chusid, AIA, Manager of Facilities and Office Services, Solomon R. Guggenheim Museum and Foundation

❯ I hope we see architecture firms continuing to offer services beyond building design. Our clients and the public cannot realize the value of an archi-

State Street Village – Campus of Illinois Institute of Technology, Chicago, Illinois. Architect: Murphy-Jahn Associates. PHOTOGRAPHER: LEE W. WALDREP, Ph.D.

tect's skills beyond designing a building if we are not out offering them. If we do not do this, other allied professionals will continue to capitalize on these opportunities to expand services, thus narrowing the definition of the architect and continuing to diminish our value.

Ashley W. Clark, Associate AIA, LEED AP, SMPS, Marketing Manager, LandDesign

What Do You See as the Future for the Architecture Profession? (Continued)

❯Moving from a period of time when the profession teetered on becoming irrelevant through the celebration of the monumental, the profession will advocate for the value of design and how design of systems, spaces, and places can improve our citizens, communities, cities. The profession will continue to expand influence on the broad field of design as the collaborative and integrative skill sets that architects possess will be utilized in new applications and fields.

Katherine Darnstadt, AIA LEED AP BD+C, Founder and Principal Architect, Latent Design

❯Architecture as a profession is changing. It is not just about buildings in an isolated sense anymore. Context, the environment, social implications, and funding sources are all important aspects of the profession. The why of the building is as important as the how.

Makenzie Leukart, M.Arch. Candidate, Columbia University

❯It is not just about the planet, it is about *people*. The next generation of designers is facing a world where green design is increasingly a fundamental value and issues like population change and resiliency are at the forefront of the conversation. Architects have a huge capacity to improve the lives of people. Those with the least amount of access actually stand to benefit the most from the services of an architect. Our diverse skill set positions us for incredible impact. As a nation, we need to harness the creativity of architects and find a way to be at the forefront of decision making and problem solving. As architects, we are public artists, and as such we have a responsibility in our work to better the environment sustainably and socially.

Rosannah B. Sandoval, AIA, Designer II, Perkins + Will

 NOTES

1. *Future Work Skills 2020* (Phoenix, AZ: Institute for the Future for University of Phoenix Research Institute, 2011).
2. Green Building Certification Institute, 2009. Retrieved August 31, 2013, from www.gbci.org.
3. R. Hyde, *Future Practice* (New York: Routledge, 2012).
4. *Integrated Project Delivery: A Guide* (Washington, DC: AIA, 2007).
5. James Cramer, *Global Success Comes in All Sizes,* 2012. Retrieved May 19, 2013, from www.di.net/articles/global-success-comes-in-all-sizes/
6. James P. Cramer and Scott Simpson, *The Next Architect: A New Twist on the Future of Design* (Norcross, GA: Greenway Communications, 2007).

APPENDIX A

Resources of an Architect

The following are professional associations, recommended reading, and websites that may be of assistance in your quest to become an architect. In all cases, you should contact them for further information. Many of the associations have state or local chapters that may also be helpful.

COLLATERAL ORGANIZATIONS

These first five associations (AIA, AIAS, ACSA, NAAB, and NCARB) are commonly known as the *collateral organizations* and represent the primary players with the profession—architects, students, educators, the accrediting agency, and the state registration boards.

The American Institute of Architects (AIA)
1735 New York Ave., N.W.
Washington, DC 20006
(202) 626-7300
www.aia.org

Comprising over 80,000 members in almost 300 local and state chapters, the AIA is the largest association for the architectural profession; its mission is to promote and advance the profession and the living standards of people through their built environment.

American Institute of Architecture Students (AIAS)
1735 New York Ave., N.W.
Washington, DC 20006
(202) 626-7472
www.aias.org

The mission of the AIAS is to promote excellence in architectural education, training, and practice; to foster an appreciation of architecture and related disciplines; to enrich communities in a spirit of collaboration; and to organize architecture students and combine their efforts to advance the art and science of architecture.

Association of Collegiate Schools of Architecture (ACSA)
1735 New York Ave., N.W.
Washington, DC 20006
(202) 785-2324
www.acsa-arch.org

The ACSA is the membership organization that represents the over 100 U.S. and Canadian schools offering accredited professional degree programs in architecture; its mission is to advance architectural education through support of member schools, their faculty, and students.

National Architectural Accrediting Board (NAAB)
1101 Connecticut Ave., N.W., Suite 410.
Washington, DC 20036
(202) 783-2007
www.naab.org

The NAAB is the sole agency authorized to accredit U.S. professional degree programs in architecture. While graduation from an NAAB-accredited program does not ensure registration, the accrediting process is intended to verify that each accredited program substantially meets those standards that, as a whole, constitute an appropriate education for an architect.

National Council of Architectural Registration Boards (NCARB)
1801 K St., Ste. 700-K
Washington, DC 20006
(202) 783-6500
www.ncarb.org

The NCARB is the organization of the 55 states, territorial, and district registration boards that license architects, and the preparer of the Architect Registration Examination and the certification process that facilities reciprocity of individual licenses between jurisdictions.

ARCHITECTURE-RELATED ASSOCIATIONS

Alpha Rho Chi (APX)
www.alpharhochi.org

APX is the only national professional-social co-educational fraternity established to encourage closer fellowship and a greater interest in the study of architecture and the allied arts.

American Architectural Foundation (AAF)
(202) 787-1001
www.archfoundation.org

The AAF educates individuals and communities about the power of architecture to transform lives and improve the places where we live, learn, work, and play. Through our outreach programs, grants, scholarships, and educational resources, the AAF inspires people to become thoughtful and engaged stewards of the built environment.

American Indian Council of Architects and Engineers
www.aicae.org

The American Indian Council of Architects and Engineers advances the role of Native American professional engineers, architects, and design professionals in practice and encourages them to advance their professional skills and to pursue careers as professional engineers, architects, and design professionals.

American Society of Architectural Illustrators (ASAI)
(760) 453-2544
www.asai.org

The ASAI is an international nonprofit organization dedicated to the advancement and recognition of the art, science, and profession of architectural illustration. Through communication, education, and advocacy, the Society strives to refine and emphasize the role of illustration in the practice and appreciation of architecture.

American Society of Golf Course Architects
(262) 786-5960
www.asgca.org

The American Society of Golf Course Architects is composed of leading golf course designers in the United States and Canada actively involved in the design of new courses and the renovation of older courses.

Arquitectos
The Society of Hispanic Professional Architects
www.arquitectoschicago.org

Arquitectos exists to promote professional and economic development, membership, and community assistance and to further enrich the architectural profession through different cultural views and practices.

Asian American Architects and Engineers Association (AAa/e)
(213) 896-9270
www.aaaesc.com

The AAa/e is committed to providing a platform for empowering professionals working in the built environment in personal and professional growth, business development and networking, and leadership in our community.

The Association for Computer-Aided Design in Architecture (ACADIA)

www.acadia.org

Formed in the early 1980s, ACADIA is an international network of digital design researchers and professionals. They facilitate critical investigations into the role of computation in architecture, planning, and building science, encouraging innovation in design creativity, sustainability, and education.

Association of University Architects

www.auaweb.net

This special group of architectural professionals is focused on the development and enhancement of our university campuses. University architects plan for the future and carefully build and renovate facilities for current needs.

Congress for the New Urbanism (CNU)

(312) 551-7300

www.cnu.org

The CNU is the leading organization promoting walkable, mixed-use neighborhood-based development; sustainable communities; and healthier living conditions.

National Academy of Environmental Design (NAED)

www.naedonline.org

The NAED provides the leadership and expertise required to accomplish complex research projects on issues such as climate change, resource depletion, and energy security.

National Organization of Minority Architects (NOMA)

(202) 686.2780

www.noma.net

The NOMA has as its mission the building of a strong national organization, strong chapters, and strong members for the purpose of minimizing the effect of racism in our profession.

Royal Architectural Institute of Canada

(613) 241-3600

www.raic.org

Established in 1907, the Royal Architectural Institute of Canada seeks to build awareness and appreciation of the contribution of architecture to the physical and cultural well-being of Canadians.

Society of American Registered Architects (SARA)

(888) 385-7272

www.sara-national.org

Founded in 1956, the SARA provides a professional society for licensed architects to unite as a common voice to work together for the betterment of the profession; the advancement of all mankind and sustainability of the environment; and foster the Golden Rule of "Architect Helping Architect."

Tau Sigma Delta

www.tausigmadelta.org

Tau Sigma Delta provides a national collegiate honor society open to students of all American colleges and universities wherein an accredited program of Architecture, Landscape Architecture, or Allied Arts is established. The society derives its Greek letter name from the first letter of each of the words of its motto, Technitai Sophoikai Dexioti: Tau, Sigma, and Delta. The motto means "Craftsmen, skilled and trained."

Union of International Architects (UIA)

33 (1) 45 24 36 88

www.uia-architectes.org

The UIA is an international nongovernmental organization founded in Lausanne in 1948 to unite architects from all nations throughout the world, regardless of nationality, race, religion, or architectural school of thought, within the federations of their national associations. The UIA represents over a million architects throughout the world through national architectural associations that form the 92 UIA Member Sections.

United States Green Building Council (USGBC)
(800) 795-1747
www.usgbc.org

The USGBC is a nonprofit organization committed to a prosperous and sustainable future for our nation through cost-efficient and energy-saving green buildings.

ASSOCIATIONS—RELATED CAREERS

Architectural History

Society of Architectural Historians (SAH)
(312) 573-1365
www.sah.org

Founded in 1940, the SAH promotes the study, interpretation, and conservation of architecture, design, landscapes, and urbanism worldwide for the benefit of all.

Construction

American Council for Construction Education (ACCE)
(210) 495-6161
www.acce-hq.org

The ACCE is a leading global advocate of high-quality construction education programs, and to promote, support, and accredit quality construction education programs.

Architecture + Construction Alliance (A+CA)
www.aplusca.org

The mission of the A+CA is foster collaboration among schools that are committed to fostering interdisciplinary educational and research efforts between the fields of architecture and construction, and to engage leading professionals and educators in support of these efforts.

Associated Schools of Construction
(970) 988-1130
www.ascweb.org

The Associated Schools of Construction is a professional association for the development and advancement of construction education, where the sharing of ideas and knowledge inspires, guides, and promotes excellence in curricula, teaching, research, and service.

Construction Management Association of America (CMAA)
(703) 356-2622
www.cmaanet.org

The CMAA promotes professionalism and excellence in the management of the construction process. The CMAA is leading the growth and acceptance of construction management as a professional discipline that can add significant value to the entire construction process, from conception to ongoing operation.

Construction Specifications Institute (CSI)
(800) 689-2900
www.csinet.org

The CSI advances building information management and education of project teams to improve facility performance.

National Association of Women in Construction (NAWIC)
(800) 552-3506
www.nawic.org

Founded in 1953, the NAWIC is dedicated to enhancing the success of women in the construction industry by building educations, careers, futures, and lives.

Design (Graphic, Industrial, Furniture, Lighting)

American Design Council
(212) 807-1990
www.americandesigncouncil.org

The American Design Council is an alliance of individual professional associations interested in advancing a shared agenda to promote effective design.

American Institute of Graphic Arts (AIGA)
(212) 807-1990

www.aiga.org

The professional association for design, AIGA is the place design professionals turn to first to exchange ideas and information, participate in critical analysis and research, and advance education and ethical practice.

American Society of Furniture Designers (ASFD)
(910) 576-1273

www.asfd.com

Founded in 1981, the ASFD is the only international nonprofit professional organization dedicated to advancing, improving, and supporting the profession of furniture design and its positive impact in the marketplace.

Industrial Designers Society of America (IDSA)
(703) 707-6000

www.idsa.org

The IDSA is the voice of the industrial design profession, advancing the quality and positive impact of design.

International Association of Lighting Designers (IALD)
(312) 527-3677

www.iald.org

Founded in 1969, the IALD promotes the visible success of its members in practicing lighting design.

Society for Environmental Graphic Design (SEGD)
(202) 638-5555

www.segd.org

The SEGD exists to educate, connect, and inspire the global, multidisciplinary community of professionals who plan, design, and build experiences that connect people to place.

Historic Preservation

Heritage Documentation Programs (HDP)
National Park Service

Department of the Interior

(202) 354-2135

www.nps.gov/history/hdp

The HDP, part of the National Park Service, administers HABS (Historic American Buildings Survey), the federal government's oldest preservation program, and companion programs HAER (Historic American Engineering Record), HALS (Historic American Landscapes Survey), and CRGIS (Cultural Resources Geographic Information Systems).

National Council for Preservation Education (NCPE)
www.ncpe.us

The National Council for Preservation Education (NCPE) encourages and assists in the development and improvement of historic preservation education programs and endeavors in the United States and elsewhere.

National Trust for Historic Preservation
(202) 588-6000

www.preservationnation.org

The National Trust for Historic Preservation is a privately funded nonprofit organization that provides leadership, education, and advocacy to save America's diverse historic places and revitalize our communities.

Interior Design

American Society of Interior Designers (ASID)
(202) 546-3480

www.asid.org

The ASID is a community of people—designers, industry representatives, educators, and students—committed to interior design.

Council for Interior Design Accreditation
(616) 458-0400

www.accredit-id.org

The Council for Interior Design Accreditation ensures a high level of quality in interior design education through three primary activities: (1) set standards for postsecondary interior design education, (2) evaluate and accredit college and university interior design programs, and (3) facilitate outreach and collaboration with all stakeholders in the interior design community.

Interior Design Educators Council (IDEC)
(317) 328-4437

www.idec.org

The IDEC advances interior design education, scholarship, and service.

International Interior Design Association (IIDA)
(888) 799-4432

www.iida.org

The IIDA is committed to enhancing the quality of life through excellence in interior design and advancing interior design through knowledge.

Planning/Landscape Architecture

American Planning Association (APA)
(202) 872-0611

www.planning.org

The APA brings together thousands of people— practicing planners, citizens, elected officials—committed to making great communities happen.

American Society of Landscape Architects (ASLA)
(202) 898-2444

www.asla.org

Founded in 1899, the ASLA is the national professional association representing landscape architects. The ASLA leads, educates, and participates in the careful stewardship, wish planning, and artful design of our cultural and natural environments.

Association of Collegiate Schools of Planning (ACSP)
(850) 385-2054

www.acsp.org

The ACSP is a consortium of university-based programs offering credentials in urban and regional planning.

Council of Landscape Architectural Registration Boards (CLARB)
(703) 319-8380

www.clarb.org

The CLARB is dedicated to ensuring that all individuals who affect the natural and built environment through the practice of landscape architecture are sufficiently qualified to do so.

Technical/Engineering

Accreditation Board for Engineering and Technology, Inc. (ABET)
(410) 347-7700

www.abet.org

The ABET is a nonprofit, nongovernmental organization that accredits college and university programs in the disciplines of applied science, computing, engineering, and engineering technology.

Acoustical Society of America (ASA)
(516) 576-2360

acousticalsociety.org

The ASA is the premier international scientific society in acoustics, dedicated to increasing and diffusing the knowledge of acoustics and its practical applications.

American Association of Engineering Societies (AAES)
(202) 296-2237

www.aaes.org

Multidisciplinary organization of engineering societies dedicated to advancing the knowledge, understanding, and practice of engineering. AAES member societies represent the mainstream of U.S. engineering, more than one million engineers in industry, government, and academia.

American Society of Civil Engineers (ASCE)
(800) 548-2723
www.asce.org

The mission of the ASCE is to provide essential value to members, their careers, its partners, and the public by developing leadership, advancing technology, advocating lifelong learning, and promoting the profession of civil engineering.

National Society of Professional Engineers (NSPE)
(703) 684-2800
www.nspe.org

In partnership with the State Societies, the NSPE is the organization of licensed professional engineers (PEs) and engineer interns (EIs). Through education, licensure advocacy, leadership training, multidisciplinary networking, and outreach, the NSPE enhances the image of its members and their ability to ethically and professionally practice engineering.

Society of Building Science Educators
www.sbse.org

The Society of Building Science Educators is an association of university educators in architecture and related disciplines who support excellence in the teaching of environmental science and building technologies.

DEDICATED TO ARCHITECTURE

ACE Mentor Program
(703) 942-8101
www.acementor.org

The ACE (Architecture, Construction, Engineering) Mentor Program stands for mentoring high school students and inspiring them to pursue careers in design and construction.

Architecture & Design Education Network (A+DEN)
www.adenweb.org

Founded by the American Architectural Foundation (AAF) and the Chicago Architecture Foundation (CAF), the A+DEN is a collaborative association of like-minded organizations in the fields of architecture and design, committed to promoting innovative architecture and design education for teachers and students in grades K–12.

Association of Architecture Organizations (AAO)
www.aaonetwork.org

The AAO is a member-based network that connects the many organizations around the world dedicated to enhancing public dialogue about architecture and design.

Chicago Architecture Foundation (CAF)
(312) 922-3432
www.architecture.org

The CAF is dedicated to advancing public interest and education in architecture and related design. Because no art other than architecture so vividly expresses what Chicago is and where it is going, the CAF educates the public to expect the highest standards from Chicago's built environment.

CUBE: Center for Understanding the Built Environment
(520) 822-8486
www.cubekc.org

The CUBE brings together educators with community partners to effect change, which will lead to a high-quality built and natural environment, one and interdependent.

Graham Foundation for Advanced Studies in the Fine Arts
(312) 787-4071
www.grahamfoundation.org
The mission of the Graham Foundation is to nurture and enrich an informed and creative public dialogue concerning architecture and the built environment.

Learning by Design

c/o The Boston Society of Architects

(617) 391-4000

www.architects.org/LBD

A core element of the Boston Society of Architects' K–12 design education and design awareness program, Learning by Design gives children the opportunity to express their ideas about their built and natural environments.

National Building Museum

(202) 272-2448

www.nbm.org

Created by an act of Congress, the National Building Museum is the only institution uniquely dedicated to exploring the what, who, how, and why of American building. The National Building Museum seeks to broaden public understanding and appreciation of our building heritage by providing people with a variety of skills needed to better understand and shape the built environment.

COMMUNITY SERVICE

AmeriCorps

(202) 606-5000

www.americorps.gov

AmeriCorps is a network of national service programs that engage more than 50,000 Americans each year in intensive service to meet critical needs in education, public safety, health, and the environment.

Architects, Designers, and Planners for Social Responsibility (ADPSR)

(510) 845-1000

www.adpsr.org

The ADPSR works for peace, environmental protection, ecological building, social justice, and the development of healthy communities.

Architecture for Humanity

(415) 963-3511

www.architectureforhumanity.org

Architecture for Humanity promotes architectural and design solutions to global, social, and humanitarian crises. Through competitions, workshops, educational forums, partnerships with aid organizations, and other activities, Architecture for Humanity creates opportunities for architects and designers from around the world to help communities in need.

Association for Community Design (ACD)

www.communitydesign.org

Established in 1977, the ACD is a network of individuals, organizations, and institutions committed to increasing the capacity of planning and design professions to better serve communities. The ACD serves and supports practitioners, educators, and organizations engaged in community-based design and planning.

Design Corps

(919) 637-2804

www.designcorps.org

Founded in 1991, Design Corps is a private nonprofit that was created to coordinate design services that help create responsive affordable housing. Respect for those housed, the local communities, and cultures involved are encouraged. Motto: Design for the 98 percent without Architects.

Habitat for Humanity

(229) 924-6935

www.habitat.org

Habitat for Humanity International is a nonprofit Christian housing ministry that works to build or renovate homes for the inadequately sheltered in the United States and in 20 countries around the world.

The Mad Housers, Inc.

(404) 806-6233

www.madhousers.org

The Mad Housers, Inc., is an Atlanta-based nonprofit corporation engaged in charitable work, research, and education. Their primary endeavor is building temporary, emergency shelters for homeless individuals and families regardless of race, creed, national origin, gender, religion, age, family status, sexual orientation, and the like.

Peace Corps
Paul D. Coverdell Peace Corps Headquarters
(855) 855-1961
www.peacecorps.gov

Established in 1961 by President John F. Kennedy, the Peace Corps has shared with the world America's most precious resource—its people. Peace Corps volunteers serve in 72 countries in Africa, Asia, the Caribbean, Central and South America, Europe, and the Middle East. Collaborating with local community members, volunteers work in areas like education, youth outreach and community development, the environment, and information technology.

Public Architecture
(415) 861-8200
www.publicarchitecture.org

Established in 2002, Public Architecture is a nonprofit organization that identifies and solves practical problems of human interaction in the built environment. It acts as a catalyst for public discourse through education, advocacy, and the design of public spaces and amenities.

Public Interest Design
www.publicinterestdesign.org

Public Interest Design.org is principally a blog about a growing movement at the intersection of design and service.

Rose Architectural Fellowship Program
www.enterprisecommunity.com/rose-architectural-fellowship

The Enterprise Rose Architectural Fellowship offers a select few of the nation's finest, early-career architects the opportunity for firsthand training and experience in sustainable community design work.

Social Economic Environmental Design (SEED)
www.seed-network.org

SEED® is a principle-based network of individuals and organizations dedicated to building and supporting a culture of civic responsibility and engagement in the built environment and the public realm.

RECOMMENDED READING

ACSA. (Ed.). (2009). *Guide to Architecture Schools* (8th ed.). Washington, DC: Association of Collegiate Schools of Architecture. ISBN 0-935-50269-5.

The Guide to Architecture Schools provides a valuable resource for individuals seeking to pursue an architectural education. Its primary content is a compilation of two-page descriptions of the over 100 universities offering accredited degree programs in architecture. In addition, the resource contains an introduction outlining the history of architectural education, high school preparation, selecting a school, architectural practice, and accreditation.

Anthony, Kathryn. (2001). *Designing for Diversity: Gender, Race, and Ethnicity in the Architectural Profession*. Champaign, IL: University of Illinois Press. ISBN 0-252-02641-1.

This landmark book offers insight into the issue of diversity as it relates to the profession of architecture. As one reviewer stated, "a must read."

Anthony, Kathryn. (1991). *Design Juries on Trial: The Renaissance of the Design Studio*. New York, NY: Van Nostrand Reinhold. ISBN 0-442-00235-1.

Design Juries on Trial unlocks the door to the mysterious design jury system—exposing its hidden agendas and helping you overcome intimidation, confrontation, and frustration. It explains how to improve the success rate of submissions to juries—whether in academic settings, for competitions, and awards programs, or for professional accounts.

Architecture for Humanity. (2012). *Design Like You Give a Damn* [2]: *Building Change from the Ground Up*. New York, NY: Metropolis Books. ISBN 0-810-99702-9.

Design Like You Give a Damn [2] is a compendium of innovative projects from around the world that demonstrate the power of design to improve lives.

Bell, Bryan. (2003). *Good Deeds, Good Design: Community Service Through Architecture*. Princeton: Princeton Architectural Press. ISBN 1-568-98391-3.

Good Deeds, Good Design presents the best new thoughts and practices in this emerging movement toward an architecture that serves a broader population. In this book, architecture firms, community design centers, design-build programs, and service-based organizations offer their plans for buildings for the other 98 percent.

Bell, Bryan, and Wakeford, Katie. (Eds.). (2008). *Expanding Architecture: Design as Activism*. New York, NY: Metropolis Books. ISBN 1-933-04578-7.

Expanding Architecture presents a new generation of creative design carried out in the service of the greater public and the greater good. Questioning how design can improve daily lives, editors Bryan Bell and Katie Wakeford map an emerging geography of architectural activism—or "public-interest architecture"—that might function akin to public-interest law or medicine by expanding architecture's all too often elite client base.

Bizios, Georgia, and Wakeford, Katie. (2011). *Bridging the Gap: Public Interest Internships*. Self-Published.

Bridging the Gap, a collection of 19 essays, brings together the best in current practice and thinking regarding public-interest architectural internship and advocates for new models that will have the power to profoundly change the architectural profession and our communities.

Boyer, Ernest L., and Mitgang, Lee D. (1996). *Building Community: A New Future for Architecture Education and Practice*. Princeton, NJ: Carnegie Foundation for the Advancement of Teaching. ISBN 0-931-05059-6.

Commissioned by the five collateral organizations involved with the architecture profession, this independent study focused on architectural education and practice; its conclusion developed seven essential goals or designs for renewal.

Cary, John. (2010). *The Power of Pro Bono: 40 Stories about Design for the Public Good by Architects and Their Clients*. New York, NY: Metropolis Books. ISBN 978-1-9352-0218-9.

The book presents 40 pro bono design projects across the country, with first-person perspectives from architects and their nonprofit clients. The selected works span six categories: Arts, Civic, Community, Education, Health, and Housing.

Ching, Francis D. K. (2012). *Introduction to Architecture*. Hoboken, NJ: John Wiley & Sons. ISBN 1-118-14206-3.

Presents the essential texts and drawings of Francis Ching for those new to design and architecture. The book explains the experience and practice of architecture and allied disciplines for future professionals.

Ching, Francis D. K. (2007). *Architecture: Form, Space & Order*. Hoboken, NJ: John Wiley & Sons. ISBN 0-471-28616-8.

This classic visual reference helps both students and practicing architects understand the basic vocabulary of architectural design by examining how form and space are ordered in the built environment. Using his trademark meticulous drawing, Professor Ching shows the relationship between fundamental elements of architecture through the ages and across cultural boundaries.

Cramer, James P., and Simpson, Scott. (2007). *The Next Architect: A New Twist on the Future of Design.* Norcross, GA: Greenway Communications. ISBN 0-975-56548-6.

The Next Architect takes a fresh look at our fast-evolving profession, starting with the proposition that everyone is an architect, both enabled and empowered to help shape tomorrow's world. Tomorrow's successful practitioners must be adept at collaborative design techniques and comfortable working at warp speed. This book challenges the next generation of design professionals to make full use of their talents to build a better, healthier, and more prosperous world.

Cuff, Dana. (1991). *Architecture: The Story of Practice.* Boston, MA: MIT Press. ISBN 0-262-53112-7.

In this book, Cuff delves into the architect's everyday work world to uncover an intricate social art of design. The result is a new portrait of the profession that sheds light on what it means to become an architect, how design problems are construed and resolved, how clients and architects negotiate, and how design excellence is achieved.

Earley, Sandra Leibowitz. (2005). *Ecological Design and Building Schools.* Oakland, CA: New Village Press. ISBN 0-976-60541-4.

The only directory of its kind in North America, this comprehensive guide features an annotated listing of schools and educational centers offering programs in ecological architecture and construction. Included also is a 10-year overview of sustainable design education, tables comparing school programs, and listings of instructors, green building organizations, selected textbooks, and publicly available curricula.

Frederick, Matthew. (2007). *101 Things I Learned in Architecture School.* Cambridge, MA: MIT Press. ISBN 978-0-262-06266-4.

As stated on the book jacket, this is a book that students of architecture will want to keep in the studio and in their backpacks; it provides a much-needed primer in architectural literacy.

Ginsberg, Beth. (2004). *The ECO Guide to Careers that Make a Difference: Environmental Work for a Sustainable World.* Washington, DC: Island Press. ISBN 1-55963-967-9.

This publication provides an overview of career choices and opportunities and identifies development employment trends as the environmental community looks forward to the pressing needs of the twenty-first century.

Hyde, Rory. (2012). *Future Practice: Conversations from the Edge of Architecture.* New York, NY: Routledge.

Conversations with practitioners form the fields of architecture, policy, activism, design, education, research, history, community engagement, and more, each representing an emergent role for designers to occupy.

Kim, Grace. (2006). *The Survival Guide to Architectural Internship and Career Development.* Hoboken, NJ: John Wiley & Sons. ISBN: 0-471-69263-8.

A concise, helpful guide to understanding the choices and decisions you will confront on the road from student to practitioner. Whether you are currently an architecture student, starting the internship process, taking the registration exams, or beginning your own firm, this book demystifies the process for you.

Kostof, Sprio. (Ed.). (1977). *The Architect.* New York, NY: Oxford University Press. ISBN 0-195-04044-9.

A collection of essays by historians and architects, *The Architect* explores and surveys the profession of architecture from its beginnings in ancient Egypt to the modern day.

Lewis, R. K. (2013). *Architect? A Candid Guide to the Profession.* Boston, MA: MIT Press. ISBN 9-780-26251884-0.

Using three sections: (1) "To Be or Not To Be ... an Architect," (2) "Becoming an Architect," and (3) "Being an Architect," the author provides an inside look at the profession, its educational process, and weighing the pros and cons of becoming an architect. Written by Roger K. Lewis, an emeritus professor of architecture from the University of Maryland, the book is excellent reading for an aspiring architect.

Linton, Harold. (2012). *Portfolio Design* (4th ed.). New York, NY: W. W. Norton & Company, Inc. ISBN 978-0-393-73253-5.

More than any other, this book provides critical information on creating, preparing, and producing a portfolio, an element necessary for architecture students in applying to graduate programs or seeking employment.

Mann, Thorbjoern. (2004). *Time Management for Architects and Designers: Challenge and Remedies.* New York, NY: W. W. Norton & Company. ISBN 0-393-73133-2.

Addresses the special time management issues that confront designers. It offers students and professionals guidance in recognizing and understanding these problems and developing effective strategies for overcoming them.

Marjanovic, Igor, Ruedi Ray, Katerina, and Lokko, Lesley Naa Norle. (2003). *The Portfolio: An Architecture Student's Handbook.* Oxford, England: Architectural Press. ISBN 0-7506-5764-2.

Gives practical advice for the creation of the portfolio covering issues of size, storage, lay-out, and order. Further, it guides the student through the various forms a portfolio can take: the electronic portfolio, the academic portfolio, and the professional portfolio, suggesting different approaches and different media to use in order to create the strongest portfolio possible.

Marjanovic, Igor, Ruedi Ray, Katerina, and Tankard, Jane. (2005). *Practical Experience: An Architecture Student's Guide to Internship and the Year Out.* Oxford, England: Architectural Press. ISBN 0-7506-6206-9.

In order to give you a real insight into professional experience, this guide includes real-life case studies from students who have been through the experience and from practices that have taken them on. It guides you through the steps of finding a placement, outlines the norms and expectations for internship in different countries, and discusses codes of office behavior and professional ethics.

Masengarb, Jennifer, and Rehbien, Krisann. (2007). *The Architecture Handbook: A Student Guide to Understanding Buildings.* Chicago, IL: Chicago Architecture Foundation. ISBN 0-962-05627-8.

Focuses on the design and construction of residential architecture. Through hands-on activities, *The Architecture Handbook* teaches both the fundamentals of architectural design and technical drawing. Students also build knowledge and gain skills through group design projects, sketching, model making, mapping, research, critical thinking, problem solving, and class presentations.

Ockman, Joan, and Williamson, Rebecca. (2012). *Architecture School: Three Centuries of Educating Architects in North America.* Cambridge, MA: MIT Press.

This book, published in conjunction with the centennial of the Association of Collegiate

Schools of Architecture (ACSA), provides the first comprehensive history of North American architecture education.

O'Gorman, James F. (1998). *ABC of Architecture*. Philadelphia, PA: University of Pennsylvania Press. ISBN 0-812-21631-8.

ABC of Architecture is an accessible, non-technical text on the first steps to understanding architectural structure, history, and criticism. Author James F. O'Gorman moves seamlessly from a discussion of the most basic inspiration for architecture (the need for shelter from the elements) to an exploration of space, system, and material, and, finally, to an examination of the language and history of architecture.

Parnell, Rosie, and Sara, Rachel. (2007). *The Crit: An Architecture Student's Handbook*. Oxford, England: Architectural Press. ISBN 0-7506-8225-6.

This fully updated edition includes advice and suggestions for tutors on how to model a crit around a broad range of learning styles to ensure that the process is constructive and beneficial for all architecture and design scholars.

Patt, Doug. (2012). *How to Architect*. Cambridge, MA: MIT Press. ISBN: 978-0-262-51699-0.

In *How to Architect,* Patt—an architect and the creator of a series of wildly popular online videos about architecture—presents the basics of architecture in A-Z form, starting with "A is for Asymmetry" (as seen in Chartres Cathedral and Frank Gehry), detouring through "N is for Narrative," and ending with "Z is for Zeal."

Piper, R. (2006). *Opportunities in Architectural Careers*. Lincolnwood, IL: VGM Career Horizons. ISBN 0-07-145868-9.

Part of the extensive "Opportunities In" series by VGM Career Horizons, *Opportunities in Architectural Careers* aims to assist the reader to learn more about the purpose of architecture in today's environment, understand what an architect does, and grasp the many career opportunities in architecture. Targeted at high school students, the book provides a good picture of the architecture profession and the tasks of an architect.

Pressman, Andy. (1993). *Architecture 101: A Guide to the Design Studio*. New York, NY: John Wiley & Sons. ISBN 0-471-57318-3.

Introduces students to the design studio and helps them to develop a process by which they can complete design projects. Covering every practical element of this central experience, from setting up that first day to landing that first job, this important work features contributions from some of the most distinguished names in architecture.

Pressman, Andy. (2012). *Designing Architecture: The Elements of Process*. New York: Routledge. ISBN 0-978-0-415-59516-2.

Designing Architecture is an indispensable tool to assist both students and young architects in formulating an idea, transforming it into a building, and making effective design decisions. This book promotes integrative and critical thinking in the preliminary design of buildings to inspire creativity, innovation, and design excellence.

Pressman, Andy. (2006). *Professional Practice 101: Business Strategies and Case Studies in Architecture*. New York, NY: John Wiley & Sons. ISBN 0-471-68366-7.

Provides fresh light on the many issues involved in the operation of an architectural practice—from how a firm is structured to how it manages projects and secures new business. Case studies, new to the this edition, augment each chapter as does a wealth of material including coverage of a topics on architectural practice.

Rasmussen, Steen Eiler. (1959). *Experiencing Architecture.* Cambridge, MA: MIT Press. ISBN 0-262-68002-5.

Profusely illustrated with fine instances of architectural experimentation through the centuries, this classic manages to convey the intellectual excitement of superb design.

Swett, Richard N. (2005). *Leadership by Design: Creating an Architecture of Trust.* Atlanta, GA: Greenway Communications. ISBN: 0-9755654-0-0.

Leadership by Design investigates the unique civic leadership strengths of the architecture profession. Drawing upon the compelling history of the profession, both past and present, as well as from his own singular experience as the only architect to serve in Congress during the twentieth century, Swett has produced an insightful volume that is both inspiring and instructive.

WEBSITES

These websites are directly related to the topic of this book and are current at the time of publication. You can explore the many other architecture-related websites as well.

ARCHCareers.org

www.archcareers.org

ARCHCareers.org is an interactive guide to careers in architecture designed to assist you in becoming an architect! It assists you in learning more about and understanding the process of becoming an architect—(1) education, (2) experience, and (3) exam.

ARCHCareers Blog

archcareers.blogspot.com

A companion to ARCHCareers.org, Dr. Architecture maintains this blog on architectural education and the process of becoming an architect. Questions posed are answered and resources are highlighted.

ARCHDaily

www.archdaily.com

Founded in March 2008, ARCHDaily is the online source of continuous information of the latest architectural news: projects, products, events, interviews, and competitions among others.

Archinect

www.archinect.com

The goal of Archinect is to make architecture more connected and open-minded, and bring together designers from around the world to introduce new ideas from all disciplines.

Architect—the magazine of the AIA

www.architectmagazine.com

The magazine of the American Institute of Architects offering architecture news, market intelligence, business and technology solutions, continuing education, building products, and other resources for architects.

Architectural Record

archrecord.construction.com

Architecturalrecord.com supplements the monthly magazine with expanded multimedia project stories, in-depth interviews with giants of architecture, daily news updates, weekly book reviews, green architecture stories, and archival material, as well as links to people and products and access to online continuing education credit registration.

ArchNewsNow

www.archnewsnow.com

ArchNewsNow.com delivers the most comprehensive coverage of national and international news, projects, products, and events in the world of architecture and design.

ARCHSchools

www.archschools.org

A companion website to the Guide to Architecture Schools compiled by the

Association of Collegiate Schools of Architecture (ACSA), ARCHSchools provides a valuable resource for individuals seeking to pursue an architectural education. It provides the opportunity to search architecture programs and review descriptions on over 100 universities offering accredited degree programs in architecture.

Design Careers and Education Guide
ucda.com/careers.lasso

Thinking about an education or career in design? Browse this guide to help you decide which specialty(ies) you are most interested in pursuing. Each specialty has a general description and education and career perspectives.

Design Disciplines, Whole Building Design Guide
www.wbdg.org/design/design_disciplines.php

A branch of the Whole Building Design Guide, Design Discipline assists in understanding how building design disciplines are organized and practiced. Disciplines included: Architecture, Architectural Programming, Fire Protection Engineering, Interior Design, Landscape Architecture, Planning, and Structural Engineering.

DesignIntelligence
www.di.net

DesignIntelligence contains a wealth of timely articles, original research, and essential industry news. The organization also publishes an annual review called "America's Best Architecture and Design Schools."

Directory of African American Architects
blackarch.uc.edu

The Directory of African American Architects is maintained as a public service to promote an awareness of whom African American architects are and where they are located.

Discover Design: A Student Design Experience
www.discoverdesign.org

Created by the Chicago Architecture Foundation, DiscoverDesign is an educational tool intended for high school classrooms as well as independent students users.

Emerging Professional's Companion (EPC)
www.epcompanion.org

Launched in 2004, the EPC is an online internship resource for emerging professionals. Primarily intended as a means for interns to supplement and bolster their knowledge as soon-to-be-licensed architects and to earn IDP credit, the EPC can also be used by students to gain exposure to practice issues while still in school, or even as an accompaniment to co-op or part-time employment before they graduate.

Great Buildings Collection
www.greatbuildings.com

Great Buildings is the leading architecture reference site on the web. This gateway to architecture around the world and across history documents a thousand buildings and hundreds of leading architects with photographic images and architectural drawings, integrated maps and timelines, 3D building models, commentaries, bibliographies, web links, and more, for famous designers and structures of all kinds.

International Archive of Women in Architecture
spec.lib.vt.edu/IAWA

The purpose of the International Archive of Women in Architecture is to document the history of women's involvement in architecture by collecting, preserving, storing, and making available to researchers the professional papers of women architects, landscape architects, designers, architectural historians and critics, and urban planners, as well as the records of women's architectural organizations from around the world.

Portfolio Design

www.portfoliodesign.com

A companion to the ever popular publication by
the same name, Portfolio Design, the website
includes essential information on the digital
and multimedia direction of portfolios today.
Portfolio Design shows you how to assemble a
portfolio that will display your talents and qualifications to the best advantage.

The 1%

www.theonepercent.org

The 1%, a program of Public Architecture, connects nonprofits with architecture and design
firms willing to give of their time pro bono.

APPENDIX B

Accredited Architecture Programs in the United States and Canada

This list is up to date as of the publication date. For an up-to-date list, contact National Architectural Accrediting Board: www.naab.org.

ALABAMA

Auburn University
College of Architecture, Design and Construction
School of Architecture, Planning, and Landscape
    Architecture
Auburn, AL
cadc.auburn.edu/apla/
B.Arch.

Tuskegee University
The Robert R. Taylor School of Architecture and
    Construction Science
Department of Architecture
Tuskegee, AL
www.tuskegee.edu/academics/colleges/school_of_
    architecture_and_construction_science.aspx
B.Arch.

ALASKA

None

ARIZONA

Arizona State University
Herberger Institute for Design and the Arts
The Design School
Tempe, AZ
design.asu.edu
M.Arch.

Arizona, University of
College of Architecture + Planning + Landscape
    Architecture
School of Architecture
Tuscon, AZ
www.architecture.arizona.edu
B.Arch.; M.Arch.

Frank Lloyd Wright School of Architecture
Scottsdale, AZ/Spring Green, WI
www.taliesin.edu
M.Arch.

ARKANSAS

Arkansas, University of
Fay Jones School of Architecture
Fayetteville, AR
architecture.uark.edu
B.Arch.

CALIFORNIA

Academy of Art University
School of Architecture
San Francisco, CA
www.academyart.edu/architecture-school
B.Arch—Candidate; M.Arch.

California at Berkeley, University of
College of Environmental Design
Department of Architecture
Berkeley, CA
arch.ced.berkeley.edu
M.Arch.

California at Los Angeles, University of (UCLA)
Department of Architecture and Urban Design
Los Angeles, CA
www.aud.ucla.edu
M.Arch.

California College of the Arts
School of Architecture
San Francisco, CA
www.cca.edu
B.Arch.; M.Arch.

California Polytechnic University–San Luis Obispo
College of Architecture and Environmental Design
Architecture Department
San Luis Obispo, CA
www.arch.calpoly.edu
B.Arch.

California State Polytechnic University–Pomona
College of Environmental Design
Department of Architecture
Pomona, CA
www.csupomona.edu/~arc
B.Arch.; M.Arch.

New School of Architecture & Design
San Diego, CA
www.newschoolarch.edu
B.Arch.; M.Arch.

Southern California Institute of Architecture (SCI-ARC)
Los Angeles, CA
www.sciarc.edu
B.Arch.; M.Arch.

Southern California, University of
School of Architecture
Los Angeles, CA
arch.usc.edu
B.Arch.; M.Arch.

Woodbury University
School of Architecture and Design
Burbank, CA/San Diego, CA
www.woodbury.edu
B.Arch.; M.Arch.

COLORADO

Colorado at Denver, University of
College of Architecture and Planning
Denver, CO
www.ucdenver.edu/academics/colleges/
architectureplanning/
M.Arch.

CONNECTICUT

Hartford, University of
College of Engineering, Technology, and
Architecture
Department of Architecture
uhaweb.hartford.edu/architect
M.Arch.

Yale University
School of Architecture
New Haven, CT
www.architecture.yale.edu
M.Arch.

DELAWARE

None

DISTRICT OF COLUMBIA

The Catholic University of America
School of Architecture and Planning
Washington, DC
architecture.cua.edu
M.Arch.

District of Columbia, University of
College of Agriculture, Urban Sustainability and
Environmental Sciences
Department of Architecture and Community
Planning
Washington, DC
www.udc.edu/college_urban_agriculture_and_
environmental_studies/divisions
M.Arch—Candidate

Howard University
College of Engineering, Architecture, and
    Computer Science
School of Architecture and Design
Department of Architecture
Washington, DC
www.howard.edu/ceacs/departments/architecture
B.Arch.

FLORIDA

Florida A&M University
School of Architecture
Tallahassee, FL
www.famusoa.net
B.Arch.; M.Arch.

Florida Atlantic University
College of Architecture, Urban and Public Affairs
School of Architecture
Ft Lauderdale, FL
www.fau.edu/arch
B.Arch.

Florida International University
College of Architecture + The Arts
School of Architecture
Miami, FL
soa.fiu.edu
M.Arch.

Florida, University of
College of Design, Construction and Planning
School of Architecture
Gainesville, FL
soa.dcp.ufl.edu
M.Arch.

Miami, University of
School of Architecture
Coral Gables, FL
www.arc.miami.edu
B.Arch.; M.Arch.

South Florida, University of
School of Architecture and Community Design
Tampa, FL
www.arch.usf.edu
M.Arch.

GEORGIA

Georgia Institute of Technology
College of Architecture
School of Architecture
Atlanta, GA
www.arch.gatech.edu
M.Arch.

Savannah College of Art and Design
Department of Architecture
Savannah, GA
www.scad.edu/architecture
M.Arch.

Southern Polytechnic State University
School of Architecture and Construction
    Management
Department of Architecture
Marietta, GA
architecture.spsu.edu
B.Arch.

HAWAII

Hawai'i at Manoa, University of
School of Architecture
Honolulu, HI
www.arch.hawaii.edu
D.Arch.

IDAHO

Idaho, University of
College of Art and Architecture
Department of Architecture and Interior Design
Moscow, ID
www.caa.uidaho.edu/arch
M.Arch.

ILLINOIS

Illinois at Chicago, University of
College of Architecture & the Arts
School of Architecture
Chicago, IL
www.arch.uic.edu
M.Arch.

Illinois Institute of Technology
College of Architecture
Chicago, IL
www.iit.edu/arch/
B.Arch.; M.Arch.

Illinois at Urbana-Champaign, University of
College of Fine and Applied Arts
School of Architecture
Champaign, IL
www.arch.illinois.edu
M.Arch.

Judson University
School of Art, Design, and Architecture
Department of Architecture
Elgin, IL
www.judsonu.edu
M.Arch.

The School of the Art Institute of Chicago
Department of Architecture, Interior Design, and
    Designed Objects
Chicago, IL
www.saic.edu/degrees_resources/departments/
    aiado
M.Arch.

Southern Illinois University Carbondale
College of Applied Sciences and Arts
School of Architecture
Carbondale, IL
architecture.siu.edu
M.Arch.

INDIANA

Ball State University
College of Architecture and Planning
Department of Architecture
Muncie, IN
www.bsu.edu/architecture
M.Arch.

Notre Dame, University of
School of Architecture
Notre Dame, IN
architecture.nd.edu
B.Arch.; M.Arch.

IOWA

Iowa State University
College of Design
Department of Architecture
Ames, IA
www.arch.iastate.edu
B.Arch.; M.Arch.

KANSAS

Kansas State University
College of Architecture, Planning, and Design
Department of Architecture
Manhattan, KS
www.capd.ksu.edu/arch
M.Arch.

Kansas, University of
School of Architecture and Urban Planning
Department of Architecture
Lawrence, KS
www.saup.ku.edu
M.Arch.

KENTUCKY

Kentucky, University of
College of Design
School of Architecture
Lexington, KY
www.uky.edu/design
M.Arch.

LOUISIANA

Louisiana at Lafayette, University of
College of the Arts
School of Architecture and Design
Lafayette, LA
soad.louisiana.edu
M.Arch.

Louisiana State University
College of Art and Design
School of Architecture
Baton Rouge, LA
design.lsu.edu/architecture/index.html/
B.Arch.; M.Arch.

Louisiana Tech University
College of Liberal Arts
School of Architecture
Ruston, LA
www.arch.latech.edu
M.Arch.

Southern University and A&M College
School of Architecture
Baton Rouge, LA
www.subr.edu/index.cfm/page/260/n/333
B.Arch.

Tulane University
School of Architecture
New Orleans, LA
architecture.tulane.edu
M.Arch.

MAINE

Maine at Augusta, University of
College of Professional Studies
Augusta, ME
www.uma.edu/bachelor-of-architecture.html
B.Arch—Candidate

MARYLAND

Maryland, University of
School of Architecture, Planning and Preservation
Architecture Program
College Park, MD
www.arch.umd.edu/architecture
M.Arch.

Morgan State University
School of Architecture and Planning
Baltimore, MD
www.morgan.edu/sap
M.Arch.

MASSACHUSETTS

Boston Architectural College
School of Architecture
Boston, MA
www.the-bac.edu
B.Arch.; M.Arch.

Harvard University
Graduate School of Design
Department of Architecture
Cambridge, MA
www.gsd.harvard.edu
M.Arch.

Massachusetts Amherst, University of
Department of Art, Architecture and Art History
Architecture + Design Program
Amherst, MA
www.umass.edu/architecture
M.Arch.

Massachusetts College of Art and Design
Department of Art/Art History
Boston, MA
www.massart.edu
M.Arch.

Massachusetts Institute of Technology
School of Architecture and Planning
Department of Architecture
Cambridge, MA
architecture.mit.edu
M.Arch.

Northeastern University
College of Arts, Media, and Design
School of Architecture
Boston, MA
www.architecture.neu.edu
M.Arch.

Wentworth Institute of Technology
College of Architecture, Design, and Construction
    Management
Department of Architecture
Boston, MA
www.wit.edu/arch
M.Arch.

MICHIGAN

Andrews University
School of Architecture, Art, and Design
Berrien Springs, MI
www.andrews.edu/arch
M.Arch.

Detroit Mercy, University of
School of Architecture
Detroit, MI
www.arch.udmercy.edu
M.Arch.

Lawrence Technological University
College of Architecture and Design
Department of Architecture
Southfield, MI
ltu.edu/architecture_and_design
M.Arch.

Michigan, University of
Taubman College of Architecture and Urban
    Planning
Ann Arbor, MI
www.tcaup.umich.edu/arch
M.Arch.

MINNESOTA

Minnesota, University of
College of Design
School of Architecture
Minneapolis, MN
arch.cdes.umn.edu
M.Arch.

MISSISSIPPI

Mississippi State University
College of Architecture, Art, and Design
School of Architecture
Mississippi State, MS
www.caad.msstate.edu/sarc
B.Arch.

MISSOURI

Drury University
Hammons School of Architecture
Springfield, MO
www.drury.edu/architecture/
M.Arch.

Washington University in St. Louis
Sam Fox School of Design and Visual Arts
College of Architecture
St. Louis, MO
www.arch.wustl.edu
M.Arch.

MONTANA

Montana State University
College of Arts and Architecture
School of Architecture
Bozeman, MT
www.arch.montana.edu
M.Arch.

NEBRASKA

Nebraska-Lincoln, University of
College of Architecture
Department of Architecture
Lincoln, NE
architecture.unl.edu/programs/arch/
M.Arch.

NEVADA

Nevada-Las Vegas, University of
College of Fine Arts
School of Architecture
Las Vegas, NV
architecture.unlv.edu
M.Arch.

NEW HAMPSHIRE

None

NEW JERSEY

New Jersey Institute of Technology
College of Architecture and Design
School of Architecture
Newark, NJ
architecture.njit.edu
B.Arch.; M.Arch.

Princeton University
School of Architecture
Princeton, NJ
soa.princeton.edu
M.Arch.

NEW MEXICO

New Mexico, University of
School of Architecture and Planning
Architecture Program
Albuquerque, NM
saap.unm.edu
M.Arch.

NEW YORK

City College of the City University of New York
The Bernard and Anne Spitzer School of
    Architecture
New York, NY
www.ccny.cuny.edu/architecture/
B.Arch.; M.Arch.

Columbia University
Graduate School of Architecture, Planning and
    Preservation
New York, NY
www.arch.columbia.edu
M.Arch.

Cooper Union
Irwin S. Chanin School of Architecture
New York, NY
www.cooper.edu
B.Arch.

Cornell University
College of Architecture, Art, and Planning
Department of Architecture
Ithaca, NY
www.aap.cornell.edu/arch
B.Arch.; M.Arch.

New York Institute of Technology
School of Architecture and Design
Old Westbury, NY
iris.nyit.edu/architecture
B.Arch.

Parsons The New School for Design
School of Constructed Environments
New York, NY
www.newschool.edu/parsons/
M.Arch.

Pratt Institute
School of Architecture
Brooklyn, NY
www.pratt.edu/arch
B.Arch.; M.Arch.

Rensselaer Polytechnic Institute
School of Architecture
Troy, NY
www.arch.rpi.edu
B.Arch.; M.Arch.

Rochester Institute of Technology
Golisano Institute for Sustainability
Architecture Program
Rochester, NY
www.rit.edu/gis/architecture/
M.Arch.—Candidate

State University of New York at Buffalo
School of Architecture and Planning
Department of Architecture
Buffalo, NY
www.ap.buffalo.edu/architecture
M.Arch.

Syracuse University
School of Architecture
Syracuse, NY
soa.syr.edu
B.Arch.; M.Arch.

NORTH CAROLINA

North Carolina at Charlotte, University of
College of Arts + Architecture
School of Architecture
Charlotte, NC
www.soa.uncc.edu
B.Arch.; M.Arch.

North Carolina State University
College of Design
School of Architecture
Raleigh, NC
ncsudesign.org
B.Arch.; M.Arch.

NORTH DAKOTA

North Dakota State University
College of Engineering and Architecture
Department of Architecture and Landscape
    Architecture
Fargo, ND
ala.ndsu.edu
M.Arch.

OHIO

Bowling Green State University
College of Technology
Department of Architecture and Environmental
    Design
Bowling Green, OH
www.bgsu.edu/colleges/technology/undergraduate/
    arch/
M.Arch.—Candidate

Cincinnati, University of
College of Design, Architecture, Art, and Planning
School of Architecture and Interior Design
Cincinnati, OH
www.daap.uc.edu/said
M.Arch.

Kent State University
College of Architecture and Environmental Design
Architecture Program
Kent, OH
www.kent.edu/caed/
M.Arch.

Miami University
College of Creative Arts
Department of Architecture + Interior Design
Oxford, OH
www.muohio.edu/architecture
M.Arch.

Ohio State University
Austin E. Knowlton School of Architecture
Columbus, OH
knowlton.osu.edu
M.Arch.

OKLAHOMA

Oklahoma State University
College of Engineering, Architecture and Technology
School of Architecture
Stillwater, OK
architecture.ceat.okstate.edu
B.Arch.

Oklahoma, University of
College of Architecture
Division of Architecture
Norman, OK
arch.ou.edu
B.Arch.; M.Arch.

OREGON

Oregon, University of
School of Architecture and Allied Arts
Department of Architecture
Eugene, OR
architecture.uoregon.edu
B.Arch.; M.Arch.

Portland State University
College of the Arts
School of Architecture
Portland, OR
www.pdx.edu/architecture
M.Arch.

PENNSYLVANIA

Carnegie Mellon University
School of Fine Arts
School of Architecture
Pittsburgh, PA
www.cmu.edu/architecture/
B.Arch.

Drexel University
Antoinette Westphal College Media Arts and Design
Department of Architecture and Interiors
Philadelphia, PA
www.drexel.edu/westphal/undergraduate/ARCH/
B.Arch..

Marywood University
School of Architecture
Scranton, PA
www.marywood.edu/architecture/
B. Arch.—Candidate

Pennsylvania State University
College of Arts and Architecture
H. Campbell and Eleanor R. Stuckeman School
    of Architecture and Landscape Architecture
Department of Architecture
University Park, PA
www.arch.psu.edu
B.Arch.; M.Arch—Candidate

Pennsylvania, University of
School of Design
Architecture
Philadelphia, PA
www.design.upenn.edu/
M.Arch.

Philadelphia University
College of Architecture and the Built
    Environment
School of Architecture
Philadelphia, PA
www.philau.edu/schools/add
B.Arch.

Temple University
Tyler School of Art
Architecture Department
Philadelphia, PA
www.temple.edu/architecture
B.Arch. (thru June 2016); M.Arch.

PUERTO RICO

Polytechnic University of Puerto Rico
The New School of Architecture
San Juan, PR
www.pupr.edu/arqpoli/
B.Arch.

Pontical Catholic University of Puerto Rico
Ponce, PR
website.pucpr.edu
B.Arch.—Candidate

Puerto Rico, Universidad de
Escuela de Arquitectura
San Juan, PR
http://arquitectura.uprrp.edu/
M.Arch.

RHODE ISLAND

Rhode Island School of Design
Division of Architecture + Design
Department of Architecture
Providence, RI
www.risd.edu/academics/architecture/
B.Arch.; M.Arch.

Roger Williams University
School of Architecture, Art, and Historic
    Preservation
Bristol, RI
www.rwu.edu/academics/schools-colleges/saahp
M.Arch.

SOUTH CAROLINA

Clemson University
College of Architecture, Arts and Humanities
School of Architecture
Clemson, SC
www.clemson.edu/caah/architecture/
M.Arch.

SOUTH DAKOTA

South Dakota State University
College of Arts & Sciences
Architecture
Brookings, SD
www.sdstate.edu/arch/
M.Arch.—Candidate

TENNESSEE

Memphis, University of
Department of Architecture
Memphis, TN
architecture.memphis.edu
M.Arch.

Tennessee–Knoxville, University of
College of Architecture and Design
School of Architecture
Knoxville, TN
archdesign.utk.edu
B.Arch.; M.Arch.

TEXAS

Houston, University of
Gerald D. Hines College of Architecture
Houston, TX
www.arch.uh.edu
B.Arch.; M.Arch.

Prairie View A&M University
School of Architecture
Prairie View, TX
www.pvamu.edu/architecture
M.Arch.

Rice University
School of Architecture
Houston, TX
www.arch.rice.edu
B.Arch.; M.Arch.

Texas A&M University
College of Architecture
Department of Architecture
College Station, TX
www.arch.tamu.edu
M.Arch.

Texas at Arlington, University of
School of Architecture
Architecture Program
Arlington, TX
www.uta.edu/architecture
M.Arch.

Texas at Austin, University of
School of Architecture
Austin, TX
soa.utexas.edu
B.Arch.; M.Arch.

Texas at San Antonio, University of
College of Architecture
Department of Architecture
San Antonio, TX
www.utsa.edu/architecture
M.Arch.

Texas Tech University
College of Architecture
Lubbock, TX
www.arch.ttu.edu/architecture
M.Arch.

UTAH

Utah, University of
College of Architecture and Planning
School of Architecture
Salt Lake City, UT
www.arch.utah.edu
M.Arch.

VERMONT

Norwich University
School of Architecture and Art
Northfield, VT
programs.norwich.edu/architectureart/
M.Arch.

VIRGINIA

Hampton University
School of Engineering and Technology
Department of Architecture
Hampton, VA
set.hamptonu.edu/architecture/
M.Arch.

Virginia Tech
College of Architecture and Urban Studies
School of Architecture + Design
Blacksburg, VA
www.archdesign.vt.edu
B.Arch.; M.Arch.

Virginia, University of
School of Architecture
Charlottesville, VA
www.arch.virginia.edu
M.Arch.

WASHINGTON

Washington, University of
College of Architecture and Urban Planning
Department of Architecture
Seattle, WA
www.arch.washington.edu
M.Arch.

Washington State University
College of Architecture and Engineering
School of Design and Construction
Pullman, WA
www.arch.wsu.edu
M.Arch.

WEST VIRGINIA

None

WISCONSIN

Wisconsin-Milwaukee, University of
School of Architecture and Urban Planning
Department of Architecture
Milwaukee, WI
www4.uwm.edu/SARUP/
M.Arch.

WYOMING

None

INTERNATIONAL

American University of Sharjah
College of Architecture, Art and Design
Department of Architecture
Sharjah UAE
www.aus.edu/caad
B.Arch.

Lebanon American University
School of Architecture & Design
Architecture and Interior Design Department
Beirut, Lebanon
sard.lau.edu.lb/aid/
B.Arch.—Candidate

CANADA

This list is up to date as of the publication date. For an up-to-date list, contact the Canadian Architectural Certification Board: www.cacb-ccca.ca.

British Columbia, University of
School of Architecture + Landscape Architecture
Vancouver, British Columbia
www.sala.ubc.ca
M.Arch.

Calgary, University of
Faculty of Environmental Design
Calgary, Alberta
evds.ucalgary.ca
M.Arch.

Carleton University
Azrieli School of Architecture and Urbanism
Ottawa, Ontario
www.arch.carleton.ca
M.Arch.

Dalhousie University
Faculty of Architecture and Planning
Halifax, Nova Scotia
www.dal.ca/architecture
M.Arch.

Laval Université
School of Architecture
Quebec, Quebec
www.arc.ulaval.ca
M.Arch.

Manitoba, University of
Faculty of Architecture
Winnipeg, Manitoba
umanitoba.ca/faculties/architecture
M.Arch.

McGill University
School of Architecture
Montreal, Quebec
www.mcgill.ca/architecture/
M.Arch.

Montreal, Université de
School of Architecture
Montreal, Quebec
www.arc.umontreal.ca
M.Arch.

Ryerson University
Department of Architectural Science
Toronto, Ontario
www.arch.ryerson.ca
M.Arch.

Toronto, University of
John H. Daniels Faculty of Architecture, Landscape and Design
Toronto, Ontario
www.daniels.utoronto.ca
M.Arch.

Waterloo, University of
School of Architecture
Waterloo, Ontario
uwaterloo.ca/architecture/
M.Arch.

APPENDIX C

Career Profiles

Tanya Ally
Architectural Staff
Bonstra | Haresign Architects
Washington, DC

Murrye Bernard
Managing Editor
Contract Magazine
New York, New York

Cody Bornsheuer, Associate AIA, LEED AP BD+C
Architectural Designer
Dewberry Architects, Inc.
Peoria, Illinois

H. Alan Brangman, AIA
Vice President of Facilities, Real Estate and
   Auxiliary Services
University of Delaware
Newark, Delaware

Jordan Buckner
Master of Architecture/Master of Business
   Administration Graduate
University of Illinois at Urbana-Champaign
Champaign, Illinois

William J. Carpenter, Ph.D., FAIA
Associate Professor
School of Architecture, Civil Engineering
   Technology and Construction
Southern Polytechnic State University
Marietta, Georgia
President
Lightroom
Decatur, Georgia

Andrew Caruso, AIA, LEED AP BD+C, CDT
Firmwide Head of Intern Development and
   Academic Outreach
Gensler
Washington, DC

Megan S. Chusid, AIA
Manager of Facilities and Office Services
Solomon R. Guggenheim Museum & Foundation
New York, New York

Ashley W. Clark, Associate AIA, LEED AP, SMPS
Marketing Manager
LandDesign
Charlotte, North Carolina

Katherine Darnstadt, AIA, LEED AP BD+C
Founder and Principal
Latent Design
Chicago, Illinois
Director
Architecture for Humanity–Chicago

Kathy Denise Dixon, AIA, NOMA
Principal
K. Dixon Architecture, PLLC
Upper Marlboro, Maryland
Associate Professor
University of District of Columbia
Washington, DC

Kimberly Dowdell
Project Manager/Director of Marketing
Levien & Company
New York, New York

Thomas Fowler, IV, AIA
Professor and Director, Collaborative Integrative-
    Interdisciplinary Digital-Design Studio (CIDS)
College of Architecture and Environmental Design
California Polytechnic State University–San Luis
    Obispo
San Luis Obispo, California

Robert D. Fox, AIA, IIDA
Principal
FOX Architects
McLean, Virginia/Washington, DC

Nicole Gangidino
Bachelor of Architecture Candidate
New York Institute of Technology
New York, New York

Amanda Harrell-Seyburn, Associate AIA
Instructor, School of Planning, Design, and
    Construction
Michigan State University
Lansing, Michigan

Carolyn G. Jones, AIA
Principal
MulvannyG2
Belluvue, Washington

Elizabeth Kalin
Job Captain
Gensler
Minneapolis, Minnesota

Brian Kelly, AIA
Associate Professor/Director, School of
    Architecture
University of Maryland
College Park, Maryland

Grace H. Kim, AIA
Principal and Cofounder
Schemata Workshop, Inc.
Seattle, Washington

Nathan Kipnis, AIA
Principal
Nathan Kipnis Architects, Inc.
Evanston, Illinois

Anna A. Kissell
Master of Architecture Candidate
Boston Architectural College
Boston, Massachusetts

Shannon Kraus, FAIA, MBA
Principal and Senior Vice President
HKS Architects
Washington, DC

Mary Kay Lanzillotta, FAIA
Partner
Hartman-Cox Architects
Washington, DC

Jessica L. Leonard, Associate AIA, LEED AP
Campus Planner/Intern Architect
Ayers Saint Gross Architects and Planners
Baltimore, Maryland

Makenzie Leukart
Master of Architecture/Master of Historic
    Preservation Candidate
Columbia University
New York, New York

Clark E. Llewellyn, AIA, NCARB
Director of Global Track and Professor
School of Architecture
University of Hawaii at Manoa
Honolulu, Hawaii

Joseph Mayo
Intern Architect
Mahlum
Seattle, Washington

Danielle Mitchell
Bachelor of Architecture Candidate
Pennsylvania State University
University Park, Pennsylania

John W. Myefski, AIA
Principal
Myefski Architects, Inc.
Glencoe, Illinois

Joseph Nickol, AICP, LEED AP BD+C
Project Manager
Urban Design Associates
Pittsburgh, Pennsylvania
Founder
Street Sense
Pittsburgh, Pennsylvania

Lauren Pasion
Architectural Designer
Studio E Architects
San Diego, California

Jennifer Jaramillo Penner
Master of Architecture Graduate
University of New Mexico
Regional Associate Director
AIA Western Mountain
Albuquerque, New Mexico

Amy Perenchio, Associate AIA, LEED AP BD+C
Architectural Designer
Zimmer Gunsul Frasca Architects LLP
Portland, Oregon

Kathryn T. Prigmore, FAIA
Senior Project Manager
HDR Architecture Inc.
Alexandria, Virginia

Elsa Reifsteck
Bachelor of Science in Architectural Studies
    Graduate
University of Illinois at Urbana-Champaign
Champaign, Illinois

Robert D. Roubik, AIA, LEED AP
Project Architect
Antunovich Associates Architects and Planners
Chicago, Illinois

Rosannah B. Sandoval, AIA
Designer II
Perkins + Will
San Francisco, California

Kevin Sneed, AIA, IIDA, NOMA, LEED AP BD+C
Partner/Senior Director of Architecture
OTJ Architects, LLC
Washington, District of Columbia

Lynsey Jane Sorrell, AIA
Principal
Perimeter Architects
Chicago, Illinois

Karen Cordes Spence, Ph.D., AIA, LEED AP
Associate Professor
Drury University
Springfield, Missouri

Sean M. Stadler, AIA LEED AP
Design Principal
WDG Architecture, PLLC
Washington, DC

Sarah Stein, LEED AP BD+C
Architectural Designer
Lee Scolnick Architects & Design Partnership
New York, New York

Amanda Strawitch
Level 1 Architect
Design Collective, Inc.
Baltimore, Maryland

Leigh Stringer, LEED AP
Senior Vice President
HOK
New York, New York

Eric Taylor, Associate AIA
Photographer
Taylor Design & Photography, Inc.
Fairfax Station, Virginia

Jennifer Taylor
National Vice President
American Institute of Architecture Students
Washington, DC

Elizabeth Weintraub
Bachelor of Architecture Candidate
New York Institute of Technology
Queens, New York

Allison Wilson
Intern Architect
Ayers Saint Gross
Baltimore, Maryland

INDEX

If you enjoyed this book, you may also like these:

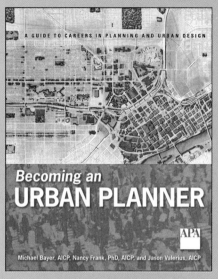

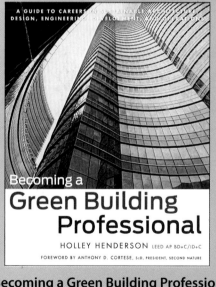
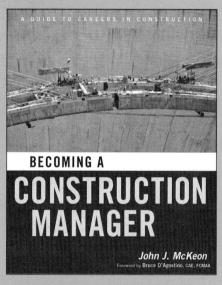